The Man That Never Was
Daniel Defoe: 1644-1731
A Critical Revision of his Life and Writing

St Stephen's Parish Church, Etton, Northamptionshire

John Martin
A Peer Reviewed Book
Foreword
Professor Kevin Barry

A bold and provocative work of scholarship.Defoe scholars will be enthralled.

Dr.Glen Reynolds
University of Sunderland

A Heritage Publications Book

Copyright © John Martin 2013

Cover design by Susan Curran

British Library Cataloguing Publication Data.
A catalogue record for this book is available from the British Library

ISBN 978-0-9543172-4-9

'Heritage Publications is a trading mame of APL Limited
Registered in England No. 06564978

Dedication

To my beloved wife Larisa for her understanding and sympathy

Biographical Truths and Untruths

The fact is that biographical untruths are accepted [by readers] if they have been said two or three times and fit in with expectations. There are sanctions of disapproval if you [the biographer] offer truths that are uncannonical. You can't start by writing 'Gerald Hopkins was a homosexual midget.'

The Art of Literary Biography
Norman White, 2003

Contents

Foreword

This is a work that provides two complementary approaches to the study of Daniel Defoe. We discover in these pages a search for documentary evidence of Defoe's birth and early life, and we are invited to join in an exploration of the hypothesis that Defoe's fictional writings are indirect forms of autobiography. The contribution to scholarship made by John Martin is fundamental insofar as the book provides documentary evidence in support of a hypothesis that Daniel Defoe was born in 1644 a full fifteen years earlier than is generally accepted. Northamptonshire replaces London as the scene of his early life. Such evidence allows scholars to re-investigate the nature of Defoe's childhood and family. His early years may be rewritten on the basis of this material and recurrent themes in his fictional narratives. There are in Defoe's writings generic and also particular clusters of events figuring childhoods that now can be argued are similar to his own. Furthermore a recalibration of his date of birth allows us to consider whether or not his private and public narratives, and those of others, recount events that may be coincident with probable adventures in Defoe's later career.

Defoe was, for good reason, a liar. Since the eighteenth century his biographers have wrestled with this fact. His need to dissimulate became, it may be argued, less strong after his 'pardon'. That said he had established habits of intrigue as a criminal, a politician and an author. Such a complexity of character, public and private, has ensured that that all biographies to date have had (or ought to have respect for) a speculative tone. The proposal that Defoe was born more than a decade earlier than had been supposed and the sketching out of a quite different history call previous accounts into question. The authorship of certain works doubtfully attributed, the reasons for the sudden publication of others, the documentary nature of the fictions and their coherence with events in Defoe's longer life, all become newly problematic.

John Martin has introduced new perspectives to the study of Defoe's career. Within the constraints of a hypothetical reading of Defoe's extraordinary and unprecedented modes of writing, this study offer scholars fresh evidence for a re-reading of Defoe's life and work.

Barry Kevin.
Professor Emeritus, School of Humanities
NUI Galway, Ireland.

November, 2012.

Preface

What is now proved was once only imagined.

The Marriage of Heaven and Hell
William Blake, 1790

This book is a revisionist biography of the life of Daniel Defoe and a consideration of the ways in which new biographical information about him affects literary consideration of his written work and in particular his fiction.

There are a number of fine modern Defoe biographies written by respected academics such as Paula Backscheider and Max Novak[1] and I have written a full length work.[2] Naturally the question arises as to the need for another one. There is a resistance to it. Literary biographers incline towards what might be called a physiocratic definition of biography: that there are one or two definitive works to be written about a subject; that this body of knowledge can be addressed by a known system; and then, so to speak, the book can be closed. This is far from being true about biography in general and for the enigmatic and troublesome Defoe it is manifestly unhelpful.

The specific need for this book is occasioned by my discovery in 2009 that Daniel Defoe was born fifteen years earlier than had previously been supposed and to a father about whom little or nothing is known. Defoe was baptised as the son of Daniel Foe and his wife Ellene in Etton, Northamptonshire in 1644.[3] He was not the son of James Foe and born in London in 1659/60 as had been previously been supposed. James Foe was his uncle. The record of his baptism had not previously been discovered because biographers were looking in the

---

[1] Backscheider, Paula. *Daniel Defoe, His Life*, The Johns Hopkins University Press, 1989 and
Novak, Maximillian, E. *Daniel Defoe: Master of Fictions*, Oxford University Press, 2001..
[2] Martin John. *Beyond Belief: The Real Life of Daniel Defoe*, Accent Press, 2006-2009.
[3] NRO. Etton Parish Baptism Records, 1587-1700.

wrong place at the wrong time. Defoe had a sister Mary and a brother Thomas of whom nothing has been known. I maintain in this book that the discovery has a major impact on all biographical accounts and interpretations of Defoe's written work.

It is not often that such a discovery is made about a prominent and important writer. It is highly inconvenient to academics and to general readers alike. No biographer would choose to make it. The belief that Defoe was the son of James Foe is received wisdom and held to be true by a wide reading public despite the absence of a baptism record. Biographers throughout the ages have felt bound to use the assumption and to write their works around false conjectures. I have been as much at fault as anyone. However, I would point out in my defence that I knew there was something wrong. In *Beyond Belief*, written in 2006, I wrote, 'What is least probable is most commonly believed: that Daniel Defoe was born in 1660/1 in Cripplegate, London into a small nuclear family of firm Presbyterian and dissenting beliefs.' [4]

It is difficult and troublesome to disturb the received wisdom of nearly 300 years. Following my discovery, no one doubts that a Daniel Foe was born to a father of the same name in Etton in 1644. However, some literary critics have sought to maintain that this Daniel Foe must have been a cousin of the real Defoe born to James Foe, and suggest that this small Etton family of Foe's had two sons named Daniel Foe. There is no evidence to support this conjecture and substantial objections to the proposition.

I summarise the main reasons for disbelief. First, I have provided a Chart for this Foe, Etton family. Over two generations all the children in the family were baptised in the Church of England. Secondly, it was the usual practice in the seventeenth century to ensure the inheritance of the elder son by naming him after the father. If James Foe had produced a son he would, probably, have named him James not Daniel. Thirdly, no one has ever suggested that Daniel Defoe had a cousin of the same name. There is no written evidence anywhere of the existence of two cousins named Daniel Foe. It is suggested that a second Daniel

---

[4] *Beyond Belief*, 22.

Foe might have died young or, perhaps, migrated. I have made a serious search of Parish Records of marriages and burials throughout England and seventeenth century migration records in an endeavour to find this mythical second Daniel Foe. They do not exist. What does exist is Defoe's father's will of 1647, when Defoe was three years of age, which names him and his sister Mary as beneficiaries and identifies James Foe as his uncle.

Defoe deliberately hid the facts of his origins and early life. He endeavoured throughout his entire life to keep his birth and early experiences in the period 1644-1680 a secret. Many gifted people in his time, and later, did the same.[5] In the absence of any evidence of a birth to James and Alice Foe, a web of speculation has been woven by biographers. Defoe was successful in hiding his origins by the deliberate adoption of a number of ruses. Those academic commentators who act on the assumption of Defoe's basic honesty will have difficulty in accepting the changes I outline on the chronology and circumstances of his life.

Put simply, biographical accounts of Defoe's early life are untrue in their entirety. For example, much has been made of an upbringing in London. However, it is my understanding that apart from a short period in 1660-1662 Defoe was not resident in London until 1680 and that it follows from this that several assumptions important to descriptions of his life as a child and young adult are incorrect. Defoe was not born into a devout Presbyterian home, nor educated in Stoke Newington Academy for Dissenters, was never a member of any Church, and not a witness to major events in London in the period, such as the Great Plague and Fire of London, 1665-1666 and the Dutch fleet sailing up the Thames in 1672.

Defoe had very good reasons for this secrecy and was highly gifted in the subterfuge he created. It is entirely understandable that Defoe

[5] There is uncertainty about the parentage of many early eighteenth century writers: for example, Richardson, Swift, and Samuel Johnson. At a later date Nerval used a false identity when he came to Paris. He never used his father's surname. See, Holmes, Richard. *Footsteps: Adventures of a Romantic Biographer*, Flamingo, 1995, 241.

deceived many commentators and biographers – although not some and not all of them all of the time. In this account I discuss a number of compelling reasons for him hiding his origins and whereabouts for the first 36 years of his life. I identified some, but not all, and not the most important, of these reasons in *Alien Come Home*, 2009.[6] Subsequently, I have continued research on this period of his life.

The findings of my earlier work, although controversial, have not met with any credible refutation. However, literary criticism of my work raised five objections to 1644 as his date of birth. I have debated these with numerous members of the Daniel Defoe Society and I address them in appendices to this work. They are as follows: the belief that Defoe attended the Newington Green Academy for Dissenters in 1674-1678; Defoe's own claim of a 'paternal' link to James Foe in an application for membership of the Worshipful Company of Butchers in 1689; a description of Defoe as 'son' in James Foe's will in 1706; and commonsense objections that it would have been difficult for Defoe to disguise the fact that he was fifteen years older than he said he was, and continue to write, when he was in his eighties. It is essential also to my narrative to show that Defoe married Jone Reade in Barbados in May, 1681. There is a belief by some that Defoe attended five sermons of John Collins in London in 1681. If this is so he would not have had the time to travel to Barbados.

I am aware that although there are no other stated objections to my findings scholars have deep reservations that need to be discussed. The principal cause of unease about changes to the narrative of Defoe's life is a widespread belief in the received wisdom incorporated in the corpus of knowledge about Defoe assembled over 280 years. It is felt that in its essentials the corpus, a considerable collection of writings, texts and spoken materials, must be right.

There is a lack of understanding among literary critics about how such a corpus is created and its reliability. It is believed by most scholars that the corpus is based on incontrovertible historical and

[6] Martin, John. *Alien Come Home ,The Story of Daniel Defoe's Missing Years*, 1644-1680, Anglian Publishing, 2009

cultural facts. It comes as an unpleasant shock when it is suggested that, for the most part, it isn't. There are widespread misunderstandings about the nature of historical facts and their transmission. It is thought by many scholars that a fact is a fact; but the life of a fact is a complex matter. Like gossip, facts that travel rarely remain stable. They may be perpetuated and re-formed in myth, folk tales, anecdotes, and victim psychology. Historical research reveals that 'facts' about persons are often invented, altered or removed in historical accounts depending on who is telling the story, and why.

It is an inescapable truth that all biography is a work of the imagination. Despite this truth some Defoe literary critics assert that the only evidence they take cognisance of in an account of Defoe's life is unimpeachable documentary evidence. They are deluding themselves and others. When their work is examined it can be shown that the man they are writing about, the Defoe they describe in his early life, never existed. Most accounts are replete with conjecture, circular reasoning, non-sequiturs and assertions of authority.

I do not deny that in general existing Defoe biographies are well-based in good evidence; but I do assert that the information they provide about his life to 1680 is without evidential foundation. Beyond 1680 there is evidence from many written sources, in particular State Papers and published works, of Defoe's status as a polemicist and involvement in the major issues of his time. Obviously this evidence is of importance in understanding his life. However, ignorance of Defoe's early life leads to the making of false assertions about his later years; in particular it acts as a bias and distortion in literary readings of his writings.

It must be true that sound documentary evidence is to be preferred to conjecture. In this work I provide such evidence for his early life; but I also make use of conjectures. I believe that conjectures when used in conjunction with documentary sources are acceptable if they have the capacity to explain. In particular, a conjecture is particularly persuasive where the evidence as a whole points to, or is part of, a pattern of behaviour.

The second unconscious objection to changing Defoe's biography is the fear that in doing so Defoe will be shown to be of a lesser importance and interest as a writer and polemicist. I do not think that new information makes him less of a person. After 10 years of serious enquiry on my part, I reach a conclusion that he was a man of genius and ingenuity who led a remarkable life in an important period of English political and social history. Defoe's literary reputation rests securely on his authorship of *Robinson Crusoe*, a felicitous work of the imagination, and his polemical support for representative government.

Defoe's recognised fiction was created mainly in a burst of creative activity in a mere 5 years in the period 1719-1724 when he was an old man. However, I offer proof in my account here of the writing of fiction and biography as early as 1709. This concentration of creative endeavour has never been adequately explained. I suggest that as Defoe was writing about events in his own life he could not publish any of these works until he had been granted an 'Exception' from prosecution for past crimes by the Whig administration in 1718. Even then he needed anonymity and subterfuge to hide the basic facts of his life. Much of Defoe's literary output beyond 1719-1724 is accounts of piracy, travel and adventure, subjects his actual life experiences equipped him to tell. Academic critics have struggled to explain Defoe's ability to write about these subjects so knowledgeably and well.

General readers and academics may think less well of Defoe fictions as a result of my work. I would be sorry if that were an outcome. However, I do not understand the reasons for thinking it. It is not my opinion. I believe the contrary: that the truth is remarkable and Defoe's treatment of it extraordinary. As so often, 'the truth' is important to the appreciation of any writer and his works.

There will never be complete agreement about Defoe's character, nor should there be; but in many respects scholars can and do agree that his behaviour was often reprehensible. My work adds fodder to those who think Defoe to be of bad character. I am sorry for it. It is not a biographer's duty to make out that a subject of enquiry is a better or worse person than he is generally thought to be. I seek to present and explain Defoe and not to praise, reduce or judge him; but in my considered opinion Defoe was not what is commonly described now, and then, as a 'good fellow'. He was, however, an entirely remarkable man of high intelligence and inventiveness, admirable literary skills and insatiable curiosity about 'the meaning of things'. I find it easy and sufficient to settle for this.

The third, and most human, reason for hesitancy in accepting a correction to the chronology of Defoe's life rests on the effect of change on the academic reputations of scholars. Academic careers and reputations are hard-earned. No one wishes to radically revise 30 years of lecture notes and to start again. However, academic integrity requires it. There are compensations in doing so. Changing the chronology and circumstances of Defoe's life helps solve many problems confronting Defoe critics and deepens literary understanding.

Defoe scholars have an understandable desire to increase the importance of Defoe studies by attributing more written works to him. This is a very great pity. Inevitably this tendency has led to absurdities and a critical reaction in the form of an onslaught on the authenticity of many works assumed to be written by Defoe. A mountain of works has been ascribed to him. Most of them were written anonymously or not claimed by Defoe in his lifetime. It is not desirable to mince words. A debate on the canon initiated by Furbank and Owens has shown that it has been put together by questionable scholarship. Faulty ascription has consequences. Much has been made in the past of the interpretation of works that can now be shown either not to be, or unlikely to have been, written by him. Consequently, any Defoe scholar worth his salt has to grapple with ascription problems. In 1988 Furbank and Owens first questioned the authenticity of the canon[7] and in 1998 they suggested that the number of attributions should be limited to some 250 works, a reduction of three hundred.[8] In the earlier of these works they wrote:

The Defoe canon is remarkably strange and not very satisfactory…It contains, indeed, as odd and as strange an assortment of texts as,

---

[7] Furbank, P.N. and Owens, W.R. *The Canonisation of Daniel Defoe*, Yale University Press, 1988.
[8] Furbank, P.N. and Owens, W.R. *A Critical Bibliography of Daniel Defoe*, Pickering and Chatto, 1998.

perhaps, has ever been attributed to one author...from the very beginning something may have gone wrong...some error crept in begetting over the years a long series of further errors... [9]

Today most scholars accept the main drift of the attributions and de-attributions of Furbank and Owens with some degree of relief. In general I follow their judgements. However, I have three important reservations. First, while having considerable doubts about stylometrics as a methodology for determining authorship, I believe that the stylometric analysis conducted at the University of Houston under the direction of Professor Irving Rothman is thought-provoking. This work has made a case for ascribing an additional 80 works written wholly or in part by Defoe to be added to the Furbank and Owens attribution list. I believe, following Furbank and Owens, [10] that stylometrics is an art rather than a science. However, stylometric analysis can alert critics to the possibility of any given work being written by Defoe. However, certainty that Defoe was the author of a particular work requires specific internal and external evidence.

The act of correcting Defoe's chronology and the circumstances of his early life results in a number of startling conclusions and consequences. I am able to ascribe additional works to the Defoe canon and I list them in an attachment to this work. The ascription of such a work as *A General History of the Pyrates* illustrates the advantages of correcting Defoe's biography. The argumentation advanced by Furbank & Owens, Arne Bialuchewski and others is deficient by absence of any decisive internal or external evidence. I am able to prove that significant parts of this work were written by Defoe – and could not have been written by any other author - by using new biographical knowledge of Defoe's activities and wider family connections.

Secondly, and consequently, to take the argument further, I maintain that internal evidence and, to some extent, the quality of the writing is crucial in determining authorship. Given that all Defoe's work is an expression to a greater or lesser extent of his real-life experiences,

---

[9] Furbank and Owens, *Canonisation*, 1.
[10] Furbank and Owens, *Canonisation*, 176-183.

accurate biographical information is not merely useful but essential to an understanding of *any* Defoe work. I have mentioned the role of such evidence in offering a sound proof that Defoe was the author of *A General History of the Pyrates*, and I conclude also, that despite doubts raised by Furbank and Owens, that the *King of the Pyrates* is rightly attributed to him

Thirdly, I suggest that further thought must be given to the issue of how much of a given work must be proved to be Defoe's to make it safe to attribute a work to him. Arthur Secord points out that in an early version of *Memoirs of a Cavalier*, Defoe is described as 'editor'.[11] I believe that the first part of *Cavalier* is Defoe's but that the remainder is an edited version of the work of another.[12] This assertion is possible and believable because by correcting the account of Defoe's early life I have produced the evidence to substantiate the first part. Similarly, although contrariwise, it will be obvious to an enquirer from a reading of my book that doubts raised about the authenticity of *Moll Flanders* and *Roxana* are improbable.[13]

I certainly agree with Furbank and Owens when they write 'some errors crept in, [to Defoe scholarship] begetting over the years a long series of errors.' It is the gravamen of my work that among these errors is Defoe's date of birth. The speculation about the date and circumstances of his birth can be traced back to a conjecture in the work of George Chalmers in 1790. Chalmers believed that Defoe's membership of The Worshipful Company of Butchers by patrimony was a proof that Defoe was the son of James Foe. In this he was confused (see Attachment 5). However, he had come to understand that there was some kind of family link between James Foe and Defoe, as indeed there was, and the assertions of his parenthood 'grew like Topsy

---

[11] Secord, Arthur, W. *Robert Drury's Journal and Other Studies*, University of Illinois Press, 1961.

[12] Attachment, for the conjecture that the manuscript or notes were in the papers of Sir John Fenwick, Second Baronet, Defoe's 'uncle' in 1696.

[13] See Marshall, Ashley. 'Did Defoe Write *Moll Flanders* and *Roxana*?' Philological Quarterly 89 (2010), 209-41.

from this limited position to the proof that he was his biological son.[14]

I accept that the use I make of Defoe's works for biographical purposes is controversial. It is my central contention that all Defoe's fictional works, and some part of the non-fictional, are autobiographical in intent: that is, Defoe is giving the reader embellished accounts of his own life. Defoe does not follow the conventions of the realistic novel by respecting linear time. What he gives his readers are episodic accounts of his various heroes. Defoe is the hero of his own life. In reality he is always writing about himself even when, or especially so, he is narrating as a woman. When these various fictional accounts are compared and put together they can be seen as giving a comprehensive, although incomplete, unwieldy, and untrustworthy account of his life. This outline does not make Defoe's understanding of his own life 'true' in any realistic meaning of the word. No one of right mind could think it. However, there is good documentary evidence to prove many of the particulars on which his various accounts are based as I seek to demonstrate.

Notwithstanding this explanation, I am among the first to recognise that establishing the 'truth' about Daniel Defoe's extraordinary life is not easy for a host of reasons. Among these difficulties, and accepting that all biographers are indebted to their predecessors, are past biographical errors of judgement of English cultural and social history. It is my contention that many errors in Defoe biography arise by intent: that is, the wish of the writer to cast Defoe's life in the most favourable light. Some errors arise from the avoidance of knowledge of our cultural past and of the evidence offered by contrary propositions and not from ignorance of them.

I am aware that some literary critics may accuse me of the sin of reductionism: that is the breaking out of constituent parts of Defoe's fictions and the use of simple concepts to the detriment of the whole. I do not do this. I am illustrating the autobiographical content of his works and not denying their artistic whole. Others are better qualified than me to make artistic judgements.

[14] Chalmers, George. *The Life of Defoe*, London, 1790.

Seventeenth century England was conditioned by social and moral experiences that are strange to a modern reader. However, Defoe's life needs to be assessed by reference to the cultural contexts of his time even though their lasting value can be established only by reference to the sensibilities of our own. It has always been the case that modern readers have to be prepared to develop a literary understanding of works of fiction without the guides that they carry over from the study of later periods. Readers of Defoe works are required to learn new words and terms and to extend and modify their vocabularies. Over the years editors, in a desire to be helpful and widen readership, have tidied up Defoe's works by cutting out miss-spelling, repetitions and some of the dross. It is a difficult and necessary task but sometimes it results in a loss of authenticity. Readers are best advised to read originals or early texts whenever possible.

In the chronicling task there are problems with dates. Until 1752 England used the Julian calendar whereas Scotland used the Gregorian calendar from 1660. The Julian calendar differed in two ways: it was eleven days ahead, and the New Year began on March 31. In this work I use the Julian calendar and assume the New Year to begin in January.

Names are an issue. It was the practice of Defoe's time to spell a name as it was pronounced. This led to many written versions of any birth name. Defoe used aliases. He started out in life as a Foe, spelt in a number of ways, and used it when exiled abroad in 1662-1680. Later, when in London, he adopted the name of Defoe by which he is known now. I do not believe it was ever an English family name. It is highly probable that it is derived from a sixteenth century Flemish name such as de Faux. The use of this prefix in France and Flanders tended to denote place and to have an agricultural context. In English today it carries an aristocratic social distinction. To an eighteenth century Englishman it denoted a Huguenot Protestant derivation.

Defoe scholars do not appear to be aware of important differences in cultural practices in the Early Modern period compared with modern times, at least not so in their Defoe studies, and are apt to misuse family descriptions. First, there are difficulties in the use of surnames. Defoe's brother and sister, as was usual at the time, followed the matrilineal line of descent and used their mother's name of King. This practice has complicated the task of tracing them. King is a common surname whereas Foe is comparatively rare. However, their mother's first name of Ellene and grandmother's name of Rose were uncommon. It has been estimated that in the seventeenth century less than 1 percent of girls were baptised Ellene in all its many versions.

Secondly, families and family relationships may not be what they seem to be. A failure to understand the use of family terms is at the heart of many misunderstandings in Defoe scholarship. An earlier generation of biographers gave credence to the view that nuclear families were steadily replacing marriages of convenience in the seventeenth century while others argued for a continuous evolution to modern forms of family organisation.[15] The evidence as it has now emerged suggests that, contrary to both these viewpoints, kinship and family establishment remained the main determinants of the definition of a family throughout the seventeenth and first half of the eighteenth centuries. A family establishment included many diverse dependents, such as servants, apprentices and co-resident relatives. A father was the head of the family and not necessarily a biological father to all in his household. Similarly a mother could be the female head, a 'nurse' or 'childminder' and not necessarily related to the father. Brothers and sisters might not share the same parents and could be step relatives. Nephews and nieces turn out to be cousins and vice versa. A same sex union is sometimes called a 'marriage' in certain contexts while a master may be a father, the captain or owner of a ship or a dominant sexual partner.

Defoe biographers seem not to have understood the various forms of marriage practiced in the Early Modern period. A church marriage was needed to establish inheritance rights but private treaty marriages, known later as 'common law' marriages, were normal and usual and

[15] Stone, Lawrence. *The Family, Sex and Marriage in England*, 1550-1870, London, 1977.
Habbakkuk, H.J. *Marriage Settlements in the Eighteenth Century*, London, 1950.

multiple marriages were common. Private treaty marriages conveyed all the rights of a church marriage other than inheritance rights and were at the convenience and mutual acceptance of the parties. [16]

There is a failure in Defoe studies to understand, or more probably to accept, Defoe's sexual orientation. Eighteenth century scholars have a sophisticated understanding of gender identity and sexuality across the Early Modern period but they do not often use this knowledge in Defoe studies. The evidence that the gender split between men and women did not exist in its modern form until the second half of the eighteenth century is compelling. I can sense the recoil when I write that in modern terms Defoe was bi-sexual with a liking for sex with men often for the giving and receiving of patronage: but this did not make him abnormal or a person to be despised. He was sexually involved with boys and young men; but, in seventeenth century perception, this did not make him a paedophile. For much of his adult life he had three wives and children by them all: this did not make him a bigamist and he never was. As a young man he had sex with his sister Mary and later with his daughter Sophia, but this did not make him a criminal: incest was not a criminal offence in England until 1908. He cross-dressed throughout his life; but this did not make him a transvestite in the meaning of the term today; any television viewer can see and enjoy cross-dressing in his living room and, in England, at his local pub. Defoe received money directly or indirectly from sex with men: this did not make him a prostitute. Everyday experience suggests that such practices are commonplace in our own times.

There is naivety in any biographer readily accepting Defoe's written words as proof of something or other. Defoe was a great liar and dissembler. William Minto, writing in 1879, knew that much was wrong in the various chronicles of Defoe's life. He suggested that Defoe 'was a great liar, a truly great liar perhaps the greatest that ever lived'. He gave future biographers wise counsel that most

---

[16] For an example, see Defoe, Daniel. *Colonel Jack*, (1722. Hamish Hamilton, 1947), 279.

have ignored by adding, 'We can hardly believe a word he says without independent corroboration.'[17]

Modern Defoe biographers tend to be pessimistic about whether more can be discovered (that is, more than they have found out). Peter Earle, who knew a great deal about Defoe, wrote in 1976 that an adequate biography would be impossible because of the obscurity and subterfuge with which Defoe enclosed his life and the lack of documentary evidence. By evidence, Earle meant the stuff of biography: reminiscences, correspondence, the trace of him in the records and memories of others, the very particulars of a life lived.[18]

Earle was a little too pessimistic. Recent biographies have revealed new particulars of Defoe's life. Moreover, Defoe gives his readers hints about the truth in almost all of his writing. Freud wrote that criminals leave clues to their crimes because at an unconscious level they wish to be punished. After a crime the perpetrator cannot resist talking or writing about it.

The barriers to uncovering the truth about Defoe's secret life are formidable and in some ways more difficult than in 1976 when Earle wrote his biography. Over the last few decades there has been a steady erosion in original archived material and its loss is of real concern to all those with a desire to uncover the truth about the past. However, there is enough material still and skilled archivists to guide in its use.

The first task of the historian in uncovering the past is to ask the right questions. The maxim needs to be, 'ask, seek, and you may find'. A failure to ask relevant questions results in barren research and no answers. The researcher then becomes convinced that nothing can be found. It may be that in uncovering the past the searcher will find the trail to be broken. A good biographer assumes that the path can be found again by proceeding in what he believes to be the right direction. I am indebted to previous biographers. Paula Backsheider, Max Novak and Irving Rothman have been invariably patient and helpful in answering my questions and debating my conclusions and Defoe

---

[17] Minto, William. *Daniel Defoe*, London, MacMillan, 1879, 1.
[18] Earle, Peter. *The World of Defoe*, 1.

scholarship is indebted to them. I have not read any of the established biographies of Defoe, and they are numerous, without learning something important about his life. Many of the earlier biographies are highly idiosyncratic and amusing and I believe they all feed the imagination.

xxvi

Acknowledgements

I have been assisted by numerous people. Rita Harris, my research assistant, has been indispensable to me. Sheldon Rogers shared with me his discovery of a Defoe marriage in Barbados. Dr Pat Stafford explored the barren records of Barbados and gave me valuable information on Edward Singleton. Paolo Da Rosa was valiant in conducting research in Portugal and Brazil. Numerous Defoe scholars have been helpful in detailed critical onslaughts on my work. Many of these criticisms were constructive. In particular Paula Backscheider, Max Novak, Irving Rothman, and Manuel Schonhorn have been helpful to me over 10 years of study. Kevin Barry and James Canton read my text and offered constructive suggestions. Alex Seltzer helped me with information on South Carolina.

Archivists in several libraries have been of significant assistance. I pay a special tribute to the professionalism of the British Library and the National Archives in Britain. The Essex Record Office coped admirably with a stream of enquiries while the Boston Public Library, the Huntington Library, and the William Clark Memorial Library were highly professional in facilitating my research. I thank the British Library, and the Essex and Northamptonshire Record Offices for their permission to use material shown in the Illustrations.

The Vicars of St Stephen's Church, Etton and St Leonard's, Lexden, Colchester were helpful. Randal Bingley, a local Essex historian of distinction, gave me proof that William Lee was partially mistaken in his endeavours to locate Defoe's home and the actual site of Defoe's brickworks in Tilbury; a likely origin of the name Man Friday in Defoe's neighbour in Tilbury, John Friday; and a clue to the identity of his black slave Toby who Defoe introduces to readers in *Religious Courtship*.[19] I am grateful to my son David Martin, BA (Cantab), an

---

[19] Bingley Randal. *Journal of the Thurrock Local History Society*, Vol.27, 1985.ERO. D/SR. 1 Court of Sewers. Defoe, Daniel. *Religious Courtship*, (1722. Derby and Jackson, Nassau St., 1857).

experienced reader of text, for reading and correcting my work.

In this work I draw upon research I have carried out since 2002, and published in *Beyond Belief* and *Alien Come Home*, but it relies in the main on an entirely new and substantial research programme in 2009-2012.

Abbreviations

BL.   British Library
ERO. Essex Record Office
H.   Healey
MA. London Metropolitan Archives
NRO.Northamptonshire Record Office
NA.   National Archives

Chronology

The Unknown Time-line

1644 Daniel Defoe, baptised Daniel Foe, on December 3, 1644 at Etton, Northamptonshire the son of Daniel Foe and his wife Ellene.

1645 Defoe's sister Mary baptised Mary Foe on March 14, 1645 at Etton, daughter of Daniel Foe and his wife Ellene.

1647 Defoe's brother Thomas baptised Thomas Foe on November 14, 1647 at Etton the son of Daniel Foe and his wife Ellene.

1647-8 Death of Defoe's father Daniel Foe on the family farm at Etton, probate of will dated October 20, 1647. Posthumous birth of Thomas. Disappearance, probably deportation to New England, of Ellene Foe. Daniel and Mary moved into the Parish Care of St. Leonard's Church, Lexden, Colchester, Essex. Thomas probably taken into the care of the family of Nicholas and Mary Wildbore in Braintree, nr Colchester, Essex in 1648. (Thomas marries Elisabeth, daughter of Nicholas and Mary in 1681).

1654 Trial year in the care of a Lawrence family in Colchester for Defoe when ten years of age.

1658 Defoe and his sister Mary taken into the care of John and Ann Lawrence in East Tilbury, Essex.

1662 Possible birth of a son Daniel to Defoe by his sister recorded in St Mary's, Chadwell, East Tilbury, Essex.

1662 Defoe embarks on a version of the Grand Tour with William Penn, the Quaker founder of Pennsylvania, Robert Spencer, the future Second Earl of Sunderland and Whig grandee, and the Earl of Crawford.

1663 Probable capture, when deserting, in The Portuguese War of Restoration and transfer under restraint for five years in Brazil, a Portuguese colony.

1663-1680 Works on, and then owns, plantations in the north and south of Brazil.

Develops a business as a merchant, and slave trader along the trans-Atlantic route between New England, Africa and Europe using

Barbados as a staging post. Meets Captain Edward Singleton, a sugar surveyor with Quaker connections on the island.

1680-1682 Attempts to resettle in England as a London merchant.

1681 Marries Jone Read, a religious migrant to Barbados from South Carolina, in May 1681. She dies there in December, 1681. Probable birth of a son.

1682-4 Travels to Barbados and New England with his sister Mary, She stays there for 8 years. Re-settles in London. Marries Mary Tuffley by Special Licence so obtaining a dowry and inheritance rights.

1690 Enters into a relationship and then 'private treaty' marriage with Elisabeth Sammens by whom he has two children. Defoe has a family establishment with her in the City of London.

1693 Enters into a relationship and then 'private treaty' marriage with Mary Norton by whom he has five children two of whom survive to adulthood. Defoe regards himself as living in Essex.

1694 Defoe creates a home with Mary Norton first in Chadwell, East Tilbury and then in Colchester.

1696 Captain Singleton tried for 'passing off' goods as French, fined and gaoled in the Fleet.

1699-1700 Travels with his sister Mary to New England. Probably, Defoe is re-united with his son by Jone Reade. Defoe claims an inheritance in South Carolina.

1701 Captain Singleton appointed William Penn's representative in Barbados.

1705/6 Defoe embarks on the trip to Brazil and Madagascar in a successful search for Avery's diamonds as described in his *Farther Adventures of Robinson Crusoe*.

Note. This is not a summary of all the many things incurring in Defoe's life and that of his extended family in the period but of the most important happenings unknown to most readers.

Illustrations

His Early Life

Chapter 1

Origins

The end I say of everything is in the beginning, and you must look to the end, or you will never begin right.

Review, VIII, 514
Daniel Defoe

In an earlier work I wrote, 'Daniel Defoe's life is the biographer's nightmare.'[20] I have not changed my mind. All attempts to write his life are strewn with error. The gravest error in biography is to cast a subject in your own image and in recent years accounts of Defoe's life have suffered as a consequence of this fault. Biographers suffer from an irresistible urge to think well of their subjects as indeed do their readers.[21] Some biographers, including many academics writing about Defoe, get more personal as they go on. It might be objected to their accounts that each book leads them closer to writing about themselves. The desire to see Defoe cast in a favourable light is strong but despite it Defoe's biography remains dogged by the issue of his character.

What is true is that Daniel Defoe lived an incredible life. He was a foundling taken into parish care, a petty thief in his youth, exiled as a soldier of fortune, planter, sailor, merchant, slave trader, pirate, money launderer, a friend of the mighty in the land of his birth - and a prodigious writer of rare genius. Defoe gained vast amounts of money in his lifetime and seemingly spent and lost it all. It is recognised by most of his biographers that he was reckless and careless in the businesses he started and the dangers he ran. Late in his long life Defoe was pursued by an 'old enemy'. For a long time this was thought to be a creditor, a Mrs Brooke, who was pursuing him in the courts, but I have offered a proof that he was being blackmailed and that all his efforts to pay off his enemy had failed.[22] This last pursuit by Mrs

---

[20] *Beyond Belief*, 1.
[21] *Beyond Belief*, 5-6.
[22] *Beyond Belief*, 272.

Brooke was in a long line of frustrated creditors. After his first bankruptcy in 1692, Defoe was pursued by creditors for the rest of his life. They believed that he had succeeded in hiding assets, and they were right. Defoe was jailed many times for his debts. Powerful enemies would buy up debts from those of Defoe's many creditors some of whom could not afford the legal expense of pursuing him, and they succeeded many times in getting him arrested and imprisoned. Defoe died penniless, or to be more accurate, unable to realise all the monies due to him or to dispose of his assets. He died intestate having disposed of his ready assets in his lifetime. He had done his best to provide for many of his numerous children and succeeded in doing so for some; but so far as is known, no one grieved in public at his parting although tears may have fallen behind closed doors. Mrs Brooke, the last of Defoe's dogged pursuers, was anxious to get at his assets no matter how trivial and told a court that Defoe's legitimate heir, his son Benjamin Norton Defoe, could not be found. She believed that either he was dead or that he had migrated to America. He was not dead for I have traced him in Essex at a later date.[23] According to Wilson, late in his life Defoe's son Daniel also migrated to South Carolina.[24] Why might these sons have gone to America? What were they seeking there? Was Benjamin Norton Defoe seeking money for his hard pressed father and, if so, from whom and how? Defoe was buried in Bunhill Fields in the City of London. It was a cemetery for religious dissenters where Defoe as a revisionist journalist and polemicist truly belonged. He was given an unmarked grave without a headstone. His poor public reputation took a hundred years to resurrect. At some time in the nineteenth century, Defoe was moved on to a grave with a headstone. Later he was given a grander spot with a marble obelisk the expense of which had been met by public subscription. When his coffin was dug up it was found at rest with two others containing the skeletons of unnamed women thought to be of importance and related to him.[25]

---

[23] *Beyond Belief*, 306, n.241.
[24] Wilson, Walter. *Memoirs of the Life and Times of Daniel De Foe*, 3 vols., London, 1830, 645.
[25] *Beyond Belief*, 274.

My narrative tells a story that has never been told. It starts in a way that seems hardly credible and continues in a manner that will be hotly disputed. Maybe on a cold winter day, by the warmth of a wood fire, good ale, and a friendly presence, Defoe recounted it. But if so these words would have been regarded by the listener as the maundering of an old man on his way out of this world and greeted with nods and murmurs.

It is an inescapable fact that the writer known today as Daniel Defoe was baptised when living at the family farm in Etton, Northamptonshire to Daniel Foe and his wife Ellene (possibly born Lawrence). This farm, now named Church Farm, abuts the church itself. The distance from the farm house door to the church is a mere thirty metres.[26] In all probability his grandfather, also called Daniel Foe was a first generation Huguenot migrant from Flanders.

The Foes in the Northamptonshire/Lincs/Huntingdonshire border areas, and there are not many, appear to be related in some way to Thomas and Cecilie Faux who acquired a long lease of the nearby Manor House at Peakirk and Glinton, with its extensive lands, from the Diocese of Peterborough in 1529. In 1593 the lease was acquired by a Robert Wildbore. The Wildbore family had many intimate links to the Etton Foes. The Manor House was renovated in 1650 in the 'Dutch style' when William Wildbore acquired the lease with the assistance of John Foe his apprentice.

There is no extant record of the marriage of Rose to Daniel Foe, the grandfather, and therefore no documentation of her married name. There is no baptism record for Defoe's father in Etton. There were four children in the family: Daniel (1615?), Mary (1625), Henry (1628) and James (1630). Rose married two more times: first to Solomon Faul, by whom she had two surviving children, Rose and Michael, and secondly, to Thomas King, both described as yeoman farmers. Thomas brought a son John into the marriage by an unknown wife thus the couple had the care of three children. The origins of Ellene King are a mystery. There is no evidence that Ellene was the natural born child of Rose King. It is

---

[26] See Illustration.

my belief that Rose was a niece of Thomas Lawrence, Mayor of Colchester in 1643/4 and 1655/6 and that Ellene was born Ellene Lawrence, daughter of William Lawrence, Thomas's brother. If this is so the relationship between Rose and Ellene was that of cousins.

There is no record of Defoe's grandfather's birth in England. If, say, he had lived a 'normal biblical' life span of seventy years, he would have been born around 1560 some thirty years later than the date of Thomas and Cecilie Faux's lease of the Manor House. However, while the personal histories of the two families were very different there were family associations. It is possible that Daniel Defoe's grandfather had multiple marriages. Defoe's claim that he had an elder brother renders it an open question.[27]

Thomas and Cecilie made no use of the prefix De in their name. Among the Foe's living in villages around Peakirk, Glinton and Etton, I can find only one family, a De Few, doing this. In sixteenth century France the prefix de or du denoted place. In the Auvergne region of France there is a small town of Le Faux. The use of Faux or any of its English derivatives as a surname would denote that a family originated in Le Faux.

Daniel Foe changed his name to De Foe in London in the early 1700's when he bought a Coat of Arms from the Royal College of Arms. He believed that he was entitled to show Arms through his paternal inheritance and that his action would tell others that he was a gentleman. On many occasions he claimed that he had an ancestor on his father's side of the family named 'De Beau Faux'.'[28] The use of the term De Beau in this context, both in France and England, meant a person of great stock or heritage whose family in medieval times was entitled to raise troops as a vassal of a reigning monarch. I believe that Defoe's claim was true, although unexplained; but whether or not it was true, the claim might explain his offer to Queen Anne to raise a regiment in the English cause when his subject loyalty to her was questioned in 1702-1703. I

---

[27] Defoe, Daniel, *Robinson Crusoe*, (1719. Ed. Thomas Keymer, Oxford World's Classics), 2007, 5.

[28] See Attachment. Cavalier: Defoe's Elder Brother.

produce evidence that he did assist in the forming of a Regiment at this time.[29] I believe that his paternal inheritance influenced and directed some of his most important actions.

It is probable that Defoe's grandfather was a first-generation immigrant most likely of Huguenot belief fleeing from France in the sixteenth century. Defoe was then a third-generation Huguenot. As such the Foe family were Strangers, in the terminology of the age, and were exiles in England, the country they had chosen as a refuge. Stranger had a distinctive meaning and the knowledge of it is important to an understanding of Defoe's life.

In Norwich, where I am writing this, there is a Strangers Museum and a Strangers Hall that date back to 1322. In this year the authorities in Norwich invited a group of Dutch and Flemish Huguenot traders to settle in the town for the prosperity that their advanced technology, access to capital, and prowess in weaving manufacture and trading would bring. A Stranger was the name given to a member of this group and it was applied to other areas of the country where successive waves of Huguenots settled. The pace of Huguenot immigration quickened in later centuries and became a flood in 1680. Estimates of numbers entering England have varied but perhaps 50,000 came in the period 1680-90, that is eight percent of the population as a whole.[30] The impact and influence of Huguenot migration in the Lincolnshire/Northamptonshire/ Cambridgeshire border areas is obvious. In Etton and the surrounding countryside Huguenot family and place names are common to the present time.

A daughter Mary was born to Daniel Foe on March 14, 1645 and a second son Thomas was born posthumously on November 14, 1647.[31] Although the Etton Register clearly identifies Daniel Foe and his wife Ellene as the parents of Mary the gap of four months between the baptisms of Daniel and Mary suggests that either one or other of the

---

[29] See Illustration for his military commission.
[30] Cottrett, Bernard. *The Huguenots in England: Immigration and Settlement,* Cambridge University Press, 1992.
[31] NRO. Etton Parish Register, 1587-1700.

children must have had a mother other than Ellene or that Daniel's baptism was delayed. The names of these siblings, or any other putative brothers and sisters, are without trace in Defoe's writings. However, he does refer to a brother in his correspondence.[32]Defoe was silent also about the names of all his nearest and dearest. As he was a man who created millions of written words this silence about his origins must be regarded as extraordinary. It requires an adequate explanation.

Defoe does not tell his readers where he was born. In all his written output, fictional or non-fictional, with the sole exception of *Moll Flanders*, which describes *Moll* being brought up in Colchester, Defoe does not mention a place of birth or upbringing for his fictional heroes. There is no mention of Etton in his encyclopaedic *Tour of the Whole Island of Great Britain*.

Defoe's father died in 1647 before the birth of Thomas. There are no local property records that tell the enquirer what happened to the farm in 1647. The Foe family held a lease. At the time of Defoe's birth there were three farms in Etton and only one was held as freehold. Probably the freehold of the Foe farm was held by the Diocese of Peterborough. After the death of Daniel Foe this farm would have been rented to someone else but there are no extant rental records to show the subsequent tenant.

At this time inheritance rights passed through elder sons. As was usual, the name Daniel ran in the line of family inheritance; Defoe's grandfather was a Daniel and two of Defoe's sons were so named. As the farm had to be worked, Defoe, at three years of age, could not succeed to it and neither of his uncles James and Henry, who had left the farm to take up apprenticeships in London, was interested in returning there.

Etton was a small and pleasant village at the time and is now reduced to little more than a hamlet. The land farmed there is lowland and in places beneath sea level as it drains towards fenland, Great Wash and the North Sea. The land is an early example of open-field

---

[32] H.29. Letter to Halifax, 5 April 1705. When Defoe refers to Robert Davis he calls him his brother-in-Law. See H 36.

agriculture where, as the name implies, the original strips are aggregated in open fields. In 1650 the land was farmed in strips. The open field method of farming is called the Midland System by agronomists and as it requires fewer people to work the land is associated with low levels of habitation.[33] The Compton Survey of 1676 found that Etton together with the neighbouring parish of Easton on the Hill had a population of 258 people whereas the Census of Population, 1991 lists Etton as having a population of a mere 158 souls, despite the population of England as a whole having increased ten fold since the seventeenth century. Archaeological research in the south eastern corner of the St Stephens Church graveyard suggests that Etton suffered grievously from the visitation of the plague that may have reduced its population significantly.

At the time Etton and the neighbouring villages came within the Consistory Court of Peterborough which, 'as the crow flies', is ninety-four miles from London. The migration of his uncles James and Henry to London was not unusual. They had to seek their fortunes elsewhere in common with many enterprising neighbours and there was no more obvious place than London. They were among the first of the Foe family to do so. However, the Foe family was not in the migration vanguard. A survey of the population of the City of London in 1630 does not list a single Foe.[34]

Huguenots migrating to England sought escape from Roman Catholic kings and princes who persecuted them for their Protestant beliefs. They thought of England as a place where they could practice their religion and which would be an economic haven for their talents and capital. Sixteenth century Huguenot migrants, who were smaller in numbers than in later periods, settled easily into English life and inter-married with the locals.

French cultural historians name this vast movement of Protestants as a Diaspora but the emigrants themselves when in England described

---

[33] This countryside inspired John Clare, the pastoral poet, who was born in Helpston and educated in Glinton.
[34] MA. Dale T.C. *The Inhabitants of London in 1638*, Society of Genealogists, 1931.

themselves as the Refuge. The modern meaning of this word is a shelter from pursuit, danger and trouble and contains the connotation that it might be temporary, to be reversed when the persecution stopped. There was no seventeenth century recognition of the word refugee.[35]

In the technical sense of the word Defoe's birth as a third generation Huguenot made him an English citizen but nevertheless when he moved elsewhere in the country he would have been regarded as a foreigner. As a foreigner the migrant could not become a freeman and so acquire inheritance rights although his personal property could be protected by the processes of common law. Limited civil rights could be obtained through apprenticeship of a Guild but it did not necessarily follow that this would give you the right to vote.

Restrictions were placed on the rights of foreigners, if not in a Guild, to trade. Taxation could be double the domestic rate. Navigation Acts passed in the period 1651-1663 gave preference to English traders and ships. These matters were of consequence to Defoe and help to explain his attitudes and behaviour. To my knowledge, and after considerable research, Defoe was never on an English voting roll, did not hold the freehold of any land or property he lived in or worked, and was never a member of any Church.

Leaving the country for any significant period of time created trading difficulties for migrants. If they were merchants the Navigation Acts made it impossible for them to trade legally with England in non-English ships and in some instances a returning migrant might find it difficult to trade normally.

One way out of these difficulties was to marry an English citizen who might possess, inherit, and own freehold property and who came with a marriage dowry. Defoe was an expert on dowries. A possible loophole provided by the Navigation Acts was to establish a Colonial identity by living in one and marrying. A marriage certificate was evidence of residence. I believe Defoe did this in Barbados in 1681. As is usual with Defoe, there were multiple reasons for his decision to marry.

---

[35] Cottret, 36.

In *Roxana,* Defoe was to write that *Roxana* was born in Poictiers and her parents were first generation political refugees banished from France. *Roxana* contrasted the wealth and sincerity of her parents with the 'starving Creatures who at that time [1683] fled hither for Shelter on account of Conscience, *or something else'*. Defoe meant by this that they were paid to come.[36] He is suggesting that his family background was one of wealth and social position, responsibility and religious conviction.

As an adult, Defoe defined himself, his sense of home, family, religion and political beliefs, by reference to his continental origin. He lived in Huguenot communities in Essex, London and on the continent of Europe for many years and among his heroes were those who triumphed on behalf of Protestant dissent. He stood aside from the Anglican Church and had a visceral dislike of princes, kings and the Roman Catholic Church. Huguenots distrusted kings and their Catholic religious beliefs.

In England Huguenots cautiously aligned themselves with distinct causes. They supported Parliament, and were opponents of monarchical power; espoused foreign wars to limit the powers of absolute princes and the Roman Catholic Church; and were proponents of standing armies and strong navies both to protect their trading interests abroad and England from invasion. Defoe was active as a propagandist in all these causes. It centred him in the dissenting movement in England without ever making him one in the strict English interpretation of the word.

In 1647 there was an urgent problem of what to do with a three year old boy who had lost his father and had been 'deserted' by his mother. Daniel Foe had to be brought up somewhere and by someone. His father left a will. It was proved on October 20, 1647. He left eighty pounds to his son Daniel and fifty pounds to his daughter Mary to be given to them when they were twenty-one years of age, ten pounds each to his brothers James and Henry payable when they were twenty-four years old, and ten pounds to the poor of Etton. His wife Ellene was

---

[36] Defoe, Daniel. *Roxana,* (1724. Penguin Classics, 1987), 37, n. 2.

appointed Executrix of his will and it was witnessed by Rose King and Abiel Buddle. Daniel Foe asked his 'beloved friends' Randle Wildbore the elder and John Ewen 'to give their friendly care to this my will'.[37]

By his donation to the poor made to his Parish Church, Defoe's father signalled his adherence to mainstream Protestant religious belief, to the Church of England. The Foe family in the Lincs/Huntingdonshire/Cambridgeshire border areas at this time did not behave as dissenters in the English Civil War and under the Stuarts, although a Quaker executor of a Foe will is discovered in early parish records.[38]

There is evidence that the Foe and Wildbore families had been close over sixty to seventy years. There are a number of Wildbore/Foe marriages conducted in Glinton, Essex and the City of London.[39] Randle Wildbore, Junior was Randle's grandson by Nicholas Wildbore and Mary Love the sister of Alderman William Love who won a Parliamentary seat in the City of London and who was much admired by Daniel Defoe. Mary died in 1684. In her will she named Richard and John Ewen, the sons of Randle Wildbore's trustee, as her kinsmen. In 1680 Mary's daughter Elizabeth married Thomas King, Defoe's brother. They had three children.[40] As was common in the seventeenth century, the paternal name of Foe was assigned to the male heir and Mary and Thomas followed the matrilineal line of descent.

Randle's sons had become merchants and were members of London-based Guilds but their principal homes were in Colchester and small market towns, such as Braintree and Coggeshall, around it. In some instances their sons continued to work family farms in Northamptonshire. John Ewen occupied a substantial residence in the picturesque village of Dedham, seven miles north of Colchester, in

---

[37] NRO, Etton. Will of Daniel Ffoe, proved October 20, 1647.[Ref .P.W .Book M, F.176].

[38] Wright, Thomas. *The Life of Daniel Defoe*, Randolph and Company, New York, 1894, 3.

[39] Parish Records, St Botolph's, Aldgate, London, Dec.12, 1692. Marriages: Richard Wildbore and Parnell Foe.

[40] The Will of Mary Wildbore, widow of Nicholas Wildbore, of All Hallows, Lombard Street, 18 August, 1684.

glorious countryside that was to be immortalised in the paintings of Constable.

Abiel Buddle was the vicar of Helpston some five miles to the west of Peakirk and Glinton where Randle Wildbore, Junior farmed. A graduate of Magdalen College, Cambridge he had been the occupant since 1615.[41]

Defoe's mother Ellene King did not swear to administer her husband's will and Abiel Buddle signed in her place. There are number of possible reasons for this and there may have been more than one applying here. She may already have left the farm. However, the most probable explanation is that Ellene was a Quaker and refused to swear an oath as a matter of principle. It is often argued that Rose King, her putative step mother, was a Quaker but there is no evidence that she was and nothing suggests it in this will. It may be that the difficulty with Ellene was anticipated. If Ellene's beliefs were well-known in Etton, Peakirk and Glinton their vicars may have been unwilling to have anything to do with Ellene and her children and if so they would not have been involved in the making of Daniel Foe's will. More likely is that Randle Wildbore, Senior was a parishioner of Abiel Buddle's and the making of a promise to act as a trustee was best solemnised in his presence.

Quakerism and individual Quakers were important to Defoe throughout his life. Early Quaker adherents were not quiet about their beliefs. A nineteenth century chronicler described their behaviour as follows:

> The followers of George Fox were generally of a very different spirit from the Friends of the present day. In the delirium of the new freedom in religion many ran into unwarranted excesses; and the excitement of the times stirred within them a spirit of intense antagonism, not always to existing evils but often in utter disregard of social order and proprietary.[42]

---

[41] Alumnae Cantabrigiensis.
[42] Dale, Bryan. *The Annals of Coggeshall*, London, 1860.

And writing about the behaviour of James Parnell in Coggeshall, a small town five miles from Colchester, he states that Parnell in the first flush of a new-found evangelism, protested loudly in the Parish Church there that the vicar was a 'false prophet and a deceiver.' There was a scene of great disorder in the church which led to Parnell's arrest, subsequent trial and imprisonment and a premature and untidy death. Parnell became an early Quaker martyr in Colchester and beyond. Anecdotally, it is said that Parnell stripped naked and ran down the street in Coggeshall proclaiming the coming of the spirit of the Lord.[43] At this time, as I maintain and seek to demonstrate in this work, Daniel Defoe was living in Colchester five miles away and John Owen, a vicar of the very same church in 1651-1656, was to become a significant person in his life.

The issue for the Foe and King families, and for Randle Wildbore and John Ewen, the trustees of Daniel Foe's will, was what to do with the children. Thomas King, Ellene's step father, might have been expected to take them in but he didn't. When in 1630 Rose King had lost her husband, the paternal grandparent of the Foe family at Etton, she remarried to a Solomon Faul and had two surviving children by him; and following his death she had married Thomas King who brought into the union a child from a previous marriage. Thomas does not have seemed to be willing to take in the three young Foe children. Perhaps there was no room to accommodate them or, more simply, he chose not to do so for personal reasons.

Thomas King died in 1658. He has been described as a poor farmer. However, in his will Thomas described himself as a Gentleman, which implies resources of at least £60. He left Rose a small annual annuity and relieved his son Michael of a debt owed by him. There is no mention in the will of Ellene.[44]

It did not seem possible for the Foe family to do anything for the

[43] Simpson, *William. Going Naked as a Sign*, London, 1660.
Braithwaite, William C. *The Beginnings of Quakerism*, Cambridge University Press, 1955.
[44] PCC. PROB. 11/284. Will of Thomas King, Gentleman of Botolphbridge, Huntingdonshire, 20 November, 1658.

three children. The two uncles, Henry and James, were young apprentices making their way in London while their aunt Mary had recently married a Richard Lambton and in 1647, the year of Daniel Foe's death, had her first child John.[45]

In these circumstances the only option open to Ellene King and Daniel Foe's trustees was to put the children into the care of a parish. They may have tried to do this locally but if so they failed. There are several possible reasons for this. In *Captain Singleton*, Defoe suggests one. He writes, 'I believe I was frequently moved from one town to another, perhaps as the parishes disputed my supposed mother's last settlement. Whether I was so shifted by passes I know not...' [46]

The births of these three children were recorded in Etton and the two elder children lived there at the time of their father's death. Thomas may have been born elsewhere if Ellene had moved out of the farm after the death of Daniel Foe but in that case she would most probably have had a claim for parish relief in Peakirk, Glinton or Orton Longueville where the King family lived and worked. With goodwill the local parishes could have sorted out the problem. Even if the children were put into the care of different local parishes they would have been so close to one another that distance would have been of limited consequence for continuing parental contact and care.

It may be that one reason for lack of goodwill was that Ellene was a troublesome Quaker and the parishes were keen to get rid of her; and, of her own volition, she may have wished to pursue a life as a missionary Quaker.

In his fiction Defoe, as the narrator, gives accounts of his central characters as they begin their lives. While they differ in some details, these accounts when considered together have a remarkable similarity and tell the same story. In them a father dies or disappears, a mother abandons her children, the hero is taken into the care of a parish having been moved from one parish to another, and is cared for by various 'nurses', and is then brought up in a non-caring family environment. If

---

[45] See Chart.
[46] *Captain Singleton*, 2.

there were different and varying accounts of Defoe's fictional beginnings they could all be greeted as pure narrative devices of a creative writer and it could be assumed that each description suited a particular end. However, their commonality suggests that they are more than that. The various descriptions can be described as bitter. The narrator is telling the readers that life placed him in an impossible situation and that this accounted for the extraordinary life he had to live in order to make his way in the world.

Defoe appears to be aware that something more explicit about his family background is to be expected from an author. In *King of the Pirates* Captain Avery tells his readers:

> I shall not trouble you with anything of my original and first introduction into the world. In the present account of my birth, infancy, youth or any of that part which, as it was the most useless part of my years to myself so it is the most useless to any that shall read this work to know, being altogether barren of anything remarkable in itself, or instructing to others.[47]

However, the account given by Defoe in *Moll Flanders* is an exception. Defoe spends all of one hundred pages describing *Moll's* upbringing in Colchester where it is well-known he spent a great deal of his adult life. If it is maintained, however, that Defoe is writing about his own upbringing it is necessary to produce particulars of his life there to substantiate any interpretation. For reasons that I have advanced, it is far from easy to do so.

In explaining that *Moll Flanders* is a disguised and embellished account of Defoe's own life, I encounter a great deal of immediate and heart-felt opposition for *Moll* has been well-liked over nearly three hundred years. Publisher's blurbs invariably portray *Moll* along the following lines: 'Born and abandoned in Newgate Prison, Moll Flanders is forced to make her own way in life. She duly embarks on a career that includes husband hunting, incest, bigamy, prostitution and

---

[47] Defoe, Daniel. *King of the Pyrates*, (1719. Hesperus Press, 2002), 7.

pick-pocketing, until her crimes eventually catch up with her. One of the earliest and most vivid female narrators in the history of the English novel, Moll recounts her adventures with irresistible will and candour – and enough guile that the reader is left uncertain whether she is ultimately a redeemed sinner or a successful opportunist.' [48]

In a later chapter I discuss *Moll Flanders* from both the narrative and autobiographical points of view. However, I stress here, and contrary to current literary theory, that *Moll* is Defoe's alter ego and that in the book he is writing about his own life as a child. In *Moll Flanders* Defoe writes:

> The first account that I can recollect, or could ever learn was that as I was born in such an unhappy Place, I had no Parish to have recourse to for my nourishment in my infancy, nor can I give the least Account how I was kept alive, other, than I have been told some *Relation of my Mother* (italics mine) took me away for a while as a Nurse but at whose Expense or by whose Direction I know nothing of it.

The wording is significant. In the family law of the time the child was owned by the father. In this instance the placing of the children would require the consent of the trustees Randle Wildbore and John Ewen acting for the father. The children were not placed with the father's paternal relatives about whom nothing is known. *Moll* recalled:

> I had wandered among a Crew of those people called Gypsies…It was at Colchester in Essex that these people left me…I remember…being taken up by some of the Parish Officers of Colchester…I was now in a Way to be provided for: for tho' I was not a Parish Charge upon this or that part of the Town by Law yet as my case came to be known and that I was too young to do any work, being not above three years old, Compassion mov'd me, and I became one of their own, as much as if I had been born in the Place.[49]

---

[48] Defoe, Daniel. *Moll Flanders*, (1722. Penguin Books, 1989).
[49] *Moll Flanders*, 45.

In *Captain Singleton* Defoe writes:

> My good gypsy mother, for some of her worthy actions no
> doubt, happened in time to be hanged; and as this fell out
> too soon for me to be perfected in the strolling trade, the
> parish where I was left, which for my life I can't remember
> took some care of me... [50]

It is usual for Defoe to dismiss further consideration of a character
by indicating their death but *Moll* completes her story:

> My mother was convicted of a felony for a certain petty
> theft scarce worth naming, viz. having an opportunity of
> borrowing three pieces of fine Holland of a certain draper
> in Cheapside. The circumstances are too long to
> repeat...[but his mother having pleaded she was seven
> months pregnant] she obtained the favour of being
> transported to the plantations [in New England] and left me
> ...in bad hands...

Ellene had been seven months pregnant with Thomas on the death
of her husband Daniel Foe. If it is assumed that she was committed to
Newgate for a minor crime, it is possible that Thomas was born there.
In *Moll Flanders* the narrator tells the reader that she/he was born at
Newgate. As I explain elsewhere, Defoe shifts gender and personal
identity in his fiction at his convenience and will. If the allusion here
is to the birth of his brother Thomas, the parish clerks in Etton and
Colchester might well have wished to dispute any responsibility for
the child and for the latter to have requested a Pass.[51]

Given the incapacity of Ellene to act, it is possible to argue that
Randle Wildbore and John Ewen, the trustees of Daniel Foe's will,
decided that the Foe children had to be moved to Colchester where his
mother's relatives, and their numerous families, could look after them.
However, if so, there was a need to reduce the considerable cost of
bringing them up and that required parish relief.

---

[50] *Captain Singleton*, 2.
[51] *Captain Singleton*, 2.

It has not been clear previously that Ellene King may have been entitled to claim this relief in Colchester. It seems that *his mother's relatives* were in a position to help out. My research indicates the distinct possibility that Ellene King's maiden name, when she married Daniel Foe, was Ellene Lawrence, and Rose King, nee Lawrence, was her cousin. I believe that there is a good case for arguing that Ellene was born to a William Lawrence in 1606 in the Parish of St James, Colchester.[52]

In the section Family Trees, I set out the family trees of the numerous Lawrence and King families of importance in Defoe's history. As I have stated, at this time the name Ellene in all its varieties (Hellen, Ellen etc.) was comparatively rare in England and in Colchester. It is thought that less than one per cent of girl's names came into this category. There are no Ellene's in any of the Lawrence, Foe, and King families known to me other than the two Lawrence families I name.[53] Similarly, although it is a more common name at the time, the family line of Alderman Thomas Lawrence is the only Lawrence family in the area using the name of Rose.

These Lawrence families were established as wealthy gentlemen landowners and merchants in Essex, Huntingdonshire and elsewhere from the mid-twelfth century and the family had inter-married with the gentry of Colchester and throughout Essex for over a hundred years by the time of Defoe's birth. There were numerous links between the Lawrence, Foe and Wildbore families in Colchester and throughout Essex over sixty years of Defoe's life.

Of importance to this story is that in fourteen of the ninety-four years in the period 1625-1719 five members of the Lawrence family were Mayor's of the Colchester Corporation and some of these were notable in the wider world of British politics. Thomas Lawrence, the Mayor in 1643/4 and 1655/6, was a remarkable man who played a significant role in the English Civil War and became a Member of

---

[52] See Chart.
[53] See the Charts provided in this book.

Parliament and supporter of the Protectorate in 1646.[54] However, he was not the most distinguished of the Lawrence's. A relative of Alderman Thomas Lawrence, Henry Lawrence, was a cousin and an intimate of Oliver Cromwell. He became the President of Cromwell's Council and was his landlord for a time.[55]

Defoe's account of how *Moll* was taken into parish care is not believable. While his explanation includes elements of a real story, as it stands it is incomplete and artfully misleading. In 1650 parish care for the poor and needy was regulated by a series of Acts of Parliament and in particular the Poor Relief Act, 1601. These Acts distinguished between vagrants and beggars, and the 'deserving poor' requiring help for no fault of their own. Practices varied between the 15,000 English Parishes covered by the Acts. Some information about parishes in Colchester, and in particular from St Leonard's, is available from Essex archives.[56]

In Colchester at this time parishes 'looked after their own'. Parishes stipulated that to receive aid a person needed to prove a family connection in a particular parish and a record of family residence varying from one to three years. Where there was a dispute between parishes the local Magistrates decided the issue. A system of Passes enabled a person whose family resided elsewhere, that is outside Colchester, to be considered for relief in the place of a child's birth or original family residence. In Defoe's description of events *Moll* does not know whether a Pass was involved or the issue determined by Magistrates.

On the face of it, therefore, *Moll* would not qualify for parish relief in Colchester. Defoe's narrative recognises it for he writes that the Colchester authorities took pity on him. Simply expressed this is most unlikely. Defoe stretches credulity further in his account. In *Moll Flanders* a number of families, including that of the Mayor himself, took an interest in *Moll*, supported her financially and offered

---

[54] The Family History of Gerald Dow.
[55] ERO. List of Lawrence Family Colchester Mayors. See Chart.
[56] ERO. D/P 245/8/2. Parish Book of St Leonard's 1653-1685.

accommodation from time to time. *Moll* describes her fear of losing parish support and being put out to work from the age of eight years – that is, in my chronology for Defoe, 1652/3. *Moll* cried every day in fear of being put to work. Defoe writes, 'This moved my good motherly nurse, so that from that time resolved I should not go to service yet; so she bid me not to cry, and she would speak to Mr Mayor, and I should not go to service till I was bigger.'

It is not clear to the reader how it would come about that this humble nurse would have had access to the Mayor or even if she gained an audience with him why the fate of one child among hundreds living in similar conditions would have been of interest to him. The obvious person with whom to raise the issue of service and financial support would have been the local parish clerk or one or other of the parish supervisors of work.

Defoe then gives the reader a long account of the relationships between *Moll* and the Mayor's family and in particular his daughters who regularly visited *Moll's* family. Again Defoe does not give any explanation. Why would the Mayor's family have any interest in this foundling? The daughters expressed their amusement that *Moll* wished to be raised as a gentlewoman. In *Moll's* account when parish relief was stopped the Mayor's family, who were already giving her money, made good the loss by regularly bringing additional money on their visits. Why would they do this? Defoe does not offer an explanation.

In Daniel/*Moll's* tenth year, that is 1654-1655, around the time of Thomas Lawrence's second term as Mayor, 'one of the ladies' invited *Moll* to stay with her and her children for a period of a year.

In real, rather than fictional life, there is a simple explanation for the otherwise unlikely support of the Mayor's family. Thomas Lawrence, the Mayor, was the brother of William Lawrence a wealthy Colchester merchant. If William's daughter Ellene was Defoe's mother then she was a niece to Thomas Lawrence the Mayor and, therefore, he may have accepted a kinship obligation to support one or other of the three

King/Foe children, Daniel, Thomas and Mary (Moll) King.[57] As Defoe's story is told it becomes clear that there are numerous and important links between the Foe family and the Lawrence's. It is unlikely that these links can be regarded as accidents of life. When taken together, it is highly probable that these families were inter-related.

The immediate responsibility for ensuring the welfare of the three King children rested with Randle Wildbore, Daniel Foe's 'loving friend'. He had four sons, William, John, Nicholas and Robert. They were all merchants in varying states of prosperity, members of Guilds with trading interests and premises in London, and substantial homes in Colchester, Braintree and Coggeshall.

The family member best placed to help with the children was that of Randle's brother Robert, who had a home in Lexden, Colchester, for his son William, Randle's nephew, was the parish clerk of St Peter's Parish Church. William Lawrence, Ellene's putative father, had a dwelling in Lexden. The family was living there in 1638.[58] A John Foe and another William Wildbore, to whom John Foe was apprenticed, also lived there at a later time.[59]

There were many William Wildbore's living in Essex at this time but we know that the Parish Clerk, of St Peter's. Colchester was Randle's nephew by a happy chance. When this William died in 1697 there was an annotation placed on the Parish record of his death. It read 'clerk of this parish aged about 80'. There is a record of the birth of Robert's son William in 1618 in St Peter's. It is this William, therefore, and no other who died in his eightieth year.[60] It might, therefore, have been possible for either the Wildbore or Lawrence families to make a claim for parish relief arising from birth or family residency for Ellene in either of the Parish's of St Leonard's, Lexden where Robert Wildbore had a home, or in St Peter's where his son William officiated. The residential qualification in St Leonard's is more persuasive to me.

[57] ERO. D/DCW 4/336 Will of William Lawrence, clothier of Colchester, March 17, 1609.
[58] ERO. 1638, Feb 17. Will of William Lawrence, gent of St Leonard's, Colchester.
[59] ERO. Parish Records of St. Leonard's.
[60] ERO. Parish Records of St. Leonard's.

Randle Wildbore's own will[61] gives support to the finding that it was his nephew William who was charged with the giving of parish care to young Daniel. The will was proved on January 17, 1657 in Glinton, Northamptonshire and witnessed by two John Wildbore's and by Robert Coles. There are a large number of John Wildbore's in the extended Wildbore family but I assume that these two were Randle's son John and his son of the same name. It is noteworthy here that it was a John Foe who had helped William Wildbore acquire the lease of the Manor of Peakirk and Glinton in 1650 and that his family was resident also in the parish of St Leonard's in Lexden.[62] Robert Cole was Randle's son in law from marriage to his daughter Anne. The will was executed by his wife Emma.

There was very little money to go round. Randle had numerous sons and grandchildren. He left money to only two cousins (nephews in modern usage), Randle, the son of Nicholas Wildbore (who was named after him and so passed on the family name) and *William Wildbore's child* (italics mine). It would normally be expected of a parish clerk that any marriage and children of his would be legitimised in parish records. There are no such records for William in Colchester, Essex or elsewhere. He was a bachelor.

It seems most unlikely that the name of this child was not known by the family members present at the witnessing of the will. I believe that at this solemn moment Randle was seeking to perpetuate his own family name and that of his deceased friend Daniel Foe and that the child was Daniel Defoe.

Why this act of secrecy? It is surprising because a will is a public document and it is important to give the exact name or identity of a beneficiary because of the possibility of legal challenge. In Lexden, Colchester, young Daniel was in the care of the Parish. Randle was acting prudently and attempting to make sure that the money he was giving did not go into the coffers of the Parish. *Moll* tells her readers that in 1658, that is the year following Randle's death, she had

[61] NRO. PROB 11/272. Will of Randle Wilbore of Glinton.
[62] ERO. Parish Records of St. Leonard's.

accumulated the grand sum of twenty-two shillings at the point at which she moved out of the care of the Parish into the home of an unnamed family but that this money was taken away from her.

It is possible, therefore, to deduce the process of giving parish care to the Foe children This process must have included some or all of the following elements: a family link to the Colchester Lawrence families including those of Ellene and Rose King; some link with the Mayor at the time, Thomas Lawrence; a link between Randle Wildbore and Robert Wildbore, living in Lexden; a kin connection between Thomas Lawrence, the Mayor at the time, and Ellene and Rose King; Thomas's willingness to help out; and last but not least, the subsidising of the cost, perhaps by contributing alms to the Parish Church of St Leonard's.

The children were lodged with a 'nurse' who was paid by the Parish to board and look after them. In his fictions Defoe is deeply critical of the practice of boarding out poor and abandoned children with 'nurses' and 'child takers' and there was much to be critical about. In *Roxana* Defoe writes:

> I was at first sadly afflicted at the Thoughts of parting with my Children, and especially of that terrible thing, their being taken into the Parish-keeping, and then a hundred terrible things came into my Thoughts; viz. of Parish-Children being Starved at Nurse; of their being ruin'd, let grow crooked, lam'd and the like, for want of being taken care of, and this sunk my very Heart within me.[63]

But in *Moll Flanders* he had no such criticisms of his 'nurse' and is complimentary of the woman chosen to take care of the children. He writes:

> In the provision they made for me, it was my very good hap to be put to nurse, as they call it, to a woman who was indeed poor but had been in better circumstances, and who got a little livelihood by taking such as I was supposed to be, and keeping them with all the necessaries, till they were at a

---

[63] *Roxana*, 52.

certain age, in which it might be supposed they might go to service or get their own bread. This woman had a little school, which she kept to teach children to read and to work; and having as I have said lived before that in good fashion, she bred up the children she took with a great deal of art, as well as with a great deal of care. But that which was worth all the rest, she bred them up very religiously, being herself a very sober, pious woman, very housewifely and clean, and very mannerly, and with good behaviour. So that in a word, accepting a plain diet, coarse lodging, and mean clothes, we were brought up as mannerly and as genteelly as if we had been at the dancing school.

These descriptions have the hallmark of a deal and of a special arrangement: the 'nurse' is something of a family retainer. While the Parish financed the board of these children, Defoe's education appears to have been financed by Daniel Foe's Trustees. Perhaps, the selling of the farm lease with its working tools and utensils raised some additional funds which could be used to pay for the children's upbringing. In *Colonel Jack*, Defoe writes:

> ...my father was a man of quality, and she (my nurse) had a good piece of money given her to take me off his hands, and deliver him and my mother from the importunities that usually attend the misfortune of a having a child to keep that should not be seen or heard of. My father, it seems, gave my nurse something more than was agreed for, at my mother's request, upon her solemn promise that she would use me well and let me be put to school, and charged her that if I lived to come to any bigness, capable to understand the meaning of it, she should take care to bid me remember that I was a Gentleman; and this, he said, was all the education he would desire of her for me, for he did not doubt, he said, but with some time or other the very hint would inspire me with thoughts suitable to my birth, and that I would

certainly act like a Gentleman if I believed myself to be so.[64]

It is possible to take the view that in *Moll Flanders* Defoe is writing exclusively of *Moll's* life as a fictional character, or alternatively of his sister Mary. However, an enquiring reader does become aware that although Defoe is narrating as a woman, there is no doubt that as narrator he is referring to a 'him', that is Defoe himself. For example, at this time girls were not given an education when in parish care and only very rarely by parents or guardians. Defoe is referencing himself. In the Colchester parishes of that time children in care were expected to work. Colchester was a centre of the wool and silk trade. Some Colchester parishes had their own woollen looms and even those without them took in work from producers that did not wish to carry out some work themselves. In *Moll Flanders*, *Moll* learns to sew and mend as a seamstress and earn income towards her keep. If Defoe is narrating solely about himself it remains possible that he did work of this kind.

In *Captain Singleton* Defoe writes that 'the first thing I can remember of myself afterwards [losing his mother] was that I went to a parish school, and the minister of the parish used to talk to me to be a good boy; and that though I was but a poor boy, if I minded my book [the bible], and served God, I might make a good man'.[65]

And this is what had actually happened to young Daniel Foe for his father's friends, Randle Wildbore and John Ewen, had been charged with the responsibility of seeing that money bequeathed to Daniel was used by them to support him. In the background, as seems probable from the various fictional accounts, the Wildbore and Lawrence families did do something to support the three children and the young Defoe retained the hope that he would 'inherit' his family fortune and become a gentleman.

It requires some further explanation that Defoe, when narrating in the first person, describes events through the person of his sister as well

---

[64] *Colonel Jack*, 3.
[65] *Captain Singleton*, 2.

as himself. In a previous book, I suggested that in all his fictions, written as personal histories or memoirs, Defoe is writing of events in his own life and that he is capable of the most breath-taking ability to change gender and personal identity in his narration without even the showing of a seam.

It is possible that Daniel Foe's trustees shared the burden of looking after the three children. I argue that in 1658 when Defoe was taken into the household of a family he was accompanied by his sister Mary. However, until this time Mary could have been housed by Nicholas Wildbore, Randle Wildbore's son, who was a rich merchant, and his wife, Mary Love or some other and unknown family.

I have learnt to trust Defoe's use of dates (other than his necessary addiction to add fifteen years) subject to the recognition of some obfuscation. He writes tortuously in *Roxana*:

> After I had been married about four years [1688], my own Father died, my mother having been dead before [Mary Wildbore/Love died in 1684] ...[he left a legacy] in the hands of my Elder Brother [Defoe, Thomas being the younger], who running on too rashly in his Adventures, as a Merchant, failed and lost not only what he had but what he had for me too, as you shall hear presently... [Defoe's bankruptcy in 1692] Within two Years of my own Fathers death, my husbands Father also died.

Nicholas Wildbore died in 1664 and someone else must have assumed responsibility as the Head of the family. This person might have been John Ewen, a trustee of Defoe's father's will.

As Thomas the younger brother married into the family of Nicholas and Mary Wildbore it is possible that at some time the children might have been farmed out to three families. These statements have to be interpreted using the family terms of the time. *Moll* is not writing about biological parents but the heads of family establishments she called her family.

Defoe's personality traits arose from this troubled and difficult upbringing as a child in Essex. He lived in and around Colchester for over sixty years of his life and his character was formed there. In Colchester some parishes, although not I believe St Leonard's, obliged children in care to prominently display on their outer garment a capital letter 'P' so identifying them as poor and recipients of parish care. Indignities such as this and of other public attitudes to the poor would have shaped the life Defoe led as a young boy and the complex adult and great writer he was to become. The young Defoe was not at the heart of things in a great capital city, and not born into a ruling elite with pretensions to be numbered among the mighty; but Colchester was not a bad place to be and it was not a disaster to be born a Foe, a Lawrence or a King.

Chapter 2

Childhood

Fate certainly thus directed my beginning, knowing that I had work to do in the world, which nothing but one hardened against all honesty or religion could go through...

Captain Singleton, 1722
Daniel Defoe

There is a commonality, as I have illustrated, in Defoe's various fictional accounts of his narrator's beginnings. In these stories a father dies early, a mother abandons her children, the hero or heroine is taken into the care of parish authorities and is moved from one parish to another and cared for by various 'nurses' and children are brought up in non-caring family environments. Relatives and place of birth are never referred to by name and little information is given to the reader to enable the true circumstances to be identified.

The beginnings of his narrators are accompanied by curious emotions. Like *Cinderella* and *Oliver Twist* the hero is entitled to something better.

As a young boy these emotions must have been difficult to sustain. At any time bad behaviour might have cut him off from his 'true' destiny and it would have been God's judgement that had cast him adrift. In practical terms, if no Wildbore or Ewen or any of his parents relatives stepped forward to take care of him at the age of fourteen the Church would have paid for an apprenticeship for him and he would have become a tradesman and lost to literature and posterity.

If the quotation at the head of this chapter is an expression of the feelings of the young Defoe at the conscious beginning of his life, it is understandable but questionable. It poses a number of issues. What on earth can he mean? Does he mean that if God had chosen to cast him adrift that all his struggles to survive and re-write his personal history were a denial of God's providential judgement? What was the work Defoe had to do in the world and why did it require dishonesty and sinful behaviour to undertake and fulfil his mission?

If this young boy believed that his fortune was to be restored by acquisitiveness, and that it could not be done at all without aggrandisement and dishonesty, then each step he took on such a road would be against God's will. God would punish him for all the actions he was bound to take. God saw and knew everything and his will could not be denied.

The constant reference to a pre-enlightenment Old Testament God, and in particular God as the ultimate reference of all things temporal, is unattractive to most people in our time. If it is believed, as Defoe did, that punishment was certain and that no act of contrition could grant redemption for wrong-doing, then, and ultimately, there was not much point in acting against one's true nature.

It has not been appreciated that Daniel Defoe lived at least part of each of sixty years of his long life in Essex. He was brought up in the county and returned there several times as an adult. He earned his living in and from Essex for most of his adult life. In the *Tour Through the Whole Island of Great Britain* Defoe did not mention Etton and its environs. He skirted the entire area. But he did write confidently of Colchester:

> COLCHESTER is an ancient Corporation: the town is very populous; the streets fair and beautiful; and though it may be said to be finely built, yet there are abundance of very good and well-built houses in it...The River Colne, which passes through this town, is navigable within three miles of town for ships of large burthen; a little lower it may receive even a royal navy. And up to that part called the Hithe, close to the houses, it is navigable for hoys and small barks...The town may be said to subsist by the trade of marking bays, though indeed the whole county [of Essex] large as it is, may be said to be employed, and in

part maintained, by the spinning of wool for the bay trade of Colchester and its adjacent towns.[66]

These adjacent towns included Coggeshall, which specialised in silk, and Braintree. Colchester makes claim to be the oldest town in Britain dating settlement back to pre-Roman times. The town was given a Royal Charter as far back as 1189. Corporation dignitaries have occupied Offices of State. It never was a town to ignore. In the years 1550-1600 a large number of weavers and cloth makers from Flanders settled in and around Colchester and to this day there is a Dutch quarter. These immigrants helped establish Colchester as one of the most prosperous wool towns in England.

In particular the Parish of St Leonard's was prosperous as it is now. It's care of the poor was financed by a stream of bequests from wealthy merchants. Today there are many fine seventeenth and eighteenth century buildings in the Parish which were financed by merchants. St Leonard's Church is opposite a wildlife park once owned by a local merchant and now bequeathed for public use.

There were numerous Foe's, Lawrence's and Wildbore's listed in the records of St Leonard's and its neighbouring parishes. While the Lawrence families were long-established with firm roots in the community, the Wildbore's had flourished more recently as producers and merchants of wool products. They were part of an emergent merchant class that was among the real victors in the English Civil War. The merchants of Braintree, Coggeshall and Colchester were London-based. It was fifty-nine miles from Colchester to east London and sixty-five miles to the centre. If a person travelled by horse, carriage or wagon he could leave this part of Essex early in the morning and be in London premises in the afternoon. It was entirely possible to work four days in London and have three days at the weekend in the country.

---

[66] Defoe Daniel. *Tour Through the Whole Island of Great Britain*, (1724-1726. Penguin Classics, 1986), 57-60.

A growing number of merchants could enjoy the intoxication and freedom of making money from trade and still have time and resources to own farms, manor houses and fine estates in the country. They could become gentlemen from humble circumstances.

Trade had become international and Essex was well-placed to trade with the Low Countries. However, it was risky. International cargoes could be lost in storms at sea or captured by the navies of hostile states, Spain and France and the Low Countries. There was a whole new world of financial speculation. Fortunes could be won and lost in dealing rooms at the toss of a coin.

The Civil War had been fought and won to protect the rights and interests of this growing class of merchant trader. A man earning his living in this way was interested in low taxes, good roads and a foreign policy that protected his goods and ships on the high seas. The Civil War had given this class a taste of rights, freedoms and self-government, and parliaments that promoted its economic interests. They had no wish to lose these advantages under a restored monarchy. Many of these local merchants were citizens of London with parliamentary voting rights gained by the ownership of property and membership of Guilds.

The county of Essex, like most others, was divided in its allegiances in the Civil War. On the whole it was for Parliament but for a time in 1647 Colchester was held by Royalist forces. The City was besieged by a Parliamentary army.

The Foe/King children came into the City at the end of this siege and the buzz of the 'occupation' must have been a feature of Defoe's early life there. The Civil War experience strengthened the resolve of the citizens of this ancient City. In the end the citizens of Colchester had opposed absolutism and attempts by central government to control their civil and religious affairs whether by monarch or republic. They had no time for either and resolved to protect and defend their democratic rights. Defoe writes in the *Tour* that, 'The government of the town is by a mayor, high steward, a recorder, or his deputy, eleven alderman, a chamberlain, a town clerk, assistants and eighteen common-council men.'[67] These men were powerful not only in their own town but as Members of Parliament and occasionally great Offices of State. A Corporation Recorder, Earl Cowper, was twice Lord High Chancellor of England.

The Essex detestation of absolutism in all its forms was strong in Colchester. John Evelyn described the town as 'swarming in sectaries' but with a preference for congregational worship. At the time of Defoe writing the Colchester section of the *Tour*, the City had eight Anglican churches and five non-conformist meeting houses, two of which were Quaker, as well as Dutch and French churches.

The Wildbore and Foe families were representative of this feisty Colchester population. There is evidence that some were Quakers and many migrated to New England as religious dissenters of some description. Those that left Essex were ambitious for a new life in the New World where they believed they could make their own rules and worship as they pleased; but the majority were content enough to worship in the Anglican Church, which became broad enough to accommodate them.

The Foe family, Flemish in origin, hated absolutism centred upon Roman Catholicism. They maintained that Catholicism was an agent of political and social control. In his adult life Defoe was tolerant of all religious belief other than Catholicism, at least in his public statements, whether expressed in its Roman form or by the High Church faction of the Church of England. Defoe's hatred was visceral and he agitated against Rome in public as if his life was dependent upon the struggle.

There is little evidence that Defoe was influenced by Presbyterianism as has been thought by earlier biographers. From an early age he set his soul against all paternalistic methods of religious control and positioned himself somewhere in the centre of the broad mass of religious dissenters.

Leading merchants and citizens of Colchester, which included many Wildbore families, did not think of themselves as provincial parvenus but

---

[67] *Tour*, 59.

as citizens of the world. They believed that their fortunes were determined by the influence exercised by England in this wider world. To the east lay the great and stormy waters of the North Sea, just visible on a sunny day from one hundred and twenty miles of Essex coastline. The threats to the shipping lanes that carried their goods and liberties came from a European continent perilously close to their shores. Politically, in his long life, Defoe was to set himself against the ambitions of the major Catholic European powers, France and Spain, who sought the control of English sea routes. In his life-time Defoe spoke for the majority of his fellow English merchants in their opposition to continental absolutism; and for a much smaller minority of dissenters, never more than ten per cent of the entire population, who maintained their demands for full equality and social justice.

It is possible and usual to read the early life recounted in *Moll Flanders* entirely through *Moll*; but not, I maintain, when she/he was 'taken in by a family' when Defoe and his heroine was fourteen years of age. Either Defoe on his own, or with his sister, spent ten to thirteen years in modest accommodation, most probably in a small two bedroom workman's cottage owned by the church in Lexden, within walking distance of St Leonard's Parish Church, and to the north west of Colchester. I am less sure of the habitation of Thomas King. There is no allusion by Defoe anywhere to be found in *Moll Flanders* that the infant Thomas was accommodated with them. In 1648, as an infant of a few months, he would have needed a wet nurse. As he was to marry into the family of Nicholas Wildbore, Randle Wildbore's son, it might be the case that this family took him in as a baby.

The circumstances of the two children were humble; but in Lexden the poor rubbed shoulders with the prosperous. Lexden was a centre for the wool trade. It was a cottage industry. In everyday concourse merchants and their factors were a common sight in the streets and byways as they scurried around in their business of getting product made and shipped to the market. The street-names evoke the wool trade to this day. Some part of this product was destined for the nearby ports of Ipswich and Harwich. The burgeoning wool trade provided a living for the Foe, Wildbore and Lawrence families in Defoe's early life, and their interests extended to London in the south, Hull to the north, and to the European continent to the east.

It is impossible to deny that the adult Defoe had a prodigious knowledge of the wool trade and of the every day interests and problems of manufacture: the marketing and finance of textile products, the economic and navigational problems of sea-going merchants, the maritime activities of the Dutch, Spanish and Portuguese navies, and the dangers of piracy. In East Tilbury, close to Defoe's brickworks in the 1690's, the estate of the Manor House of East Gubyons, owned in the family line of Edward Lawrence, included woollen looms.[68] Defoe's adult activities included his own woollen manufacture. As a foundling desperately seeking a place in a hostile world, it is easy to imagine the young Defoe resolving to find out how his relatives earned a living and to seek to become a part of their world. He must have done this with very great intensity and high intelligence.

Nathaniel Lawrence, to whom Defoe was related, owned many trading vessels which were berthed at nearby Ipswich.[69] In Defoe's teens a daytime trip to the port must have carried a thrill and excitement of its own. It might have been possible for him to board one of these ships and later in life to cadge a sea voyage just as Defoe reveals in his fiction. Seamen on board ship, and in many an inn, would have been a source of strange tales of adventure; naval encounters with pirates and the warships of the French, Dutch and Spanish navies; exotic places and their riches; of black men and slavery; of plundered wealth, gold and silver coinage, diamonds and other precious stones. A penniless man might venture forth on one of these ships and return very rich; but he would have to fight for these riches and young men had best learn quickly to defend themselves and to be able to dispose of the opponents they would encounter.

Britain is a union of small islands and no citizen is much more than a day trip from the sea. The appeal of life as a voyager and seaman is

---

[68] ERO. D/DC 23/633-644 Deeds concerning the Manor of Gobyons, East Tilbury.
[69] ERO. Will of Nathanial Lawrence the Elder of Colchester, 15 August, 1712.

deep in the bones of every Englishman. Quite early it must have become rooted in Defoe's mind that the ultimate escape and refuge from a life that offered him too little was to be at sea. In the *Journal of the Plague Year* the great sailing ships are berthed upstream in the Thames. They could not trade, for their entry into foreign ports had been blocked by occupants in fear of disease. In themselves they were pure and free of infection. If one could only swim out and board a ship one could escape the dangers of a land-borne life. Travel to the continent of Europe meant more than adventure, trade and riches to Defoe. It was, in a sense, a going back home, an association with the places and religious and political causes that had shaped the early history of his father's Foe family.

In the sixty years of his life Defoe spent in England he resided and worked in Colchester, Tilbury and their surrounds. A few miles to the north-west of Colchester lies the village of Great Tey, where Defoe co-habited with Mary Norton, and where after his death in 1731 his son Benjamin Norton, who had twice married in the Parish Church there, had a peddlers licence. To the east of Great Tey, lies Fordham where Defoe leased land from the Corporation of Colchester. This land was worked beyond his death by his son Daniel; and in a straight line is the Queens Head at Fordingstreet, where his brother Thomas lived and worked a farm until his death in 1716, and where Defoe stayed from time to time.

It is not difficult to imagine the lives these children lived and Defoe has described some of it in his fiction. Defoe was given a boy's education. He was taught to read and write by their 'nurse' who, if the account in Moll Flanders is to be believed, was a pious woman. At the time the principal purpose of education was religious: and the intention was to enable children to come into God's purpose for humanity as a whole and for them personally. Writing involved the copying out of the Bible and punishment was to do it some more. Defoe writes that as a child he copied out the Pentateuch (the first five books of the Old Testament). It reads like a punishment or a task of preservation but it was most probably a normal part of any child's education at the time.[70]

---

[70] *Beyond Belief,* 36, 40.

37

Reading was confined then, with exceptions for the very rich, to the Bible and to Psalters, to the writing out of biblical texts, and the reading of literature about martyrdom. It was a time of emotionalism in religion: pietism, mysticism and quietism. All these traditions influenced Defoe.

Mary could not been given the same education as a boy, or indeed, any education. Girls were expected to busy themselves with domestic tasks and the common occupation for a working class girl was to enter domestic service. *Moll's* story as told by Defoe tells the reader that she worked as a seamstress and even when taken into a wealthy merchant's family she was expected to continue this work.

At the age of fourteen Defoe was to receive a good house-education. One indication for the reader that Defoe is the subject of *Moll's* story is that *Moll*/Mary would never have been given such an education. This disparity of treatment by gender may well have been the root of Defoe's adult conviction that life treated women harshly and that they should not be denied fair life-chances.

The two children, if together in Lexden, would have cuddled up together in a single bed for warmth. When the weather was particularly cold the 'nurse' might have kept the fire going and all the family would have slept around the hearth. Eating would have been restricted to scraps for breakfast and one family meal a day which required all the children to be present. In between times they would have been hungry. When Defoe writes that his mother was vexed if he did not clear the plate it was probably the reaction of a hard-pressed 'nurse' who was aware that the children would not get another chance to eat that same day. This way of living brought the children together; each was dependent on the other. Daniel as the elder son had a particular responsibility to look after his sister. Nowhere in Defoe's work does the reader hear what they said to each other as young children.

Given Defoe's proclivity to project himself onto others, the story he tells about himself in *Captain Singleton* is helpful to an understanding of his state of mind and the life he was leading. The dates given by Defoe in his fiction always have a real-life connotation and they do so in *Captain Singleton*. Defoe writes that when he was a little boy of about two years of age he was stolen and then resold to a beggar woman and then to a Gypsy. Afterwards at a time that he could not remember he was taken into the care of a parish. Defoe was three years of age when he was taken into the care of the Parish of St Leonard's. This time sequence is the same as given by Defoe in *Moll Flanders*. The Gypsy mother gave him the name of Bob Singleton. Thus Bob Singleton was not the narrator's real name but a name that he had 'acquired' and decided to use after he had been 'abandoned'.[71]

The term Gypsies refers to people who travelled about the country, did not accept the usual conventions of social behaviour, and who were rebellious of all civil attempts to exert authority over them. Quakers were sometimes referred to as Gypsies. Early Quakers rejected all paternal authorities and were thought licentious. David Blewett in his notes to an edition of *Moll Flanders* comments that, the actual words used by Defoe are important. Defoe wrote, '*those people they call Gypsies*'. Blewett comments, 'True Gypsies were thought to have come originally from Egypt (hence their name), but it was widely believed that many vagabonds blackened their faces and those of their stolen children in order to appear as Gypsies.' [72] Defoe's Gypsies are not real at all but invented by him for narrative purposes just as he invented Captain Bob. Defoe is expressing that his feelings about the sudden 'abandonment' by his family after his father's death was akin to being stolen and that his brother had disappeared before he had any memory of him.

It is my contention that Mary's life is strongly alluded to in *Moll Flanders*. She became a domestic dogsbody who earned her living from sewing. In Defoe's writings he shows empathy for women. He must have become painfully aware that his sister's life was one of extreme difficulty and he sympathised with her. It is my belief that he developed a physical relationship with Mary and that as his and her story is told it becomes clear that the relationship was sexual.

---

[71] *Alien Come Home*, 37.
[72] *Moll Flanders*, 430, n.9.

In Defoe's fiction he develops many situations where there are triangular relationships usually involving two men and a woman. In real life there is evidence that this is how he lived his life. It would not have been thought strange in the seventeenth century where poverty, cramped living spaces, and lives spent in isolated rural communities made incest common and widely tolerated.

The children would have had to learn to forage in the fields. Wood needed to be collected for the fire and the fields and rivers were a source of food. Social historians maintain that at the end of the seventeenth century, as the urban population grew, up to thirty percent of people had no roof above their heads but slept rough in fields and hedgerows. This figure may be exaggerated but it is certainly true that many people did live rough and went to sleep hungry.

In the summer and autumn food could be foraged from open land and forests: fruits, berries and herbs could be gathered in abundance. In harsh winters it was not only birds and wild animals that died of hunger but poor people without the money for provisions. It was no wonder that the poor stole to keep alive. However, the Foe children were cared for by a good, pious woman who would have come down on them heavily if they were blatantly stealing from farms. An easier way to steal was to follow the path of the nearby River Colne into the town and to filch from local traders in the market. There were rabbits to be snared in the fields and fish to be caught in the river, activities that were legal so long as the acts did not involve trespass on private property.

An easier way to get food was to steal the money to buy it. In bustling markets there were rich takings to be had from picking pockets in the gathering city crowds. Once the necessary skills had been acquired there were opportunities to make serious money. However, you had to be very skilful to lift purses and if you were caught doing it the punishments were severe. There is a wealth of information about petty theft in all Defoe's fictions and, assuming the biographical nature of his fiction, it seems highly likely that he grew up as a petty thief and became an accomplished one.

If a little money was not enough you could gain more by being a member of a gang. If you were brave enough, there were more spectacular deeds of burglary and assault you could perform. In *Captain Singleton* Defoe writes, 'I was exactly fitted for their society indeed [of sailors] for I had no sense of religion upon me....I was preparing to be as wicked as anyone could be, or perhaps ever was...' In *Colonel Jack* Defoe writes, 'We were hopeful boys...and promised very early, by many repeated circumstances of our lives that we would be all rogues... [and using the third person to distance himself] Singleton tells the reader that he set out in the world so early, that when he began to do evil he understood nothing of the wickedness, nor what he had to expect...'

In *Moll Flanders*, *Captain Singleton*, *Colonel Jack* and *Memoirs of a Cavalier*, there is a common pattern: petty theft, graduating to more serious crime, appearances before Justices of the Peace and an ability to talk oneself out of trouble – and a growing fear that it was all getting too much and that the narrator would finish up hanged.

It is usual for young boys to pass through a period when they make a nuisance of themselves and commit crimes out of bravado. Typically such boys grow through this period to emerge as honest and responsible citizens. However, Defoe's narratives suggest a passage of crime that was more serious. In *Colonel Jack*, after describing Jack's drift into petty crime, Defoe writes:

I never took this picking of pockets to be dishonesty but, as I have said above, I looked on it as a kind of trade that I was to be bred up to, and so I entered upon it, till I thus was made a thief involuntarily, and went on to a length that few boys do without coming up to the common period of that kind of life, I mean to the transport ship or the gallows.

Through his characters Defoe shows that he was well-spoken and seemed, to observers, to have been carefully brought up as a thoughtful and honest boy with a sense of religious responsibility. *Colonel Jack* put it this way:

> For my particular part, I got some reputation for a mighty
> civil, honest boy; for if I was sent on an errand, I always did
> it punctually and carefully, and made haste again; and if I
> was trusted with anything, I never touched it to diminish it,
> but made it a point of honour to be punctual to whatever was
> committed to me, though I was errant a thief as any of them
> in all other cases.

Defoe is suggesting to his readers that the respectable image he created in his life was not real; it was invented as a ruse to cover up the 'real boy'. The projection of this image had utility in that the impression of being a trustworthy boy gave him cover when he was caught out committing a crime. *Colonel Jack* tells his readers that, '...some of the poorer shopkeepers would often leave me at their door, to look after their shops till they went up to dinner, or till they went over the way to an ale house, and the like, and I always did it freely and cheerfully, and with the utmost honesty'.

Defoe's characters are sturdy boys able to look after themselves. They did not pick quarrels but if conflict was unavoidable they knew how to fight. It was a last resort for Defoe's characters because they were able to talk themselves out of almost any predicament. In their youth Defoe's male heroes learnt to swordfight. In his adult life Defoe carried a sword in public. Defoe's characters wished themselves to be cautious and slow to take offence or to put themselves in a position where they might be seriously injured or killed. It is easy to imagine this as the advice or admonition given by a fencing instructor; but in his life Defoe, by his own admission, was rash, quick-blooded and hasty in picking quarrels and thus was constantly in danger.

There was a problem for young Daniel Foe of where to hide money and other booty, for if he took stolen goods and money back into his home the 'nurse' would surely have found it and created a mighty fuss. She might have been compelled by conscience to take this booty from him and endeavour to return it to the rightful owners. Whatever she did would have put him in severe danger. In *Colonel Jack*, Defoe describes movingly an evolution of immense importance to him. He wished to look good and to clothe himself better. The first use he made of ill-gotten wealth was to buy clothes and improve his appearance. He ate out and began to look and behave as a young gentleman.

In understanding Defoe it is important to keep track of his fictional heroes thieving and deception. Delinquency was at first no more than mischief and of a minor seriousness; but the habit of thieving led to serious crime when he was a teenager staying in London without the day to day guidance of mentors. The seeds grown in childhood developed into the practice of substantial and sophisticated deception as an adult. Defoe had learned that the best way to hold on to money, or to create it when he had none, was to use letters of credit and bills of exchange. These schemes to invent money were developed to meet the need to finance overseas trade and to provide cash during the inevitable delays in receiving payment for goods transported by ships overseas. Whether one was able to finance a business this way at acceptable interest rates and discounts was dependant – as it is now – by a credit rating. Good reputation was a condition of business.

As a merchant making his way Defoe needed to be well-regarded just as in Colchester, as a boy, he needed goodwill from shopkeepers. The sums involved were much larger and losses arising from the dishonouring of bills more damaging. In *Colonel Jack* and *Moll Flanders* Defoe tells his readers how these more sophisticated scams worked.

Gaining trust was the key to the successful working of a scam. People needed to trust you before they lent money and if they were doubtful you were required to have good security and accept a charge on your goods. All con artists have to develop the art of appearing trustworthy. Few practitioners were more skilled at it than Defoe.

These dichotomies must have puzzled Defoe's 'masters'. When Defoe was working for a patron such as Lord Somers, Robert Spencer or Lord Harley he could be expected to perform to high standards and usually did. Others had to be reassured. Harley had to tell Queen Anne that Defoe was a good man really. Defoe recognised that if someone was paying you, it was right to perform. These performances were part of his life, but for him much else was 'going on.' His real purposes and aims, some of which were blatantly dishonest and immoral, were as important to him - and often more so. These other purposes almost always involved the drive to aggregate and hide wealth and to be recognised as a gentleman of means.

What was 'the work he knew he had to do in the world which nothing but one hardened against all honesty or religion could go through'? This boy had been born the eldest son of a respectable farmer who came within the definition of a gentleman. On the death of his father it was his duty to care for the widow and his siblings. In the Foe family, as the elder son of an elder son he had a superior family status to that of his uncles James and Henry. However, when his father died he was a mere three years of age and there was no estate to inherit. He was cast into an indifferent world, sustained by parish relief and the whims and consciences of his father's friends and distant relatives.

It is not necessary to reach deep into a psychoanalytic school of reasoning to be aware of the complexity of the emotions experienced by the young Daniel Foe. What seems obvious is that Defoe did not complete the rite of passage which in a 'normal' progression leads from an Oedipal desire to replace the father and come into possession of the mother and to a partial renunciation of the early desire to be possessed by and approved of by the father.

Bergler maintains that the taking of great risks, that is gambling, revives childhood memories of grandeur. He suggests that gambling against the evidence of logic, intelligence and morality comes from an unconscious desire to lose money.[73] Tarpy argues that such risk taking is always associated with an unresolved Oedipal complex.[74]

Instinctively Defoe would have felt that he had replaced his dead father by his mother only to be abandoned by her. His original sin of 'killing' his father was not rewarded in any way and surely he would be punished for it.

---

[73] Bergler, Edmund. *The Psychology of Gambling*, New York, 1974.
[74] Lea, B.E.G., *The Individual in the Economy*, Cambridge University Press, 1957.

Human desires are transgressive and unknown. In our lives we are driven to approach and then to avoid objects of desire; and what makes us feel most alive is the act of risking our lives. When and where security is offered as an alternative to risk, and perversely, it is risk that is embraced and surprise, dread and fear which replaces repose. There is always something or someone we seem to value more than the safety of our own lives, and more than life itself. A religiously educated seventeenth century man believed that for this waywardness and sin he would be punished in this life and the next and he believed that this punishment was both right and certain.

It cannot be denied that for Defoe risk-taking was irresistible. Paula Backscheider writes: 'As a businessman he was essentially a gambler, excited by new deals, new prospects. What we see in many of the speculations is an almost compulsive interest in taking risks and acquiring wealth.'

Defoe's maturation, and in particular the issue for him of sexual identity, must have been highly complex. Leo Abse argues, from an imperfect biographical understanding, that Defoe never completed the rite of passage from child to adult and that any study of his risk taking, extravagancies, crushing guilt and extraordinary feminine identification and bisexual practices is best explained by his childhood.

In some ways Abse takes too little notice of the nature of sexual identity in the seventeenth century. It is generally agreed now that gender difference, the distinctions between male and female, did not exist in its present form until the second half of the eighteenth century. It did not mean much to claim a man to be homosexual, bisexual or heterosexual. There were other social and gender sexualities and social signifiers. Defoe was in contemporary language a sodomite and a person capable of intense passion for men.

At a practical level, in the absence of a welfare state, individuals looked to their families and the wider network of kinship for help in bad times and assistance to make their way in the world. If a family member married into money the wider family rejoiced; if he married badly or unwisely he would be the subject of obloquy.

Defoe believed he had the obligation to restore his family fortunes, to bring his scattered family together and to protect and enhance the fortunes of those nearest to him. It was not an easy task to 're-possess his mother' because she had either died or had been deported to New England. Nor was his starting position among the parish poor of Colchester much help. But his life was not without promise. The Wildbore and Ewen families were pledged to help, his uncles James and Henry, traders and merchants in London, could be expected to take some regard of him, and God had not entirely deserted him. Defoe at a moment of stress was able to write, 'The God that gave me brains will give me bread.' Defoe was a very, very, clever boy. He must have realised he was highly astute at an early age and that he was going to need all his wit to make his way in the world.

Chapter 3

The Foe, King, Wildbore and Lawrence Families

My original may have been as high as anybody's, for aught I know, for my mother kept very good company, but that part belongs to her story more to mine.

Colonel Jack
Daniel Defoe, 1722

In various writings Defoe refers to his ancestry inherited through his father, perhaps from multiple marriages, but in the quotation above he is referring to his mother's ancestry. While his isolation as a child in the care of a parish must have been deeply dispiriting to him his descriptions of abandonment may not be literally true in all respects. While it seems undeniable that he felt the emotions he wrote about in real life, it is probably true that many adults cared about him.

The 'conventional account' of Defoe's life concentrates on his Foe relatives, and their family friends and acquaintances, some of whom are important to any narrative of Defoe's life. However, there were hardly any of these people accessible to Defoe until he spent time in London at the age of sixteen. Bastian is alone in identifying linkages with the Wildbore families[75] but he makes no mention of the very many Lawrence family connections or the importance of his mother's relatives, the very many King families. No adequate explanation of Defoe's life can be given without discussion of them. In this work I give numerous examples of the inter-linkages of these families in Defoe's story. In a series of charts, I sketch out some of the families of importance to Defoe over eighty-six years of his life. I summarise the links of greatest importance at this point to make it easier for readers to follow the narrative.

Foe Families

At the time of Defoe's birth there were very few Foe families in

---

[75] Bastian, 43.

England. It appears that most of them were concentrated in eastern England. In the Consistory Records of Huntingdonshire, Ely and Northamptonshire over the period 1449-1739 there are fifteen Foe and Foe derivative families.[76] In 1638 there were no Foe's in the City of London but by the 1660's there were some half a dozen. Probably there were no more than thirty Foe and Foe derivative families in the whole of England. As it is possible to trace the origins of at least twenty of these families in Northamptonshire and Ely, it is highly likely that Defoe had knowledge of almost all of them.

The only Foe family known to me in Colchester was that of John Foe, a direct descendant of Thomas and Cecilie Foe, who was apprenticed to William Wildbore. This William became the lease holder of the Manor of Peakirk and Glinton in 1650. A John Foe, most likely a descendant of Thomas and Cecilie, was a member of the Parish Council of St Leonard's, Lexden, Colchester in 1720. [77] Apart from Defoe's uncles Henry and James, I have been able to find only two other Foe families in the City of London in 1695-1696: those of Thomas Foe and William Foe, who lived with a woman described as a widow, and whose establishment included a maid called Susannah Foe. Thomas is most likely a descendant of Thomas and Cecilie Faux, for the name Thomas runs in the family, while a William Foe is recorded in the records of the Consistory of Northamptonshire.[78]

Backscheider believes that to these Foe families can be added another, a London based merchant called Du Foe and his wife Jane. Backscheider concludes a discussion of Du Foe by asserting that his wife Jane (birth name unknown) was a cousin of Defoe's.[79] I do not know of any Jane Foe who might be Defoe's cousin. My own belief is that Du Foe was a trader of French nationality handling merchandise to and from France, and that Defoe's motive in intervening to try to rescue his widow Jane from a charge of attending an illegal religious assembly was trade rather than family allegiance. Strictly speaking, the prefix for

[76] Wright, 3.
[77] ERO. Parish Records of St. Leonard's.
[78] Wright, 3.
[79] Backscheider, 43, note 4.

a surname based on place in France, such as Faux, is masculine. Du Foe is grammatically correct and as such normal to a French citizen. After her husband's death Jane Foe continued with his business. These Foe families constituted a limited kinship network in London for Defoe but he makes no direct mention of any of them by name in his written work.

Lawrence Families

The Lawrence families known to Defoe were wealthy merchants and landowners based in Essex, Hertfordshire and Kent. All these counties are frequently mentioned in Defoe works. Some of them could link their ancestry to Henry Lawrence, who became President of Oliver Cromwell's Council in 1654.[80] This link is important to Defoe's story for a number of reasons. Of greatest interest is that in 1656 Henry Lawrence was elected a Member of Parliament for both Caernarvonshire and Colchester and ceded his Colchester seat to Thomas Lawrence, twice the Mayor of Colchester during the time that Defoe was growing up there. Charts for the Lawrence families are provided in this work together with a list of Mayors. This list includes four Lawrence family members. In addition to the Mayoralty these families provided Aldermen and key officials to the Corporation of Colchester.

Henry Lawrence became the Minister of Plantations in Cromwell's Republic and owned plantations in New England and Barbados. His son John first owned plantations in Barbados and later became a very rich planter in Jamaica. The family link would have been talked about in the homes of his relatives and Henry Lawrence would have been regarded as a role model inspiring Lawrence families to migrate to make their fortunes. The Dow family site records three members of a Lawrence family, John, William and Thomas, migrating to New York State.[81] Unfortunately there are many Lawrence families with three brothers of this name and I have been unable to identify the right one.

There are three main groupings of these Lawrence families of

---

[80] *Dow Family History.*
[81] *Dow Family History.*

importance to Defoe: first the family of Alderman Thomas Lawrence (who died about 1594) and his wife Agnes; secondly, the numerous families of their children; found mainly in Colchester, Coggeshall and surrounding small towns; and thirdly the family of Edward Lawrence who owned the Manor House of East Gubyons in Tilbury and were settled in considerable numbers in St Albans, Hertfordshire and West and East Farleigh in Kent. A difficulty in establishing these links to Defoe is the commonality of their first names; there are numerous Mary's, John's, William's and Thomas's. Records of their marriages often do not exist and may have been destroyed or not kept. In some instances, when marriages were arranged by private treaty, there were no records. Wills are a useful source of family information but they were not always made and those that were and are extant rarely give a complete picture

To clarify some of these issues I have provided footnotes to the Charts. However, to be clear, I summarise below the links with the Lawrence families which I can prove by documentation or suggest by conjecture.

I have provided good documentary proof that Defoe and his sister Mary were taken into the care of St Leonard's Parish Church, Lexden, Colchester, Essex. This being so, the events Defoe describes, as narrator, in *Moll Flanders* are important accounts of the upbringing of the two children in the fourteen year period 1648-1662.

In this period the Mayor of Colchester, Thomas Lawrence, and his daughters helped the two children financially by bringing them money and by placing sewing tasks with the 'nurse' some of which may have been undertaken by Mary. They were visited also by other families in the town who, I conjecture, were Lawrence families related to the Mayor.[82]

When Defoe was fourteen years of age, he was surprised that yet another family came forward to help him. I conjecture that this family was that of John and Anne Lawrence who were resident in East Tilbury

---

[82] *Tour*, 59, n.18.

and who, for a time, were occupants of the Manor Houses there and in Mucking and Waltons.[83] The successors of Edward Lawrence retained ownership of the Manor House for over a hundred years. Mary King, formerly Mary Lawrence, describes James Lawrence as her beloved father in her will dated 27 May, 1695.[84] James was a Mayor of Colchester in 1706, 1711, 1713, and 1719.[85] From Mary's will it can be seen that when widowed she married a man called Rowland and when widowed again she married Edward King.[86] Her daughter, Mary Rowland, married a man called Moses Martin.[87] When she was left a widow she married Francis King, Defoe's nephew through his brother Thomas.[88] This being so, and tortuous although the trail turned out to be, Defoe was a distant relative through marriage to James Lawrence.

It follows from this kinship link that even if were not true that there were Foe family links with the children and grandchildren of Alderman Thomas Lawrence, through Defoe's grandmother Rose and mother Ellene, which I maintain there were, there were kinship links with them all from 1702 through the marriage of Francis King and Mary Rowland.

A John Lawrence, son of the elder Mary Lawrence, married into the family of Sir Isaac Rebow, MP. Defoe mentions Rebow in the *Tour*.[89] Defoe writes, 'The government of the town is by a mayor, high steward, a recorder or his deputy, eleven alderman, a chamberlain, a town clerk, assistants, and eighteen common council-men. Their High Steward [this year, 1722] is Sir Isaac Rebow.' Defoe notes that Sir Isaac Rebow was a parliamentary representative of Colchester for most of the last thirty years. Thus both James Lawrence and Sir Isaac Rebow

---

[83] ERO. Deeds concerning the Manor of Gobyons, East Tilbury.
[84] ERO. D/ABW Will of Mary King, of Colchester, 27 May, 1695 which names her children
[85] See Chart.
[86] ERO. Parish of All Saints, Colchester, 25 June, 1679, Marriage of Edward King single man to Mary Rowland, widow, both of St Peters, Colchester.
[87] ERO. Parish of Mile End, Colchester, Moses Martin and Mary Rowland, Mile End, dated 30 June 1690.
[88] ERO. Parish of St Mary the Virgin at the Walls, 16 June, 1702, Francis King and Mary Martin.
[89] *Tour*, 59.

were distant relatives and kinsmen on Defoe's mother's side of the family.

The year 1722 is significant in Defoe's story not only for the publication of several books but for the acquisition of a Colchester estate on a long lease. At two Council meetings in 1722 the Corporation agreed to lease to Defoe one hundred and twenty acres of land on highly beneficial terms, Nathaniel and James Lawrence, as senior Aldermen and past Mayors, and Sir Isaac Rebow as Recorder, were present.[90] Two Nathanial Lawrence's, father and son, were Mayors of Colchester on seven occasions in the period 1672 -1710. It was the son who was present in 1722.

There is evidence that both Defoe's uncles, Henry and James Foe, were related or linked in some other way to Lawrence families. In 1666 a Mary Lawrence married John Lee, clearly identified in the pubic record as an apprentice of Henry Foe, a saddler in the City of London.[91] This Mary Lawrence could be the Marie Lawrence born to a Henry Lawrence in St Albans in 1641 who would have twenty-five years of age in 1666.[92]

The identity of James Foe's wife Alice remains elusive. As quoted elsewhere, in the *Journal of the Plague Year*, HF the narrator, and usually thought to be Defoe's uncle Henry, writes about saying good bye to his brother, James, as he departs from the City. He says, 'My brother, who had already sent his wife and two children [note no son, for there is evidence that he had two daughters] into Bedfordshire, and resolved to follow them, pressed my going very earnestly';[93] and later, 'so I took my leave of my brother, who went away to Dorking, in Surrey, afterwards fetched a round farther into Buckinghamshire or Bedfordshire to a retreat he had found there for his family.' Bastian suggests that James Foe went to Dorking to attend the funeral of his

---

[90] See Chart: A List of Colchester Mayors.
[91] Saddlers Company. Apprenticeship Lists, 1664, Lee, Jonathan, son of John, Kidderminster,
Worcestershire to Henry Foe, 28 July 1664.
[92] Defoe, Daniel. *Journal of the Plague Year*, (1722. Penguin Books, 1966), 31.
[93] See Chart: Parish Records of St Albans.

friend Lawrence Marsh on 24 July. He writes of the incident in *Moll Flanders* that from Little Brickhill the next town along the post road was St Albans twenty miles from the town. I comment here that Defoe/*Moll* met his Old Governess in Brickhill. If it is assumed that this governess was something of a family retainer teaching children within the Lawrence family. it could be implied that James Foe might have thought his children would be safer at or about Little Brickhill, forty miles from London, than in Dorking, a lesser distance of twenty-six miles. In the event the plague did reach St Albans. More likely, I think, is that he decided that they would be safer with his relatives.

In what sense could the Lawrence family at St Albans be Defoe's relatives? Alice Foe's maiden name is unknown. She might well have been a Lawrence. Alice was a relatively rare name. However, there were three in the family line of the Edward Lawrence families who had settled in West Farleigh in Kent. An Edward Lawrence married an Alice and the name was passed down over three generations. In correspondence towards the end of his life Defoe refers to moving between various London lodgings and a village in Kent. [94] A John Avery, possibly the father of Captain Avery, married an Alice Lawrence in Leigh, Kent, close to the Lawrence families in West Farleigh on August 4, 1634.[95]

Wildbore Families

There were many Wildbore families in Colchester and nearby towns who would have been aware of Defoe in his childhood in Essex. While the primary role in bringing up Defoe and his sister Mary were the Lawrence families, acting out of kinship to him, the Wildbore families in performing their roles over a thirty-three year period, 1647-1680, did so out of friendship, honour and personal regard for Defoe's father Daniel Foe.

William Wildbore, the Parish Clerk of St Peter's, Colchester, had a special role as a 'guardian'. Robert Wildbore, the brother of the Randle Wildbore acting as trustee of Defoe's father's will, would have passed on

[94] H. 251.
[95] Parish Records of St. Margaret's, Leigh, Kent.

news of Defoe's progress. Randle died in 1658 and looked to his son Nicholas to ensure that Daniel Foe's will was respected and executed as a matter of honour.

I have conjectured that Defoe's brother Thomas King was brought up in the Braintree home of Nicholas Wildbore, fifteen miles from Colchester, because he married Nicholas's daughter Elisabeth. in 1680 and had children by her. Nicholas Wildbore died in 1664 and his family moved to London. His wife Mary, born Love, died in 1684, but that was time enough to ensure that the money due to both Daniel Defoe and his sister Mary under their father's will was paid to them. John Ewen, most probably the son of the trustee of Defoe's father Daniel, was the trustee of Mary Wildbore's will. I conjecture also that Mary Wildbore was the Widow referred to in *Robinson Crusoe* and for whom he had so warm a regard.

King Families

Later in this book I provide a proof that Defoe's printer Morphew was sued by Defoe's nephew Francis King. I believe this proof to be self-sufficient. While not wishing to fall foul of my own complaint that in Defoe scholarship the use of non sequiturs is common, I believe that it follows from my proof that this is evidence that Defoe's brother and sister followed the matrilineal line of descent and used their mother's surname of King in their adult life. If as I conjecture, Defoe's father had previous marriages, then Defoe was a half-brother to Mary, James and Henry – and, if so, Mary and Thomas may have claimed something of their maternal heritage in using the name of King.

This assertion should not cause surprise. In some parts of Britain the use of surnames was rare until the seventeenth century. A principal cause of change was the need to distinguish elder from other sons as legitimate heirs. The patriarchal rights of elder sons were strengthened in inheritance law toward the end of the seventeenth century. An elder son could be distinguished from other children by the exclusive use of the father's surname. It was common for other children to use the mother's surname.

I do not know whether there was a family agreement to do this with the Foe children or whether there was an agreement among the children. In general the task of identifying a person in the seventeenth century caused difficulties. It was difficult to produce documentary evidence for Mary Norton, a Defoe wife by private treaty, because she followed the matrilineal line of descent and used her mother's name. Benjamin Norton Defoe, felt the need to use two surnames, or his parents did, to distinguish himself as Defoe's legitimate heir while claiming matrilineal descent. Sometimes Benjamin described himself as Mr Norton. It follows from these practices that as King is a common surname, and parish records are imperfect, it is difficult to establish the identity of all Defoe's relatives on his mother's side of the family. There were a large number.

The issues involved in finding his kin are considerable. Fortunately, I repeat my conviction that when Defoe writes about his relatives in his fictions, he offers a logic for the reader to establish who they are which, if followed by a biographer, can lead to their identification. However, there are many other Defoe written sources involving the use of family terms that remain difficult to identify.

Despite these difficulties it is possible to describe the life led by Defoe's brother and sister, Thomas and Mary. The links to Yorkshire, in particular Hull and York, are important and there are links also between Lawrence's and King's in Essex and Yorkshire Not all the possible connections can be proved but there are enough provable links to establish the family network.

Chapter 4

Finding a Space

[His father told him that] ...the middle Station of Life was calculated for all kinds of Vertues and Kinds of Enjoyments...that this Way Men went silently and smoothly thro' the World and comfortably out of it...

Robinson Crusoe
Daniel Defoe, 1719

In the task of unravelling Defoe's actual life from his fiction a recurring difficulty of interpretation arises from his ability to shuffle his characters by changing their identity, role and gender. This ability to displace himself by appearing to be other than he was enables Defoe to tell his story while avoiding the reader's judgement of his actions. In his actual life this ability to effortlessly change character infuriated his friends and enemies. When these disguises and evasions became apparent the natural reaction of many was to revile Defoe for dishonesty and slipperiness of character.

As I have started to explain, *Moll Flanders* is an important and crucial account of Defoe's early life. In it Defoe is telling his own story but he writes this into an alter ego of his sister Mary. It is difficult to unscramble these accounts, for this is Defoe's intention: to tell the reader unpalatable truths while slipping out of the frame of reference so that the reader's sympathy is engaged and the excitement of the moment can be shared.

In *Moll Flanders* account of her life, when she/Defoe reached the age of fourteen, a serious decision had to be made about her/his future for all parish relief was withdrawn at this age. The parish would expect him to earn a living in trade. The parish records of St Leonard's show that it financed apprenticeships at the age of fourteen.[96] It was a critical point in young Daniel's life for without the intervention of others his hopes of becoming a gentleman would disappear.

---

[96] ERO. Parish Records of St. Leonard's.

Defoe needed a Wildbore, Foe or Lawrence family to step up to the breach and, if a Wildbore, to honour Randle Wildbore's pledge to provide for his future. Arguably there was money set aside for the purpose. If the execution of Daniel Foe's will had been conducted conscientiously the £80 set aside for Defoe, if invested or saved, might have grown in value. However, it would not become available to him under the terms of his father's will until he reached twenty-one years of age.

In *Moll's* account there was an agonising period of indecision while his 'families' discussed what to do for him. The Lawrence families, who I believe had been looking out for him, hesitated at the vital moment while other adults in his life must have considered whether they could help. Defoe writes, 'I was frightened out of my wits almost, for I was, as it were, turned out of doors to the wide world.'

Defoe's account is confusing. He writes:

> The young ladies, Mr. Mayors daughters, would come and see me… they brought others with them…when they came to understand that I was no more maintained by the public purse as before,, they gave me money oftener than formerly; and as I grew up they brought work for me to do [for which money was paid]…One of the ladies took so much fancy to me that she would have me home to her house [for a week.] And on the 'death' of the nurse she sent her maid to take me away. I was no sooner …but the first lady, that is to say, the Mayoress that had sent her two daughters to take care of me; and another family which had taken notice of me sent for me after her. Madam the Mayoress was angry that her friend had taken me away from her, as she called it …for as she said, I was hers by right, she having been the first that took any notice of me. But they that had her would not part with me.

Moll's account, if taken literally, is unbelievable. *Moll* by her own account is a foundling. She becomes the centre of attention of a number of wealthy families including that of the Mayor of Colchester. These families compete keenly with each other to bring her up within their households and to bear the full expense of doing so. In my interpretation, this is the full expense of at least Daniel and Mary. Why on earth would any of these families do this unless they were relatives or bound by some other fealty?

It is my contention that the Mayor of Colchester referred to by *Moll* was Thomas Lawrence the son of an Alderman Thomas Lawrence who died in 1594. This son became the MP for Colchester in 1646 and thus a member of Cromwell's Protectorate. Henry Lawrence, who became President of Cromwell's Council in 1653, was elected as the Colchester MP earlier in the same year but stood aside for Thomas and took up a seat in Caernarvonshire. Henry was a distant cousin of Cromwell's, who was a tenant of his on farming land in Cambridgeshire.[97] This event tends to suggest that Thomas and Henry were related in some way.

The host family that took Defoe in had, according to Defoe, the generosity and goodwill to provide boarding and education as befitted an English gentleman. However, here and elsewhere, it is obvious that he is not narrating as *Moll* but as himself. He does not write 'gentlewoman' for if so it would be obvious to the reader that as a girl she would not have been given such an education, if given one at all.

Several of the Lawrence family trees are provided in charts in this work. The Lawrence's in Essex, Hertfordshire and Kent recognised each other as kinsman. They moved from one part of the country to another with equanimity and in the knowledge that they would be recognised, welcomed and assisted. They inter-married. On the whole these families were successful as merchants and landowners. They took up civic responsibilities. To be taken in by any one of these families, and treated as an equal, was to be accepted by them all. Defoe must have felt exhilarated and thrilled by this turn of events. It transformed his life expectancies and ushered him into a different world.

The first, and the obvious host candidate family to take in

---

[97] Dow Family History.

Moll/Daniel, was that of Thomas Lawrence the Mayor of Colchester in 1655. However, *Moll*/Defoe tells the reader that this was not the family.

Secondly, but also likely, is the family of one of Alderman Thomas Lawrence's many sons, that is the brothers of Thomas the Mayor, who in their turn had many children who lived in and around Colchester. Of these the most likely was the family of William Lawrence, Alderman Thomas's nephew. I have already conjectured that Ellene, William's niece, was Defoe's mother. William Lawrence, the father, was a wealthy merchant with several ships owned and berthed in Ipswich. However, there are arguments against this family as a choice of host: if Defoe's biological mother was born into this family and they had made no move to house them earlier it does seem improbable that they would have changed their mind. It can be argued that they acted at first out of a sense of family shame. Of course, time mellows and the family may have had a change of heart. However, as Defoe expresses surprise at the family who took him in, I am inclined to think not.

Defoe's actual choice of words is helpful. He writes of 'a family that took notice of me'. This expression might cover a more formal process of correspondence and meetings. I think it likely that James and Henry Foe might have become involved in some way in this family issue; and the Wildbore family, charged with the trusteeship of his father's will, would surely have been asked to express a view. Despite the willingness of the Mayor's family to take in Defoe it was another alternative that won the day.

I believe that the family that took in Defoe was that of John and Anne Lawrence, descendants of Edward Lawrence who at this time were residents of the Manor House of East Gubyons, East Tilbury. There are many reasons for this belief that are best discussed elsewhere in my narrative. The point I stress at this time is that this family had family connections in St Albans in Hertfordshire and East and West Farleigh in Kent. Defoe mentions these connections in several fictions and I discuss them in my narrative.

It is obviously helpful to my narrative account to link Defoe to the family line of Edward and Henry Lawrence who had established themselves in Tilbury and St Albans. Henry Lawrence, the President of Cromwell's Council, whose family roots partly originated in St Albans was deeply involved in colonial ventures in the New World. In 1632 he acquired land in Connecticut and later he farmed 10 acres in Barbados with the labour of indentured servants and slaves. Oliver Cromwell appointed him Minister of Plantations. Henry's son John migrated to Barbados and later to Jamaica where he became a rich plantation owner.[98]

It was Henry Lawrence who set in motion a land grab in the New World. The Lawrence's were participating in a remarkable trans-Atlantic English colonial network between Europe and America and the Caribbean and Africa. This network fed a growing population in Europe by the labour of migrants and their indentured servants and slaves in the New World.

This trans-Atlantic colonial network could be entered at many points in a chain: by traders based in London as well as planters in Barbados and migrant communities in New England. Settlers in Barbados and New England needed indentured servants and slaves to work their plantations. The plantations were capital intensive and without cheap labour their working would have been uneconomic. The opportunities opened up for the Lawrence's and the migration possibilities must have been agitated about in the Lawrence families; they became part of the stuff of adulthood for young Defoe.

I do point out at this point that there is no doubting Defoe's very long association with Tilbury culminating in the major investment he made into a brickwork's there. In my narrative Defoe spent some part of up to fifty years in homes and work places in Tilbury. No biographer has been able to explain how, why and when Defoe was able to make large investments into his brickworks. I am influenced in my conclusion by a single piece of information from Defoe's alter ego, *Roxana*.[99] In this fiction, Defoe writes that her/Roxana's father died four years into the marriage. Her Father (actual not biological) left her

---

[98] Dow Family History.
[99] *Roxana*, 41.

Elder brother in charge of it. He promptly lost her money in reckless trading. John Lawrence of East Tilbury died there in 1688, that is four years after Defoe's marriage to Mary Tuffley. Unfortunately, either he did not make a will or it is not extant.

The family household of John and Anne was financially able to help Defoe and his sister if need be. Through *Moll*, Defoe tells his readers that he/she was with her new family from fourteen to sixteen years of age and that he/she was given 'all the advantages for my education that could be imagined'. This household had 'masters to come to the house to teach' and *Moll*/Daniel was given the education of a wealthy merchant's son. It does seem obvious that the narrator and subject of the tale is a man.

The account of *Moll's* education is consistent with the description given by Defoe of *Crusoe's* education. Defoe tells his readers that, 'My Father, who was very ancient, had given me a competent Share of Learning, so far as House-Education, and a Country Free-School generally goes, and designed me for the Law, but I would be satisfied with nothing but going to sea.' The description was derided by Charles Gildon, who in seeking to label *Robinson Crusoe* as an account of Defoe's own life, stated that he had never heard of such a misleading account of someone's education. Crusoe's account is compatible, however, with that given in this work; St. Leonard's had provided Defoe with Free School Education and a Lawrence family with House-Education.

There is no 'silver bullet' linking Defoe to John and Anne Lawrence. However, the circumstantial evidence that it was this couple who acted as the host family is overwhelming and thus makes the conjecture highly likely.

Chapter 5

Identity, Sexuality and Family

Freud...insisted in is his essay on creativity [that when] he set up sign posts pointing to the source from which the artists creativity sprang... it was a destination that could not be reached.

Leonardo da Vinci
Standard Edition of the Works of Freud, vol.11.
Quoted by Leo Abse, *The Bi-sexuality of Daniel Defoe*, 2006

So far in this narrative my task has been to display Daniel Defoe to the point when as a young man he broke away from the familiar to launch himself upon the world. However, the reader expects something more from a biographer than display. I hope that I have conveyed something of the extreme difficulty of Defoe's upbringing without suffocating the reader with psychological jargon and judgements but I am conscious that it is not enough

At 18 years of age most people are shaped for the world they are to occupy. They will become more like themselves. Much of what is expected of them has already been asked and their character and personalities formed. What sort of a person was Defoe when on the cusp of adult life? As the life he was to live was extraordinary, Defoe at 16-18 years of age must have been remarkable in himself.

I have made the point that in his fiction Defoe has told his readers about his beginnings in life and that there is a consistency in these various clusters of information.. Fortunately Defoe, in several accounts of the life of the teenage and early adulthood of his fictional characters is also consistent: he has helped his enquirers out. In seeking to establish his character traits and behaviour I am conscious of the need to avoid circular reasoning. Much is known about his behaviour after the year 1680 and I do not wish to read these insights back in time in a simplistic manner.

Defoe had to fashion an identity for himself. He had no hand-downs.

He had no recollections of either of his parents and had been placed in a community in Colchester as a castaway amidst a sea of traders and merchants. His uncles James and Henry, after completing their apprenticeships were busy merchants in London. I daresay they had not forgotten this young boy entirely but in the flux of life they took refuge from responsibility by accepting he was being cared for by others.

He must have admired some of the adults he encountered in Lexden but none, I suspect, substituted as a role model for a missing father. In Lexden there were many people of Huguenot origin and they looked to friends and traders on the European continent. Having been abandoned by his immediate family, Defoe jumped a generation of Englishness to his family roots on the continent and put himself on the outside of things English. It is not a handicap to a creative person to be placed, or to place himself, on the outside of things looking in. In doing this Defoe may have sought to identify with kinsmen created by his grandfather's early marriages and to a continental European tradition of dissent.

Living with his sister Mary in Colchester, Defoe seems to have recognised emotionally that despite his station in life adults, both women and men, were attracted to him. He was hungry for acceptance and belonging. It may be that his sister Mary received more attention than he did. She may have been attractive and appealing. She was certainly useful because she could make and repair clothes. There was a place for her in any household with a little money to spare whereas he was a burden, an expense and, as he grew up, a nuisance. If he was to be approved by adults, and particularly men, shouldn't he be more like Mary? Mary was his immediate family and his own. If she was sweet on him and solicitous for his future she may have been malleable to his wishes.

What is clear is that the young Defoe was intelligent and, in a masculine sense, sturdy and able to look after himself physically. *Colonel Jack* tells the reader that, 'I passed among my comrades for a bold, resolute boy and one that durst fight anything.' However, he was prudent and 'therefore shunned fighting as much as I could …and brought myself off with my tongue... [as] 'a man as while I was a boy.'[100] The *Cavalier* tells us that he removed himself from physical danger as a soldier. [101] The Colonel, in *Colonel Jack*, refused the provocation of a duel.[102] The drawing of swords in a quarrel with Nathaniel Mist did not result in a duel. The carrying of a sword, said to be a habit of Defoe's, was then an assertion of masculinity. He was not 'to be messed with'. It is difficult for admirers of Defoe, among whom I number myself, to accept that his fictional heroes while polite and respectful to adults and civil authority in their demeanour, were thorough-going rogues. In numerous fictions Defoe tells the reader that he believed himself to come from a perfectly respectable and moneyed background but that fate had dealt him a cruel blow by removing both his parents. He had been obliged to others for his very existence. He needed to behave well and be thought a respectable and civil boy because the consequences of being thought bad were dire. He would be thrown onto a scrapheap. But beneath this pleasant demeanour his heroes, and I suggest Defoe himself, were willing to do almost anything to achieve their objectives in life – money, and the appearance of it, and respectability.

Defoe's characters are useful to other people but take the first opportunity to take advantage of any trust placed in them. They enjoy this deceit. *Captain Singleton* tells the reader, 'I was reputed to be a mighty diligent servant to my master, and very faithful. I was diligent indeed, but I was far from honest; however, they thought me honest, which, by the way was their very great mistake... [a good old parson had told him that he knew that from the age of eight or nine that he was rumbled and] I was preparing to be as wicked as anyone could be.' So this young boy hid malicious and malevolent motivation behind a mask of respectability. He was deceptive but he didn't deceive all those who knew him well.

His characters are short of money. When they get some, it is

---

[100] Defoe, Daniel. *Colonel Jack*, (1722. Hamish Hamilton, 1947), 7.
[101] Defoe, Daniel. *Memoirs of a Cavalier*, (1722. J.M. Dent, 1937). Quoted by Bastian, 78.
[102] *Colonel Jack*, 223.

hoarded. Others try to get it off you and sometimes they succeed. If you have money not only do you not get hungry but you can buy respectability with good clothes. These adventurous boys used money to buy clothes and live like gentlemen. If you have a great deal of money there is the need to aggrandise, hide and protect it. On the other hand you can flaunt it. If you have too little money it is acceptable to get some by petty thieving. Stealing from others becomes habitual. You do not wish to get caught out, for the punishments are severe, and so subterfuge is used to deceive people. Other people object to this behaviour and there is a need to trick them. Defoe's characters become confidence tricksters. In all this anti-social and dishonest behaviour the narrator himself draws limits. Gang activity and the committal of serious crimes are avoided because if caught the punishment could be execution.[103]

Defoe's characters are anti-heroes disrespectful of authority and when they are opposed they become aggressive. In later and well-chronicled accounts of events in Defoe's life, it is difficult not to conclude that he displays a need to provoke situations which arouse resistance and opposition. It is almost as if he and his characters are only really alive when they possess a total sense of being in opposition.

Defoe's characters are compulsive gamblers and risk-takers and each action is accompanied by a sense of excitement and eroticism.[104] The issue of Defoe's sexuality has been inadequately considered by biographers and such consideration as there is does not seek to place his behaviour by using the cultural and gender terms of the times. I suggest that there has been a misunderstanding of what can be meant by sexual preference in the seventeenth century and an inadequate appreciation of kinship and the patronage system.

I have suggested earlier that the evidence points to incest with his sister Mary that started when they were both very young. There may have been similar behaviour with his brother. I do not know. There is evidence that this eroticism was expressed in cross-dressing and as a

---

[103] *Colonel Jack*, 76.
[104] Abse, 39-40.

sodomite. There are many descriptions of Defoe as an adult that suggest that he was a beau in the language of a later age.[105]

More controversially I interpret Defoe's fiction to suggest that many of the sexual affairs he describes in his fiction are passionate affairs he conducted with men. These observations are particularly true of *Moll Flanders* and *Roxana* where I have been able to identify some of these men. It is unusual for a male author to write two successive and successful fictions as true histories of a woman and so thoroughly to enjoy the experience. In certain fictional situations when Defoe is identifying himself as a woman he needs to be seduced. Playing this role put him in command of the situations he created.

I have argued in other works, particularly those on Swift, that sex was often demanded as a price for patronage.[106] This knowledge is disagreeable to those wishing to admire Defoe: it must sometimes have been disagreeable to him. I do not wish to be judgemental. It is not the function of a biographer to abhor but to identify and explain.

More controversially I have argued in a previous work,[107] and I do so here, that Defoe had a sexual interest in young people that in modern terms would be thought unhealthy and wrong. In his time, sex with minors was legal once a child reached the age of twelve. Children were legally the property of their parents and it was often thought right to punish them severely to 'keep out' the devil. These punishments were disliked by children and parents alike. However, it was a Christian duty to use punishments no matter how upsetting. Defoe writes about punishment in *Family Instructor* and *Religious Courtship*. A sensitive reading of these works suggests that Defoe was upset at having to beat his children. I argue in my work on Swift that Laetetia Pilkington was traded for commercial advantage by her father. I am not suggesting that Defoe behaved in this way but that it would not have surprised him that others of his acquaintance did so.

---

[105] See comments of John Kelso, 291 in this work.
[106] Martin, John. *The Man Himself: A Life of Jonathan Swift*, Anglian Publishing, 2009.
[107] *Beyond Belief*, 264.

I argue that Defoe was addicted to shunamitism, the belief that he could prolong his life by sleeping with young people whether it involved sex or not. Francis Bacon argued for and practiced shunamitism. His claims were taken seriously. Given the everyday experience of Defoe's life, when sharing beds with others was common in over-crowded houses and at inns, it is not entirely surprising that he slept with others. This practice in Defoe's life, when allied with certain proclivities, got him into trouble with the law and subjected him to blackmail. I discuss his terrible difficulties in *Beyond Belief*.[108]

I am reluctant to judge Defoe. I am wary of all emphatic and dogmatic conclusions about gender and sexual practices in the early modern period. The best evidence shows that the current understanding of gender differences between men and women did not apply in general until the middle of the eighteenth century and that the transition from a kinship system to the nuclear modern family occurred much later than has been supposed. Attitudes to children, women and young people were callous and brutal in the seventeenth century.

I believe that there is considerable conjectural evidence that Defoe needed triangular relationships: two men and a woman and sometimes the reverse. In actual life he enjoyed one over many years with Elisabeth and Nathaniel Sammens. I discuss this relationship later in this book. Defoe gives the reader a fictional triangle in *Roxana*. I suggest that the roots of this preference may be found in the early loss of his parents and the emotional need to reclaim them both

In his childhood Defoe seems to have been separated from his brother Thomas while knowing about him. If so Defoe would have experienced his absence as a loss. Defoe may have experienced this 'loss' as abduction. When Defoe writes about being stolen by gypsies he may have been drawing upon his own experience of being 'lost' when three years of age and his brother having been stolen. There is evidence that later in life the two brothers were close and at that from 1694 onwards they were living together in Tilbury and Colchester.

---

[108] *Beyond Belief*, 259-269.

This emotional need for a younger brother was met by Defoe in attachment to young black slaves. The most famous of these is the fictional Man Friday in *Robinson Crusoe*. Defoe introduces the reader late in his life to the 'real' Man Friday in the form of the young slave from Barbados living in his family. In *Family Instructor* Defoe reveals to the reader the character of Toby. There are other examples. In *Robinson Crusoe*, Defoe attaches himself to the young slave Xury only to sell him off when it was convenient to do so.

I argue that Defoe had a strong sexual preference for younger men, I first discussed thus theme in *Beyond Belief*,[109] and I develop it further in this account. When embarking on a fact finding tour for Harley in 1705 he was accompanied by several young men. He changed them when it suited him to do so. It was almost as if he was rewarding himself for months of abstention while in prison. Attachments to boys and young men, presents the modern reader with extreme difficulties. Young black slaves became fashionable in the Early Modern period.

Defoe was itinerant. He was brought up without a permanent home or one that we would recognise to be one in our own time. The places he laid his head at night were those that were convenient to him. Defoe confesses this to his readers. This is not to argue that he did not have places that served him well as homes and to which he returned from time to time. However, there was always another place and other locations that were important to him. Throughout his life he was constantly on the move.

In places where he rested for some time, Defoe created wives and had children. Some of these marriages were legal church weddings and some private treaty arrangements. It was entirely lawful to cohabit with another person and enter into a private treaty with them amounting to a marriage. The only difference between such a marriage and a church wedding was that these wives never acquired inheritance rights for themselves or their children. A list of Defoe's women and children is provided in a chart. I identify two legal wives and two others. This

---

[109] *Beyond Belief*, 42-43, 60, 80-81, 93, 159-160, 204, 215-217, 239-242, 260-261, 272-280.

evidence comes as a shock to previous biographers who have imagined that Defoe had in Mary Tuffley a loyal and 'loving' wife for forty-seven years.

However, over a long life Defoe was committed to the locations of importance to him and spent considerable time in them. Consequently, he was loyal, in his own way, to the wives and children he had accumulated. The relationships with these children can be traced in his fiction. Of course many of them were neglected and he felt guilt and regret stemming from his own uncertain family upbringing. In the end he provided for their needs, or something amounting to them.

Chapter 6

Great Adventure

He [his father] told me that it was for Men of desperate Fortunes on one Hand, of aspiring superior Fortunes on the other, who went abroad upon Adventures, to rise themselves by Enterprize, and make themselves famous in Undertakings...

Robinson Crusoe
Daniel Defoe, 1719

In one of the most memorable passages in *Robinson Crusoe* Defoe describes the advice given to him by a 'wise and grave father' on worldly ambition. This unknown person was not his biological father but a senior male in his family. His 'father' advised him that the position in life he occupied was the middle station and that happiness lay in *Crusoe* accepting this and avoiding the extremes of life. *Crusoe's* education had equipped him for trade or a profession such as law but at seventeen years of age he dismissed these possibilities as coming too late in his life.[110]

Defoe had been given the education of a prosperous merchant's son. It equipped him well for the world he was to occupy. However, it almost certainly had one serious disadvantage for any man with serious pretensions to make something of himself as a gentleman: instruction was given in English. The hallmark of a gentleman was Latin and a prestigious education gave a man the art of communication in the language. All his life Defoe defended himself from sniping from his political opponents that he was ill-educated for lack of mastery in Latin. In the *Compleat English Gentleman* Defoe sought to refute the necessity of knowing and conversing in Latin.[111]

---

[110] Defoe, Daniel. Ed. Thomas Keymer, *Robinson Crusoe*, (1719. Oxford's World's Classics, 2007), 5-6.
[111] Defoe, Daniel. *The Compleat English Gentleman*, (partial version, 1729. Ed. Bulbring, London, 1890).

An English gentleman possessed land and to one extent or another lived off the cultivation of it and the rents paid by others for the right to farm it. The early death of his father deprived Defoe of the opportunity to inherit land or the capital to buy it. He needed to seek his fortune elsewhere.

As a young boy he would have seen the large and imposing trading ships and men of war gliding down the River Colne and he writes movingly of ships anchored at harbour at Ipswich and Harwich.[112] In his youth he could listen to amazing yarns and tales of adventure from sailors and merchants recounted in many an inn. It would have seemed to him that the pickings and dangers of petty theft were nothing compared to the riches that could be gained from war, colonising the weak, or trading in the exotic products of foreign lands.

In the *Tour* Defoe writes of his early experiences in visiting Ipswich and Harwich, major ports for the coastal trade, and Tilbury, an emerging centre for shipyard repairs. Bastian believes that Defoe spent a winter in Ipswich. There is no doubt that he had early memories of his experiences there. He writes about the great collier ships that carried coals from Newcastle to London.

At this time Lexden was a centre of the cloth trade in Colchester and organised as a cottage industry. It was entirely natural for the young Foe children to look to romantic destinations abroad rather than the hard work of their immediate neighbours, and to London, a capital city, and to the European continent across the grey and turbulent seas so close to them. The very same merchants that gathered-in the bays from their workshops traded world-wide with strange and foreign parts. They would have had a thousand and more tales of their adventures to tell young children.

In the four year period 1658-1662 it is highly likely that Defoe saw something of his uncles James and Henry in London. He had two methods of travel to London; by sea from Ipswich or Tilbury or by wagon or coach by road. Hitching a ride and persuading someone to put him up when he got there would not have been a problem.

---

[112] *Tour*, 66-67.

In *Robinson Crusoe, Captain Singleton* and *Colonel Jack* Defoe wrote about this period in his life. In *Captain Singleton* Defoe writes nonchantly that, 'the town where I was kept, whatever its name was, must be not far off from the seaside; for a master of a ship ...carried me to sea with him on a voyage to Newfoundland...'

He did not get there quite so easily in *Robinson Crusoe*. Defoe writes: But being one Day at *Hull*, where I went casually one of my Companions being going to Sea to London [prompted] me to go with them.' They experienced a storm and the vessel almost capsized to his terror. And then later when in *Yarmouth* Roads they experienced an even greater storm and the ship capsized. The father of the young man who had brought him upon the ship issued a dire warning. 'Young man, Says he, never go to sea any more, you ought to take this for a plain and visible Token that you are not to be a Seafaring Man.' And then prophetically he asked, 'What are you?' And on what Account did you go to sea?' And then after *Crusoe* had spun him a story declaimed, 'I would not set my Foot in the same ship with thee Again...depend upon it, if you do not go back, where-ever you go, you will meet with nothing but Disasters and Disappointments till your Father's Words are fulfilled.'

Defoe had kinsmen in Hull. A number of Lawrence families had second homes in Hull and there is evidence that his sister lived there. Despite the emphatic warning Defoe had been given, and his conviction that God's providence had determined his status in the world as 'a castaway', *Crusoe* was undeterred. He hesitated but plunged on. He made his way to London by road and with the help of his relatives raised the money to embark again on a long sea voyage with 'an honest and plain dealing Man.' [Captain]

I do not believe that these events were as continuous and immediate as described in *Robinson Crusoe*. It is more likely that between the ages of fifteen to eighteen Defoe experimented with going to sea against the good advice of his 'family' who wished him to settle for a comfortable and respectable life in England. During this period he spent time in London with 'relatives' such as his uncles James and Henry, and with the Wildbore and Lawrence families.

In the end he did go abroad on a great adventure but not as outlined in *Crusoe*. Even *Crusoe* did not encounter the continuous opposition of his family for he collects the not inconsiderable sum of £40 to finance his first venture. Defoe writes that, 'I had mustered together by the Assistance of my Relations whom I corresponded with, and who, I believe, got my Father, or at least my Mother, to contribute so much as that to my first Adventure.'

It has been believed that *Crusoe's* ill-fate was as a consequence of disobeying his father. It was certainly a dire sin for a Puritan to do this. God, in his Providence, would certainly punish such a sinner. However, at this point in Defoe's life who could be considered his father? The punishment had already taken place because he was cast out of God's loving care as an infant. Perhaps, among the very many excitements that drove him on was the hope, if not the expectation, that he could find his mother across the threatening grey seas and through the mighty winds and thus thwart God's punishment: that was Defoe's real sin, the determination to thwart God's providence, and the inevitability of the further punishment that would follow whatever his super-human efforts to defy his will.

In *Crusoe*, Defoe slips in an important allusion to his teenage companions when they were on the loose in London in the period 1660-1662. He writes simply that, 'It was my Lot first of all to fall into pretty good Company in *London*, which does not always happen to such loose and unguided young Fellows as I then was.[113] This good company were his fellow companions described in *Colonel Jack* and *Memoirs of a Cavalier*.

In a previous work, *Alien Come Home*, I argued that among this 'Company' was Robert Spencer, the future second Earl of Sunderland and leading Whig statesman, and William Penn, the son of Admiral Penn, and the future founder and proprietor of Pennsylvania. Unbelievable though it might seem at first consideration, there were many touching points of possible contact between the three young men when they came together in the period 1660-1662. As I have argued,

---

[113] *Robinson Crusoe*, 16.

these three embarked on a version of the Grand Tour in July, 1662 from which Defoe did not return to England until 1680.

If the application for parish relief in *Moll Flanders* was in the name of Ellene King, the mother, as I think it must have been, Mary would have been known as Mary (or the diminutive *Moll*) King. As I mentioned in the earlier chapter Defoe establishes a situation of competitiveness between two 'brothers' for the sexual favours of Mary/*Moll* the young girl taken into the household of an unnamed family who, I argue, was Defoe's sister Mary. In this new home Mary, while one of the family, was expected to earn her living by sewing for them.

The elder 'brother' in this narrative was called *Robin*. At this time, Robert Spencer was nineteen-twenty, Mary King fifteen-sixteen and Defoe sixteen-seventeen years of age..

Moll favoured the advances of the elder 'brother' for whom she felt love and passion and gave herself to him. *Robin*/Robert explained to *Moll* that he could not marry her or anyone until he had come into his very substantial family fortune. Robert Spencer became the second Earl of Sunderland on his twenty-first birthday in October, 1662. Defoe has difficulty in managing his narrative account. *Robin* becomes a distant figure and not really a 'brother' at all. In the period 1661-1664 Robert Spencer went on European tours on three occasions. He was very rich indeed and at one point in the story he gives *Moll* the large sum of 500 *louis* in consideration of the freedoms he had taken with her. Was this money actually going to Mary/*Moll* at all or was it Defoe who needed the money? As the story unravels it is clear that he needs money to establish himself in life and. in particular, to finance an adventure overseas with Robert Spencer. Did he encourage Mary to give sex to Robert with the fancy and untrue story that he might marry or commit himself in some way to her? In reality Robert Spencer was expected by his family to marry for money and family advantage.

Moll's story is continued in *Captain Singleton*. Captain Bob and his companion William the Quaker are unable to return to England for fear that ill-gotten wealth will expose them to prosecution. Defoe describes a preliminary to return. A letter is sent to a sister (said to be William's) to ascertain what has happened to her since Captain Bob left England. She tells him that after waiting a while she had moved to London where she married and had children. *Moll* tells her readers that her family had moved to London where they received an invitation to Robin's wedding. Robert Spencer married Anne Digby in 1665.

Moll explains that she accepted the attentions of the younger 'Brother' in the household that had taken her in. She 'married' him and had two children in the period 1661-1662. The frontispiece to the original version of *Moll Flanders* tells the reader that she did 'marry' her own Brother. It reads that she was, 'five times a Wife (whereof once to her own Brother)'. There is an obvious deduction to be made: Defoe fails to maintain the fictional basis of his narrative. *Moll* had no biological Brother in the household that had taken her in. The relationship she describes with a 'brother' must then have been with Defoe. Incest was not a crime but it was a sin. If revealed it would make a baptism by an Anglican vicar somewhat difficult. But that does not rule one out.

If it is maintained, as I assert, that Defoe is telling readers through *Moll's* account, that he had two children by his sister Mary, the claim has to be tested against particulars. How can it be true that Defoe had children by his sister? In research for her biographical account, Paula Backscheider discovered an unusual baptism record in Chadwell St Mary dated July 27, 1662. It read 'Daniel son of a stranger'. I have examined it.[114] This parish is not 'any old place'. The Church is within comfortable walking distance of the Manor of East Gubyons which was owned by the family of Edward Lawrence from 1560, and a ten minute walk from Defoe's brick and pantile business. Defoe was to live in the Parish of Chadwell St. Mary from the late 1680's to 1705.

There is a consequence in names. Nationally, Daniel was not a rare name. However, it was uncommon in the Tilbury area. It was the practice of the Defoe family in Etton to name first born sons after the father. In Defoe's case from grandfather to father, then to him, and

---

[114] *Backscheider*, 3-4.

from him to the first born sons of his multiple relationships. His first born child by Elisabeth Sammens was called Daniel.[115] The baptism coincides with Defoe's departure on a version of the Grand Tour by the end July, 1662. On the other hand, to call someone a Stranger carried the distinctive meaning of being unknown in the parish. The person seeking a baptism could have been a seasonal farm worker from another parish. However, the death of John Lawrence in 1688 was recorded in the neighbouring Parish of East Tilbury. Logically, a servant visiting the church from East Tilbury could be unknown to a vicar at Chadwell St Mary. It may be that once Defoe had departed the area it was possible to baptise the baby and so save his immortal soul.

This is not an incontrovertible proof that this baby boy was Defoe's by his sister Mary; but it is a persuasive conjecture. The child could have died in its infancy, been brought up by John and Ann Lawrence, adopted or put into care. The prospects of survival would have been precarious if he had been put out to a child-minder.

Defoe describes versions of his sister's story in *Moll Flanders*, *Captain Singleton* and *Roxana*. When *Moll* moved to London she was courted by several tradesman and, in particular linen drapers, and eventually married one. *Moll* describes herself as having 'a tolerable fortune in my pocket' that meant that she could pick and chose. She describes her husband as 'this amphibious creature, this land-water thing called a gentleman-tradesman,' and a 'rake, gentleman, shopkeeper and beggar, all together.' *Moll* tells the reader that her new husband, coming into a lump-sum of money at once fell into such a profusion of expense, that all I had, and all he had before…would not have held out above one year.

Her husband bought a coach and horses with footman and took her on trips to Oxford and Northamptonshire. Mary King had relatives in Northamptonshire. In the end *Moll's* husband bankrupted himself and left her without support in London when she changed her name and living quarters and adopted the name of Moll Flanders.

---

[115] *Beyond Belief,* 23.

Moll/Mary's father, Daniel Foe, left her the sum of £50 to be given to her at the age of twenty one, that is in 1666. According to 'his sisters' account in *Captain Singleton*, she moved to London after Defoe left for his continental adventure in 1662. It seems probable then that Mary would have been paid this sum (together with interest) when she was in London and that this is the 'dowry money' *Moll*/Mary was describing in her account.

In *Roxana* Defoe writes that his heroine was married off by her father to an Eminent Brewer at the age of fifteen with a dowry of £2,000. She lived for eight years with this husband before he went bankrupt and then another three years before he fled to France. Thus this marriage was over and *Roxana* penniless by 1695.

My estimate of the date the 'sister' and her uncle wrote to *Captain Singleton* is 1679-1680.[116] The 'sister' tells him that she had been left a widow with four children and kept a little drapers shop in the Minories in the City of London. A letter was written to an 'uncle' to confirm this information. The date of the 'sisters' marriage and the birth of children are consistent with my account of his sister's real marriages.

In what follows I rely on a judgement that in *Colonel Jack* Defoe gives the reader an embellished account of his adventures with Robert Spencer and William Penn. In the account of it that I give now, I produce evidence that this was so and not only that they were friends together in 1660-1662 but for the rest of their lives.

Defoe writes that following the 'death' of his nurse, that is after his age of fourteen, he and two other 'Jacks', so called because they were always together, resolved 'that they would all be rogues'. For about two years they lived a life of villainy and petty crime.

Defoe describes the 'Jacks' as bastards. It is a free and different interpretation than any we would accept today. Robert Spencer's father was killed in September, 1642 at the Civil War Battle of Newbury. He became a soldier and diplomat. The elder Jack, Captain Jack in Defoe's narration, became a soldier. In Defoe's narrative Captain Jack, is described

---

[116] *Alien Come Home*, 34-35.

at the time as being plain Jack 'for some years after, till he came to preferment by the merit of his birth, as you shall hear in its place'. Defoe writes of knowing someone who was to come into a fortune:

I knew a private Gentleman, whose father had sett him up worth 200,000l [louis d'or £10,000 in old French francs at a conversion rate of 20 francs to the £1]. and bid Him sett up for a Gentleman…Once I saw a calculation made from his own Presence; for I had so far an Intimacy with his Affairs, by which it appear'd. that in twenty five years more, had he liv'd so long, he must have been worth two Millions Sterling.[117]

Defoe writes that their adventures lasted over three years. Towards the end *Colonel Jack*, the Defoe of my story, realised that if he continued his career as a petty thief he would be caught and executed or deported. He took matters into his own hands and decided to flee from London.

It has been possible to demonstrate that these 'three Jacks', Robert Spencer, William Penn and Daniel Foe, went on a version of the Grand Tour together. I first wrote about it in an earlier work, *Alien Come Home*.[118]

It is accepted by biographers that Defoe went on a version of the Grand Tour at the age of seventeen to eighteen. Bastian who writes persuasively about the places Defoe visited assumed that as Defoe was born around 1660 the Tour took place in 1678. He was right about Defoe's age at the time, seventeen, but wrong about the date. Defoe went on his tour at end July, 1662. Bastian believed that he was financed by the Gentleman quoted above. He was. I conjecture, and seek to prove, that this Gentleman was Robert Spencer, the future Earl of Sunderland and Whig grandee.

Bastian's starting point is my own. The genesis of the Tour is described in Defoe's *Memoirs of a Cavalier*. Defoe writes:

At seventeen years of age my tutor told my father an academic

---

[117] Quoted in Bastian, 67.
[118] *Alien Come Home*, 26-30.

education was very proper for a person of quality and he thought me very fit for it: so my father entered me for…College in Oxford, where I continued three years. I thought I had stayed long enough for a gentleman, and with his leave I desired to give him a visit.

His father then decided to marry him off and to make a settlement of £2,000 a year on him. He responded, 'I confess I thought that a gentleman ought always to see something of the world before he confined himself to any part of it.' His father gave him leave to travel upon the condition that 'he would promise to return in two years or farthest, or sooner if he sent for him.' The young gentleman continues:

While I was at Oxford [1660-1661] I happened into the society of a young gentleman, but of a low fortune, being a younger brother, who had instilled in me the first desires of going abroad, and who, I know passionately longed to travel, but had not sufficient allowance to defray his expenses as a gentleman. We had contracted a very close friendship, and our humours being very agreeable to one another, we daily enjoyed the conversation of letters. He was of a generous free temper, without the least affectation of deceit, a handsome proper person, a strong body, very good mien, and brave to the last degree…He sent me word he would go with all his heart. My father, for I sent for him immediately to come to me, mightily approved my choice; so we got our equipage ready, and came away for London.

I believe that this passage is an embellished account of moments in Defoe's life in which he uses a role reversal to disguise the fact that he is writing about himself. If so who was the subject of this passage, and who the gentleman? Robert Spencer and William Penn were both students at Oxford in 1660-1661. They were sent down in disgrace for robustly opposing the attempt by the University to compel the wearing of surplices following the accession of Charles II. Penn and Spencer supported the Christchurch Chaplain John Owen who held services in people's homes.

John Owen was the Vicar of Coggeshall in 1655 and a former Chaplain to the Republican armies in the siege of Colchester in 1648. Defoe had many associations with Coggeshall. The narrator, the *Cavalier*, states that he was seventeen years of age at the time. Defoe was not eighteen years old until December. Spencer did not come into his fortune at twenty-one years of age until October 1662.

Robert Spencer as the elder of the three Jacks was dubbed the Captain in *Colonel Jack* and in that narrative two of these Jack's (Spencer and Defoe) left England by boat together. The father in the *Cavalier* would be Robert Spencer's step-father and guardian Robert Smythe. A role reversal took place in Defoe's fiction. The narrator must be the person aged seventeen years of age. Possibly, the use of *Cavalier* in the title has a root in Defoe's relative in Northumberland, Philip de Lorraine.[119] This consultation took place some months before Robert Spencer acceded to his title and fortune and he needed the consent of his guardian to travel abroad.

As I have commented, it is generally accepted by Defoe biographers that Defoe embarked on the Grand Tour when he was eighteen years old`, that is according to them, in 1678 and by me in 1662. It is known from Pepys *Diary* that Penn's Grand Tour started at end July,1662;[120] from several biographical accounts that Robert Spencer made three continental tours between 1661 and 1664.Of these trips he was accompanied by William Penn on one occasion in 1662. There is correspondence between Penn and Sunderland that proves it. In a letter to Sunderland, Penn thanks him for his discretion in keeping the events in Paris a secret. [121]

Robert Spencer and Defoe met up on the road to Paris with William Penn and William Lindsay, the Earl of Crawford, who belonged to a Scottish Covenanter's family. We know that this to be so because

---

[119] See Attachment, Defoe's Elder Brother. The Dukes of Lorraine had used the title of Cavalier from mediaeval times

[120] Pepys, Samuel. *Diary of Samuel Pepys*, Bell and Sons, 1971,Vol. 3, 132.

[121] Peare, Catherine, *William Penn*, Dobson Books, 1956, n. 38.

William Penn describes it [122] as does Defoe in *Memoirs of a Cavalier*.[123] They came to Paris as a group of five gentleman and two servants. It was usual to travel in a group in France for mutual protection. In Amiens, Defoe tells his readers they learnt some new pick-pocketing techniques so adding to his accounts of such activities in *Colonel Jack* and *Moll Flanders*.

Peare writes about Penn's activities in France: 'Here is a gap about which almost nothing is known. The record of his stay in Paris is blank.' Besse, a writer of a contemporary biography states that 'Penn attended the French Court at Fontainebleau.'[124] According to Defoe in *Memoirs* they (he and his companions) stayed in Paris for three weeks, 'to see the court and what rarities the place afforded'.

Their stay in Paris was cut short by a dreadful event the consequences of which shaped Defoe's life. Defoe's *Cavalier* writes that as he was walking before the gate of the Louvre, where he hoped to see the Swiss Guard parade, 'a page came up and speaking in English said, Sir, the Captain [Defoe's description of Spencer in *Colonel Jack*] needs your immediate assistance.' Defoe continues:

> I, that had not the knowledge of any person in Paris but my own companion whom I *called Captain,* [as in *Colonel Jack* and italics mine] had no room to question, but it was he that sent for me and crying out hastily to him [the page], 'Where?' followed the fellow as far as possible. He led me through several passages which I knew not, and at last through a tennis-court into a large room where three men, like gentlemen were engaged very briskly two against one. The room was very dark, so that I could not easily know them asunder, but being fully possessed before of my Captain's danger, I ran into the room with my sword in my hand. I had not particularly engaged any of them, not as much made a pass at any when I received a

---

[122] BL1575/435. Penn, William. *No Cross, No Crown*, Collected Works, Vol. 272, London 1726.

[123] *Memoirs of a Cavalier*, 3-4.

[124] Quoted in Peare.

very dangerous thrust in my thigh, rather occasioned by my too hasty running in than a real design of the person; but enraged at the hurt, without examining who it was hurt me, I threw myself upon him, and ran my sword through his body.

Later Penn was to write about an incident in Paris in a publication entitled, *No Cross, No Crown.* He wrote:

I was once myself in France…set upon about eleven at night, as I was walking to my lodging, by a person that way-laid me, with his naked sword in his hand, who demanded satisfaction of me for taking no notice of him, at a time when he civilly saluted me with his hat, tho' the truth was I saw him not when he did it. I will suppose he had killed me, for he made several passes at me, or I in my defence had killed him, when I disarmed him as the Earl of Crawford's servant saw, that was by.

These two accounts of a duel have key elements in common: a visit together to Paris in July, 1662 when Spencer was twenty and Penn and Defoe seventeen years old [actual and fictional ages]; a duel there resulting in one account in a death or possible death, of a man/ French courtier; the size of the travelling party; a visit to the Court; a return to lodgings; the page/servant as a witness; and regret, embarrassment and mental turmoil caused by the incident.

Defoe's further account is revealing. At the tennis court, two men stood gazing, and the page had disappeared. He discovered that the Captain [Spencer] was not there, and so he ran away and made his way back to his lodgings where he found him present and unharmed. He [Defoe] was badly hurt and soon had 'a roomful of people about me.' Outside the streets were full of people 'inquiring after the person who had killed a man at the tennis court'. He was moved to another house under cover of darkness. In ten days time he was well enough to flee Paris with the Captain – although it turned out that he should not have moved so quickly as his wound reopened.[125]

---

[125] *Alien Come Home*, 27-31.

As with all attempts to disguise the whole truth, these descriptions quickly reveal inconsistencies. According to Defoe when he arrived at the tennis court there were three men fighting and the Major [Penn] had fled. The page had also disappeared. Who then was the 'friend' still confronting the two hostile Frenchmen? Spencer? Arguably, Defoe's actions had assisted Penn to escape with the page and saved Spencer from serious injury or even death. Defoe made his escape separately. On the way back to his lodgings Penn was challenged by a courtier seeking the killer. He writes that he was able to disarm his challenger. If so he must have been carrying a sword. As likely he and the page were able to convince the challenger that they had nothing to do with the incident.

Both Spencer and Penn had good reason to flee the scene. They had arrived in Paris with letters of introduction to the Court and to diplomats in Paris. At this time both fathers, for Spencer a step-father Sir Robert Smythe, had diplomatic family alliances with the restored Charles II and family loyalties to the monarch. Spencer's actual father, Henry Spencer, was a Royalist soldier and killed in the Civil War while his mother, Lady Dorothy Sydney, had taken care of Charles 1's children at Penhurst after his death. Penn's father was personally rewarded by the new monarch for his part in bringing him back to England. In a sense both men were Cavaliers. The sending down of both youths from Oxford for refusing to wear the surplice thought appropriate by the new monarch was embarrassing to the families although, no doubt, there must have been an understanding that it was difficult for fathers to control every action of high-spirited off-spring. Spencer's step-father had allowed him to be in France only on the strict instruction that he could be called back on short notice. At this time England was in alliance with the French and any diplomatic incident could be seen as damaging to the Crown. A diplomatic incident in France would have rendered both fathers persona non grata there. Penn returned home while Spencer and Defoe wended their way south from the capital as described by the *Cavalier*.[126]

It will be obvious to the reader that if there were no other evidence

---

[126] *Memoirs of a Cavalier*, 14 -21.

that Defoe was born in 1644 - and there is in abundance - this account of the visit to France with Spencer and Penn in July, 1662 would suggest it. However, the assertion of Defoe's date of birth is not a prime mover for this account - but an implication of it. I maintain the narrative presents a highly persuasive conjecture supported by good documentary evidence.

EXILE

Chapter 7

The Voyage Out

I found no better shift before me...than to enter myself as a soldier...

Colonel Jack
Daniel Defoe, 1722

It is generally accepted on Defoe's own protestations and behaviour that he had served as a soldier. In the conventional account of his life, and on the conjecture made by others that he was born in 1659/60, it is incredibly difficult, if not impossible, to find a time when he might have done this.

Defoe incurred ridicule when he rode as a trooper in the Royal Regiment of Volunteer Horse at the first Lord Mayor's Show of the reign of William III in 1689. These troopers, it was said, 'were for the most part Dissenters'. It is claimed also by numerous biographers, although on very shaky evidence, that Defoe had taken part in the Monmouth Rebellion in 1685.

If these protestations were the only evidence for Defoe's military service, the possibility could be safely dismissed. However, there is convincing documentary evidence. The National Archives in London have a record listing Daniel Defoe as a cavalry officer in the British army. He is shown as a Captain Lieutenant in Captain Desborde's Regiment of Dragoons raised in Portugal in 1702-3(?). I reproduce the information about this Commission as an Illustration. There is evidence that the process of raising up to six regiments for support of Portugal in the forthcoming War of the Spanish Succession, 1702, began in 1701/1702. In the entire English Army Commission Registers from 1661-1714 Daniel Defoe's name is the only Foe/Defoe listed.[127] In May, 1702 Portugal joined the Grand Alliance against France.

---

[127] NRA. Dalton. Charles. *English Army Lists and Commission Registers*, Vol.V1, 1707-1714,
London, Eyre and Spottiswood, 1904, 268. See Illustration.

In this venture Defoe was accepting the leadership of a Huguenot soldier. Something is known about Captain Peter Desbordes. He was a French Protestant exile from France resident in London, who became a naturalised British subject by resolution of the House of Commons in March, 1699.[128] Desbordes had a distinguished military career and rose to the rank of Lieutenant Colonel.

The six regiments raised by Desbordes were paid for by the English Treasury. Defoe qualified for a pension paid by the Treasury. According to the English Registers, Defoe was drawing a pension in 1722. It was possible to buy a commission in the British and Portuguese armies at the time, and many did, but it seems unlikely that Defoe would have been acceptable to Desbordes without evidence of military experience, and/or, family status.

When *Colonel Jack*, aged no more than seventeen years, was 'on the loose' in London, he professed to have been able to speak knowledgably about recent European wars and the diplomatic relations that determined them. He was speaking of the European dynastic wars that are named and described as the Thirty Years War, 1621-1648. Defoe's account of the conflict in *Memoirs of a Cavalier* and in conversation as a young man is of the latter stages of this long war.[129] At this time, 1660-`1662, Defoe may have had access to private libraries with historical accounts of this war and the later English Civil War- perhaps that of Robert Spencer's family.

The war at various times involved most states across the European mainland of Europe and on the high seas. Mostly it was fought out on the soil of what is known now as Germany. Naval warfare reached across the Atlantic to the Caribbean and New England in a struggle for colonial advantage.

The causes of the conflict and the foreign policy objectives of each of the combatants were complex and changing. Sometimes the conflict is seen as religious and arising out of the Protestant reformation and the

---

[128] *Journal of the House of Commons*, 1660-1690, Vol.1.

[129] It can be argued that this is evidence of a post-Oedipal crisis described by Jacques Lacan's *Symbolic Order*, a period of illusory unity and mastery of the world.

counter pressure of Roman Catholic states. Religious differences were important but the war was caused more by the dynastic aspirations of kings, princes and nations than any other factor.

Specifically, it is possible to identify three main causes for this long and damaging War. The first, and perhaps the most important, was a struggle between France and the United Provinces and the House of Hapsburg (Spain and Austria) for territorial control and influence. Secondly, and in particular, the political weakness of the German remnants of the Holy Roman Empire invited the attention of predators anxious for influence and control. Thirdly, the naval war was fought by the major European powers to colonise territories both for their wealth and for the benefits of the trade created by linking Europe to Africa and the New World. Vast quantities of goods were moved through an Atlantic corridor to the advantage of both merchants and settlers.

The Thirty Years War was brought to an end by the Peace of Westphalia, 1648, which gave independence to various territories: to the Swiss, through the formation of the Swiss Confederation, a Northern Netherlands, and a German Confederation of Princes, in which Prussia exerted a dominant influence, and which was to become modern Germany in 1871.

The Peace did not bring an end to conflict; it took a different form. The Habsburg Empire through the Kingdoms of Austria and Spain and France now engaged in a long conflict for territorial protection, influence, trade and colonial possessions and glory. England became locked into conflict with the Dutch for supremacy at sea.

Early in the period the Dutch gained an advantage over all its rivals at sea and fought successful sea battles in European waters against France and England to assert it. All nations sought the right to ship goods to and from their ports and colonies in their own ships. In England in 1651, 1654 and 1663 Parliament enacted Navigation Acts with the purpose of banning foreign ships from transporting goods from outside Europe to England or its colonies. The objective at this time was to challenge the position of the Dutch who dominated the

European merchant trade. It became illegal also for English colonial merchants to sell certain goods to other nations.

While Defoe could not have taken part in the Thirty Years War, as the account in the *Memoirs* would imply. However, I do think he could have participated in the Portuguese War of Restoration, 1662-1663, in a force of English auxiliaries. As a consequence of the war Portugal achieved its independence from the Hapsburg Empire. It was an involvement which led Defoe to a personal disaster. While serious for him, the duel in Paris would only have been a temporary setback, but the consequence of his involvement in the Portuguese War, was to be his exile from England until 1680. This period of time, 1662-1680 accounts for eighteen years of *Robinson Crusoe's* exile. Over three years in a rush of fictions, *Robinson Crusoe* (1719), *Farther Adventures of Robinson Crusoe*, (1720), *Memoirs of a Cavalier*, (1720), *Captain Singleton*, (1720), *Colonel Jack* (1722), and *Moll Flanders* (1722) Defoe gives an account of his life. I regard them as feeding into a 'monomyth' unique to him. Each fiction goes over some of the same ground while extending the account by period and event. Taken together they have the effect of a vast and self-justifying outpouring of hidden truths, passions and revelations.

In *Memoirs of a Cavalier* Defoe discusses his involvement in military action. The *Captain*/Spencer did not take part in any fighting and, as is known, he returned home to England. This war, given the date, could only have been the Portuguese War of Restoration, 1662-1663. An English expeditionary force of some two thousand cavalry and foot soldiers was led by men of Cromwell's Old Guard, now out of a job. The early stages of the war went badly for the Portuguese. In the chaos men withdrew from the battle lines in order to survive. The *Cavalier* makes a good case for the assertion that all wars 'involve lions led by donkeys'. In order to save their lives, men melted from the battle ground. In the end all turned out well and the Portuguese gained a victory.

The Portuguese military commanders may have found the distinction between withdrawal and desertion to be too fine for them. Deserters and 'cowards' were shipped under constraint to Brazil to provide much-needed labour on plantations. This is what happened to the unfortunate Defoe.

Robinson Crusoe, Captain Singleton and *Colonel Jack* feed into Defoe's monomyth and essentially tell the same story. According to Joseph Campbell a monomyth is an all-male quest as 'old as the hills' as a literary genre.[130] Defoe's heroes proceed at seventeen to eighteen years of age to make 'voyages out'. They travel to Portugal, Brazil and Virginia under some form of restraint. In *Robinson Crusoe* the narrator is transported to Brazil and in *Colonel Jack* to Virginia as an indentured labourer; in *Crusoe* and *Colonel Jack* they are engaged in sugar production; and they have a shared experience in trading goods and slaves from trading points along the trans-Atlantic trading routes, from Portugal, Spain and England to Africa, South America, the Caribbean and New England.

Colonel Jack is helpful to a biographer. Following upon the hint of desertion in the *Memoirs*, in *Colonel Jack* some soldiers have actually deserted and were then press ganged into a ship sailing for Virginia. The narrator was eighteen years old, as would have been Defoe if he had deserted in 1663. On boarding this ship *Colonel Jack* tells the reader that he would not see the shores he had left (England) for nigh on twenty years, the period of time I conjecture for Defoe's exile -1662 to 1682 - when he decided finally to settle back into England. In England Defoe is careful to sever the *Colonel* from his past. He tells his readers that he could not '*remember his name or his parentage.*' (Italics mine). He was pressed into service on a plantation in Virginia for five years as a punishment for military desertion.

On board ship the *Colonel* produces a valuable bill of exchange which earlier in the story he explained had been given him in London by a gentleman in return for a money deposit. The *Colonel* sought to use the bill to buy his freedom from the master of the ship. However, this Captain preferred to receive cash from a merchant in Virginia who would place the *Colonel* with a plantation owner. It is difficult to believe the *Colonel's* account. It has a certain slipperiness and self-justification. The

[130] Campbell, Joseph. *The Hero with a Thousand Faces*, (1949. Fontana Press, 1993).

ship master's threat must have been to return Jack and his companion to the military authority from which they had deserted. The account of the transition from ship to plantation, as described by Defoe, lacks conviction.

Colonel Jack knew that he deserved his fate. As he reflected on it, he thought that he had been brought into this miserable condition as a 'slave' by some strange directing power as a punishment for the wickedness of his younger years. It was a harsh judgement of himself as a young man of eighteen years of age.

However, he was lucky, as he describes his fate, in the character of the plantation owner. *Colonel Jack* produced his bill of exchange to his new master who was inclined to believe his story. The bill was sent to London to be cashed and in the meantime *Colonel Jack* was appointed an overseer of slave labour.

At this point in the story Defoe uses a clever narrative device. He is concerned to show that *Colonel Jack* was not at the bottom of the social pile. A group of branded felons were delivered to the plantation. His master explained to them that whatever had happened in the past they had the opportunity now to make amends and make something of themselves. He came to a young fellow of not more than seventeen or eighteen years of age (a common Defoe narrative device here for talking about himself). His warrant mentioned that though he was a young man he was an old offender who although several times found guilty of crimes had always been respited or pardoned. He had been whipped and branded yet nothing would do him any good. Defoe is using the narrative device of two arrivals, both of which he is a part, and which are separated in time. This enables him to distance himself from an army and an event - at some time he may have been branded.[131]

This device enables the *Colonel* to think well of his master for he concluded that he was aware of all these things but nevertheless had trust in him. His master, as presented by Defoe, was of a tender and compassionate nature, but it required another supervisor to teach the

---

[131] *Beyond Belief*, 255.

Colonel, and to persuade the master, that harsh beatings were unnecessary.

The bill had a face value of £92 and after deducting £42 for the cost of collecting it from London there was enough money for the purchase of land on which the *Colonel* cultivated tobacco and vegetables on his own account. However, while the bill was redeemed, the cargo it purchased was lost at sea with very little recovered. *Jack* was left with the arduous task of working the land to repay the loan he had received out of profit. *Colonel Jack* tells us that he was in the service of his master for five to six years, that is, 1663-1669 in my narrative.

While Virginia was the *Colonel's* destination and his stay was there, I believe that the period of forced constraint was elsewhere. At some time in his story Defoe does travel to Virginia but not I think in the 1660's. It is my argument that the events he describes at this stage of his life took place in Brazil, a Portuguese colony. I am strengthened in this conviction by Defoe narrating that his heroes were transported to Brazil in a Portuguese man of war. Defoe gives just enough information to produce convincing fictional accounts of living in Brazil.

Crusoe was rescued on the high seas by a Portuguese ship when he was escaping from a period of slavery by 'The Moors at Sallee' and put ashore in All Saints Bay in Brazil with some goods and weapons he had been able to salvage. The friendly Portuguese Captain then undertook a mission to travel to London, contact a Widow who held money to his account, and buy stock and utensils to its value without remuneration (which might be thought to be an unlikely story). The Captain brought back valuable goods and a young black slave, who he had bought for £5 pounds, and an indentured English servant. By selling some of this stock *Crusoe* had the capital to start up in business as a sugar planter. The reader is told that the value of the goods shipped to him was £100. If the £5 for the slave is deducted, the amount received from London would be £95, a sum identical to that received by *Colonel Jack* from London. It is reasonable to assume that Defoe was describing the same event in two different fictions.

Who might the Widow be? In his will Daniel Foe leaves his son Defoe the sum of eighty pounds and Randle Wildbore and John Ewen were entrusted to see that he received it when aged twenty-one. Defoe was twenty-one in 1665. Randle Wildbore died in 1658. Nicholas Wildbore, his son, may have accepted the responsibility of passing the inheritance from his father to Defoe. Before leaving on his Grand Tour, Defoe may have created a bill of exchange. Nicholas Wildbore died in 1664 leaving a widow Mary (nee Love) who subsequently moved to London. This being so, Mary Love was the widow entrusted with the responsibility of getting the money to Defoe. If a modest rate of interest is added to the principal of eighty pounds it could have grown to a hundred pounds by 1665 a period of eighteen years. It follows from this explanation that Defoe's relatives and kinsmen in London would have known about his incarceration in Brazil by 1665.

The Portuguese had shipped sugar cane to Brazil from Portugal from the beginning of the sixteenth-century. North East Brazil became the leading production centre of the trade. In Brazil the plantations were first worked by settlers and the local indigenous people. However, slaves were preferred to free men because of the long hours of labour and minimal subsistence costs of using them.

In *Farther Adventures*, Defoe describes something of this local workforce and their inter-marriage and servitude to planters through the character of Will Atkins. Defoe uses the characters he invents, or the people he encounters, to tell the reader something of himself.

Much to his chagrin Defoe had become a planter. He grew tobacco. He had the co-operation of his neighbour who was a Portuguese citizen brought up in England. By steady application he had some degree of success. But it was not enough for him. He could not resist the temptation of making big money in the slave trade.

Crusoe tells the reader that after four years of prosperous trading he discussed a proposal with some Merchants and Planters to fit out a ship to Guinea to buy negroes for use on the plantations as slave labourers. They required this venture to be kept secret. The slaves bought would be used only on their plantations and he, *Crusoe*, was to have a fair share of them without having to provide any capital or stock. Defoe writes that *Crusoe* was responding to a request from others but he gives the impression, nevertheless, that the proposal was his in the first place. Earlier in his story *Crusoe* tells the reader of other slave trading ventures of his.[132] He was experienced and willing. Slavery had become essential to the economics of sugar production in Brazil and the Caribbean and slaves could fetch high prices in both these territories.

From the outset of his seventeen years of habitation in Brazil, Defoe bought and used slaves in the production of tobacco and sugar. When Defoe writes about slavery and the exploitation of slaves on plantations he is writing directly from his own experience. Over a life-time this experience embraced tobacco and sugar production in Brazil, Barbados and Virginia. Defoe was a staunch defender of slavery throughout his life both as an individual and through shareholdings in the South Sea Company and the Royal African Company. The slavery abolitionist cause had little support in Britain, other than among Quakers, until the nineteenth century when the trade became unproductive and conscience caught up with economics.

In various places in his written work Defoe expresses his concern for the welfare of slaves and their fair treatment but he evades moral responsibility for his involvement in the trade by the use of a well-known shibboleth; namely, that when slaves were asked whether they wanted freedom they chose servitude. It is of course true that a slave, or former slave, could have no genuine freedom unless the law of the land gave it.

There have been various estimates of the number of black Africans enslaved by Europeans, mainly the British, French, Portuguese, Spanish and Dutch, and transported to the New World. In the three hundred years between the sixteenth and nineteenth centuries up to ten million slaves underwent the grim journey. Some twenty percent or more died in passage and many others within a short period of time of their slavery on a plantation. They were easy to replace.

---

[132] *Robinson Crusoe*, 59.

In Defoe's lifetime the economic advantage of sugar and tobacco production, perhaps not truly viable at all without slave labour, shifted to the West Indies. Britain brought sugar cane to Jamaica around 1617 and to Barbados from 1630. These colonies required settlers, capital and labour. As the sugar demand from Europe grew exponentially so did the need for slaves. It has been estimated that by 1667, when Defoe first entered the trade, there were over seven hundred owners of plantations in Barbados alone using over 80,000 slaves. They included members of the Lawrence family who at various times had acquired land in South Carolina, Barbados and Jamaica.

By the 1680's thirty percent of the adult population in Barbados were Quaker migrants from South Carolina and Europe. Quakers argued the case for slaves to be admitted to Sunday worship in Meeting Houses. They were fiercely opposed by settlers on the grounds of the loss of their output. As Defoe spent time on Barbados it might be supposed that he was influenced by Quaker arguments. William Penn, Defoe's companion on the Grand Tour, was not against slavery. The Penn family was not against the purchase, sale and maintenance of slaves as domestic servants, and William Penn needed a plentiful supply of them to assist his new settlers make a success of their ventures in the New World.

As the sugar and slave trades moved north to the Caribbean islands and New England, Defoe moved with it. His interests were broader than the trading of slaves and the selling of sugar. The needs of the migrants settling in New England had to be met by imports to and exports from Europe, in particular England. There were two main trans-Atlantic trade routes. The Dutch were first in setting up a West Indian company with fortified trading posts in West Africa and with links to slave traders in the interior. England, Spain and France followed their example. Slaves were shipped from other parts of Africa as well. These slaves were shipped to the plantations that were the ultimate buyers in the West Indies and New England. In return the produce of the New World was exported to Europe. These trading routes and rights were protected by national navies. The English and the Dutch fought a series of naval wars to establish supremacy over the sea routes. In the end a rough geographical sphere of naval influence was established with the Dutch achieving supremacy off the African coast and the English dominance in the Caribbean and New England. Yet despite naval agreements the Dutch were never squeezed out of trade with New England and the English navy succeeded from time to time in achieving some success off the coast of Africa and eventually complete dominance of the North Sea and the coastline of Britain.

Brazil was not the ideal location for a merchant trading with England, New England, and the rest of Europe. Successive English administrations, by a series of Navigation Acts, in particular those enacted in 1660-1663, attempted to obtain the largest possible share of the trans-Atlantic trade for English traders. If Defoe was to prosper in the trade he needed to own an English ship, defined by the Acts as the ownership of at least twenty-five percent of the vessel's hull. He began to think, therefore, that London would be a better and safer trading base.

Chapter 8

Piracy

The crime of piracy is against the universal law of society... [a pirate] being hosti humanis generis....by declaring war against all mankind, all mankind must declare war against him.

Commentaries on the Laws of England
William Blackstone

The pent up anger in the young Defoe had led to delinquency and alienation. He did not want the life that was open to him in England. In Brazil there were other displaced Europeans like him. They came from everywhere and nowhere seeking their fortunes and through hard work and the exploitation of others, indentured servants and slaves, earned a living from the ownership of land. Defoe could become a recognised person in Brazil in 'a middling sort of way' in a society that did not despise him. It was not enough. He wanted to achieve a fortune, to be noteworthy and recognised by others as a worthy and even distinguished man. If he could not achieve this in England and Brazil there was an alternative society open to him through piracy. He could set his face against all those who had denied him a place and live by new values and judgements that respected his own – and become rich.

If *Captain Singleton* is to be believed, Defoe consciously welcomed the opportunity to declare war against his society by leading a life that involved him in piracy. He declared war first, and the Brazilian authorities, acting as Portuguese colonial enforcers, responded by declaring war on him. However, Defoe had self- conscious limitations. He did not wish to carry the pursuit of wealth to the point of self-destruction. Wealth was of no use to him if it led to a horrible death

The legitimate trans-Atlantic trade was pillaged by many seeking to live off it. Whatever the international agreements, all trading activity was subject to interference by the national navies of the Dutch,

Spanish, and Portuguese. A regular and legal trader along these routes could have his vessel attacked by foreign navies with the loss of cargo, ships and crew. Not the least of the predators were pirates who gathered in great numbers in the Caribbean, Africa and the East Indies.

Slave trading was illegal unless within the terms of an Asiento. In Brazil the Portuguese navy guaranteed that trading in slaves was subject to its control. A return journey from Brazil to Africa took many weeks. Keeping your crew provisioned and a large number of slaves fed for several weeks were considerable tasks. It must have been tempting and necessary to raid a merchant ship for its provisions in order to stay alive. Ethically, it could be argued, that if you were raided, a tit for tat retaliation of some kind was justified.

Defoe was highly knowledgeable about piracy and mercantile trade and wrote much about pyrates. For many years *A General History of the Pyrates*, 1724, an important contribution to an understanding of the history and the life of pirates, was attributed to him. Latterly credence has been given to the authorship of the work by Nathaniel Mist whose printer Charles Rivington registered the book with His Majesty's Stationery Office under the name of Charles Johnson, now thought to be a Mist pseudonym. To add to the difficulty of ascription, Defoe was working for Mist at or around the date of publication in 1724. It is said, without documentary evidence, that Mist sailed as a merchant sailor in the West Indies and had the experience needed to write the book. Nevertheless, I believe that Defoe had the major hand in it and that he and Mist collaborated on the book. I provide a conclusive proof that this is so in a chapter in this book. There is no doubt in my analysis that Defoe wrote *King of the Pirates*, 1720, *Captain Singleton*, 1720 and *Robinson Crusoe*, 1719 and the *Farther Adventures of Robinson Crusoe*, 1720. When these books are compared, it can be seen that they cover the same ground of merchant and piratical experiences in the Caribbean and Madagascar.

The nearest that Defoe comes to admitting piracy in his fiction is in *Captain Singleton*. The title page reads as follows:

Containing an account of his being set on Shore in the Island of Madagascar, his settlement there, with a Description of the Place and Inhabitants: Of his Passage thence, in a Paraguay, to the main land of Africa, with an account of the Customs and Manners of the People: His Great Deliverances from the barbarous Natives and wild Beasts: of his meeting with an *Englishman, a Citizen of London, among the Indians*, (italics mine) on his Return to Sea, with an Account of his many Adventures and Pyracies with the famous Captain Avery and others.

In *King of the Pyrates*, Defoe offers a personation of Captain Avery and a spirited and sympathetic defence of his actions. In the *Farther Adventures of Robinson Crusoe, Crusoe* returns to Madagascar. What all the books have in common is piracy, Captain Avery and Madagascar. Crusoe tells his readers that he achieved, at a high point, £1,000 a year from his plantations in Brazil but that this was but a fraction of the money he made on a single adventure in the waters of the trans-Atlantic routes.

A difficulty for Defoe biographers is to distinguish between fiction and reality. Did Defoe become involved in piracy? Was Captain Singleton a real or imagined person? Did Defoe know Captain Avery and become involved with him, meet Captain Kidd, and enter into a life-long friendship with William Penn as I have suggested?

Captain Singleton

There was a real-life Singleton, Edward Singleton, whom Defoe knew intimately for twenty to thirty years. I discuss his relationship with Defoe in a later chapter and summarise it here. The Singleton family were located in the Parish of St James, Barbados, a mile from the sea port of Bridgetown.[133] Edward Singleton became a government sugar surveyor. In 1697 he was found guilty of corruption in London and imprisoned in the Fleet. [134] Singleton was either a Quaker or a good friend to Quakerism. He was the executor of the will of Jonas Langford a wealthy plantation owner who opened the first Quaker meeting house

---

[133] Barbados Parish Records, 1660-1680, RB 3/48, 49, 50, 51.
[134] Calendar of Treasury Books, Vol.12, July, 1697, 265.

in Antigua.[135] In 1701 William Penn had sufficient confidence in Singleton to appoint him to act as an unofficial representative of his in Barbados.[136] Although Singleton may have been something of a rogue he had no reputation for being a pirate. Defoe, Singleton and Penn were both fictionalised and real characters who knew and trusted each other for thirty to sixty years.

It is my belief that Defoe uses his familiar narrative device of switching identities in *Captain Singleton*. Defoe is writing about himself when he narrates *Singleton's* story and he uses him as a front man to distance himself from his narrative crimes. The term Captain Bob, as used by Defoe to describe *Singleton*, is a colloquialism whose meaning, in the context in which Defoe uses it, is a makeshift Captain, an amateur in temporary charge of a ship. The term is used in *Robinson Crusoe*.[137]

In my opinion, awareness that there is an actual Singleton changes the story and questions the many interesting interpretations of it. This is a troublesome conjecture of mine as it raises the issue of the extent to which *Singleton's* story is a realistic account of his or Defoe's life or whether it is pure fiction in part or in whole?

While I do not wish to discuss the literary merits of the book at this point in my story, I draw the reader's attention to its two distinct narrative stages. The book shares such a split with *Robinson Crusoe*. In the first half of Singleton's story he is marooned on Madagascar for joining in a mutiny. He makes his way across Africa accumulating vast riches and once home attempts to settle in England. He remains rootless without the ownership of property, spends and loses his money and decides to return to sea. In the second half he turns to piracy off the coast of South America and in the Caribbean.

Captain Singleton/Defoe, as presented in the narrative, is a

[135] *Journal of the Barbados Museum and Historical Society*, XI: 193. The Will of Jonas Langford, Senior of Pope's Head Plantation as one of the executors.
[136] *Papers of William Penn*, Letter to James Logan dated 11 January 1701, 'Consign all thou send me to ed. Singleton in Barbados no need that RE [the official agent] knows of it.'
[137] *Alien Come Home*, 31, n.27.

thorough-going rogue. *Singleton* describes his entry into piracy as follows:

> I did not care where I went, having nothing to lose...[I] came into it without the least hesitation, either at the villany of the act [the original piracy] or the difficulty of performing it. I that was, an original thief, and a pirate, even by inclination before, was now in my element, and never did anything in my life with more particular satisfaction.

Backscheider writes about *Singleton* as follows:

> He has almost no education...no opportunity to learn any ethical code [so] he is consistently predatory and bold ...his ingenuity makes him a leader...something was 'all one' to him [and] without family, loyalties or scruples, going or staying, trading with the natives or killing them seem neutral choices. Singleton [tries to] recreate England...but is quick to say to say that his worst treatment has been in England. [He is] shocking rather than average, foreign rather than common to our experience...

As I read *Captain Singleton*, I am impressed by Defoe's considerable knowledge of ships, navigation, places and piracy. How could he have acquired such knowledge? In his Introduction to the 1977 Dover Publications edition of *A General History of the Pyrates*, Manuel Schonhorn seeks to answer the question. He argues that a 'good deal of this knowledge of trading routes and harbours and neutral ports was gained by Defoe in the 1680's when he travelled throughout most of the countries of western and central Europe as a commission merchant and importer.'[138] He points to his widespread reading of contemporary publications and his relationship with Dalby Thomas, the author of *An Historical Account of the Rise and Fall of the West Indian Collonies*. Dalby was appointed an Agent General of the African Company's Gold Coast settlement in 1703. Schonhorn points out also that it was probable that Defoe had encountered such voyagers as

---

[138] Schonhorn, Manuel. Ed. *A General History of the Pyrates*, Dover Publications, 1999.

Woodes Rogers and Alexander Selkirk. All these influences were of importance to Defoe and his written works. However, these factors do not explain Defoe's detailed knowledge of piracy and the slave trade in the Caribbean and along the American coastline and nor can it explain the intricacies of his narratives.

A reader of *Captain Singleton* arrives at the irresistible conclusion that '*Singleton*' was there. The act of stealing a ship defines *Singleton* and his gang as pirates. At first he tells the reader, 'We cruised ...chiefly upon the Spaniards.' Until the Anglo-Spanish Treaty, 1670 this was a relatively safe thing to do because it could be argued that this was in the English national interest. Together with the fictional friend, Captain Wilmot, his pirate gang acquired by piracy three good and complementary vessels and lived off the produce being carried by vessels from New England. This was a fateful crossing of the border line between buccaneering and piracy.

Defoe writes, 'Here we came to a resolution to go away to the coast of Brazil, and from thence to the Cape of Good Hope and then to the East Indies.' This was a slave route. They put in at Madagascar and then returned to Salvador da Bahia, Brazil where they not unsurprisingly encountered the Portuguese navy anchored in the Bay of All Saints (where *Crusoe* had a plantation). In a sea battle *Singleton* and Wilmot overcame a Portuguese man of war. Now they were in difficulties as wanted men.

There is a legal background to this incident. Salvador, the capital of Brazil at the time, was a major centre of the slave trade. Until the Treaty of Utrecht when an Assiento was granted to Britain, which subsequently assumed most of the trade, it was illegal to attempt a private trade in slaves. What was suggested by *Crusoe*/Defoe to the planters was illegal. Movements at sea were noticed by the authorities and the Portuguese fleet was waiting for *Singleton's* ship in Brazilian waters.

Defoe uses euphemisms and evasive language to soften the revelation of his hero's actions. *Crusoe* tells reader that in conversations he had had with the planters:

I had frequently given them an Account of my two voyages

to the Coast of Guinea, the manner of Trading with the Negroes there, such as Beads, Toys, Knives, Scissars, Hatchets, bits of glass, and the like; not only [for] Gold Dust, Guinea Grains. Elephants Teeth [tusks] but Negroes, which was a Trade at that time not far entered into, but as far as it was, had been carried on by Assiento or Permission of the Kings of Spain and Portugal, and engross'd in the Publick, so that few Negroes were brought, and those excessive dear.

Captain Singleton is ignoring these niceties and his slave dealing is illegal. Illegal trading in slaves involved long sea journeys, frequent challenges at sea and in ports, and the dangers of starvation and death. A pirate ship needed to board cargo ships from or to New England for food and general provisions because it was often dangerous to put in at a port. If the crew did not accept an invitation to join the pirate ship they were either killed or put ashore. The pirate who put men ashore ran the risk of the captives escaping from the island or territory selected and subsequently being reported by them to the authorities. *Singleton* states 'accounts had been made public of how we murdered the people in cold blood, tying them back to back, and throwing them into the sea, one half of which, however, was untrue, though more was done than is fit to speak of here.' On one occasion they had put men ashore on an island to the north of *Brazil* so evoking *Crusoe's* desert island. *Singleton* carefully evades all references to his own acts. On occasions he tells the reader that Wilmot was hard on a captured crew and that happenings were too awful to describe in detail; but he never describes his own actions.

There is a climax to *Singleton's* piracy. Defoe writes that *Singleton* boarded a large ship to find '600 negroes, men and women, boys and girls and not one Christian or white man on board.' He believed that the slaves had mutinied, killed the crew and thrown them overboard. There were signs of a struggle and blood. What on earth should they do with the slaves? The men were all for killing the slaves and throwing them overboard but *Singleton* and William the Quaker persuaded them not to do so. William entered into discussions with other countries along the American coastline and succeeded in selling the slaves and calming the authorities.

I do not believe that this incident is an actual account but if it did occur the description given is most probably an overstatement. I do not believe that *Singleton*/Defoe boarded a ship to find 600 slaves and no crew. It is far more likely that he attacked the ship and killed its crew and then found himself with a large number of slaves with no easy way of disposing of them. I do not believe that William Penn/*William the Quaker*, engaged in piracy in the way described. There are other and better explanations for his involvement in *Singleton's* story.

It is understandable that many readers would be entirely unconvinced by any literal representation of Captain Kidd, Captain Avery and John Wilmott - most probably a fictional representation of the Second Earl Rochester- in *Singleton's* narrative, while recognising that these people were of intense interest to Defoe. Nor would they be impressed by Defoe's plagiarising of Robert Knox in *Historical Reflections* which Katherine Frank has commented upon.[139] For a start, the dates are all wrong. William Penn could not have been in Barbados until end 1682 at the earliest. However, it is possible that Defoe met Penn on his first visit to Pennsylvania after becoming the proprietary owner of the state. As I discuss later, Defoe's wife Jone Reede died in Barbados in December 1681. Defoe was in a legal position to claim all she possessed, and most probably did so in 1682.

Captain Avery

Similarly, and most intriguingly, did Defoe encounter Captain Avery and become involved in some way in helping him to his own advantage? I believe that he did. As Katherine Frank makes clear *Singleton's* fictional encounter with a white gentleman in Africa is an allusion to Avery who, as Defoe writes in *King of the Pyrates*, escaped from justice by travelling across Africa. Katherine Frank suggests that *Singleton's* description of a dishevelled white gentleman stumbled

---

[139] Frank, Katherine, *Crusoe: Daniel Defoe, Robert Knox and the Creation of a Myth*, The Bodley Head, London, 2011.

across in central Africa was based on a description Robert Knox offered of his father in Ceylon. As usual Defoe was precise. This white man 'was not above thirty-seven or thirty-eight years of age.' Defoe suggests that he had been there in his present state for two years. In *A General History of the Pyrates* Defoe suggests that Avery was born near Plymouth at a date before the Peace of Ryswick [1697]. There is an actual Parish Record showing that an Avery was born in August, 1659 in Newton Ferrers, near Plymouth.[140] The actual date Defoe was using in *Captain Singleton* must at the earliest have been 1698. If some thirty-eight years is added to the conjectured date of Avery's birth then a birth around 1659 is possible. Through this allusion it can be seen that Defoe knew of an actual or supposed date of Avery's birth, a fact that has eluded many enquirers. However, if we follow Aitken's maxim and subtract or add twenty-seven years we would arrive at a birth in the 1630's. This conclusion results in an issue. In 1720 when Defoe published *Captain Singleton* he knew the precise date and place of Avery's birth whereas in *A General History of the Pyrates*, published four years later in 1724, he didn't. Defoe resorts to an imprecise statement about his birth.

Defoe was able to arrive at the precise date for at least two reasons. First, he may have been related to Avery through the Kent branch of the family line of Edward Lawrence; and secondly, it is my view that as a result of his own seafaring activities Defoe encountered many pirates and maritime adventurers of different hues and knew how to contact them in London and other English ports.

Defoe's accounts of Captain Avery's escape from justice and the steps he took to realise the value of the booty he had acquired, which was mainly in diamonds and gold coins, differ in *A General History* and *King of the Pirates*. Following the first of these accounts Avery succeeded in acquiring control of all the booty, slipped two ships that had taken part in the capture of the *Ganj-Sawaii* and whose crew were entitled to a fair share of the prize, landed others in New England

---

[140] Parish Records of Newton Ferrers, Devon. Baptisms: 1659, Aug.23. Henry son of John and Anne Evarie.

where some of the men decided to stay with a limited number of diamonds as their share of the booty; and then left suddenly without notice. He landed in Dublin where eighteen of his original crew were subsequently granted a Royal Pardon. Avery found it difficult to sell the diamonds in Ireland because of his fear of detection. He went to Bideford in Devon, changed his name and told some of his relatives he was there. He consulted a Friend in England who advised him to try and sell his diamonds in Bristol. His Friend advised him that he knew a group of dealers in Bristol who might be interested in buying the diamonds. This Friend went to Bristol and negotiated a deal there for him. Subsequently a group of Bristol merchants travelled to Bideford and negotiated terms with him for the sale of all his diamonds and some gold. Avery was to be paid monthly sums but the promised payments were first irregular and then stopped. Even when money was received the amounts were so small that he could hardly live off them. Avery became desperate and decided to take the risk of going to Bristol to have it out with these merchants. To his dismay he was told by them that he would not receive any more payments. He was told that if he objected to this they would report him to the government in London and he would be arrested and punished for his crimes. By now Avery was fearful of recognition and arrest, penniless and desperate and decided to return to Ireland. From Ireland Avery, according to Defoe, continued to plead his case but in vain. Eventually and at a date not revealed by Defoe he took a ship to Plymouth and walked one hundred miles to Bideford where he soon became ill and died.

The issue of whether Defoe was the Friend who advised Avery and went to Bristol on his behalf is not easy to resolve. Assisting Avery, and living off the proceeds of his piracy, would have been regarded by the courts as serious crimes. Moreover, Defoe would not have wished to give publicity to any other piratical crimes in which he had been involved. I suggest that the minimum requirement for a proof of Defoe's involvement, would be to show that he could have been in Bideford and Bristol at the right times to fit his narrative.

Bideford and Bristol

Defoe, in his trade as a merchant in the 1690's, used West Country ports. It would have been comparatively easy for him to enter Bideford by sea or by land. Bastian who has recorded much of Defoe's trading in the period places a ship docking in Plymouth on Defoe's behalf. He records a listing in the London Gazette of Jan. 1-4 1692 containing the item: 'Plymouth, Jan.31. Yesterday arrived here the *Desire* of London, with Wines from Lisbon.' This ship was owned by Defoe.

Defoe was in Bideford and Bristol in July, 1705 on a tour arranged to provide intelligence for Harley. Backscheider has provided a useful map of his journeys on this tour. Bideford was a small town, although a significant port, and it is difficult to comprehend the reasons for Defoe's visit. [141]

Bristol

Thomas Wright has provided readers with a useful anecdote. He writes:

> In order to escape his creditors he [Defoe] took refuge in Bristol, where he lived at the Red Lion Inn...in Castle Street. Here he got the name of the 'Sunday Gentleman,' because his appearance on that day, and that day only, in fashionable attire 'a fine flowing wig, lace ruffles, and a sword by his side – being kept indoors during the rest of the week by fear of the bailiffs.' He adds that after some parley a composition was agreed to. If the 'composition agreed to' followed the 1692 bankruptcy, the timing of the visit was in the 1690's. If the composition was under the Bankruptcy Act, 1706 the event of Defoe being there was a date before 1706. Of course Defoe's secrecy may have had nothing to do with creditors, other than a desire to have money to buy them off, but maybe the secrecy was required because he was engaged in the secret business of interesting Bristol merchants in buying diamonds. [142]

Captain Kidd

---

[141] Backscheider, 185.
[142] Wright, 38.

Captain Kidd was one of the most notorious seventeenth century pirates. Defoe introduces him to readers in passing when he writes in *Captain Singleton* that when joining his first pirate ship that 'he had at last brought me to concert with the most famous pirates of the age, some of whom have ended their journals at the gallows.' On his first pirate ship there was 'one whom we called Captain Kidd who was the gunner.' I do not know whether Defoe met Kidd. There is no evidence one way or the other to answer the question. However, the fate of Kidd who was tried, found guilty and publicly executed, became the gossip of London. In a sense all London had met Kidd for as Defoe writes, 'Wherefore about a Week after [the verdict} Captain Kidd, Nicholas Churchill, James How, Gabriel Loff, Hugh Parrot, Abel Owen, and Darby Mullins were executed at Execution Dock, and afterwards hung up in Chains, at some Distance from each other, down the River, where their bodies hung exposed for many Years.'

As I have suggested. Penn and Defoe went on a version of the Grand Tour when in their teenage years. In *Captain Singleton* an important conversation occurs between William the Quaker from Pennsylvania (William Penn) in Barbados which I believe is a reference to conversations with Penn and Defoe in the period 1680-1683 and which possibly took place on the island.[143] The issue *Singleton* raises with William was what to do with the wealth which they both had acquired. Could they both return to England with this plunder? Defoe writes that, 'William and I consulted what to do with ourselves…we decided to do so in the open fields, where no one would hear.' Would God permit them to keep such wealth? William responds by remarking that as they had acquired it and as, by its nature, it could not be returned, God would expect them to use it well. *Singleton* had told William that he accepted that he was a rogue and a thief by his very occupation as a pirate and that he deserved to be hanged for it. Rather than suffer such a fate he would take his own life. William persuaded Bob that there was no need to do that and that they should work out together what to do. In reality their mutual concern was, I suggest, that *Singleton* had been

---

[143] *Captain Singleton*, 232-244.

involved in some mix of the following: illegal slave trading, the possible killing of crews in vessels seized on the high seas, and the stealing of cargo(s). These crimes were punishable by a gruesome death. These problems could catch up with you in an unexpected manner if you allowed crew and passengers to survive by putting them off on a desert island. If these people managed to get off the island and return to England they night report you to the authorities.

William maintained that despite this the problems could be overcome. A plan of action was discussed. They agreed that when back in England:

1. They would be strangers to each other in public

2. Defoe would reveal nothing of what happened over these years except to his sister

3. The truth of it all should never be spoken or written about in public

4. When in public they should speak in a foreign tongue

5. They should always act as 'brothers' and would help each other.

In the conversations between these two men, Defoe/ *Singleton* and William Penn, the former raised the issue of his sister. Her plight is described as being the difficulties of William's sister. The details given match those of Defoe's sister Mary who he had left in Tilbury. Although abandoned by Defoe, and movingly, Mary sent the sum of five pounds to help him get back to England. I conjecture that following Singleton's narrative Penn had arranged for Mary to receive a substantial sum of money to enable her to move to a new address. *Moll Flanders* tells her readers that she had come into money from a previous husband. It is difficult to understand how this could have come about as she had been left with nothing but debts from her earlier marriage. [144] This transaction could be described as a form of money laundering.

---

[144] *Captain Singleton*, 244.

The need for secrecy and the usefulness of speaking in a foreign tongue while in England is duplicated in *Colonel Jack*. Defoe writes:[145]

> I had nothing to do now but entirely to conceal myself from all that had any knowledge of me…I lived single indeed and in lodgings, but I began to be very well known…I passed for a foreigner and a Frenchman, and I was infinitely fond of everyone take me for a Frenchman…I went also to Flanders, upon which seeing my certificate of exchange I was called Colonel Jacque… [I] got a French servant to do my business. I lived in this private condition. I continued about *two years*… [His business consisted only in the selling of his merchandise. Italics mine] in receiving and disposing of tobacco, of which I had about 500 to 600 hogsheads a year from my plantations, and in supplying my people with necessaries as they wanted them. In this private condition I continued about two years more, when the devil owing me a spleen since I refused being a thief, paid me home with interest by laying me a snare. [A woman who enticed him into marriage].

As written by Defoe, *Singleton* states that he appreciated that his return [permanently] to England could cause trouble for William [if Defoe was prosecuted for his misdeeds William's name might be raised]. But William responds that he would take this risk. There is a happy ending. William rides off with *Singleton* to a golden horizon while Defoe/*Singleton* 'marries' a sister [Mary, Defoe's sister].

In writing in this way, Defoe was exaggerating and embellishing his own acts of piracy, to the point at which some readers might think that in commenting upon them at all I am falling short of the necessary distinction between the reality of the life Defoe lived and his fiction. Perhaps I am but I think not. I assume that Defoe was seriously concerned that he would be brought to justice at some time and fearful of the retribution that he knew would follow. When looked at soberly, I

---

[145] *Colonel Jack*, 208.

suggest to the reader that over a period of twelve years, 1668-1680, Defoe did fall short of the highest legal standards in his conduct as captain of a ship. Many seamen would have known something about Defoe's merchant activities. They might turn up at any time in any tavern or coffee house that Defoe was known to visit.

Return

Chapter 9

London: A Life in Transition

*She had resolv'd ... that it was absolutely Necessary to change my Station,
and to make a new Appearance in some other...Place where I was not known,
and even to pass by another Name if I found occasion.'*

Moll Flanders
Daniel Defoe, 1722

When Defoe returned to London in 1680 it wasn't clear to him whether
he could shift the centre of his business activities to the City of London
and make something of his life. He was reunited with his sister Mary
(*Moll*). If *Captain Singleton*/Defoe is to be believed, and with William
Penn's help, his sister Mary(*Moll*) had moved to a new address and was
to be found in a place four miles from London. Defoe always keeps his
readers guessing at his residency. However, when he meets *Moll* again
it is explained by her to the reader that she needed to change her place
of abode and even her appearance if it were necessary to do so.

This new residence may have been in Tooting, now a suburb of
London, five miles from the centre. Bastian states that on the death of
Walter Lodwick in 1662 he left a large house in Tooting to his widow
Elisabeth. She married again to David Clarkson a family friend of the
Foe's. Mathew Clarkson, a half-brother, acted as Defoe's factor in New
York in the 1680's and petitioned for the post of Secretary for New
York in 1689. Bastian writes:

> He [Mathew Clarkson] supported his petition with a
> certificate to testify to his character as a factor; and one of
> the eight who signed it was Daniel Foe. Two others James
> Moyer and Robert Knight probably had connections with
> Defoe. The remaining five were all close relatives of the
> petitioner – his brother David Clarkson, his half brother
> Thomas Lodwick; his cousins, David King and John Rowett;
> and Gerald van Heythusen, who was either his uncle... or

the latter's nephew. Thomas Lodwick signed Defoe's Marriage License in 1683.[146]

In 1680 this large house might have been occupied by a gregarious group of men, women and children. In the absence of the men, busy with trade and often abroad, the women might have been a little loose. If this house was Mary/*Moll's* new abode, Defoe in his fiction, with a dash of over-egging, could have described it as he did in *Moll Flanders* as a 'house of ill-repute'. Thomas Wright has provided an un-attributed drawing of 'Defoe's house in Tooting'.[147]

There is a well-established legend that Defoe lived in Tooting in the 1680's and that he founded a Dissenting church at which Joshua Oldfield, the well-known Presbyterian preacher of the time, presided and was assisted by Defoe. Thomas Wright describes it as follows:

> Defoe now (1688) resided at Tooting, where he formed the Dissenters of the neighbourhood, chiefly Presbyterians, into a regular congregation, and there is no doubt that occasionally he preached among them. The church founded by Defoe met first in a private house, and afterwards in a temporary wooden building, which in 1765-1766 gave place to the Presbyterian Chapel [and more latterly] the Defoe Memorial Church.

A statement such as 'without any doubt' is characteristic of Wright. He is able to make a categorical statement without a shred of evidence. I do not think there is any truth in this legend and local historians have suggested otherwise. According to Waddington, the true inheritor of the 'Defoe' tradition in Tooting is the Congregational Church. It was on the site of the Congregational Church in Tooting High Street that Oldfield preached in 1715. [148]

Moll tells the reader that she had come into a substantial sum of money from a previous marriage and she used the prospect of this money to 'catch' a Captain who claimed to have three plantations in

[146] Bastian, 96-97.
[147] Wright, 38.
[148] Congregational History. *A History of the County of Surrey*, vol. 4, 1912.

Virginia. *Moll* was willing to give him what remained from her fortune and to migrate to Virginia with him. This person turns out to be her 'old husband'.

This new home was shared by *Moll* with other ladies. There is a hint that *Moll* and the ladies were not amiss from entertaining in the new home. Is this, in reality, what Defoe tells us about his sister when he calls her a whore?

However, if my interpretation of the dialogue between *Captain Singleton* and *Quaker William* is right, she had come into money because William Penn had sent it to her. Now Defoe wanted what remained of this money to be paid back and *Moll* returned it. They 'married' again and shipped themselves to Virginia where they lived on a plantation with his 'mother'. This mother I believe and seek to demonstrate was Defoe's 'mother in law'. The mother confessed that she had been transported to Virginia as a criminal from Newgate and showed *Moll* a brand mark on her wrist.

When *Moll* reflected on this story she came to the conclusion that her 'mother in law' must be her own mother because her story was exactly as she understood her mother's story to be and that, therefore, she had slept with and had children by her own brother. Her husband from this time became nauseous to her. In reality this was how it might have been: a 'brother and sister' reunited with a 'mother in law'.

Of course *Moll Flanders* and *Colonel Jack* are works of fiction. However, I have already argued that Defoe had an incestuous relationship with his sister Mary and so in a seventeenth-century use of the term he had been her first 'husband'. Daniel Defoe was living with his sister Mary and had children by her. It could be argued that a child abandoned by a mother, as Defoe felt himself to have been, is prone to the fantasy that he can regain and possess her. In most people all these feelings usually remain repressed and dormant. A creative writer like Defoe had access to his feelings and it might be argued he invented the whole thing. However, the documentary evidence of the baptism of a child in Chadwell St. Mary is not easily shrugged off. However, the reading I give is a simpler and more persuasive explanation of the relationships between a mother/mother in law, a daughter/sister and a husband/brother.

In *Captain Singleton* Defoe steers readers in the same direction. Money has been sent to his sister, she moved home, she expected the return of her brother; and, as I have conjectured, he was to return to her. *Moll's* money, the remnant of money, seemed to be used to buy her brother a share of a ship and enable him to return to the life from which he had fled. At least for Moll that would enable her to live in Virginia out of the reach of gossip and to make a new start. Defoe tells readers that his 'sister' stayed in America for eight years.

In seeking a better and real-life explanation there are two considerations to keep in mind. The first of these is a possible consequence of Defoe's marriage in Barbados. Defoe had married Jone Reade in Barbados in May, 1681. Seven months later, in December, she was dead. This interval of time suggests that she may have died in childbirth. There is no record of a birth and death of a baby. Defoe was back in Barbados in 1682 and the date of his stay on the island can be estimated by the voyage of William Penn to Pennsylvania in 1682. Secondly, there is the use of family terms at the time. The terms brother, sister, husband and mother did not necessarily imply biological links and could be, and usually were, relational terms within family establishments.

Some readers may prefer to regard the whole episode as fiction. However, the story I am relating is not a dramatic device to explain one work of fiction: it is woven into the fabric of three, *Moll Flanders*, *Captain Singleton* and *Colonel Jack*. Inch by inch, tale by tale, year by year Defoe is telling the reader his personal history.

Behind the story of posing as a Frenchman in *Colonel Jack* lay a real dilemma for Defoe in seeking to trade in and from London. The Navigation Acts, 1660-1663, restricted trade between England and the colonies to goods carried in English ships defined as a ship in which seventy-five percent of the hull was built in England. The tobacco Defoe brought to London and was seeking to sell may well have been brought in on an English ship. Defoe, as the narrator, quickly gets rid of the Captain of the ship that brought him back to England by explaining that he was prosecuted, found guilty of a crime and executed. Defoe's goods could be sold on to France without infringement of the Acts only if he could demonstrate that he, and the cargo, was French. If he was to use the cash earned from these sales to buy goods for supply to the English colonies they would need to be carried there in an English ship.

Customs officials were vigilant in applying the regulations and penalties were severe. An illustration of the difficulties confronting Defoe unless he changed his national status is provided by the ill-fortune of the real-life Captain Singleton. I have written that in January 1696/7 Captain Singleton fell foul of a vigilant Customs Officer and was fined 120 louis and sentenced to be imprisoned for seven months. In July, 1697 he petitioned the Treasury for his release. The Treasury minute reads as follows:

> Petition of Edward Singleton prisoner in the Fleet showing that he was kept 7 months in messengers custody on the information of one Paine of delivering French goods to Young [young?] Bromefield but that at his trial Joseph Beverton an officer [of the Customs] procured another person to swear against him on whose single evidence he was fined 120 louis, and is now in the Fleet; therefore praying a discharge and release.[149]
>
> I do not know whether Captain Singleton was doing business for Defoe in 1696/7. If he was so employed Defoe might have recognised an obligation to pay his fine.

This trading problem is revealed in *Moll Flanders*. The sea Captain who turned out to be *Moll's* 'first husband' was seeking to buy a share in a ship. He could as a Stranger and a Foreigner buy no more than twenty-five percent of any boat. This being so, numerous complications arose in how the boat should trade. One way round the regulations was to acquire the status of a Colonial citizen for which proof was needed.

In his real life, Defoe's plantations originated in Brazil, a

---

[149] NA. Calendar of Treasury Books, Vol. 12, 21 July, 1697, 265.

Portuguese colony and through time they shifted to the north using Barbados as stopping point for replenishment. In *Captain Singleton* Defoe describes Barbados as a trading station. In 1630 Barbados had become a British colony. Thus Virginia, South Carolina and Barbados, at the dates at which they appear in Defoe's fictions, are all English colonies. In writing about plantations in Virginia, Defoe is 'legitimising' himself in his fiction so as to avoid accusations of illegal trading as a Brazilian, and thus as a Portuguese national.

In 1682 Defoe would have needed to produce documentary evidence to Customs officials in London that he was a Colonial subject. Establishing your identity, without challenge, as I have repeated many times in this narrative, was difficult. Following his marriage to Jone Reade, Defoe was able to produce a marriage 'certificate' of some kind, showing him as resident in Barbados. In addition Defoe would have been able to demonstrate that his wife originated in South Carolina, a British colony.

There is no reasonable doubt that the Daniel Foe who married Jone Reade was Daniel Defoe. Although seventeenth century records of this period are sparse in the Caribbean, I have searched those that exist. There are no records of the births, marriages and deaths of Foes in the Caribbean other than an isolated example in Jamaica that I am satisfied has nothing to do with Daniel Defoe. There is no reason to suppose that this Daniel Foe was someone alone in time and space in Barbados, and, therefore, nothing to do with Daniel Defoe the writer.

From the time of his marriage to the end of his life Defoe had a close and constant interest in South Carolina. I assume that he came into an inheritance there on his wife's death in 1681 which included property and land. There is no extant will in Barbados for Jone Reade. If there was no will to state a contrary distribution of her assets, they would have passed to Defoe as the legal husband. However, to establish his claim on her estate Defoe would have had to travel to Barbados and, perhaps, to South Carolina. This is what he did.

South Carolina was of lasting importance to Defoe and his family. When in *Moll Flanders* he persuades his sister to return with him to his plantations in New England, he settles her, at least for a time, in South Carolina;[150] he wrote in defence of religious freedom for South Carolina, and a new constitution in 1706;[151] it is conjectured that his son Benjamin Norton travelled to South Carolina in 1729-1730; and his son Daniel may have settled there after Defoe's death. It is possible also that kinsmen on his father's side of the family, other than Foes, owned land there.[152]

On his return to London in 1680 Defoe was likely to have been in touch with Sunderland and Penn; they were certainly in touch with each other. William Penn made his first visit to his new state of Pennsylvania in October, 1682. If my interpretation of the conversations between *Quaker William* and *Captain Singleton* is correct, Defoe is referring to actual meetings and discussions with William Penn. They could have taken place in Barbados in 1682-1683. Commonsense suggests that it is more likely that Defoe and Penn would have discussed the subject of Defoe's permanent return to England in London.

In March, 1681, King Charles II formally signed the Charter drafted by Sunderland that gave Penn the territory of Pennsylvania, some three months before Defoe's marriage to Jone Reade. Perhaps, the two dates are inter-connected; that it was not only mercantile interests that led Defoe to Barbados but a claim or allocation of land in the New World.

It might be thought that an unspoken alliance, understanding and friendship between Penn and Defoe was unlikely with Defoe an erstwhile pirate and Penn a much-respected Quaker leader and friend of the Stuarts. It was not so. These men were on opposite sides of the same coin. Both men had been grappling with similar problems in the New World. These problems would continue to plague Penn until he was obliged to sell back Pennsylvania to the English crown.

As William Penn struggled to interest successive waves of emigrants to go to New England and settle there he had to deal with

---

[150] *Moll Flanders*, 132.
[151] Defoe, Daniel. *The Case of the Protestant Dissenters in Carolina*, London, 1706.
[152] See Attachment 7: Defoe's Elder Brother.

all the resistances to newcomers that awaited them from the receiving communities. Quaker settlers in the New World had encountered rough times: arrest, trial and punishment, including death. By the 1670's when Penn began to build his new world, Quakers had been pushed out of the new territories into the Caribbean islands.

I believe that in the period 1680-1684 an understanding was reached between the two men on how Defoe could resettle in London and avoid prosecution there. *Singleton*/Defoe had been at his wits end and had confessed that he was close to suicide. Defoe tells the reader through *Singleton* that it took him two years to settle his affairs before he could move back to London permanently. He had to find a way to money launder and shift resources into cash or cash equivalent to sustain a trading activity there.

Upon his return to England, Defoe must have been in touch with his younger brother Thomas who married Elisabeth Wildbore in May, 1680 at All Hallows Church, London. The first child of this marriage was born on 30 March 1682.[153] This interval of time was sufficient to explain Thomas's presence in Pennsylvania. In a letter to Penn, Marquand complained that Thomas King had caused difficulties for him in the task of building a home for Penn. The issue raised by Marquand reads as if Thomas King had bought land and was reluctant to sell it to him at the market price.[154]

There is no doubting Defoe's continuing interest in New England from beyond 1680. The first traceable link is in December, 1684 when Defoe tells his readers that he was present when Richard Wharton submitted to the House of Lords Trade and Plantations Committee 'proposals for the regulation of New England'.[155]

Knowledge of Defoe's trading links with New England dates from 1688. Defoe had agents in New York and Maryland and correspondents in Boston. In November, 1688 Defoe supported the petition of Mathew

[153] Parish Records of All Hallows Church, City of London.
[154] *Papers of William Penn*, vol.2, 1680-1684.
[155] Bastian, 96-98.

Clarkson for the post of Secretary for New York that gave reference to his prowess as a factor. Bastian writes that, 'Defoe himself became involved in the trade with the English colonies.' Certain family names and known family links continue to come up: for example, the Colbron, Lodwick and Abbott families. The latter two families were known to have friendly links with James Foe.

Defoe's interests were not limited to colonial policy and trade. According to the South Carolina Historical Society he wrote in support of dissenters, including Quakers, threatened by persecution.[156] These were links established externally to America. What is missing are details of his stay there. It is not possible for a man and his family to live and work land in a country, no matter how secretive his life, without revealing evidence of his presence to others. Defoe did his best to cover his tracks in America but his presence there can be uncovered by good research. Ironically, American scholars have sought him out in England and neglected his presence in America.

---

[156] Brinsfield, John W. *Daniel Defoe: Writer, Statesman, and Advocate of Religious Liberty in South Carolina Historical Magazine,* Vol.76, July 1975, 101-111.

Chapter 10

Repentance, Re-invention and Re-settlement

Without lifting a finger, just by being born twenty years sooner, Lorin Jones had destroyed Polly Alter as a painter...And Polly could not do anything about it [but could she?] She could suggest that there is a choice between being a good person and a good painter, and that Jones had chosen the darker path.

In 'Life for a Life'
The Truth About Lorin Jones
Alison Lurie

It has always been difficult to re-invent a person; but it was easier to do it in the seventeenth century than now when the demands to identify people are all-embracing. However, it is achievable still. On July 8, 2008 the world's press reported the arrest in Belgrade of the Serbian nationalist Radovan Karadzic. It was thought that his story was so bizarre it was impossible to make it up: in common parlance 'truth was stranger than fiction'. A man wanted for fifteen years on charges of genocide, war crimes, and crimes against humanity had been living quietly in Belgrade, the capital city, for many years.

Before he became a fugitive, Karadzic had been instantly recognisable as a result of his international exposure in the world's media. In Belgrade he lived under an assumed name. In a sense Karadzic repented in that he turned his life to healing. He gave lectures on alternative medicine, Christian Orthodox spirituality and meditation, and offered treatments for depression and impotence. He looked quite different from his known and familiar appearance and his new image was fit for his new purpose; he was 'bushy and white in peace, and bouffant and clean shaven in war'. In Belgrade Karadzic had work colleagues who respected him and harboured no suspicions of his past. Many people knew of his new identity and in the end that was the reason for his detection. Fifteen years of public anonymity is a long time to survive on the run. Inquiries by journalists into how he survived reveal that he had a supporting network of relatives and friends who knew about his metamorphosis. Theories have been advanced that he had allies in the Serbian government administration that protected him.[157]

Defoe could not resettle in London without some if not all of the cover achieved by Karadzic. In the period 1680-1684 he must have been watching with keen interest the political progress of Robert Spencer. Would Spencer climb the political greasy pole to the top? He made it. Would Penn achieve his ambitions in the New World and thus be able both to protect Defoe in London and advance his interests in the New World? He did. Defoe with great adroitness managed a protection transition from Sunderland to Harley around 1698. It lasted sixteen years until 1714. Following Harley's fall Defoe struck a deal with the Whigs to continue his immunity from arrest and punishment for all crimes he might be alleged to have committed up to 1716.

The support of these powerful men was never unconditional. They expected favours in return. More than any other man, it was Sunderland who supported Defoe's efforts to fashion a place in London as a polemical journalist in 1683-1700. By the end of the period he was arguably the leading Whig propagandist. Defoe had to 'deliver the goods' by being effective in his polemics. He was. Penn's conditions have been set out in the previous chapter. Defoe was expected to act in Penn's cause by speaking up in the Quaker interest. He served Penn's cause to an extent that is not generally recognised. But Penn asked also for something else from Defoe that was difficult for him to achieve; he urged upon him redemption and a genuine attempt to seek God's help to change his life for the good.

In London Defoe attempted to honour his agreement with Penn. He sought redemption for his sins. It is difficult to make a judgement about the depth and sincerity of his attempt to do this. Defoe retained his overwhelming mental preoccupation with wickedness and the impossibility of redemption but he did seem to recognise that he had made a promise. Penn would have told Defoe that if his intention was

---

[157] Hawton, Nick. *The Quest for Radovan Karadzic*, Hutchinson, 2009.

genuine, if he sought God's Grace, then God would help him to live a Christian and better life.

It might be thought cynical (but isn't it true?) that when confronting a parole board a convict might do anything; almost anything, to demonstrate his sincerity. If a confession would get a man out of gaol, or for Defoe the avoidance of the disgrace of a public trial, he might be expected to give it a thought or two. He needed to become and look respectable and attempt to keep his activities secret, and by his own account that was what he achieved.

I doubt that 'the reprieve' led to a change in Defoe's character or behaviour. It is often said that experience and age leads a man to wisdom; but in reality it more often than not leads to caution. Defoe learnt something about tempering his natural volatility of behaviour but he remained the man he had always been. The impossibility of character change was to plunge Defoe into further crises and in the end, over twenty years later in 1703, to the Pillory. At this humbling point in Defoe's life many commentators claim to have noticed changes in Defoe: he became quieter with himself, chastened and maybe more religious in the sense William Penn had urged upon him. I do not believe he had a profound character change but rather that he drifted into religiosity, a condition of being or seeming to be religious. In the twenty-first century there is little appetite for the condition and to call a man religious would not be to offer him a compliment. In the seventeenth-century it was otherwise: it was considered to be right and proper that men should be respectful of things religious. A public display of piety, if falling short of the otiose, was welcome in a man.

More profoundly and truly Defoe recognised that he could not save himself. He was told by others that God could save him if he sincerely repented and changed his ways, asked for God's forgiveness and sought his Grace. However, even if he did these things, the question remained for him of whether he could ever do what God demanded of him. He did not think that he would be able to make the changes that he assumed God demanded. In the end, and despite his self-protestations, Defoe did not convince himself.

Defoe sought to change his appearance in public. Descriptions of him by contemporaries suggest that he always took great care and expense to fit himself out as a gentleman in a long wig and fashionable clothes. He wore a sword in public. He changed his name. In Essex he continued to use the name Foe for much of his life but in London he adopted the name of Defoe. He cultivated a public image at fashionable coffee houses and among the literati and politicians of his age. In Essex he endeavoured to live like a gentleman with a carriage and coat of arms. He had portraits painted by fashionable portrait artists that portrayed him as a gentleman. In this deportment he could be seen with the statesmen and politicians of his age without adverse comment about his appearance.

It was never clear where Daniel Defoe lived. At any one time he was maintaining two or three households and had numerous lodging points and bolt holes in London and elsewhere. In *Colonel Jack* when a messenger from his first wife found him and presented him with a bill of £30 for immediate payment, the Colonel's first feeling was one of annoyance that his lodgings had been found. When late in Defoe's life, as described in *Roxana*, her daughter (in reality Elisabeth White the daughter of Defoe's Stoke Newington tenant) came looking for her/him, she told the woman she had found (Mary Norton) that wherever she/he went, she knew where to find him, and that he could not escape her.

It has been difficult for biographers to write about Defoe's personal life except in London. Historians and political observers are naturally interested in historical happenings and social events in the capital about which so much is known. Writing about Defoe's life in Northamptonshire, Essex and Kent is far more difficult and seemingly less inviting and dramatic then the drama of political happenings in the capital.

At first when Defoe was back in London he was still enmeshed in the New World. In 1681/2 he was unsettled. He needed to continue his trading as a merchant. It had to be done in England and he needed to be able to work to and from London. His trading need was to link the Old

World to the New. He resettled his sister in New England. He involved himself in Penn's adventure there and sought to take advantage of it. He introduced his brother Thomas to Penn and persuaded Thomas to go to Pennsylvania and make money..

If *Colonel Jack's* narrative is to be believed, Defoe's marriage to Mary Tuffley came about in a most unexpected way. After the death of Jone Reede, Defoe was prepared to settle in New England. However, once he decided to do so there were other considerations that changed his mind. In England, Defoe would certainly have thought it helpful to get his hands on a decent dowry through an expeditious marriage. However, in reality he was totally unprepared for English family life. It may be that those who wished him well thought that he should 'settle down'. It is possible that the Tuffley family knew Defoe's uncle James. If James Foe wanted Defoe to settle in London and 'make something of his life' he may have suggested marriage with Mary Tuffley.

In 1684 Mary Tuffley was 17 years of age and the daughter of a comparatively wealthy London merchant.[158] *Colonel Jack* describes his first wife as sophisticated and setting out to entice him. Compared with the women he had mixed with on his travels in Brazil and Barbados she may well have had an appearance of refinement. It is apparent from the *Colonel's* narrative that his first wife wished to be a 'home-maker' and look after the first child of the marriage whatever the expense. It would not have been obvious to her that her husband lacked the resources to do this. She would have believed him to be wealthy with plantations overseas and the appearance of living well

At first Defoe was preoccupied with Barbados and his marriage to Jone Reade. In all probability he would not have heard about her death until April-May 1682. I believe he returned to Barbados around the time of William Penn's arrival in New England in November, 1682. It would not have been until the summer of 1683 that he would have been back in London. Within six months he was married. The allegation for the Marriage License, dated 28 December, 1683, was signed by one

---

[158] Backscheider, 30.

man, Charles Lodwick, a friend and business associate, acting alone. Lodwick became the Mayor of New York in 1694/5 and corresponded frequently with the House of Lords Trade and Plantations Committee. The allegation stated that Defoe was around twenty-four years of age when actually he was nearing forty. Who saw this licence? Perhaps, only the vicar saw it. Others, who knew the truth, may not have cared much for a small deception. Some wanted him married with the security of a large dowry, and the prompt payment of his bills. If looking the other way was a requirement, James Foe's business acquaintances may have had reasons for doing so and laughed into their ale. Marriage was a commercial matter. There were debts to be paid and cargoes to be financed.

These merchants had commercial interests to protect and they were more important than queries about Defoe's age. James Foe spent time in Portugal and may have traded in goods brought into Lisbon in ships in which Defoe had an interest. If these goods were on occasions pirated and James Foe and his friends had benefited from their receipt, they too would be vulnerable to investigation. The death for conviction of piracy was very nasty but so also was the punishment for dealing in stolen goods.

It was relatively simple, if indeed it was thought necessary, to pass off Defoe as James Foe's 'son' born in Cripplegate in 1660. If James said he was his 'son' why he must know. It is not to say, as I have explained, that he was his biological son. As for Alice Foe, she was nowhere to be seen. Daniel Foe, the colonial adventurer was re-born Daniel Foe, London merchant. When Defoe returned to Tilbury in Essex around 1685-1690, it was safe to be a Foe or a King. As *Moll* tells her readers when she returned to Colchester and its environs, none of her 'family', the Lawrence's, were found to be there. Over twenty-five years had elapsed.

Defoe was appointed to the position of Accountant to the Glass Commission in 1695 in the name of Foe. When Defoe began to spend more time in the City of London he changed his name to Defoe, acquired a carriage and a coat of arms and wore a long wig. However, he remained a Foe in Essex. When Defoe signed off the final accounts of the Glass Commission in 1712 he did so in the name of Foe.

When notices appeared for Defoe's arrest in 1703 they used a variety of versions of his name. In the first advertisement he is described as Daniel de Fooe and Daniel Fooe, in the second he had become Daniel de Foe *alias* de Fooe. Elsewhere he is described as Mr. D. De Foe. By this time, therefore, Defoe had succeeded in creating uncertainty as to his name and identity and it was known that he used aliases.

The use of the name of Defoe in London conveyed a continental Huguenot identity. Defoe had promised William Penn that he would talk in a foreign language once back in England. It was not difficult for him to do so, if indeed he did, because he must have had a smattering of several languages and, in particular, knowledge of French, Spanish and Portuguese.

I have presented evidence elsewhere that Defoe cross-dressed. It was certainly one way of disguising himself. In his usual everyday appearance Defoe was over-dressed, flamboyant and flashy. In 1706 he was attacked in an anonymous pamphlet:

> One thing Daniel, I want to know that, is whether you keep up your Beau habit, your long wig with tossels at the end of it, your Iron-bound hat, and your blew Cloak? As also whether you have left your old Wont, of holding out your little finger to show your Diamond ring.[159]

This description is replete in sexual innuendo. The writer is signalling something about Defoe's sexuality, as a preliminary to accusing him of sodomitical practices. It raises the question also of how Defoe acquired such a ring. Such a description is far removed from other possible images of Defoe on board a ship as a common sailor or when a soldier at the end of a forced march. When he grew older Defoe locked himself away in his house at Stoke Newington and limited the number of visitors. He was in constant danger of detection for the

---

[159] Quoted by Novak, 251.

exploits of his earlier life.. He was blackmailed. There is always a price to be paid to preserve guilty secrets. Defoe did his best, not always successfully, to limit it.

Almost from his very first breath Defoe felt the need to disguise himself and confuse and baffle others. He became a multi-faceted person capable of a multiplicity of selves. His life strengthened his resolve to adopt a wide variety of identities. I have written about this psychological necessity along the following lines: [160]

In Defoe's writing the reader is confronted with a confusing dichotomy between an 'ideal' world, that is justified in rational terms, and which has a religious and moral dimension, and the dark, anarchic irrationalities that his fictional characters inhabit. For Defoe the contradiction is multi-dimensional: he appears to have created new selves to cope with severe traumatic experiences in his childhood. When pain and ignominy became too much to endure, Defoe disassociated his self and departed to other places and other selves. The structure of control and management of the process was complex and unstable. It appears that the adult Defoe could function in what would seem to others to be a thorough-going, purposeful and integrated way (and with great determination) by having many sub-systems that, it appears, operated independently of a controlling self. Like an actor he was capable of performing contrasting roles with equal conviction; but unlike one, he lived out these roles in everyday life. Thus his self-identity was, in some sense an illusion. The characters of his sub-systems had as much, or greater, reality as the outward appearance he gave to the world; and he invented their daily discourse in his writing to the bafflement of those seeking to explain their numerous contradictions.

From time to time the complex problems were too much and Defoe could not cope. He withdrew and occupied protected places and sought punishment for sins real and imaginary. Even if there were no external reasons for secrecy and subterfuge, and usually there were, he needed these hidden places.

---

[160] *Beyond Belief*, 45.

In the first 36 years of his life Defoe had experienced the most remarkable events and diverse range of experiences. He had travelled throughout Europe and the New World and on voyages to many of the most remote parts of the discovered world; served as a soldier and sailor, in all probability for more than one nation state; traded in a diversity of products throughout the known world; he made great losses and occasionally huge gains, passing from riches to poverty; and he had endured the most fearful moments on ships driven through high seas and great storms. There would have been many occasions when he faced the possibility of a gruesome and unknown death.

He brought to his understanding of these events a high intelligence and acute interest in all those matters shaping the world: human, technological and industrial. He read widely. In various fictions he details his reading material. He became a distinguished graduate in the university of life where his fellow students were the grist of several working worlds.

When in London, Defoe had something to say culled from these experiences, something to add to the mainstream, errors and misunderstandings to correct, and original observations to make. He began to add this to the mainstream of a wash of pamphlets and news sheets that an enquiring London public were digesting and enjoying. He began to write. He found himself better than most. Through Sunderland he found a way of serving the Whig causes and once employed there was no better polemicist.

Chapter 11

Marriage and Family

He used me very handsomely and with good manners, upon all occasions, even to the last, only spent all I had, and left me to rob the creditors for something to subsist on.

Moll Flanders
Daniel Defoe 1722

Defoe had a complex family life in several family establishments. He had many children. Biographers have had difficulties in older accounts in determining just how many children he had and when. It has been universally accepted prior to my own work in 2006, that Defoe had one wife, Mary Tuffley, who he married in 1684 and by whom he had seven or eight children who survived birth and childhood; but until an earlier work of mine no one was able to count them accurately or to give their dates of birth.[161] The figure of seven is sourced to a letter Defoe wrote to Robert Harley in which he states the number of his surviving children;[162] but as some of his children died young the numbers would have varied through time. In his writing Defoe, not unsurprisingly, sometimes got the number wrong. There is a curiosity in determining when he had his children and by whom. In many accounts only two children were produced in the first eight years of the marriage to Mary Tuffley and then they all came in a rush. No explanation has been given for this sudden burst of fertility.

The starting point for any explanation is to accept the factual evidence that Defoe entered into a number of 'marriages' and had children by a number of women. Chadwick and Thomas Wright[163] believed that there was a deep rift in Defoe's marriage to Mary, that it quickly failed, and the couple separated or said nothing to each other for many years. Defoe hints that this was the situation in his comments

---

[161] *Beyond Belief,* 155.
[162] H. 10.
[163] Wright, 25, quotation from Chadwick.

in *The Serious Reflections of Robinson Crusoe* when *Crusoe* enters a long period of nearly 29 years without talking to his wife and family, (1685-1714?) other than to one daughter. The reality is that Defoe entered into a number of other 'marriage' relationships that involved the care of children. At some times in his life, Defoe was maintaining three family establishments. As any modern father knows, supporting three families would be an enormous financial drain on personal resources.

In reality, Defoe had as many as eleven children by five women. In a chart I set out the number of Defoe 'marriages' and the children created by them. Defoe had five marriages of various descriptions: one a marriage in church, another by Special Licence, two other marriages by 'private treaty' and an incestuous relationship with his sister Mary that in his fiction he describes as a 'marriage'.

The marriages in the first two categories were to Jone Reade (1681) and Mary Tuffley (1684 -1731) and the private consent marriages were to Elisabeth Sammens (1685-1707?) and Mary Norton (1692-1731?). Jone Reade died seven months into her marriage and it may be that she did so in childbirth. There is no parish record of a surviving child. I conjecture that the child Humphrey in *Moll Flanders*, and who I discuss in a later chapter, is Defoe's son by Jone Reade. Similarly, I believe that Defoe's children by his sister Mary, as suggested earlier, are supported but by a single baptism record in Chadwell St Mary, Tilbury in 1662.

Excluding children born to his sister, and the problematic Humphrey, Defoe had towards the end of his life five surviving children: Hannah by Mary Tuffley; Sophia and Benjamin by Mary Norton, and Daniel and Sarah by Elisabeth Sammens. Mary Tuffley had two further children, Maria and Henrietta by another and unknown man referred to in *Religious Courtship* as 'Sir Charles'.

A further four children did not survive childhood. Mary, a daughter by Mary Tuffley, died as an infant. There is a record of her death and burial in a City of London vault in 1685. [164] Martha, a daughter by Mary Norton, died in Hackney, London in 1707 and was buried in an 'unknown parish'. Two other, and unknown children by Mary Norton, died at unknown dates.

There is good documentary evidence to support these conclusions. The records of the marriages to Jone Reade and Mary Tuffley, in Church and by Special Licence respectively are available. The 'private treaty' marriage to Elisabeth Sammens is supported by a family tax record showing them living together with Daniel and Sarah their children in 1695/6.[165]

The marriage to Mary Norton, a Quaker, is supported by documentary evidence of her parent's marriage in the Colchester Quaker Record's, her father's will which names her, and a link between John Ward, Defoe's farm manager, and Mary's father, Richard Simmons. Other documentary evidence of her existence in Defoe's life includes the following: a loan she made to Defoe to help pay the rent on Defoe's farmland in 1727, for which an illustration is provided; the choice of the name Benjamin Norton Defoe for a son; several literary allusions to her in *Colonel Jack*, *Roxana*, the *Farther Adventures of Robinson Crusoe*, *Family Instructor* and *Religious Courtship*; and the observations of Alexander Pope and Richard Savage.[166]

This documentary evidence is supported by a number of persuasive conjectures some of which rely on documented material. In particular, I suggest that the accounts of various marriages given by the Colonel in *Colonel Jack* are fictionalised real events. In a later chapter I give a full account of *Colonel Jack*. However, given the importance of what Defoe reveals of his married life in the book I summarise some of the important material it offers.

Colonel Jack/Defoe suggests that his first marriage (I conjecture to

---

[164] Parish Records of St. Michael, Cornhill, 1688. The 7th day was Buryed Mary Foe the daughter of Daniell Foe and Mary His Wife in the Lower Vault in the South Isle of the Church.

[165] MA.CRO. Marriage Assessments 1695/1696, Parish of St Botolph's, City of London.

[166] *Beyond Belief*, 98-101, notes, 110-113.

Mary Tuffley) failed because she was led astray during his numerous absences by other men. The *Colonel* considers a legal divorce but decided that it would be impossible. *Colonel Jack* tells the reader that he refused to support children who were not his. The *Colonel* suggests that the two children not his were Maria and Henrietta. This conclusion is supported in *Family Instructor* and *Religious Courtship*. Legally, Defoe's position was not sound or unchallengeable because he had already received £1,500 of the dowry. Defoe told Harley that the dowry agreement was for £3,700. [167]

Nowhere in his writings does Defoe admit to a jointure and its requirement to put money aside for the benefit of his wife and children on his death. The law on a man's financial commitment to his wife and children when separated from her, and the consequential effects of separation on the payment of both dowry and jointure, is obscure. In *Colonel Jack* a man presents the *Colonel* with a bill for £30 raised by the *Colonel's* first wife and demands payment of it. The *Colonel* was dismayed and disappointed that the man had found the place he was living in and had gained entry so easily.

The visitor draws a sword on the *Colonel* and demands a duel as a matter of honour. The Constable called to the scene sagely observes that the issue between them could only be determined in a court. Later *Colonel Jack* concedes that his wife may have been acting fairly and that he loved and respected her really. The reader is left with questions. Who was the father of the two children *Colonel Jack*/Defoe was not accepting responsibility for? Could they have been the messenger's children? [168]

In her will Mary Tuffley left the bulk of her estate to her three daughters Hannah, Maria and Henrietta.[169] I conclude, therefore, that the overwhelming probability is that while Hannah was a daughter by Defoe, Maria and Henrietta were her children by another and unknown man. This unknown man is discussed by Hannah and Sophia in

---

[167] H.51.

[168] See Chapter 27, *Religious Courtship*.

[169] Will of Mary Tuffley. See Chapter 27, *Religious Courtship*,

Religious Courtship. In *Conjugal Lewdness* I believe that Defoe's description of the two girls in his Stoke Newington home expecting to benefit from a share of his estate as 'nieces' is an allusion to Sophia and Hannah.[170]

Colonel Jack was so annoyed about the behaviour of his first wife that he spied on her and contemplated divorce. It was extremely difficult for any man of plebeian background to divorce his wife. Nevertheless, I searched all the possible records to establish that he didn't. The fact of 'the other man' tends to shift some of the blame for marital breakdown from Defoe. However the breakdown came about, Defoe was left with the necessary tasks of looking after himself domestically and providing for Hannah, the surviving child of the marriage.

Colonel Jack's second wife is based on Defoe's relationship with Elisabeth Sammens, wife of Nathanial Sammens, a Spitalfields weaver and loyal friend to Defoe. This relationship is documented. The Marriage Assessments records in the City of London Metropolitan Archives show that Daniel Foe was living on the left side of Moorgate in 1695/6 in the Parish of St. Botolph's, Bishopsgate with his wife Elizabeth, their children Daniel and Sarah and one servant Hannah How. There is an entry in parish records of Sarah's baptism in the name of Nathanial and Elisabeth Sammens in April, 1697, that is, a significantly later time than the census on which the tax assessment was made.[171] It was normal practice to baptise a child as soon as possible after a birth because of the fear that a child was not saved from original sin until baptised. The entry in the parish register is peculiar. Upon a first reading it could not be found. A second search found it out of sequence between two other entries, as if it had been placed there after the event.

The Spitalfields Parish Records show that Elisabeth Sammens had six children. The explanation for Elisabeth having children by both men requires an account of the relationships between the three of them. They had been sharing the same bed, a practice that literally is not

---

[170] Beyond Belief, 272.
[171] *Beyond Belief,* 270.

surprising in a small house with several children, and the issue arose as to which man fathered Sarah. I have maintained that *Roxana* provides a clue. *Roxana* /Daniel agreed to share a bed with the landlord. *Roxana* was delivered of a son by the landlord who offered to look after it. The son is described as a 'charming child who did very well' but later the reader is told by *Roxana* that she did not really care for it. Later also *Roxana* describes herself as having two children by the landlord.

When *Roxana* returns to England she goes searching for her missing five children. Of these five, two were dead and one son and two girls living. She began her search in Spitalfields at the *Weaver's House*. There a neighbour tells her that the Mistress being *dead* [italics mine] the daughter had gone into service with a great Lady at the other end of town. I suggest to the reader that this girl was Sarah. Defoe/*Roxana* had to account for two further surviving children by the landlord and there is another girl to be identified. I argue that the missing children are those of his Stoke Newington tenant John White and not Defoe's biological children.[172]

Whatever the rift between Defoe and Nathanial Sammens in 1697, signalled by Defoe in setting up a separate family establishment with Elisabeth Sammens, and up to 1703 and Defoe's arrest and punishment in the pillory, the two men remained close friends. When on 20 May, 1703 Defoe was arrested on a warrant alleging seditious libel, he was found at Sammens home. Later, in September, 1704, Sammens was arrested for distribution of Defoe's pamphlet *Legion's Memorial*. He did nothing to incriminate Defoe as the author and for his loyalty he was sent to languish in Newgate Prison. Following this imprisonment, Sammens was obliged to work as a journeyman at a reduced wage. In a very real sense Sammens relationship with Defoe had ruined him. The relationship was mocked in public. In 1708 an anonymous pamphlet accused Defoe of an affair with Sammens wife.[173]

When Defoe returned to London from Barbados early in 1683 it is

[172] *Beyond Belief*, 269-271.
[173] BL 11601 d.20 Anon. *Legions Memorial, The Welsh Monster or The Rise and Downfall of that late Upstart*, the R-t H- ble Innuendo Scribble (assumed date, 1708).

undeniable that he spent time in London. However, it is undeniable also that he established a home and a place to work in Tilbury very early on. It is known that from around 1686, two years after his marriage, he took out leases on seventy acres of marshland with mortgages in the name of Maurescoe, Stamper and Ghisleyn in Tilbury. Eventually the land included a brickworks, and the use of a wharf and a house. Defoe excluded the leases from his bankruptcy proceedings in 1692. He succeeded in resisting the mortgagees efforts to recover their advances by first slowing them down and then by winning the Chancery case they brought against him in 1699. He achieved this by arguing that equity of redemption applied.[174] Under this principle the mortgagees could not succeed until the accumulated interest reached the actual value of the property.

Writing to Harley, Defoe stated that that the brickworks at Tilbury 'began to pay me very well ... I began to live, took a Good House , bought me a Coach and horses a Second Time.' According to gossip, and amplified during a court case taken against Defoe for overcharging on beer he sold to his factory workers from a hostelry he had set up in Tilbury, he had established a home with another woman.[175] Much later, and according to Richard Savage, the Benjamin Norton Defoe who had appeared in London as a hack writer around 1721 was 'a bastard son of Defoe's... Daniel Defoe's son of love by a lady who vended oysters.'[176]

Daniel Defoe had a private treaty marriage with Mary Norton and I have been able to unravel it. As with Defoe's other marriages I ask the questions of whether she existed, how and where she came into Defoe's life, and what evidence there is of children.

In *Colonel Jack* Defoe describes a private treaty marriage as follows:

There happened to be a young or rather middle aged woman

---

[174] The discovery is original to Sutherland, James. *Defoe*, London Methuen, 1937, 286-289.

[175] Bastian, 193-194, 222.

[176] *Beyond Belief*, notes, 110-112, in particular.

in the next town, which was but a half mile off, who usually was at my house and among my children every day...she came but merely as a neighbour and to see us, yet she was always helpful in directing and ordering things for them, and mighty handy about them *as well before my wife died as after*. [Italics mine]. Her father was one I employed [to] do business for me in ... northern parts of Britain.

Colonel Jack resolved to marry and love her. He sounded her out about her past and she confessed that when younger a good clergyman's son had made love to her but that nothing had become of it. So he married her. Jack tells the reader that his three children 'were rejoiced at it'.

He was to discover after the marriage that Moggie his wife 'made a slip in her younger days and was got with child some years before by a gentleman of a great estate in that country, who promised her marriage and afterwards had deserted her.' The situation had lasted for several years against the wishes of her father who described this gentleman as 'wicked'. She had not accepted this suitor. *Colonel Jack* says, 'But that was before I had come into the country, and the child is dead.'

This story is an embellishment of the truth and hardly credible as told. Coggeshall where Mary Norton lived and worked was not half a mile from Tilbury or Aldham, Colchester where I believe Defoe was staying at the time these events are described. The distance from Aldham to Coggeshall, but not to her father's, Richard Simmons, farm, was some five miles across the fields.

There is good evidence that Defoe was in Tilbury in the 1690's because his residency is recorded in the Book of Sewers for the district. Ralph Bingley, once the archivist of the Thurrock Borough Council, has produced a plan drawing showing the brickworks, house and ferry. The position of Defoe's house and the jetty is clearly marked. Bingley states that there is no way that Defoe could have driven a horse and carriage to his brickhouse from the jetty because of the bad condition of the pathway. He suggests that Defoe must have housed the carriage elsewhere, either at an inn, or as I investigated, the Manor House of

East Gubyons, also shown on the map. In 1703 Defoe displayed a coat of arms on the front page of his publication *The True Collection*, 1703 that anecdotal evidence suggests he had on the side of his coach. This being so it was in the 1690's that Defoe, became the 'fine gentleman' he describes in *Colonel Jack*.

The public house mentioned in the legal case brought by Maurescoe, Ghisleyn and Stamper in 1699 was called 'the House' and stood next to the wharf, a ten minute walk from his brickworks. It trades today under the name *World's End*. The House is mentioned in *Moll Flanders* and in the *Review*. Randal Bingley believes that Defoe stabled his horse and carriage at the House.

The Manor House of East Gubyons had been owned by the family of Edward Lawrence since 1565. In 1704 the Earl of Beddingfield, the London Sheriff given the task by the High Court in London of ensuring that Defoe gave good security for the recognisance of the good behaviour required of him before he could be released from Newgate, acquired a lease of the Manor House with a release after a period of a year.[177] The lease describes the Manor House as being recently in the occupation of Thomas King, who may have been Defoe's brother. It was possible, therefore, that when Defoe began his stay in Tilbury in 1692 he lived in a brick farmhouse close to the jetty and at some later date occupied the Manor House. He stayed there until 1704 when Beddingfield acquired the lease. After a release from prison, I believe he moved with his three children to the Queens Head, Aldham, Colchester that was owned by his brother.

I am inclined to think that the 'gentleman of means' in *Colonel Jack's* narrative, who had Mary Norton with child, was Daniel Defoe. *Colonel Jack* was describing a 10 year course of events. Mary Norton did not arrive in Defoe's place of work and then his home by accident but by invitation. The father who worked for Defoe was Richard Simmons, Mary's father, a member of a group of Quakers that explored the inland seas for oysters and who owned dredging boats. Richard Savage may have been right in describing Defoe's 'mistress' as an

[177] ERO. D/DC633/-644. Deeds Concerning the Manor of Gubyons.

oyster seller for Defoe might have met Mary Norton when as a merchant he was buying and selling oysters and other sea delicacies.

Colonel Jack tells the reader that he and his Moggie had five children of whom two survived. The first of the surviving children was Benjamin Norton. I have developed a great deal of information about Benjamin's activities in Essex and elsewhere in *Beyond Belief*. Benjamin was Defoe's legal heir,[178] he experienced further education at Edinburgh University,[179] is said to have had nineteen children by three wives, married bigamously,[180] and stayed in Essex after the death of Defoe.[181]

It was usual for a father to name a first son after himself and for this son to inherit. Assuming this practice was followed by Defoe, the assumption would be that Daniel was the eldest son and therefore the heir. However, Benjamin was the legal heir. This would seem to suggest one or other of two things: that Benjamin was born before Daniel and/or that Defoe privileged his marriage with Mary Norton. It is Mary Norton that he refers to constantly in his fiction. In James Foe's will he left a gold watch to Benjamin 'in the possession of his mother' but £100 is given to Daniel. In Mary Tuffley's will she leaves Benjamin a gold watch.[182] If this is the same watch it would suggest three things: first, that Defoe was not much of an executor; secondly, that James Foe was not quite sure 'who was who' at the time, and thirdly that he and Benjamin did not meet Mary Tuffley in the 25 years that had elapsed. James Foe does not name Mary Tuffley by name in his will.

Much is known about Sophia, Defoe's second surviving child by Mary Norton. She is the only Defoe child with a Church record of birth. Defoe recorded this birth at St John's Parish Church, Hackney. The record reads, '1701 Dec. 24. Sophia dau. of Daniel Defoe by Mary his

---

[178] *Beyond Belief,* 98-9, 100, 206, 218, and Charts.
[179] Backscheider, 264, 309-310, 312, 357, 593n.49.
[180] *Beyond Belief,* 94-95, 98-99, 156, 206 216, 222.
[181] *Beyond Belief,* 278.
[182] Burial Records of St John's, Hackney.

wife.' Which Mary [183] and why Sophia as a name? I suggest that Defoe wished to be able to say, were Sophia the Electress Dowager of Hanover and her family to succeed to the English Crown, that he had named his daughter after the Empress. I rely on two literary allusions for Sophia's parentage: the family conference in 1714 that enabled her to accompany her father to his new Stoke Newington home as described in *Colonel Jack*, and secondly references to her wanting to go to stay with her aunt in *Religious Courtship*. Defoe was concerned to marry her off with a dowry that in the end he achieved with Henry Baker. As stated earlier he had provided also for Hannah in life and after his death. However, he did nothing at all for Maria and Henrietta.

Martha Defoe was a child by Mary Norton and her death is recorded in the Parish Register in St John's, Hackney. She died in 1707. Her burial record is peculiar. It reads, 'Martha Defoe, a child was carried out of the parish to be buried in 1707.' The commonsense reading of this is that she died in the parish but was moved out of it because the parents wished her to be buried elsewhere. There is no record of where she was buried.

In 1687 a lawsuit instituted by Robert and Sarah Knight against their son Robert and Defoe revealed that Defoe had bought a leasehold interest in five pieces of land in the Tilbury area 'diverse years' before. Defoe leased this land to a Peter Sainthill a London doctor. However, Defoe continued to occupy the land. In August 1687, Robert Knight accepted a mortgage of £300 authorised by a factor acting for Joan Tuffley and Daniel Defoe. The document was not signed by either of them. I assume from the use of the expression 'diverse years' that Defoe was occupying land in Tilbury soon after his return to England and, perhaps, before his marriage to Mary Tuffley in January 1684. The leasehold transaction for the Tilbury land most commented upon dates from 1689. In that year, when Defoe had possession of thirty acres, he took out a further mortgage with Joan Tuffley and Sainthill as his partners, Peter Mauresco and his partner Stamper as the second party,

[183] *Beyond Belief*, 120-121. Wright misreads the Parish records. He states that there was a baptism but there was not. Baptisms are clearly described as such.

Ghisleyn as the third, and Defoe and Robert Knight the fourth. At a later date Defoe entered into the business of brick and pantile manufacture on this land. It would have involved the raising of considerable additional capital. Who helped him raise the money and how he contrived the purchase is unknown. However, it may be that he inherited money around this date.

According to gossip, and amplified in the court action for overcharging for beer sold to his workers in the brickyard, Defoe was keeping a mistress at his Tilbury home. If this was Mary Norton, as I have suggested, she must have been a very young girl. If we assume that the gossip originated well before his bankruptcy in 1692 and possibly as early as 1682/3 it would suggest that a relationship between them started in the early 1680's. I have estimated that Mary Norton was born in the early 1670's. *Colonel Jack* provides a clue to her age. Defoe writes that at the time of his marriage to Moggie some years later she was a 'young or middle aged woman'.

The three marriage relationships I describe here were of lengthy duration and they display love and affection. All the children that were biologically his were properly provided for in his lifetime. He gave them the chance to work, encouraged their legal marriages, and did what he could to ensure their well-being after his death.

Chapter 12

The Struggle for Representative Government

Presbyterians design nothing less than the ruin of the monarchy and our family...For if His Majesty does not entirely submit to them and become less than a Duke of Venice, rebellion must follow.

James, Duke of York, 1679

The 1680s was a critical period in English history and Daniel Defoe could rightly proclaim that if not at the centre of events he was an observer and a participant at the periphery. The Restoration of the Stuart family as the rightful monarchs of England in 1660 signalled that the attempt to govern England as a puritan republic had failed. The majority of people who had joined in, or at least acquiesced, a republic came to accept that the restoration of the monarchy was the best way to re-unite a divided country. They had been willing to come together with the supporters of the Stuarts to heal the bitter divisions of the Civil War. The majority wanted the country to be governed as a parliamentary democracy: they wanted a protestant king willing to share sovereignty with parliament. The English nation has never changed its mind. Charles II was willing to endorse the compromises the Restoration settlement obliged him to accept but his tolerance never extended to all those who advised him. They were concerned to win back their lands and privileges and sought the recognition, at the very heart of government, of the religious beliefs rejected by the majority in the Civil War.

To those living through the twenty-eight years of the restored Stuart dynasty and later under William III (1688-1702) it never seemed certain that the compromises of the Restoration were safe. Later these compromises became known as the Revolutionary Principles. There were those at home who found the limitations on the monarchy hateful. Across the waters the great Roman Catholic powers, France and Spain, stood ready to take advantage of a divided English nation.

On his return to London in 1680 and throughout the decade ahead Defoe found himself at the heart of a political and religious struggle fought out not only in parliament and royal palaces but on the streets. His involvement in this struggle was dependent on the help of his friends. William Penn was busy securing the future of his North American territories with the help of Sunderland who was to become First Secretary of State. Something is known about Defoe's relationship with Penn but virtually nothing of his dealings with Sunderland. Not much is known about Sunderland who has yet to find a good biographer; but the picture that does emerge is that he placed his own interests above political principles. He was as zealous and loyal in supporting the Stuarts as he was in embracing William III. The picture that emerges is that Sunderland was less concerned with principle than self-survival; he supported James II during the Exclusion Crisis and as king but switched his allegiance to the future William III at precisely the right time.

The issues of loyalty to one's master and good judgement were of importance in 1685 at the time of the Monmouth Rebellion. In the third week of June, 1685, the City clubs, coffee houses and taverns were alive with news of the armed landing in Lyme Regis, Dorset, of the Duke of Monmouth, the illegitimate and protestant son of Charles II. The invasion had been some time in coming but was no surprise when it did. Monmouth was once a favourite with Charles II, who gave his son discreet recognition at court. Monmouth was an exuberant, athletic and fun-loving womaniser who spent his life in a dissolute manner; he was more associated in the public consciousness with riding his own horse at Newmarket, and for jousting in the flesh-pots of the capital, than for acting in matters of state.

Monmouth was a protestant. This would have been of no consequence had Charles been able to provide an heir to the throne. When it became clear that Charles could not, however, people thought of Monmouth, for they realised that Charles's brother James would succeed him. No one doubted that James would return England to a Roman Catholic allegiance. As this threat to a liberal protestant

England grew, Monmouth became ambitious and permitted himself to be used as the tool of others determined to thwart Roman Catholic absolutism.

When it became obvious to Charles that Monmouth was not truly repentant of his implication in the Rye House Plot (which if successful would have led to Charles's murder on the way back to the capital from Newmarket races), he removed his son's royal protection. The net closing around him, Monmouth thought it prudent to decamp to Brussels where he was joined by his mistress, Lady Henrietta Wentworth.

Back in London confederates and envoys plotted on his behalf. Arms and a ship were bought and Monmouth's chances were debated throughout the capital. Royal spies logged every move. Honest and God-fearing men confronted the choice between involvement in a rebellion and betrayal of the 'good old cause'. Most, with a heavy heart, made the judgement that an invasion by Monmouth could only lead to failure and their own ruin or death if they should support it.

Defoe must have been was undecided about any action he should take. His heart and his purse told him to participate. A proud descendant of protestant religious refugees, his family had not made the sacrifice of leaving their own country to succumb once more to a Roman Catholic monarch. It was not what they had expected, for under the Tudor monarchs Henry VIII and Elizabeth I the protestant reformation in England had seemed secure.

As important to Defoe, however, were the prospects of royal reward and the recognition of public office. If he moved decisively to support Monmouth from the outset of his invasion from Holland, and if Monmouth were to be successful, why should he not be preferred by him? Yet, if he joined in and the rebellion was to fail, the consequences were too horrible to contemplate.

A claim was made by Defoe that he participated in the Monmouth Rebellion, and then in elliptical form thirty years after the event, in a pamphlet entitled, *An Appeal to Honour and Justice*, 1715. Defoe wrote that he was one 'that had been in arms under the duke of Monmouth.'[184] Participation seems to have been confirmed by a pardon granted to him two years later.[185] However, I do not believe that he did participate in the uprising in any real meaning of the expression.

I discussed the subject in a previous work when I suggested that the story told by Defoe in the *Journal of the Plague Year* of three men stealing from the City of London to avoid the plague offers a clue of what he might have done in June, 1685. To escape the security precautions put in place by his friend Sunderland to prevent Londoner's joining the Rebellion, Defoe would have left the City in the dead of night. He would have had to leave at a selected point of exit offering the best chance of avoiding detection by the guards mounted at the bridges and highways. Defoe would have needed to lead a packhorse out of his premises at Freeman's Yard in the midst of the night and to possess a trading licence to leave the city specifically granted to him. He would have worn a sword, but that was normal, for it was dangerous for merchants to travel alone on the highways and byways even in normal times. He would have to rely on others for a pistol. It was possible to do all this and it was subsequently estimated that 400 Londoners did leave the City to join the Rebellion despite the security arrangements.

Assuming Defoe did this on the right night and at the right moment, and if the account in the *Journal* is followed, he was one of three men who passed over an unmanned bridge into open country. Once safely away, they pitched a tent and caught up with missed sleep. Early in the morning their presence was spotted by an agitated local farmer and hastily they moved on across tangled tracks, keeping clear of highways and habitations.

They reconnoitred the first town they came upon, for their food would not last long. Special Constables were guarding the entry points to this town; at best they would be turned away as unwelcome strangers, at worst they would be taken. Finding a small wood they pitched camp by a brook, a welcome source of fresh water.

---

[184] *Appeal to Honour and Justice*, 1715.
[185] General Pardon, 1686. *Beyond Belief*, 72, n. 82.

They were seen there also and in the middle of the night they were challenged by Special Constables riding out from the nearest town. They had taken the precaution of hiding their weapons elsewhere in the wood and, for the moment, their story was accepted. They were advised to go back, however, for others might not take the same view. There was no further sleep that night as they discussed whether to go on with all the hazards of adventure or take the prudent, if cowardly, decision to retreat. There was no agreement between them and no certainty for any man.

Defoe, the narrator, left his borrowed pistol where he had hidden it and took the open road back. Late on the third day he rode into Freeman's Yard, to the relief of those who depended on him. Of course, most men would have thought him to have been prudent but Defoe would have sought his bed with a profound melancholy. When it had come to it, he had lacked the courage required of a hero.

This account is fictional and disputatious. It cannot be proved but, without falling into casuistry, I believe it to be true, on the balance of probabilities. The exact words in the *Journal* are as follows:

> The watch placed upon Bow Bridge would have questioned them… Crossing the road into a narrow way turns out of the hither end of the town… avoided any enquiry there. The constables everywhere were on their guard… because of a report that was nearly raised… that the poor people in London were up in arms and had raised a tumult… Here they were examined… To forward this fraud they obtained [from] the constable at Old Ford a certificate of them passing through Essex… directed to the next Constable.

When these men hove to for the night in a barn, they were accosted and one of them was 'challenged like soldiers upon a guard'. The travellers found themselves unexpectedly inconvenienced because the horse that carried their baggage was obliged to keep to the road while others could go across the fields. The constables remained 'obstinate'. They were denied entry to towns and had to camp in the forests. In the end they had to give up and go back to the city.[69]

There is evidence that Defoe was forced back into the city, or never left it, in his impressive recall of criminal proceedings against a person called Dangerfield whose trial began on 30 May, 1685, twelve days before Monmouth landed. The trial concluded with a sentencing on 24 July after the Rebellion had ended in failure.[186]

A question to be posed by those who argue that Daniel Defoe did take part in the rebellion is why should a young man, with a wife, children and a business to take care of, join a rebellion with so little prospect of success?

A romantic might do so, and Defoe was one, but then he lived in an age of reason when individuals were expected to behave rationally. The romantic tradition presented a world where an individual could blaze his way by the sword and alter his status and social position by the force of glorious deeds. Defoe seems to have dreamt of doing this as a young man. Judged by his collections of ancient and heroic tales brought together in his manuscript *Historical Collections*, dated 1682, Defoe gives an insight into his imagination at that time. He associated himself with warriors and accepted them as role models.[187]These images stayed with him throughout his life; throughout five successive reigns over half a century.

The revolutionary doctrine Defoe believed in and advocated allowed for 'the people' acting as a mob to overthrow any monarch not accepting a protestant king. In *Crusoe's* island kingdom, Crusoe's rhetoric is of absolutism and the submission of the subject. Defoe does not speak the language of the social contract. For *Crusoe*, an understanding between monarch and subject follows an anterior condition that presupposes that they have entered into a mutual compact, whether tacit or explicit. It is an understanding upheld by force of arms, with 'a naked Sword by my Side, two Pistols in my belt, and a Gun upon each Shoulder'.

Beliefs of this kind provide an insight into Defoe's character and his ideas. They are mythological in origin. Novak summarises the subject matter of *Recollections*. He writes:

---

[186] Bastian, 113.
[187] *Historical Collections*, 1682.

> Of the 140 separate apothegms or anecdotes, the greatest
> number concern Alexander ... with Julius Caesar and
> Augustus having three each. The Great Schanderberg, the
> Albanian hero who fought so bravely against the Turks
> appears in several stories and fifteen concern soldiers ...
> forty involve death and execution ... and many ... involving
> religious themes have their share of violence in them.[188]

At that time, 37 years before he published *Robinson Crusoe*, Defoe
may have seen himself as a romantic hero rooted in religious purpose,
in epic and certainty, who conquered the iniquitous by force in a
turbulent and dangerous world. By contrast, the tendency in recent
critical expositions of Defoe is to modernise him by relation to a Whig
version of history, to the rights of man, parliamentarianism and
republicanism. In contrast, the truth about his deepest emotions must lie
in his seventeenth-century roots.

A truly modern man can take God out of his heaven and seek his
own material advantage. To protect worldly gains made by the power
of the sword or gun was a troublesome matter. On his island *Crusoe*
sought to colonise and dominate his new world. *Crusoe*/Defoe does not
share a modern preoccupation with the dangers of executive power, but
resistance to it was to become the dominant constitutional issue for the
English parliaments of his time. Throughout his life Defoe was a
vigorous defender of monarchical control when in the hands of a
righteous monarch (one he approved of) and he became agitated when
it was challenged.

A sane man will not be wholly in the grip of romantic myths and
symbols and will draw back from the brink of acting out his
romanticism, whereas an unbalanced man motivated by biblical
certainty may not. With Defoe, no one can be quite sure where he stood
on the delicate balance between the two. This drama was played out in
Defoe's early life. Unless Defoe's belated admission of participating in
the Monmouth Rebellion is believed, there is an historical difficulty
about how his dream of glory was acted out. Most recent biographers,

---

[188] Novak, 69-70.

against the balance of probability, continue to believe in the myth of his participation in the Rebellion. It is worth considering the claim in detail in order to dismiss it.

Early biographers were sceptical. Chadwick, writing in 1859, said, 'but when Defoe affirms that he was there as a fighter, what must I say? ... he must have been thoroughly watched by the government and marked out for destruction. Defoe was not there, though he says he was.' Later, Chadwick states, in his own quixotic manner, his reason for this belief: the lack of any observation whatsoever that he was. 'If L'Estrange, Ned Ward, Tom Browne or Oldmixon, had at that time affirmed that Foe, the hosier, was a Captain or a General in Monmouth's force, I should have rejoiced to record the fact.'

Minto writes that 'he boasted of this when it became safe to do so.' Minto, in common with others, thought that the fact that graduates of the Charles Morton Academy had participated in the rebellion was circumstantial support for Defoe's involvement. However, I demonstrate in this work that Defoe never attended the Newington Academy. Sutherland was more judicious. In 1937 he wrote that 'he [Defoe] may have been gambling on Monmouth's success ... riding about in the west country [on business] and curiosity ... induced him to ride with the rebels. It is probable that he remained on the fringe. If he had fought ... he would have told us so.' In 1955 Charles Moore expressed his view that Defoe took part in the Rebellion with more certainty. 'Defoe', Moore writes, had said goodbye to his wife and had 'rode westwards through the by-lanes ... avoiding the pickets who guarded the main roads.'

In 1980 McDonald Wigfield seemed to put the matter beyond doubt when he discovered the name of Daniel Defoe among a list of those who were 'engaged in the late rebellion and to be inserted in the general pardon.' This was a fact never mentioned by Defoe. [189]

In reality, to make good an assertion of Defoe's participation in the Monmouth Rebellion there are four matters to consider: first, whether it

---

[189] *Beyond Belief*, 67-75.

would have been possible for him to leave London undetected to join the Rebellion, secondly, whether it would have been possible to participate without anyone noticing and telling others or confessing it, thirdly whether he could have escaped detention after the Rebellion had collapsed, and lastly to explain a Royal Pardon which went unpublicised for the remaining forty-six years of his life.

The government in London had been aware of the possible invasion for some months and had taken effective action to prevent dissenters in the capital from joining it. London had been seen as an important recruiting ground for the Rebellion. Dissenters had been picked out as potential rebels, their homes were systematically searched and arms and horses confiscated. Once the landing was known, soldiers were used to block off all the entries and exits to the capital. Special magistrates were appointed and over two hundred dissenters were arrested and held in custody. While it would have been possible to leave the capital it must be considered unlikely and even if it had been contrived the chances of apprehension were high.

Any supposition that Defoe was travelling westward with former schoolmates from the Morton academy is clearly wrong even when not allowing for my assertion that he never attended the academy. McDonald Wigfield[190] has been able to list over 1,500 rebels who were within the royal pardon, including Defoe and three former students of the Morton academy (Battiscombe, Jenkyns and Hewlett), who are described by Defoe as 'western martyrs' in a 1712 pamphlet.[191] Battiscombe and Hewlett came over from Holland with Monmouth. Jenkyns rode out from London but was arrested on suspicion in Ilchester and released by some of Monmouth's soldiers. If he had been accompanied by Defoe 'the whole world would have known of it'. John Shower, another Morton academy student, came from Holland, and was pardoned. None mentioned Defoe.

The supposition that Defoe could have participated in the Rebellion

[190] McDonald Wigfield, W. *Monmouth Rebellion*, Moonraker Press, 1980 59.
The Monmouth Rebels, Alan Sutton, 1985, 11, 83, 94, 155.
[191] Defoe, Daniel. *The Present State of the Parties*, 1712.

without anyone knowing about it or reporting him afterwards is absurd. There was an intense pressure on participants to confess, with the assurance of a lighter sentence. Confessions were extorted and rewards were given to informers. Confronted with this implausibility most biographers have assumed that in some way Defoe was on the fringe of events and did not 'bear arms for the duke of Monmouth' as he claimed. This assumption is not credible: if he had been involved in any way he would have been named by someone.

The hunt for the fleeing rebels was relentless and most were picked up while escaping to the nearest port, relative, or home. Each parish was instructed to 'go to every house, and produce lists of men absent and arms discovered or taken.' Money could be made from the transportation of the rebels and there was a known price on their heads. Backscheider writes, 'That Defoe had remained un-captured was simply amazing: at best a one in fifteen chance.'[192]

King James issued a General Pardon in March 1686. The pardon excepted 'all Fugitives and persons fled from our Justice of or into parts beyond the Seas or out of this Our Realm who shall not return and render themselves to Our Chief Justice before the 29 September next ensuing.' If Defoe had participated in the Rebellion and had fled abroad this would have accounted for a wish to be included specifically within the royal pardon. However, we know that he was on tax rolls and petty jury lists and gave bail to two people during the years 1685/1686 and 1687 and this reasoning would seem not to apply.[193]

The fact that he was added to a list put before magistrates for inclusion within the pardon is not concrete evidence of participation in the rebellion. The preparation of additional names in lists was notoriously unreliable and corrupt: people could pay to gain inclusion to gain Revolutionary credentials, and at any time there was a going rate. Defoe could have got himself on to a list for a payment of £50.[194]

---

[192] Backscheider, 48.
[193] *Beyond Belief*, 72.
[194] *Beyond Belief*, 73, n.85.

Defoe leaves a clue as to what might have happened in *Colonel Jack*. The *Colonel's* wife planned to obtain a pardon for him when he was in exile abroad for treasonable activities. 'She would write to a particular Friend in London, who she could depend upon to try to get a Pardon ... within the expense of two, or three, or four hundred pounds ... he should have Bills payable by such and such a person on Delivery of the Warrant for the thing.'[195] The stress here is upon the untrustworthiness of the correspondent and the request that nothing should be done unless the pardon was certain, that his involvement in the rebellion was not known, and that a pardon was only precautionary. In the event, *Colonel Jack* did not need the pardon.

In 1715 Defoe had an urgent need to restore his standing with the new Whig administration. He needed to become a 'boy scout' with the right 'badges of honour.' This need to diminish the hostility of friends and foes must have been uppermost in his mind. However, it is probably true that Defoe would have been inclined to join the Rebellion, for at the time every dissenter knew two things about Charles's brother James: that his marriage was childless, and that as time passed it was likely that he would die without an heir, and that as an avowed roman catholic he felt spiritually committed to return England to the Roman Catholic Church.

However, there is no doubt that the Duke of Monmouth was a role model for Defoe. In 1702 there were three obvious possibilities for the Succession: Edward, son of James II, and a Roman Catholic monarchy; a Hanoverian heir, in the line of the Electress Sophia; and Anne, the daughter of Charles II. In *The Succession to the Crown of England*, Defoe adds a fourth. He posed the issue of the claims of the son of the Duke of Monmouth and suggested that they be given impartial consideration.[196] In the 1680s Defoe could not predict the Succession but, in all probability, he preferred Monmouth.

It was only in 1715 when the Hanoverian line had been confirmed that Defoe felt able to mention a role in the Monmouth Rebellion. In

---

[195] *Colonel Jack*, quoted by Bastian, 122.
[196] *The Succession to the Crown of England*, 1701.

doing so, he made no mention of the royal pardon. He might have been ashamed to do so, not because of the inclusion in a pardon as such but because he had invented his participation in the rebellion. He had done nothing on an issue of importance to him when many among his friends and fellow dissenters were killed in battle or executed. It is time to face up to the probabilities. As Chadwick wrote, 'Defoe was not there, though he says he was.'

Notwithstanding the temptations to a biographer of accepting Defoe's account, I believe he made up the story of his participation. If so, what does it tell us? Of course, he was tempted to join the Rebellion for the reasons argued here. Even though he decided not to participate, he must have wanted it to succeed for he would have thought the cause to be noble and righteous. However, reason and observation would have led him to doubt the prospects of a triumph for the Duke, and cowardice, or prudence, may have played its part.

The failure of the rebellion was a setback for the dissenters who had been the dominant force in it. While Defoe turned his attention to adventure and business it must have seemed obvious to him that to succeed in life required position and place. He had faced the first test of his determination to succeed and had failed, but his analysis of his situation in life was surely right. As he had defined himself by dissent, he would be handicapped in the struggle for preferment without a protestant monarch.

Defoe only had to wait three years for the accession of William and Mary for the realisation of his dream of a protestant monarch. While no actor could fulfil the role of Defoe's warrior king, William III came very close to it. A protestant, he had fought against France and his armed foray into England, at the request of the leading Whig politicians of the day, was an invasion which, to the dissenter at least, had saved protestant England from a steady but inexorable slide into absolutism and papacy under James II.

It was a political change that occurred without the firing of a single shot. While James hesitated, William camped out in open country. When James fled, William advanced towards London; when he reached

Reading, and it was clear that there would be no armed opposition to his advance, Defoe rode out to join a gathering throng.

It was truly a bloodless revolution. Gradually, in the confusion of these historic events, it became clear to the English what had been done in their name. The people, through parliament, had asserted their right to depose a king, whether or not it was maintained that he ruled by divine right. Feiling points out that the English need not have been so surprised. He writes that: 'Between 1327 and 1688, for nine sovereigns who reigned continuously and died in their beds... there were the forced exile of three kings, the public execution of a fourth, and the foul murder of another four.' [197]

Unbeknown to most, the constitutional position had evolved to the point where parliament was willing to devolve administrative and executive power to a monarch, while retaining the right to hold him to account. It was a balance that would only achieve effective and stable government if the two worked closely and amicably together. It had become part of this balance that the monarch should sustain the vitality of the protestant religion.

It was in the interest of the European Roman Catholic powers, in particular France under Louis XIV, to destabilise any such balance between the English monarch and parliament. Throughout William's reign there was constant warfare. Against the backdrop of the English, Scots and Irish in constant civil conflict (religious, political and economic), England engaged in bitter armed struggle on land and sea. On William's arrival, Holland was at war with France. Parliament was in no position to deny William, whose involvement in England was always part of his strategic battle against France. England engaged itself in a nine year conflict until the peace of Rhyswick in 1697.

Unable any longer to bribe a royal mistress, the French concentrated on buying the House of Commons. In retaliation, the king and the court bought its own placemen and resisted the attempts of both Houses of Parliament to limit royal preferment. William used his executive

---

[197] Feiling, Keith. *A History of the Tory Party*, 1660- 1714, 2nd ed. (Clarendon, Oxford University Press, 1965), 74.

powers to promote what the public understood to be 'his foreign wars' with a resulting rise in national debt and higher taxes.

Now was the moment for Defoe to enter public life but he still had to find a way of doing so.

Chapter 13

Bankruptcy

I might instance here the miserable, anxious, perplexed life the poor tradesman lives under before he Breaks...how harras'd and tormented for money...how many, little, mean, and even wicked things will even the most religious tradesman stoop to...as his very soul would abhor at another time: and for which he goe, perhaps, with a wounded conscience all his life after?

The Compleat English Tradesman
Daniel Defoe, 1727

Daniel Defoe was not an innocent when he sought to conduct a business as a merchant from a London location. Although he had not chosen a life as a planter and merchant trader in Brazil, his experience of doing so must have given him the confidence to do something similar in England. It would prove to be more difficult. Sugar production in Brazil was capital intensive and only made financially viable by the exploitation of vast numbers of black slaves, local native populations and indentured labour. The sugar trade was demand-led in Defoe's experience of it by the huge increase in sugar consumption in Europe in the period 1650-1750. The centre of sugar production had shifted to Barbados during Defoe's exile. This change depended on a vast number of slaves.[198]

It was only natural for Defoe to think, whatever may have been his uneasy moral repugnance, that he could make a fortune by slave trading. *Crusoe* tells his reader that as a young man, that is when he was no older than sixteen to eighteen years old, he had embarked on a slave trade voyage to Africa and made £300 from his venture.[199] It is one thing to do this in Brazil where even there, as I have argued, he got

---

[198] Gragg, Leslie. *The Quaker Community of Barbados: Challenging the Culture of the Planter Class*, University of Missouri Press, 2009.
[199] *Robinson Crusoe*, 16-17.

into difficulty, and quite another to conduct such a business from London or any other English port. However, as I argue later, he did find a way to do it despite the difficulties.

Trading merchandise by ship from London as a natural extension of his experience in Brazil was difficult for a number of reasons. First, and most awkward, was that he was seen as a foreigner because of his long exile. So long as he was viewed in this way, and under the Navigation Acts, he could own no more than 25 percent of an English built boat. Sharing the ownership of a boat meant that he could not determine the composition of its crew, destination, or cargo. It most likely led to mixed cargos. There is an example of these difficulties in *Moll Flanders*. The Captain on the loose in London was looking for a boat and confessed that he was only the part-owner of one. Secondly, if he were trading with the New World, the long distances involved in shipping goods tied up his investment in cargoes for long periods of time. Financing these cargoes had become possible by the use of sophisticated methods such as bills of exchange. The cost of financing trade in this way would have been high for an unknown entrant to the market and of questionable repute. Thirdly, there were dangers in shipping cargoes along the trans-Atlantic routes. As England was in a state of war with France for much of the time Defoe was trading, English merchants and their ships were liable to attack by French vessels. In an earlier chapter I comment on *Colonel Jack* pretending to be French and conducting his trading business with France through a French agent.[200] In the Caribbean, whatever the Treaty obligations, the Dutch navy was the enemy. Defoe's enthusiastic endorsement of William III to the throne of England was based not only on religious and dynastic reasons but upon the belief that the Dutch would not act against English interests in European waters and in the New World. Fourthly, there were the external threats to cargoes by pirates and bad weather. While cargoes could be insured against these risks the premiums were high and claims often led to the breaking of the insurers before they paid out.

---

[200] *Colonel Jack*, 208.

Defoe could not have achieved much in these difficult circumstances without the help of friends and relatives and trading partners in the territories with which he traded. Bastian has revealed details of many of the names, some of whom were Defoe's kinsmen. Mathew Clarkson may have acted as a factor for Defoe in New York. When in 1694 he petitioned for the Post of Mayor of New York he supported it with a testimonial to his good character signed by Defoe and seven others: James Moyer and Robert Knight (who assisted Defoe rent land in Tilbury), his brother David Clarkson, his half brother Thomas Lodwick (a step child of David Clarkson who had alleged the particulars for Defoe marriage license in 1683), his cousins John Rowett and Gerard Van Heythusen, and a David King who was possibly a relative on Defoe's mother's side of the family. There were the Abbott's, friends of James Foe in Boston; and his own correspondents there, Joseph Beaton and John Sharp. In Maryland a Samuel Sandford acted for Defoe.[201]

Today it might be asked of any modern adventurer in Defoe's mould to explain his business model. It is easy to understand that Defoe had one. What is less clear is whether he fully understood its implications. At the outset he gathered together as much capital as he could. *Crusoe* tells his readers that he sought out his nephew, bought him a boat and made him the Captain of it.[202] Later this boat appears in other accounts. It is named the *Aurangezebe*. I suggest that the fictional nephew in *Farther Adventures of Robinson Crusoe* is a man called Francis King, a nephew to Defoe. Francis King was undeniably English in charge of an undeniably English-built ship. It is known that Defoe bought at least one other boat, the *Desire*, which appears in various points in his history. Defoe claims to have been promised a dowry of £3,700 pounds from his marriage with Mary Tuffley. Very wisely the Tuffley family seem to have held most of it back. In *Colonel Jack* there is a suggestion that he was only given £1,400.

With these sums, and others unknown, Defoe bought grazing land in

[201] Bastian, 96.
[202] *Robinson Crusoe*, 234, 256.

Tilbury. Bastian suggests that there was little short-term advantage for Defoe in buying seventy acres of land there.[203] The leases cost Defoe £1,855 pounds in 1689/90 of which he advanced £955 and borrowed £900 on mortgage from Robert Stamper, John Ghisleyn, Peter Mauresco and his own mother in law, Joan Tuffley. Bastian suggests that as the rental yield was less than 5 percent and the cost of the loans 6 percent the immediate income yield was small. In his own mind Defoe might have regarded this land as a nascent estate on which he could build a home and farm and thus have the basis of a family establishment independent of others. He was able to do achieve this but only after a devastating bankruptcy.

The purchase of fixed assets, land, ships, warehousing and the finance of working capital for long periods of time at sea, required considerable resources and extensive loans. It was possible to raise working capital through bills of exchange and letters of credit but the interest charged was high as a consequence of the risk. In the 1680's Defoe never had the resources to conduct business in this way. Some risks could be shared with other traders of a like mind and no doubt Defoe did attempt to shed risk in this way. This was a sure way to make enemies. His world was full of fair-weather friends and when the going got difficult they became enemies. These associates had short memories. Defoe might justifiably point out that people had benefited from his successes but creditors thought nothing of that. They had become used to earnings and were enraged to suffer losses. Those who thought this way thought nothing about dragging Defoe into the courts and a debtor's prison.

A hypothetical judge of Defoe's business model would need to take account of the very many actions he took to raise short-money from trade within England and the continent of Europe. Confronted with a daily lack of cash he set about trying to undertake activities for cash and to build a distribution network for products imported from the European continent. When he sallied forth from his warehouse in London he carried samples of his merchandise; and on his travels he

---

[203] Bastian, 145.

sought contacts who would act for him in different places and sales outlets that would give him orders for his merchandise. From the outset he was able to establish a trade in wines and spirits with Portugal and Spain and he was active in it for approaching 40 years.

During the period in which Defoe was trading with France, Spain and Portugal, England was in a constant state of war. Although the accession of William III in 1689 gave England relief from the dominance of Dutch ships in European waters it intensified attacks on British ships by the French navy. Defoe was able to claim his colonial status in trade with Barbados, and hence onwards to New England, but it did not cover him for direct trade to the American colonies. Neither did it protect him from the Dutch for whatever the treaty arrangements Dutch merchants persisted in their trade to the Caribbean and New England. Much of this trade could be financed with bills of exchange but as Defoe's losses accumulated interest rates would have risen and loans been denied to him. Trade not financed by Notes of some kind had to be met by him from his own cash resources or borrowed from friends. Legal disputes were expensive. The more successful he was in building his business the greater the need for liquidity. Defoe was creative in his efforts to overcome these difficulties. Sutherland and Backscheider have written about many of the ruses and devices Defoe employed when pressed for money. Sutherland discovered that between 1688 and 1692 Defoe was the subject of eight claims in Chancery suits. Some were settled against him while others dragged on until the plaintiffs either died or gave up.

For example, in July 1689, Joseph Braban a merchant of Lyn Regis, sued Defoe for £396 for goods supplied to Defoe for sale on commission. Braban was willing to compromise and gave Defoe a further nine months to pay subject to a further sum of £600 as penalty. Defoe could not pay. In the end Braban agreed to the payment of the £396 and dropped the penalty.

The restrictions of the Navigation Acts were always present. In August, 1688 Defoe was obliged to sell seventy-five percent of a ship he owned to a man called Harrison who sailed with a cargo to Portugal.

On his way back the ship was attacked and Harrison was boarded and arrested. Harrison sought payment of £62 from Defoe for his share, twenty-five percent, of the lost cargo. Defoe mounted a complicated defence. He accused Harrison of leaving without an agreed route and even denied that he had sold a share of the vessel to him. The issue was buried in claim and counterclaim.

In Defoe's defence it can be argued that at the time mercantile disputes of the kind I have been describing were legion. Nevertheless, it is true that Defoe was engaged in a great many disputes and a fair-minded observer might well have had grounds to dispute his honesty. In his disputes Defoe was willing to involve his friends and allies. Joan Tuffley, his mother in law, helped him out by advancing £300 pounds on the security of his land in Tilbury in 1687 but that did not prevent him from trying to cheat her five years later over the purchase of civet cats. This redoubtable lady sued him when she failed to recover an investment in these cats which were bred for their perfume. She alleged manifest 'fraud' and during the case she stated that Defoe was a 'gay deceiver'.

It is difficult to defend Defoe from accusations of dishonesty. Sutherland describes two cases taken out against Defoe involving a misuse of bills of exchange. In 1692, Defoe was charged with wrongfully converting a bill of exchange for his own use. 'According to the plaintiff, the clerk had picked up a bill of exchange in his master's chambers while his master lay dead in another room, and had handed it on to Defoe who gave £60 for it'. The case went against Defoe. Almost immediately, Defoe faced a similar charge. He was involved in the formation of a company to exploit the invention of a Cornish inventor, Joseph Williams, who procured a patent for 'a certain engine for diving of great use and benefit'. Joseph Williams had contributed money in bills of exchange. Williams charged Defoe with having done him out of a considerable sum of money in concert with a Thomas Williams (who was also involved in the first case). Defoe offered a plausible defence and the case ended inconclusively.

Sutherland, generously, considers that the losses sustained on the high seas from storms and attacks by privateers of foreign navies were principally the cause of Defoe's difficulties. There is confusion and uncertainty about the extent of Defoe's trade with the New World. In the early stages of his settlement back in London this trade might have been considerable; if so the losses described by Sutherland must also have been substantial. There is documentary evidence showing him trading the *Desire* from London to European ports and I have conjectured that the *Aurangezebe* traded with New England, South America and the Caribbean. While the returns from trading to the New World were great the lead times for cargoes were necessarily long, the capital tied up in the ventures was considerable, and cargoes were likely to be lost entirely in bad weather and piracy.

However, the trade most commonly associated with Defoe in the 1680's was the wholesale distribution of hosiery products. These were low-value products requiring distribution systems and mass sales to give a return. The advantages of this type of business to Defoe were considerable and it represented, perhaps, the only day-to-day income on which he could rely. As a factor he travelled extensively to distributors and retailers throughout the country. He set in motion a behaviour which became habitual, absenting himself from home and travelling by horse and carriage to places that were novel and diverting to him. He made it his practice to make contact with dissenting communities throughout the country and to gain information about their worries and concerns. In time it made him well-informed about all kinds of people, work-places and situations, a knowledge that was to inform the work that gave him fame in his lifetime and after his death, *A Tour through the Whole Island of Great Britain*.

Speculation, gambling and poor business judgement were the causes of Defoe's trading difficulties, but he, his character and behaviour, was his own worst enemy. Defoe was simply too unstable and restless a person to succeed in the taking of speculative risks in a variety of business ventures. Indeed, he wrote about a businessman such as himself in the *Compleat English Trader:*

…when he finds himself grown rich, to have his head full of grand designs, and new undertakings. He finds his cash flow in upon him, and perhaps he is fuller of money than his trade calls for; and as he scarce knows how to employ more stock in it than he does, his ears are the sooner open to any project or proposal that offers itself; and I must add, that this is the most critical time with him in all his life.

In all these pursuits it must have seemed obvious to Defoe that forming good business connections offered his best chance of success. The dissenting community offered entry to a society of fellow spirits which, while it may not have taken him far- for economic self-interest, as ever, governed individual decisions, would have 'opened doors'.

In the bars, taverns and coffee houses of London there was fellowship of another kind. There was a social and political mix to be found there. A clever fellow could get a hearing from his superiors and an ingenious one with imagination could gain knowledge of the latest speculations and earn the opportunity to participate in them.

At some time it is possible that Defoe became a Mason. It would have been difficult for him to become one because of the social exclusiveness of Masonic Lodges, but the printers and City men around him achieved membership, and Defoe would have found a way in. Membership would have been useful to him because masonry opened up a wealth of personal contacts across social boundaries, ranging from the royal family and the aristocracy to the scions of industry and commerce. Backscheider has suggested that later in his life, around 1706–7, Defoe was able to acquire access to the Scottish aristocracy during the negotiations for the Union of Scotland and England, when he was in the pay of the English government, because he was a mason. Masonic Lodges were highly secretive about their membership and proceedings (there are no extant or accessible membership lists) and it is difficult to prove whether any individual was a member. However, it seems probable that at some time before 1703 Defoe became one.

More controversially, Defoe could have been using his sexuality to gain advantage. Defoe's sexual activity is hardly likely to be logged anywhere. It is only later in his life that his homosexuality can be spoken about with a degree of certainty; but a man is not likely suddenly, late in his life, to find himself with a sexual orientation not experienced in his youth.

In the 1690's it became more dangerous for a man to be openly homosexual. The Glorious Revolution of 1688 ushered in a cultural change. The Revolution was in a sense a defeat for the French. The anonymous author of *A Satyr against the French* wrote, 'All Europe to their fashions bends the knee, In that they've gained the universal monarchy'. France was alleged to be 'the source of tyranny, anarchy, and luxury, despotic Lords and effeminising delicacies, frogs, fricasseed and coxcomb-pies'. [204]

The Stuart Court was considered to have been under French influence and now it was time for a change. Relations between men could be homosocial, and even homoerotic, but homosexual practices were to become incompatible with a more masculine political culture. Outward display was to become frowned upon as effeminate and contrary to the spirit of a mercantilist and trading age.

Instigated by the Crown-sponsored Society for the Reformation of Manners, prosecutions of homosexual practices (and executions of men committing them) doubled after 1688. Homosexual practices were seen as inherently associated with effeminacy, and thus a danger to the state. The tyranny of the state was to catch the poor and unsuspecting. For a time, high social position would guarantee immunity and 'protection' could be bought. For some, life went on as usual.

All his life Defoe was curious about the changing world around him. His intellectual output at this time must have been prodigious. There was no better place than London to become acquainted with the scientific and industrial discoveries being made. Defoe's intense and inquiring nature would have meant that he was constantly engaged.

Reckless trading was bound to cause Defoe to come to a sticky end. On 29 October, 1692 a London magistrate, Sir John Powell, was

---

[204] Anon. *A Satyr against the French,* London, Randall Taylor, 1691, 5.

presented with a straightforward petition by Walter Ridley, a haberdasher, and three other traders, Cornelius Shadwell, Jerome Whichcote and Nicholas Barrett. These traders were owed money by Daniel Defoe; they had given him time to pay and Defoe had made promises of payment that were never honoured. It was necessary to call in the debts and commit this fellow to the Fleet prison until they were paid and this is what Sir John Powell did.

Defoe had been on the slippery slope for some time, losing money in multifarious ventures, hopelessly and desperately extending his credit and resorting to whatever stratagem was to hand, regardless of its honesty. Today it is a legal offence to knowingly trade when insolvent but the penalties and outcomes are more generous to the culprit. In the seventeenth century when caught out in this way there were simpler and cruder arrangements. Naturally creditors lived in hope of a payment. Defoe made some kind of an arrangement, or paid some kind of bribe, to get out of prison. It was not difficult. Of 1,651 prisoners charged and sent to the Fleet from 28 April to 1 December, 1696, 'only three hundred prisoners had been discharged by regular procedure' and the others escaped by bribery.

However, there was no escape for Defoe from his troubles. Desperately, he tried to save himself and by October, 1692 he succeeded in persuading 140 creditors to whom he owed the enormous sum of £17,000 to agree to a composition of 15 shillings in the pound but four creditors with debts amounting to £200 refused. Accruing so large a number of desperate creditors might be thought to be disaster enough, but they were not the whole of it. Defoe omitted all the creditors he thought he could avoid. In November, two creditors, one of whom was owed the considerable sum of £700, lost patience and on their suit Defoe was committed to the King's Bench prison and then on to the Mint. He was there some time before he was able to obtain his release.

A ray of hope was to be found in the passage through the Commons of the Merchant Insurers Bill but then the bill was defeated in the House of Lords on 9 March, 1694. Defoe's name was among nineteen on that bill, and a late entry. If the Bill had been passed Defoe would have obtained relief on some of his debts if two thirds of his creditors had agreed. It remains uncertain to what extent Defoe had incurred mercantile insurance debts and when: it is possible that he may have incurred them after his bankruptcy. Defoe tells his readers that he was present at the consideration of the bill by parliament. It must have been cruel for him to witness 'his hopes go down as fast as the ships which created the losses in the first place' .

In the corridors, offices and work shops of the City of London Defoe's reputation had been lost. Clearly the money lenders would have sought some sort of an explanation for his disaster. A man might plead the times in which he lived. The City of London was full of all kinds of merchants growing their businesses and becoming rich at a faster pace than would have been possible for their forebears. It must have seemed to them all that it was possible to become a gentleman with servants, carriages and expectations. The financial world of stock jobbing, bills of exchange, private banks, lotteries and speculative projects was upon them in a raw and unregulated fashion. Why should not the aspiring Defoe become one of these merchant adventurers? He was intelligent and quick with a good head for figures, interested and well-informed, diligent and unceasingly energetic and up to date about every new service venture or development.

It can be argued in Defoe's defence that the culture in which he lived was acquisitive and, in a sense, formed by the prospects of acquiring wealth and changing personal status in society. Such an assertion raises more doubts than it solves. A conclusion that Defoe's greed was excessive is inescapable. The questions multiply. Was his avarice and desire for the riches of the world a product of too little love, attention and material sustenance as a child? Did Defoe suffer from a form of childhood anal retention against which he was defenceless and which in his adult life took the form of aggrandisement? Was he doomed to seek possessions and to retain them even when their utility to him was doubtful?

Whatever Defoe's other values and activities, it is true that throughout his life he was ceaselessly and restlessly preoccupied with the making of money. The surest route to this success for an intelligent man such as Defoe was to apply himself to a City career in which he made himself useful to others. He needed connections and to make himself indispensable to persons of place and influence. This is what he attempted and, to some extent, he succeeded in doing. Such a strategy requires patience, reliability and trustworthiness. Defoe was deficient in all these qualities. Even lacking these qualities of good character, Defoe would have succeeded if he had been accomplished enough. But in business, as in so many activities, accomplishment is the product of assiduous daily practice.

As for writing, until the lifting of the licensing laws in 1695 with their draconian policing of publishers and printers, it was difficult for a rebellious or impulsive writer to find an audience. Defoe wrote but it is not likely that by writing he could make a steady living. If he kept his identity hidden, even from the printer, there were opportunities to make an occasional profit, as described in an earlier chapter but then it would not have been known that the writer was Daniel Defoe and later, when he might have told us he was the author of this or that pamphlet or poem, he is silent.

Finally, it has been argued that Defoe became bankrupt because he devoted too much time to politics and writing. To fill the vacuum in what is known of Defoe's activities in the 1680s and 1690s, and to round their characterisation of Defoe, it has been tempting to earlier biographers to ascribe anonymous works to him. Many of these early ascriptions are now thought not to be Defoe's at all and, while it is probable that he was writing, perhaps the activity was not as great as is often supposed. George Chalmers, an early biographer, writing in 1790 states that Defoe 'did not become a bankrupt because he had taken to writing; he became an author because he had failed in business'.[205]

Today the consequences of bankruptcy in England remain severe and the act carries a moral stigma. However, now a bankruptcy puts an end to the financial troubles of the bankrupt in that all his debtors are

---

[205] Chalmers, George. *The Life of Daniel Defoe*, 5.

bound by a court order. The bankrupt need not have the consent of any of his creditors and, providing the terms of the bankruptcy are honoured by the defaulter, he will in time be free of all remaining obligations upon its termination date. However, it remains true that a debtor in modern England can find himself in prison for a debt if he places himself in contempt of a court order.

In earlier times debt was regarded far more harshly and in many places as a capital crime; in England, some bankrupts were executed for their debts late into the eighteenth-century. At the time of Defoe's first bankruptcy, any creditor could prevent a general composition with creditors and the consequence for the debtor was incarceration in prison where there was a constant fear of mutilation or death. Bribery of the gaolers was one means of escape, buying off the creditors who had caused the prison sentence another.

Once free, prisoners remained subject to the pursuit of their creditors. Other people, possibly enemies, could buy debts, pursue them in the courts and get people put out of their way. While in prison, people could not earn a living and the creditors got nothing. The creditors had a financial interest in dealing with debtors but for serious offences and for emotional reasons some preferred revenge to part-payment.

Twelve years later when Defoe had secured release from prison after his ordeal in the pillory, he was again bankrupted. In a sense the two bankruptcies were linked: the unsuccessful resolution of the first had led to the second crisis. In the 1705/6 session of parliament, after Daniel's second bankruptcy, a bill entitled, *A Bill to Prevent Frauds Committed by Bankrupts*, was passed and a commission in bankruptcy established. The Act enabled a bankrupt to achieve a situation, subject to the investigation of the commission, where creditors could be bound to accept a bankruptcy, even when some objected, and where the bankrupt could keep up to five per cent of his assets. The Act departed from past attitudes in that it benefited the creditor as well as the debtor and enabled the honest bankrupt to make a quick and complete settlement with creditors.

Defoe criticised the bill in the *Review*[97] and wrote about it to Harley. He stated that he had been advised not to seek advantage from the new act as his creditors would all come at him. Then, between 18 and 22 July a notice in the London Gazette announced that Defoe's bankruptcy was being investigated by the commission and that he had been ordered to attend a meeting. Defoe avoided attending by leaving London, but he could not do so for long. The commission had considerable powers of initiative: it could act on the evidence of others, seize records and books of account, oblige witnesses to attend and answer questions and make a wide variety of orders.

Some biographers assume that the London Gazette advertisement was placed on Defoe's initiative but it could just as well have been on that of the commission acting on its own or on the prompting of others. Certainly there were many creditors who believed that Defoe was hiding assets and they would not have been shy in coming forward.

It is not difficult to imagine the scene. In early August, the commission ordered to deal with the affairs of Mr Daniel Defoe considered the evidence for the third time. Before removing himself from London, Defoe had provided the committee with a long statement of outstanding debts, some supporting accounts, other information and a plea. From information given to the committee from other persons, the members had decided the information was incomplete. Defoe was asked to provide additional information and to address specific issues. He responded and was brought before them.

The officials were precise men charged with specific responsibilities under an Act of Parliament. They were not to be easily satisfied by generalities or rhetoric. While they did not possess judicial powers they felt themselves bound to act as if they did. Confronting them was a well-dressed man of average height and build, with a wig too long for the fashion and fatigued with travel and worry. He was not a handsome man, for he possessed a jutting chin and a disfigurement of his face, but undeniably he had presence. Despite his fatigue, he would have displayed a frenetic energy. He fidgeted with his papers and interrupted members in full flow, responded to precise questions with a flood of words, and gave answers which prompted more questions. All in all it must have been quite a performance.

These officials were not to be denied, for they knew what they wanted and had the forensic skills to find it out, but they were men of the world with other duties to perform. They did not have infinite time. In the end they gave up. Nothing could be resolved one way or another, in favour or against.

Defoe claimed the commission's findings as a famous victory against formidable enemies. He wrote to Harley stating that he had gained 'at last a Compleat Victory Over the most Furious Subtill and Malitious Opposition That has been Seen in all The Instances of the Bankrupts Act'. [206] He claimed that he had received financial relief under the Act, but the relief he spoke of was emotional. Defoe's denied creditors continued to hunt him down for the rest of his life. He was never safe from a knock on the door.

The unanswered question for all those biographers who seek to interpret the evidence of Defoe's bankruptcies to persuade readers of a good character for him arising from a sound and stable family life, a strict Presbyterian upbringing and schooling, a possible calling for the ministry, and with the secure basis of a rich dowry, is how his business activities turned out so badly? No doubt there was ill-fortune, and the hazards of war must have been a factor, but there is evidence of wilfulness, immoral business dealings and recklessness. There is far more present in his behaviour than the amorality needed for the conduct of a successful business, and nothing of the conscientious puritan.

Defoe's bankruptcy did not finish his business career, although his name was blackened in the City of London, but the easy days of persuading people that his word was 'as good as his bond' were over.

---

[206] H.124.

Chapter 14

Recovery

The God that gave me brains will give me bread.

An Elegy on the author of
the True Born Englishman
Daniel Defoe, 1704

In his many setbacks and vicissitudes Defoe showed great resilience: although cast down and dispirited he always bounced back to show new spirit and enterprise. In some respects, however, his immediate prospects were poor. His bankruptcy in 1692 prevented him from engaging in trans-Atlantic trade centred on London if it involved the raising of money. Novak quotes an anonymous writer of a pamphlet entitled *A Character of Daniell de Foe writer of the Pamphlet Called the Review*.

> Daniel Defoe the Author of the Review is no French Man, but born here in England, bred a Hosier, and followed that trade till he broke for a considerable Sum. His creditors run him into an Execution of Bankruptcy, but to no purpose he having fraudulently, as they seemed assur'd, Concealed his Effects. So that his Reputation amongst ye fair Dealers of the City is very Foule, he is a profest Dissenter, tho' reckoned of no Morals.

No doubt Defoe's first inclination was to conduct his affairs as normally as possible. He must have tried to resume where he had left off. His hosiery business in Freeman's Yard continued but the work was conducted at first by an assistant. A little later records show him as no longer there. Defoe was able to warehouse goods at Tilbury where he could receive and distribute merchandise by sea. *Colonel Jack* reveals local links with groups of traders in Essex where he could ship speciality goods throughout the country, sea foods such as oysters and building materials such as gravel from dredging in the Thames estuary.

He held on to ownership of seventy acres of farmland in Tilbury from which there was a revenue stream and developed brickworks there. General trade could be continued in Tilbury without some of the creditor pressure centred on London. However, Defoe needed to be present in London and to keep his residences wherever they were a secret.

When the next trace of Defoe is found, it is in the organisation of private lotteries from an address a few doors down from his premises in Freeman's Yard, which suggests that this part of London remained for a while at the centre of his activities. These lotteries were in the interest of Thomas Neale, a groom-porter in charge of gambling in the anteroom of the royal palace and a Member of Parliament. He had a licence to conduct them. Neale had the reputation of being something of a gambler himself. In 1692–1693 he was involved in over 37 projects from which he made a profit. He spent his money in pursuit of influence and gain.

While it would have been apparent to Thomas Neale that Defoe was a suitable person to front these lotteries, it is not obvious how the two men met. After the ascent of William III to the throne in 1689, Defoe must have believed that he could gain influence at Court through his friend Sunderland. However, Sunderland, who had became a Roman Catholic to appease his royal master, James, Duke of York was summarily dismissed by him with the words 'you have your pardon; much good doe it you. I hope you will be more faithful to your next master than you have to me'. Sunderland fled to France. Initially William III distrusted Sunderland and excluded him from the Indemnity Act, 1690. However by 1691, the year before Defoe's bankruptcy, Sunderland had been allowed to return to England and take his seat in the House of Lords. If Defoe had approached Sunderland for an introduction to the Court in 1692, he might well have been advised to contact Neale.

Defoe was named by Neale as a 'Manager's Trustee' of these lotteries and would have taken money from them. Sir Thomas Neale was also named as a Trustee. There is little doubt that these lotteries were corrupt and the public tired of them in the end. All offices of this kind and even or especially state appointments were accepted as conferring 'a licence to print money'. However, although illegal profits could be made, it was regarded as 'poor form' to overdo it. Even the great Samuel Peyps got into trouble for corrupt practices. His most recent biographer, Claire Tomalin, does not deny that he took the usual quota of pickings.[207]

Lotteries as a form of gambling were disapproved of by nonconformists of all shades. Even to this day a solid body of religious opinion frowns upon all forms of gambling. Defoe would not have wanted to be prominently associated with gambling and, to the extent that he wished at this time to retain the confidence of his non-conforming followers, he may have wished to move on as soon as possible.

Thomas Neale had an inside track to the happenings at William III's court. How he came to achieve it is not known but for the next 7 years, until he over-reached himself, he possessed in a royal licence, a permission to 'print money'; but, to make it he needed the active collaboration of the determined, conscientious and unscrupulous.

As an outsider William was dependent on the use of his royal prerogative to influence public affairs and to get things done. As the nation was drawn into foreign wars, the power of the executive expanded and opposition to the Crown grew with it. As royal policy became opposed by parliament there was an executive need to circumvent it... The rewards for collaboration with the Crown grew to fantastic extremes. A major national war effort always brings the very worst of society to the light of day and for some years under William there were rich pickings for the unscrupulous.

Defoe became one of Thomas Neale's 'bag men'. He had the qualities to succeed in the role. The evidence from his fictions discussed later suggests that Defoe and Thomas Neale may have had a long-standing sexual relationship. Defoe would have taken advantage of the relationship to share in the spoils.

---

[207]Tomalin, Claire, *Samuel Pepys: The Unequalled Self*, Penguin Books, 2003.

It is probable that Neale introduced Defoe to Sir Dalby Thomas, a fellow lottery Trustee. In 1695 Dalby became one of three Commissioners to devise and supervise the collection of the duty on glass. Dalby Thomas gave Defoe the job of accountant to the Commissioners at a salary of £100 per annum, rising to £150.

The Commission had been created to raise money for William's wars and became unpopular as the public resistance to them grew. The tax was abolished in 1699. However, the Commission was not finally to be wound up until 1712 when Defoe signed the final accounts as accountant and Harley signed them off for the government. Defoe had continued to receive a salary and was paid for the production of the accounts.[208] This was Defoe's first state appointment and he was not to mention it until 1715, nineteen years later. A great deal of public money would have passed through his hands and he would have had a share of it.

In 1695 parliament heard from King William of a plot to assassinate him planned from Paris. There was an overwhelming parliamentary majority for the actions William thought necessary to deal with the conspiracy. On 27 January 1696 William ordered all those holders of offices under the Crown to renew their oath of allegiance. A period of time to the end of May was given to conform. Defoe swore his oath in April, 1696 and his name is recorded in the Chancery record for the month ending 29 April, 1696.[209]

There are gaps in the Chancery and Exchequer records for Sacrament Certificates in the period 1695–1700 and it is not possible to trace Defoe's. It is possible that he may have deposited a certificate in a Quarter Sessions convenient to him. If so, some diligent researcher may find it. However, Defoe wrote about the experience, albeit obliquely. In the *Tour*, Defoe writes about the emotions felt by a dissenter taking the sacrament in an Anglican church:

I remember that going with some friends to show them this

---

[208] *See Beyond Belief*, 105.
[209] *Beyond Belief*, 105.

magnificent Palace...[the Royal Chapel at Windsor]...when the Dissenters were a little uneasy at being obliged to kneel at the Sacrament one of my friends... who was a Dissenter... fixed his eyes on the alter-piece... he whispered... how can your people persecute us for refusing to kneel at the Sacrament... that was not the place for him and I to dispute it... we did [later], but brought it to no conclusion, so tis useless to mention it any more.

Arguably, the dissenter in the church is Defoe, and his friend, the narrator, represents a companion or his conscience. The Royal Chapel is the symbol of a royal appointment but it is not likely that Defoe took communion there.[119] The actual occasion can only be imagined

This common misunderstanding of the nature of Defoe's appointment as accountant to the Glass Commissioners is compounded by another discovery in research for *Beyond Belief*. It is assumed that when the tax on glass was abolished in December 1699 the work of the Commission ended and staff were dismissed. However, my research shows that it did not wind up its affairs until 1712, nearly thirteen years later. The Commissioners and their staff went on being paid throughout the period. This information is to be found in the final accounting statement of the commission, dated 16 July, 1712, which was prepared by Defoe, under the name Daniel Foe, on behalf of the commissioners.[210]

In the opening preamble to these accounts it is explained that the offices were held 'until such time as they were determined' and that they (the officers) were empowered to collect the tax and 'the issuing, expending and laying out of the same [funds] to paying salaries to the said Commissioners [and] the Officers, Clerks and other employees under them in the managing and collecting the duties or for the Incident Charges of their Office... and for the accounting of all hereafter'.

In these accounts it is specifically stated that Defoe received his salary in 1700 and 1701. In 1704 and 1710 special warrants were issued

---

[210] *Beyond Belief*, 106.

for the payment of arrears of salaries and expenses. It is likely that these monies were to plug holes in the revenues collected from the late payers of duties caused by the Commissioners and officers paying themselves ahead of any counter balancing sums. In 1712 Defoe received specific remuneration for the preparation of the accounts but the amount is not stated. Thus the commissioners were permitted to spend nearly thirteen years collecting overdue taxes and winding up their affairs. During this time they were paid generous salaries out of public funds and enjoyed the benefit of additional revenue from corrupt practices.

It is of great interest and significance also that these accounts were signed off and the commissioners' affairs brought to an end by the signature of Harley, both in his name and as the Earl of Oxford. There is evidence that the relationship between Robert Harley and Defoe cooled in 1712. If it had not, would the commission have rolled on for a further two years until the new Whig administration brought it to an end?

In his lifetime, Defoe campaigned strenuously against dissenters seeking public office, their signing of the Test Act and agreeing to abide by the practice of occasional conformity, whereby dissenters could hold offices in corporations so long as they took communion in an Anglican church from time to time. In his public arguments, Defoe stated his belief that the Act debased the communion service and tempted men to equivocate on what they really believed for private gain. Defoe claimed to know more about occasional conformity than any man in Britain: he may well have been right. His pamphlet arguments, often presented anonymously, were logical, consistent and compelling and, in their personal attacks on named individuals, extremely unpleasant.

A man might reasonably object to the Test Act. However, it stood the test of time as an assurance to the public that servants of the Crown would not use their positions to assist rebellion against lawful authority. At the very least, it can be seen that Defoe's relentless attacks on individuals taking the Test were not principled. Why did he make them? Perhaps there was a kind of rage at the disappointment of being overlooked for elected office. In reality, there was no possibility, after his bankruptcy in 1692, for Defoe to achieve public office in the City of London, for his reputation was ruined. Later, despite all his requests and manoeuvrings, there was no hope of a position under the Crown elsewhere, despite his occasional statements to the contrary.

Defoe knew he was talented. He believed himself to be more knowledgeable and more energetic than the dignitaries he saw preferred, but he was distrusted and actively disliked. Perversely, throughout Daniel's journalistic career he was most venomous in attacking those individuals who occupied positions that he coveted or careers he would have liked to emulate.

In this account of his life I have largely ignored the stream of Defoe pamphlets on the Test Act and on occasional conformity. Harsh judgement though it might be, in the light of his occupation of a corrupt office under the Crown for over fifteen years, his crusade against others performing just such offices can be held to be little more than hypocrisy, jealousy and cant. Defoe would have argued that it was one thing for a rich or privileged man to behave corruptly or falsely but quite another for a poor man in need of money.

I suggest, by way of mitigation, that there are other explanations for Defoe's persistent pamphleteering against religious conformity and the Test and Corporation Acts in a variety of voices. One is visceral: every Huguenot refugee contemplated the imposition of Dragonards[211] to ensure Catholic conformity in Flanders with dread and loathing; secondly, loyalty and fealty to William Penn may have influenced him, for Quakers were the greatest victims of religious conformity in England; and thirdly, there was a constant need to make money.

Furbank and Owens express their incredulity that Defoe could write nine pamphlets against religious conformity in very different writing styles and narrative voices in a short period of time. However, if

---

[211] Dragonards were spies appointed by the Roman Catholic Church to spy on citizens to ensure religious conformity.

Defoe's objective was to create and sustain an attack on these practices as a service to Penn, and to make money by disputation, it is not possible for the critic to be dogmatic on the issues raised about his authorship of various pamphlets expressing different points of view.

In 1696, Dalby Thomas was instrumental in helping Defoe in another venture from which he made money. In the two years 1696-1697 Defoe was awarded contracts by Greenwich Hospital for the supply of bricks and pantiles to be produced at his brickworks at Tilbury. On the back of this, Defoe was awarded other contracts in Greater London. Dalby Thomas was a member of both the Grand and Fabric Committees of the Hospital and, therefore, in a position to influence the award of contracts.

It has been argued that at this time, for political and journalistic services rendered, Defoe received money from William III. Defoe would like readers to believe that he was close to the monarch for whom, it has been argued, he set up some kind of intelligence network. There were connections to the Court, of whom Thomas Neale was one, but it is doubtful whether they amounted to the relationship suggested by Defoe and some biographers. It is improbable that Defoe had in some way a special or friendly relationship with William, for the social distance between them would have precluded it. Quite apart from the determining factor of class and position, William was an austere and withdrawn figure, often absent abroad and surrounded by his Dutch advisors. For Defoe, William was something of a remote father figure, to be admired at a distance, much as it seemed the young *Crusoe* related to his father.

It has been supposed that Defoe was a member of the Royal Regiment chosen to be 'the guards for their majesties' persons' and thus in a special position at Court. The evidence for this is Oldmixon's description of a military pageant organised in honour of William and Mary on 29 October, 1689, in which Defoe took part. Defoe was there because he had made a special effort with the Butchers Guild to become a liveryman. Of course, he was there also out of a belief in a protestant monarch and the potential opportunities William's reign might offer him. Thirty years later, in one of Gildon's satires, the author imagines Defoe's fright at the thought of serving abroad in the Royal Regiment. It is not likely that Gildon knew for certain, although he may have had a suspicion, whether or not Defoe had military experience.

After a few years, Defoe must have felt much happier. For much of his time he was out of harms way in Essex. The Glass Commission gave him a steady income without demanding much from him. In Tilbury he could continue trading. His brickworks was making money. He had secured an office under the Crown and made powerful friends. He was a big man in Tilbury and was beginning to live the life to which he aspired. In London, if he were careful, he could be near any new political, religious, industrial or scientific development. He put money into property, speculated when he could, and exchanged gossip in the coffee houses, clubs and taverns. He was on the alert for any advantage or threat.

His family arrangements matched the complexity of the life he led. Mary lived with her three daughters, Hannah, Maria and Henrietta. Sarah, his daughter by Elisabeth Sammens, lived in the Sammens home in Cripplegate; but their son, Daniel, was in Tilbury with Benjamin Norton, and later Sophia, his children by Mary Norton. There were mouths demanding food in three places at the same time.

On occasions Defoe is likely to have brought his Tilbury ménage to London when he needed to be there, and for a time his Sammens ménage were accommodated in the City of London. These families and children had to be supported financially on a regular basis. Part of the answer to the question as to why Defoe was obsessed with the need to earn money is that his wives and children needed a steady flow of it.

The evidence in his fiction suggests that the marital arrangement with Mary Norton was happy and successful. She was a simple woman, semi-literate, as her writing shows, with a love of children. Her Quaker background may have made her mild and honest, straightforward and calm. Defoe may not have wanted more children but Mary did. Without Mary being wilful or cunning in any way, they may have come about perfectly normally as the result of an undemanding intimacy.

Defoe had sailed into calmer waters and easier times. On a quiet day, when looking over the Tilbury estuary where trading ships made their way to London or Harwich, his mood may have been bitter-sweet. It could not have been possible to look back without deep melancholy. However, Defoe had a keen sense of the mutability of human existence. As he looked across the steely-grey waters to those great ships on the horizon, he knew that his bankruptcy had changed some things for the worse and *for ever* but that he had come through.

The Road to the Pillory

Chapter 15

Polemics, Journalism and Political Philosophy

Queen Anne was ... a narrow-minded, bigoted woman; the tool of ambitious priests, who wished to protect or increase ecclesiastical power ... and wealth at the expense ... of the community. She showed herself the true daughter of James II. With her the church was always falling (and aspirants gathering places by following) 'the cry of the church is in danger.'

The Life and Times of Daniel Defoe
William Chadwick 1859

On the face of it had William III proved to be an exception to the rule and had turned out to be immortal, no one would have been happier than Daniel Defoe. William was unable to abolish the Test Act, for prudence demanded that he needed the support of Anglicans and the country Tories as well as Whigs and dissenters, but under his tutelage, at least at the beginning of his reign, passions subsided. Anyway, Defoe was willing to cheat. He took public office, kept quiet about it, and concentrated on the task of becoming seriously rich.

When Defoe first began to write, and why, when and what he wrote, is a subject of on-going controversy. Those biographers and academics that tend to inflate Defoe's literary importance ascribe more and earlier written works. However, I do agree with them that it is probable that Defoe was writing, in Sunderland's cause, in the 1680's. I argue in Appendix 2 that Defoe did not write *Historical Collections*, 1683 as such but copied out the work of another; but it is arguable he wrote in support of Roman Catholic Vienna against a Turkish siege in 1683, even though it is dependant on a specious statement in an *Appeal to Honour and Justice*, 1715 written 32 years after the event. If it is assumed that he was writing for Sunderland it is probable that he wrote *A Letter to a Dissenter from his Friend at the Hague*, 1687.

It is my belief that it is possible that the 'Friend' written to was Sunderland, a faithful servant of Charles II and his brother James, Duke of York. Sunderland served Charles II as Secretary of State for the Southern Department between 1682 and 1687 and in other capacities. In 1687, in an attempt to appease both Charles and James, Sunderland openly embraced the Roman Catholic faith. However, Sunderland had important and complex reservations about James from 1687 and James, becoming aware of this, dismissed him in 1688 on the grounds of his disloyalty. Sunderland fled the country.

Manuel Schonhorn writes that 'The determination of Defoe's political stance during the years he was engaged as a government pamphleteer for William III is problematic because of his extensive resort to *personae,* aliases, and satiric voices and the vexing problem of attribution...[it is to be admitted] that Defoe's varied, indirect, and camouflaged defences of the Kings policies, plotted against the divergences of critics of the Revolution then and now, defy analysis'. These seeming divergences arose not so much from Defoe's character but were a consequence of tactical manoeuvring by his political masters, and their unavoidable need to respond to the flux of parliamentary affairs; and, in particular, in the 1680's to Sunderland's difficulties with the Stuart monarchs. In an unstable political system statesmen were obliged to change sides and shuffle their alliances. Survival was as important as principle. It was Defoe's task to assist in the survival of his political masters however they trimmed their sails and shuffled their policy stances.

Defoe may have entered the arena of anonymous authorship of polemical political journalism as a 'mouth piece' for his friend Sunderland. If so it is desirable not to assume that all of the opinions expressed in these polemics were Defoe's but rather the views of his paymaster and as a way of testing opinion in parliament and the capital. It follows from his association with Sunderland that there may be other polemics not claimed as Defoe's in the period 1683-1688. If these realities are accepted the answer to the charges of inconsistency and variability in Defoe's writing lies less with Defoe but with Sunderland

and, in their turn, other members of the Whig Junto. Such conclusions do not make Defoe a journalistic hack. Everything he wrote for his masters incorporated his own flair and, to an extent, his point of view.

Sunderland's supreme achievement in semi-retirement at his ancestral home in the 1690's, where William visited, was to persuade the King to work through a Whig administration rather than to seek to work with an unstable coalition of interests. William III spent much of his time on the continent and regarded Sunderland as a principal conduit to the Whig Junto formed to consolidate its parliamentary dominance - Somers, Halifax, Wharton and Edward Russell, Earl of Orford. Elected for the first time in 1689, the Junto really only began to dominate Parliament from 1693. Sunderland had spotted them all early on in the parliament and they owed their prominence to him. In the propaganda war of the 1690's, Sunderland was able to place polemical journalist assignments to whomsoever he pleased for works written in the interest of both the Junto and the King. He often, but not exclusively, chose Defoe.

Bastian writes:

> Defoe... was becoming 'the secretary of the party' [the Whigs] and the political campaign with which he had been associated for several months would have been impossible without the organisation controlled by the Whig party managers...On the other hand, Defoe would not have embarked on any political manoeuvre without William's approval.

I suggest that in his work Bastian overstates Defoe's role. Defoe received his instructions from Sunderland or a Whig grandee of Sunderland's suggestion. It was for Sunderland to ensure that Defoe understood William's objectives and for Defoe to carry them out. There were no doubt other writers engaged in Whig propaganda and Bastian, among others, exaggerates the importance of Defoe as a prime mover and in believing that he had a 'direct line' or special relationship with William.

Defoe states in a number of places that he received money from

William for his written support of his causes. In particular it is argued that he received a direct payment of a large sum of money from William for the writing of *The True Born Englishman*, 1701; and further that this money enabled him to develop his brickworks. Although this is possible, there is no evidence of direct payment from William. It is far more likely that he would have been paid for pamphlets by Sunderland or a Whig manager for work done on behalf of the Whig cause.

Defoe's writing came to public notice with the publication of *An Essay on Projects* in 1697. It was part of his design to enrich himself by involvement in public projects.[123] The *Essay* is a collection of proposals, all of which were already in the public domain, in the form of projects for bettering society. These projects include Banks, Highways, a Pension Office, Bankruptcy, Academies (in particular an Academy for the improvement of the English language, and an Academy for Women), and the welfare of seamen.

The *Essay* is dedicated to Dalby Thomas and was produced for him. Dalby Thomas was Daniel's mentor at the Glass Commission and the person ultimately responsible for obtaining his appointment. He served on many governmental committees and commissions charged with public welfare and the raising of money for William's wars. State Lotteries and other public projects were seen as ways to raise money for the war.

Dalby Thomas's public prominence, and the career of his associate, Thomas Neale, took a nasty turn when they were arrested in 1699 and charged with embezzling funds from a lottery. Neale was expelled from the House of Commons and died in December of that year. Thomas used the influence of powerful friends to secure his release, but then was charged again for bribery in relation to a distilling bill under consideration by the House of Commons.

Defoe's *Essay* had something of the modern political 'think tank' about it. It disseminated ideas already in circulation and which might catch on in the form of a project. If they did, and as Defoe requests of Dalby, he would like to join in. The mistake that is usually made in commenting upon the *Essay* is to assume that the ideas mooted are

Defoe's. In fact they constitute Defoe's judgement of what projects might catch on and which would capture the energies of his sponsor, and, no doubt, he favoured those projects from which he could benefit.

The projects that Defoe seemed to favour were mostly dirigiste: that is, they depended upon central government initiatives to bring them about and both the capital expenditure and revenue running costs would need to be raised from the taxpayer. These projects have never been greatly favoured in England down to our present time, and those that we remember, such as the Millennium Dome of 2000, are derided.

The triennial elections from 1695 to 1701 all produced more country party Tories who were opposed to the war with France, for which they and their constituents were paying. When in 1697 the Treaty of Rhyswick brought about a welcome peace, these country members led a movement to disband the army, and 'to turn swords into ploughshares'. The Junto Whigs - Halifax, Somers and Russell now Earl of Orford- were confronted with the demand for 'a peace dividend' and the disbanding of the army. There was a need to influence public opinion to maintain a standing army and Somers, the Lord Chancellor, orchestrated the campaign.

The Whigs, through Defoe, joined the public debate in December, 1698 with a pamphlet entitled *A Brief Reply to the History of Standing Armies in England*.[124] The background to the timing of this work is that it was public knowledge that Louis XIV of France was determined to rebuild his army to take advantage of the situation which would follow the anticipated death of Charles II of Spain. William III was determined to resist the French and maintain English preparedness for war. Parliament strongly opposed the maintenance of a standing army in peacetime and a parliamentary resolution was passed reducing the army to eight thousand, so long as they were 'of his Majesty's natural born subjects'. This resolution sought the disbandment of William's trusty Dutch guards.

The pamphlet is closely argued and persuasive and seeks to persuade doubters that an effective army raised and sustained by parliament was not inconsistent with the maintenance of a free parliament under a protestant monarch, and that the alternatives of a militia and the recruitment of foreign troops would not be effective and their advocacy would send the wrong message to England's enemies.

Defoe's motives for writing the pamphlet were mixed. No doubt he believed in the arguments he advanced as they were central to his political values and the Huguenot posture he had adopted but they ran also in the same direction as his financial and family interests. He was writing in support of William III, from whom he was hoping for patronage and preferment, and in support and defence of his own trading interests that would be damaged by French and Spanish control of European seas.[125]

In writing in support of William III and the Junto, Defoe was conscious that the parliamentary tide had turned against the King and now sought to limit his use of arbitrary power. A parliamentary committee investigated the generous grants of public money given by William to his friends, and the punishment of his enemies by the policy of forfeiture of estates in Ireland. When the committee reported, it urged the rescinding of some grants and rewards and William was forced to give way.

In politics the enthusiasm of one moment often turns to disapprobation very quickly. It was only one year earlier that the Peace of Rhyswick had brought the war with France to an end. Its closure, and the attribution of it to William III, was enthusiastically greeted in London. However, William's popularity did not last and the election of 1698 confirmed a widespread public demand for a peace bonus and with it ushered in a period of parliamentary instability.

For the first time in his life, Defoe was active as a propagandist at the highest level in the production of extant works of genuine public interest, written in a persuasive and recognisable style. In the period 1698–1703 there are nineteen works that are ascribed to Defoe on a narrow range of subjects, partly political, which feed into the major parliamentary and diplomatic matters of debate at this time.

As I have argued earlier, Defoe was in touch with royal officials and it is probably true that he saw it as a profitable course of action to support both Sunderland's and the Court's point of view. A close reading of the works does give a very strong impression that on most occasions he was paid to propagate a particular line under the 'editorial direction' of others. However, the language and casuistical skills deployed were his own.

Defoe had most of the right credentials for work as a Whig propagandist. He may have claimed in private conversations to have been a 'participant' in the Monmouth Rebellion, he was a fervent supporter of the Glorious Revolution, and, after his *Essay on Projects* was published in 1697, he was seen as a proven writer on matters of public policy. Apart from the making of much needed money, he must have felt that he could make himself useful and achieve the patronage and place that was so important to him.

The task of identifying Defoe's views is made even more difficult because of the persistent tendency of those who write about him to interpret history in Whig terms and to personalise political issues. It is common to see the period 1698–1702 as a triumph for a Whig struggle to complete the achievement of the Glorious Revolution and thus to place Defoe among the modernising radicals. In reality, the main political division of the time was between the 'country party' and the Court. From 1695 there was a majority for a 'country faction', mainly landed Tories, that inch by inch sought to chip away at a royal prerogative which William was determined both to protect and enlarge.

In becoming an increasingly agitated propagandist for William, at a time when authority was drifting away from his monarch, Defoe alienated all those potential and natural allies who sought to limit the royal prerogative, enlarge parliamentary control of the political agenda, and reduce the national debt and lower taxes.

The struggle for parliamentary supremacy was bitterly fought throughout Defoe's adult life. The Stuarts had attempted to frustrate the claims of revisionists. The University of Oxford was the first to sound the trumpet against the Crown. In July, 1683 the university selected a long list of propositions from the writings of their opponents and condemned them as 'false seditious and impious …and destructive of all government in Church and State.' They went on to assert that all civil authority was derived originally from the people: that there was a mutual contract, tacit or express, between the prince and his subjects, and that 'if he perform not his duty they are discharged from theirs.' The university maintained that the sovereignty of England was in three estates – King, Lords and Commons - and the king had but a co-ordinate power and could rightly be overruled by the other two. Moreover, they asserted that it was possession and strength that gave the right to govern, and success in a cause or enterprise proclaimed it to be lawful and just.

The accession to the throne of William and Mary in 1688 was an endorsement of the university's position but the arguments of the university for limits to the exercise of the royal prerogative remained just as valid during their reign. As William, under the pressure of unceasing warfare against France for advantage on the continent, sought to enlarge his prerogative at the expense of parliament, public sentiment was against him.

Political debate at the time was lively, personal and full of invective to an extent which in modern times would be regarded as illegal on the grounds of libel or anti-racism. Journalists felt no compunction in the making of bloodthirsty attacks on public figures or each other. There was an abiding danger that the worm of government would turn and react savagely under the Sedition Act, as Defoe would discover, but, amazingly, journalists rarely drew back from savage personal attacks. While Lord Somers, if he were careful, could organise, plot and propagandise without fear of sedition proceedings (but not of impeachment) this was not true of Defoe: for even when writing anonymously, his identity as an author could be unmasked by a determined administration.

One such journalistic enemy of Defoe's, who claimed the most impeccable of revolutionary credentials, was John Tutchin. Towards the end of 1699, Tutchin joined in the attack on William and his entourage in a vicious verse-attack entitled *The Foreigners*. The verse related how the 'Israelites' (English) had freed themselves from a tyrant and replaced him by a Prince from 'Gideon' (the United Provinces), but had been mad enough to allow into the country with him a 'boorish brood', born from bogs and 'natures excrement' to pry upon the land. What had the 'Israelites' to do with such vermin as 'Benthic' (William's favourite Hans William Bentinck), who not only devoured whole provinces in 'Israel' but also presumed to divide the possessions of the unfortunate 'Hiram' (King of Spain)? What had they to do with such as 'Keppech' (another of William's favourites, Arnold van Keppel, Earl of Albemarle), who mounted to high position 'by the usual course, Of whoring, pimping, or a crime that's worse'. [that is, sodomy]

Tutchin's retort was a shrewd attack on William and the 'Court faction' and had the merit of being largely true. When the details of the secret Partition Treaties dividing up the King of Spain's possessions upon his death, made without the consent or knowledge of parliament, became public 'heads were to roll', and the knowledge of indefensible patronage, favouritism, corruption and sodomy at the very highest levels of the Court scandalised Anglicans and Dissenters alike.

Tutchin's attack upon the Court was popular and struck home, but it was not his verse that was to echo through time, but Defoe's reply. In his apologia, *An Appeal to Honour and Justice*, 1715, Defoe sought to describe his feelings when reading this attack upon William. He describes the verse as 'a vile abhorred pamphlet...in which the author...fell upon the King himself, and then upon the Dutch nation: and after having reproached his Majesty with crimes that his worst enemy could not think of without horror he sums up all in the odious name of Foreigner.'

Most of Defoe's angry reaction is cant because the essence of Tutchin's attack was true. Defoe knew that it was true because he participated as a supporter of the Court, at the edge of events. But the central theme of the poem Defoe wrote in response to Tutchin stings and sings throughout time: that is, it was nonsense to ascribe the sins of English society to the foreigners in your midst, and that to be addicted to it was to enslave yourself to an arrant absurdity that undermined the citizen's own recognition of identity. Defoe's reply, *The True Born Englishman*, published in 1701, is profound, simple, and recognised by most English people throughout time to be true: that to 'scratch an Englishman is to find an immigrant.'

For most writers, and in particular poets, it would be a dream to carry down through time a single work, a well-turned phrase, or even a single line. In the beginning, when he started to write, Defoe wished to be a poet. He cannot be fairly described as the equal of the great poets of his time, for he is too loose, clumsy, crude and plain but *The True Born Englishman* and the *Hymn to the Pillory* which followed it are memorable and they have passed down to posterity. Their fame was a signal of two things: Defoe's ability to tune in to the most singular and particular of attributes, and his involvement in the spirit of the times.

Defoe is not complimentary about his countrymen, for they are accused of the sin of ingratitude, of 'An ugly, surly sullen, selfish spirit,/Who Satan's worst perfections does inherit'. And he thinks even less of other nationalities, for the Spanish are too proud, Italians too lustful and the Germans are but drunkards. For the English, a mixture of all that is bad, there is no room for boastfulness or false conceit or disparagement of others.

The True Born Englishman is a poem with many memorable lines and succeeds in conveying passion, humour and rage. Defoe uses a compelling rhythm and movement based on repetition. But if the reader feels the better for the reading of the poem, he is also more confused: for Defoe conveys something of the very same splintering of national and personal identity which enables one to disparage a neighbour while feeling no better oneself. It was a difficulty for him and a legacy for today.

The True Born Englishman was an immediate popular success. So much so that in other publications Defoe described himself as the author of it. It went to his head. He felt that he was no longer a bystander but could with equanimity be a participant without danger to himself. Alas, he was wrong.

Defoe's political pamphleteering in the period 1697-1703 is largely confined to a single subject: the War of the Spanish Succession. There were many variants: the maintenance of a standing army, the return of a parliament of right-thinking gentlemen who need not be of the landed interest, and the desirability of settling the claims to the throne of Spain by negotiation and compromise without a war with France. Even when, on the death of James II, Louis recognised his thirteen-year-old son Edward as Pretender to the English throne, Defoe, at least in his public writings, was willing to turn the other cheek so as to maintain a focus on the Spanish issue.

This issue was one of extreme difficulty for the English nation. The controversy was in a sense a rehearsal of what was to come: the resistance to a Napoleonic Europe at the end of the century and to German domination in two twentieth-century wars and, in our own days, opposition to foreign expeditions as part of a war on terrorism. The arguments are always the same. England could never permit foreign powers to dominate the continent and to disrupt its trade and commerce and, at a time of their choosing, to invade its islands.

In these continental matters, Defoe can be seen to be serving his royal master on subjects within a legitimate area of public debate. Emotionally it was easy for him to do so, for his own identity was that of a foreign entity, a Huguenot protestant, as well as an English merchant, an eighteenth-century national equivalent of a British Muslim today.

It is significant that in this fusillade of words Defoe has nothing to say about the Act of Settlement of 12 June, 1701 which succeeded in settling the succession in favour of Anne while limiting the royal prerogative in ways which William must have found humiliating. The Act of Settlement is rightly seen as cementing the supremacy of parliament and establishing legally that a monarch ruled only so long as he recognised it. The Act has been seen as a triumph for the revisionist movement and an achievement of the Whigs, to whom Defoe was loosely aligned at the time; but in reality, as Feiling argues, it represented the constant constitutional programme of the 'country party' since the Revolution of 1689.

As Defoe did not write anything, at least which is extant, on the Act, we can but suppose his thoughts. He would have approved of the Act's legal definition of the powers of individual members of the Privy Council, that no pardon should bar an impeachment, a clause forbidding placemen to be members, and measures to protect the independence and security of tenure of judges.

On the other hand, Defoe's allegiance to his past paymaster, William, would have caused him difficulty: no future sovereign after this Act could rush England into war as William had done in 1689, or could leave England for months in time of peace, or employ foreigners in the Privy Council. In the Act of Settlement it was stipulated that Sophia, the Electress Dowager of Hanover and her family, were to succeed to the throne if neither Princess Anne nor William had any more children. In the event, William turned against Sophia and she did not succeed, but at the time it seemed that she would.

Defoe decided that he would record, not baptise, the birth of a child and name a new daughter Sophia. He did this at St John's parish church in Hackney. The record reads, '1701 Dec.24. Sophia dau. of Daniel de Foe by Mary his wife'. It is my belief that this child was by his third 'wife' Mary Norton. He had not been living with Mary Tuffley for nine years, but he was co-habiting with the second Mary in Tilbury. By merely recording Sophia's name, Defoe avoided the need for mother and child to be present. As a Quaker, Mary Norton would not have baptised her child in an Anglican church.

So why did Defoe do it? It is a question posed time and again of Defoe's actions by his biographers. There is obvious self-seeking. If Sophia was to succeed William, Defoe may have had the thought that he would be able to say that he was one of the first to recognise her significance; there could be no more loyal profession of allegiance to this new majesty than naming your own daughter after her. It was an act of fealty.

From 1697-1702 Defoe continued his practice of writing against occasional conformity. He wrote four times attacking it. He did so in the most logical and biting terms and by naming defaulters, upbraiding them for a 'new sort of religion that looked two ways'.

The desire for a place within a national church, for 'comprehension', had been an unfulfilled Cromwellian aspiration and the schism of 1661–1962 had been deeply regretted by Presbyterians even when they followed their ministers into dissent. Occasional conformity could be seen as a healing medicine although Defoe was probably right in his belief that it encouraged movement back to the Anglican Church.

In practice you make few converts by insulting people and maligning their characters. In the long run it was not legislation alone that changed men's civil rights and dignities but a toleration of differences, a lowering of tension to the point at which discriminatory laws could be changed or allowed to pass into desuetude without discontent. Men learnt to live by the civilisation of double standards.

As has been argued earlier, Defoe himself had benefited from 'occasional conformity' in that he had sworn an oath of allegiance to the Crown and attended communion at an Anglican church in order to take up and maintain his appointment as accountant to the Glass Commissioners.

To be fair to Defoe, he made a distinction between an office holder, who had to take an Anglican communion to keep or be chosen to do an official job, and a person performing a political office, such as a mayoralty, when the office holder already had an occupation. However, this is a distinction without a difference for the principle is the same. And, if we are to be strictly balanced, it can be added that Defoe was running a brick factory and obtaining money through journalism, which were his occupations at the time of his taking of an oath and attending Anglican communions.

At this time, Defoe's agitation on occasional conformity might have been caused by frustration at exclusion from City offices. It would be understandable if a failure in business, expulsion from membership of a church and potent challenges to tenets of religious belief had caused some loss of self-belief and had undermined his sense of personal identity.[128] However, it is my belief that in writing like this Defoe was honouring a pledge he had given William Penn, for Quakers were the greatest sufferers from conformity laws.

On 2 December, 1697 a man acting quickly, in fear of detection and public arrest, and with some agitation, posted a copy of Defoe's pamphlet, *An Enquiry into the Occasional Conformity of Dissenters, in Cases of Preferment*, on the door of St Paul's Cathedral. On this day, Sir Humphrey Edwin, a well-known dissenter and Lord Mayor of London, was to attend a thanksgiving service in the Cathedral. The *Post Man* reported it as a 'foolish pasquil, reflecting on the Lord Mayor' posted on the door. Did Defoe post his own pamphlet, so invoking the practice of Martin Luther and asserting the rights of protestants to dissent from established church practices? It was a histrionic gesture, of which Defoe was capable. Anecdotally, it was accepted that he did post the pamphlet.

What is undoubtedly true is that in the period 1700–1703 Defoe was not a mere man of past memories and words but of action. He supposed, albeit wrongly, that parliament would not act to defend his monarch and through him the protestant cause and that he, Daniel Defoe, must take action to ensure it.

It was a highly dangerous and foolish conclusion to reach and the actions which arose from it succeeded in alienating friend and foe alike. In this period Defoe repeatedly lost all rational control of himself, to the dismay of others and to the detriment of family, friends and himself. In November, 1700 Sir Thomas Abney had attended a service at St Paul's followed by attendance at his usual Meeting House at which John How was the preacher. Defoe reissued his 1697 pamphlet specifically addressed to How. He asked a question: 'If the Service of their Country be so dear to them, pray why should they not chuse to expose their bodies and their estates for that Service rather than their souls?' How fought back, confident that he was speaking for the majority of dissenters, and an acrimonious exchange took place.

Such a debate merely enraged proponents and opposers alike and fuelled the animosity that led, through a Commons committee, to a move to abolish occasional conformity. The Bill died a natural death with the death of William III. Logically, Defoe should have supported such a bill but when it was re-introduced in 1702 under Queen Anne but he opposed it on the ground that it was part of a fearful tightening of the screw against dissenters.

It is not known with certainty what role Defoe took in the preparation of a petition to parliament by the Kentish Petitioners urging preparation for war against France. However, in September, 1701 in a pamphlet which included the text of the petition in which the Petitioners urged the dissolution of the House of Commons because it did not act to protect them against a French invasion, he makes a vigorous defence of the Petitioners. Almost certainly the petition was part of the Whig agitation against the government orchestrated by Lord Somers, and it is probable that Defoe had been in touch with him. The House reacted vigorously to this challenge to their authority and after a five-hour debate arrested the five men of Kent who had presented the petition.

Their treatment provoked Defoe to the authorship of a far more revolutionary attempt to influence the Commons to act against its will. In *Legion's Memorial* he listed fifteen grievances against the present House of Commons and demanded in the name of all the people of England that 'all just national debts be discharged, all persons illegally imprisoned be released or bailed, John How be made to retract his aspersions on the king, vigorous resistance be given to the growing power of France, and the thanks of the House be offered to the Kentish Petitioners'. It ends, 'Our name is Legion, and we are many.'[129] Defoe professed to be acting for the people of England and he writes, 'but if you continue to neglect it [the petition], you may expect to be treated according to the Resentments of an injur'd Nation; for Englishmen are no more to be Slaves to Parliaments, than to a King'.

While these sentiments are in line with the views expressed by Oxford University that 'all civil authority came from the people', Defoe goes further: his is a threat to overturn parliament by the power of the mob. He might state that the French had bought individual Members but William had done like-wise. Parliament believed that in the ultimate reckoning a parliament man was thought likely to exercise his vote according to the national interest. Parliament was not to be set aside on an issue of judgement by a threat from the street.

There has been controversy about the method of delivery of this troublesome petition to the Commons on 14 May, 1701. The controversy requires the biographer to take a considered view about several matters. Was Defoe acting in concert with Harley in the preparation and delivery of the petition? If they were acting in concert, which is my own belief, what does it tell posterity about the personalities of both men and the nature of their relationship? The current inclination is to believe Defoe when he wrote that he marched into the House of Commons guarded with about sixteen gentlemen of quality. Such a belief increases the solemnity and significance of the occasion and the social importance not only of the act itself but to those who supported and delivered it.

In aligning himself with numerous men of quality in his presentation of the event, Defoe was repeating a common technique of his in asking the reader to assume that he was acting for numerous others and assuming an important leadership role when in fact he was acting alone. However, the presence of these gentlemen would not have prevented action being taken against Defoe.

Oldmixon gives a different version. He writes that Defoe asserted the manifesto in a letter addressed to Harley in his capacity as the Speaker of the Commons. If so, although there is no evidence, it might be assumed that Harley was willing to present the petition in his own interest but misjudged the mood of the House.

An older anecdote quoted by George Chalmers is more intriguing – and persuasive. He suggests that Defoe, disguised as a washer-woman, presented the petition to Harley as he entered the House. This older tradition suggests to the reader that Defoe might have been the sort of person who would dress-up as a woman and that Harley was a person who enjoyed the pretence of it. If this were to be true, .the incident relies on Defoe's willingness and enjoyment of cross-dressing and Harley's knowledge and acceptance of it. This anecdote is well-sourced. George Chalmers obtained it from David Polhill, the son of one of the arrested Kentish Petitioners, who had heard it directly from his father. In *Beyond Belief* I state my belief that Harley and Defoe had met each other on the introduction of William Patterson well before 1701.[212]

An anonymous writer made a vitriolic attack on Defoe and Harley for their behaviour. This writer accused them of meeting at Rummers coffee house as close friends in 1701 'where a Set of Whiggish Furies daily met' to write *Legions Memorial.* [213]

The pamphlet attacks Harley, and by implication Defoe, as a sodomite. If the writer is right in his accusations, it would imply that that Harley and Defoe concocted *Legion's Memorial* together and enjoyed the experience. If this is so, and I think that the balance of the evidence supports the conjecture, it is entirely possible that they invented a novel way of getting it to the attention of the House of Commons.

This incident requires an explanation of the nature of their friendship and collaboration in early eighteenth-century terms. In an earlier chapter I discuss Defoe's sexuality and throughout this work I have given conjectural evidence of Defoe's cross-dressing and passionate attachments to various men. Harley's sexuality is less certain. However, I give conjectural evidence in a recent book on Swift that Harley had a sexual relationship with him. In this book I point out two conclusions from gender studies: first, that there is strong and diverse evidence that eighteenth century gender splits between men and women did not occur in the way we now describe and understand them, until the second half of the century; and secondly, that the giving and receiving of sexual favours in return for patronage at earlier dates was commonplace. [214]

Harley was seeking to navigate himself from a role of Speaker of the House to Principal Secretary of State. He seems to have thought that

---

[212] Beyond Belief, 299, n.130.
[213] *The Welsh Monster.*
[214] Martin John. *The Man Himself: A Life of Jonathan Swift,* Anglian Publishing 2009.

de-stabilising the Administration worked in his favour at this time. Whether it did or not, he succeeded in climbing the 'greasy pole'.

Legion's Memorial advances the doctrine in the most clear and unavoidable polemic that parliament existed by the consent of the people and that if this position of trust was abused by default and bad faith, or by neglect, the authority of parliament could be first challenged and then overthrown. In this Defoe was restating the constitutional argument of Oxford University. But the pamphlet reads as the defeated demand of the Levellers of the English Civil War and exposed Defoe to the charge, which he denied, that he was one.

In practice, Defoe was demanding that the duty of parliament was the defence of its protestant religion, of William its protector, and of the realm which made these things possible. It was a stinging attack expressed and delivered in such a way as to confound and repel its audience – parliament, the Anglican bishops, the Tory placemen and country members – and to stir them into retreat. From the moment that those who had been attacked by the pamphlet recognised that Defoe stood behind it, they marked him out for revenge.

The political debate changed in March, 1702 when William III died as a result of falling off a horse in Windsor Park. The accession of Anne led to a dramatic change in political and religious fortunes. The Junto Whigs - Somers, Halifax and Orford - were swept from office. In came Rochester, the queen's uncle; and into the Treasury came Nottingham, a narrow-minded Anglican, as Principal Secretary of State. In the offices of state and the corridors of Westminster Palace new, and not so new, elites worked to create a parliamentary composition which would give a Tory majority, to perpetuate themselves, and to restore the fortunes of Queen Anne's beloved Church of England. The panoply of hated Dutch advisors and their hangers-on left the country.

In pulpits at university chapels and up and down the country, preachers denounced in ringing tones recusants, rebels and dissenters; now was a time for the revenge of the righteous. Among them and leading the pack was Reverend Henry Sacheverill who had published a sermon that attacked dissenters in forthright terms. It is said that 'nobody not alive at the time' could fully recognise the fears and anguish of dissenters. In the United Kingdom, it is known that this is not true, for those who lived through the troubles of Northern Ireland in the last thirty years of the twentieth century know that brand of religious bigotry only too well.

It was all too much for Defoe. How he felt is best deciphered from *Crusoe's* discovery of 'the Shore Spread with Bones', for the High Flyers of the Anglican Church threatening to bang on Defoe's door (or so he imagined it) were for *Crusoe* the native savages invading the peace of his island. *Crusoe* finds bones on a shore and a boat far out at sea but approaching the island. He writes:

> I looked up with the utmost affection of my soul ... gave God thanks... I was ...distinguished from such dreadful creatures... I continued pensive and sad [then] I thought nothing but how I might destroy some of these monsters ... I contrived to dig a hole under the place where they made their fire and put some five or six pound of gunpowder [there] ... I loaded muskets [at the place where they might land] ... [and then, much later] I saw that God [had granted me] the protection of His Providence.

In real life Defoe was not pacific. At this time, his heart was full of rage, and often despair gripped him. Just as he was poised to become a person of distinction, in serving a royal master and the true protestant cause, his hopes were confounded, to the joy of his enemies. He just had to do something about it.

Chapter 16

Public Disgrace

It was a wretched thing for a Mother thus to see her own Son, a handsome comely young Gentleman...and durst not make herself known to him.

Moll Flanders
Daniel Defoe 1722

I have conjectured that Defoe accompanied William Penn to America in September, 1699 and returned to England by August, 1700. I give an outline for my reasons in *Alien Come Home.* [215] I alter some of the detail in this account. In the chapter here on *Moll Flanders* I give my current reasoning. When I first wrote about this I supposed that the visit was mainly motivated by the emotional needs of Defoe and his sister Mary to be reunited with a son. However, on reflection I think that the principal reason for the second trip was to enable Mary to come into an inheritance in South Carolina left to her by Defoe's 'former mother in law' Jone Reade who was the fictional 'mother'. I suggest that a condition of an inheritance was that Mary had first to 'settle' in America for some period of time and that this is what she did. From this complicated transaction Defoe would have come into some badly needed money.

An absence of this length would have affected Defoe's written output. Bastian writes about the 'drying up' of Defoe's pen:

> During the eighteen months from the early summer of 1699 to November 1700 there were no political tracts: nor did he grind any of his personal axes. The only known piece of work he published during these month's was his poem *The Pacificator* which appeared on 29 February, 1700...it was the kind of thing that Defoe could have thrown off in a few winter evenings.'[216]

---

[215] *Alien Come Home*, 51-55.
[216] Bastian, 221.

Furbank and Owens suggest that if *The Pacificator* was written in reaction to any contemporary event or circumstance that it was in response to a pamphlet entitled *A Short View of the Immorality of the English Stage*, 1698. Such a reaction would have been most appropriate in 1698. The appearance of the poem in 1700 may have been at the request of Defoe prior to embarkation or an act of entrepreneurship by the printer.

Similar difficulties arise in relation to two pamphlets published by Defoe late in 1700: *The Two Great Questions Considered*, in November and *The Two Great Questions Further Considered* in December. In the latter Defoe explains that he had written the first pamphlet before Louis XIV had recognised the claim of the Duke of Anjou to the Spanish throne. This leaves open the date at which he wrote it. The date at which the claim became publicly known was 4 November, 1700.

There was a similar delay in the publication of *The True Born Englishman*. By Defoe's own account it was written in response to a poem by Tutchin published in August, 1700. Defoe's response did not appear until six months later.

Bastian comments on correspondence between King William, Sunderland and Somers. William had written to Sunderland seeking his support for the issue of a pamphlet explaining threatening political developments in Europe. On 15 September, 1699 Sutherland sent the King's letter to Somers with one of his own. He wrote that the problem needed illumination and rebutting because of 'the proceedings of the present Ministry which began at the King's return from Holland in the previous year…The breaking of the last Parliament…the care that was taken by them and their friends upon the death of the King of Spain to persuade the World that a war would undo us…' On 30 September, 1699 Somers replied that a thing of that name had been promised and on 3 October added that 'The paper desired would certainly have a good effect. It was promised, and it is to be believed to be ready printed. But for some reasons that the writer conceals, it is not yet appeared and there is a doubt when it will.' My conjecture is that Defoe sailed to America at the same time as William Penn in September, 1699. Bastian suggests that the writer commissioned by Somers was Defoe. The missing pamphlet would appear to have been *The Two Great Questions Considered.*[217]

In 1702 Defoe's position as a trusted polemical pamphleteer of the Whigs was gravely undermined by death: first, the death of William III in March and the subsequent accession of Anne to the throne, and secondly by the death of Sunderland in September. The Whigs were out of power. It had always been dangerous to write in support of a political faction but anonymity and the patronage of powerful men had shed the risk for Defoe. Defoe's protection no longer existed.

In December, 1702 an anonymous pamphlet was published in London. It was a satire written in the voice of a Henry Sacheverill, and titled *The Shortest Way with The Dissenters: or Proposals for the Establishment of the Church of England.* The author stated that for nearly fourteen years God had suffered the purest and most flourishing church in the world to be humiliated by its enemies but that now the throne was occupied by a true friend to the Church of England (Queen Anne) the day of deliverance was at hand. It continued by urging an end to a tolerance which punished recusancy by a mere fine, for it was a crime to separate from the true church. If a simple law was passed condemning any person at a conventicle to be banished and the preacher hanged there would be no more talk of disunion. 'With popery on the one hand, and schismatics on the other, how has the Church been crucified between two thieves [...] Now let us Crucifie the Thieves.'

Extreme Anglicans, including Sacheverill, greeted the pamphlet with enthusiasm while dissenters received it with dismay as a prediction of the fate that awaited them. It took but a few days for the public to realise that it had been duped. No one was pleased: Anglicans thought it a vile abuse and dissenters that it had placed honest men at risk. The Queen, identified as the prime mover of extremist measures, was outraged; new placemen and the Queen's new advisors were suspicious

---

[217] *Alien Come Home*, 56.

of what they understood as 'party moves' to de-stabilise the new administration, and the government's political opponents ran for cover.

Harley had felt obliged to advise Godolphin that the author of the *Shortest Way* had to be discovered and Daniel Finch, the austere Secretary of State of the Southern region was tasked with the search. The finger of suspicion pointed at the recently ousted Whigs. A warrant was issued for the arrest of Edward Bellamy one of the Whig's party agents and a familiar figure among London printers. He confessed to taking Defoe's manuscript to the printer George Croome. Next day Nottingham issued a writ for Defoe's arrest. Defoe's papers were to be collected from his lodgings at the Sammens and brought to him.

Defoe's attack in *The Shortest Way* was not upon an externalised form, such as an Act of Parliament. It read as a personal attack upon Queen Anne and her compliance to advisors. Unfortunately for Defoe it is possible that among his papers at the Sammens was a bawdy and insulting poem about Dr Hamilton, the Queens physician and her knighting of her by a raised leg. It reads:

> The Queen rose up, the Doctor kneeled,
> And lifting up the Royal leg,
> With gout and dropsie swell'd full big.
> Over his head she raised it high,
> As sword is brandisht in the skie
> Rise up, Sir David, says the Queen,
> The first Cunt knight that e'er was seen. [218]

Ultimately the Queen was to be guided by the advice of her Minister's on any punishment of Defoe but to the extent that she might have been persuaded to exercise a royal discretion an insult such as this was unlikely to influence her to go easy on Defoe whatever the special pleading.

Nottingham issued a warrant for Defoe's arrest. Defoe went into hiding with the hope that the whole affair would blow over. Bastian suggests that Defoe fled to Scotland, a former retreat outside the

---

[218] *Beyond Belief*, 17.

jurisdiction of the English Courts. If he had stayed there he would have been safe. It appears, however, that he had to return to London to deal with a persistent and dangerous creditor. If so, he misjudged the balance of risk, for he was arrested at Nathaniel Sammens home on information leaked to the authorities.

There began a complicated game of shadow boxing. Nottingham caused Defoe to be taken from Newgate Prison to his rooms at the Palace of Whitehall where he questioned him at considerable length. Nottingham was convinced that there was a 'party' for whom Defoe was acting. These suspicions were well-founded. The administration was in a deadly political game for survival; and one in which they would eventually lose out. But at this moment it was free to act. It was an opportunity for Defoe to do a deal. If he told all he knew of the matters he had been involved in over the past two years, and if this amounted to something worthwhile, he might escape punishment.

Defoe was released from prison on bail set so high that it might be supposed by a dispassionate observer that Nottingham's suspicions were well-founded and that behind Defoe, and those who stood as surety for him, were others of mightier means. Defoe appeared to have been highly complacent. He thought that the whole affair would play over; he spun the issue out in the hope that it would be overtaken by other affairs of greater consequence.

Then with patience running low Defoe was indicted for Seditious Libel in June, 1703 at the Old Bailey, in a trial presided over by the Lord Mayor of London, Sir Samuel Dashwood. Included among the judges were Sir Edward Ward, Sir John Fleet, Sir Edward Clark and Sir Thomas Abney, all of whom had reason to resent Defoe. Whatever the technical and legal arguments, and there were some, there was no hope of a fair trial. Defoe had been persuaded to plead guilty in the hope of leniency. He was sentenced to a fine of 200 marks, to stand in the pillory on three separate occasions for the duration of an hour, and to find sureties for good behaviour for a period of seven years. It was a heavy blow, but it could have been worse.

Defoe had been visited in prison by William Penn's son also called

William. As a result of the visit Defoe wrote the following remarkable letter to Penn from Newgate.[219]

> [I] Lett you Kno' with all the Thankfulness I am capable ...of your Extraordinary Kindness:- Concerning for your Self For me So much a Stranger to you [and] in the Manner in which they Proposed it I had No Person to Discover...not Accomplices, No Sett of Men...[and I] Entreat the Continuous of those Kind Offices you have so generously undertaken.

[Signed] An Unknown Captive

These words echo the undertaking agreed between Captain Singleton and William the Quaker in *Captain Singleton*.[220] These two characters agree with each other that on their return to England:

1. They would be *strangers* to each other in public.
2. Defoe would *reveal nothing* of what they had been involved in to others, except to his sister.
3. The truth of it should never be *spoken or written* about in public.
4. They would always act as *'brothers'* and would help each other. (Italics mine).

Penn told Lord Godolphin that Defoe would make a full confession. Godolphin wrote to Nottingham on 17 July as follows:

> Mr William Penn came to see mee to tell me that he had acquainted my Lord Privy Seal [Buckingham] that de Foe was ready to make oath to your Lhp. of all that he knew, and to give an Account of his Accomplices...provided he may be excused from the punishment of the pillory, and not produced as Evidence against any person.

Penn was on friendly terms with Queen Anne because he had known her when young and because of Penn family support of her father Charles II. Remarkably, Penn had urged Defoe to tell the truth

[219] H.7.
[220] *Captain Singleton*, 244.

by which he meant to confess the names of those who employed him to write the *Shortest Way* and for what reasons. Nottingham would also have hoped to get Defoe to reveal what else he knew of the alleged sins and omissions of the Whig administration.

Defoe wrote a humble supplication to the Queen excusing himself of any intent to commit an offence of sedition and to name anyone else. William Penn achieved the impossible: he persuaded the Queen to grant Defoe a full audience at Windsor Castle. A carriage collected him from Newgate and took him to Windsor Castle on 21, July. The Queen and the administration were not impressed by Defoe's bland protestations of loyalty. What they wanted was a full confession with names. Writing about this audience Nottingham stated, 'As to de Foe the Queen seems to think…that his Confession amounts to nothing.'

I have maintained, and sought to prove, that Penn and Defoe had been close friends for 40 years and that they were pledged to keep their relationship a secret. It can be argued that there was nothing remarkable about Penn's help to Defoe at this point. Penn was a champion of dissenters and regularly advised them how to protect themselves against prosecution. However, to my knowledge, Penn had never sought to obtain a royal audience for any of them. Penn's intervention at this point was prudent and careful. There was no public knowledge of what he was doing and he did not visit Defoe in prison.

I have also set out a proof that *Captain Singleton*, Defoe's alter ego in the fiction of that name, was a real person with a relationship to both Penn and Defoe. In his correspondence Penn alludes to Defoe although, in accordance with their agreement, he does not mention him by name. In a letter to Charlwood Lawton, his America agent, dated July 5 1701, Penn wrote:

> Shall wee after all our Noble Hazards and Many Disappointments on our Essays and after making Colonies for the Crown at our Own Cost be made and Treated as Less Creatures than the Mayors of the Meanest Corporations of England and Ireland may as Criminals and Publick Enemies and Every Little Mercinary Toole Countenance agst our

Merritt upon the Crown for our Industrious and Successful Adventure, If it must be thus Commend to the Eng:men a Satry.

And in a second letter to the same man dated August 18, 1701, he wrote:

But if those Little Tools [his opponents in Pennsylvania] Can find Credit there that Have none here to ruin the Meritorious, the Author of the True born Eng:man a satyr.

The Editors of Penn's *Papers*, express the view that both these allusions are to Daniel Defoe and his work *The True Born Englishman*. 221

The linkage of Penn to Captain Singleton is established by the following letter James Logan sent to Penn dated 11 January 1701 'Consign all though send me to ed. Singleton in Berbados [Barbados] no need to tell RE [Robert Egerton, the official agent] knows it.222

I regard the account I have given of the relationships between Sunderland, Penn, Singleton and Defoe as an important element of the proof I offer of the birth of Defoe in 1644. In asserting this I am relying on a definition of evidence as applied in an English court which permits circumstantial evidence to be admitted when it falls into a comprehensive and thus defensible pattern. Clearly, the proof I have advanced of Defoe's birth is strongly supported by unimpeachable documentary evidence; but the relationships between the four men is a mixture of documentary evidence and conjecture. This evidence presupposes three of the people, all of a similar age, embarked on a version of the Grand Tour in 1662 and that they were collaborators between 1680 and 1702.

On the face of it, there is no rational explanation for so crass and ill-judged an intervention in the affairs of state at so inflammable a moment as the publication of *The Shortest Way*. It was a crucial misjudgement arising from a sense of injury and personal vanity. In the

---

221 *Alien Come Home*, 69-70.
222 Penn, William. *Papers,* Vol. 4, 58, 66, and n. 7.

first place it was plain wrong to assume that the immunity from legal prosecution that Defoe enjoyed while writing in defence and support of William and his administration could somehow be extended to him when he was attacking an administration he opposed, for even his powerful political associates lacked such an immunity.

Defoe seems not to have understood that an attack upon a royal official or, in Queen Anne's case, Anglican bishops and priests, was treated in law as an attack on the royal personage appointing them. Defoe's explanation that he was attacking the extremes of Anglicanism did not run, for Anne herself was part of the extreme.

There were intellectual errors and confusions. They raise the issue of Defoe's intellectual perspective and the need – seemingly endless- to 'look both ways'. *The Shortest Way* was an ingenious and convincing satire in an age of satire. Defoe genuinely believed that it was through satire that the 'truth' could be revealed. Moreover, he believed that there was such a 'truth' and that he had in *The Shortest Way* revealed it. This was his defence. He posed a question to himself. What had he done? His defence was that he had revealed (proven, really) the proposition he had addressed. Defoe tended to assume that the 'truth' was a quantifiable entity and could be proved if the mind was addressed to it. Not for him the proposition that not every problem has a solution, or any acceptance of the notion that once an intellectual position was arrived at it should be treated as a provisional outcome.

In 1705 in replying to a particularly nasty attack on him by Lord Haversham, Defoe suggested that he might more likely have ended in the peerage than in the pillory had William III continued to live. In defending himself from Haversham, Defoe makes a claim for himself. He writes, 'I was ever True to one Principle, I never betrayed my Master or my Friend; I always Espoused the cause of Truth and Liberty, was ever on one side and that cause was ever right; I have Liv'd to be ruined for it, and I have Liv'd to see it Triumph over Tyranny.' These are brave words, indeed, but even when allowance is made for the occasion and the rhetoric, the informed reader knows this defence to be simplistic and wrong.

It is possible to argue that in *The Shortest Way* Defoe was making a serious attempt to deflect the new administration from a change of policy and to persuade Queen Anne to shift her general position closer to the Whigs by ridiculing extremist advisors. If so, it was a serious intellectual endeavour which miscarried because of the fever of the time.

Defoe hints of his involvement with 'a party' in *Hymn to the Pillory*. The poem was circulated by his supporters at the pillory. In it he asserts that he was being punished for not betraying his friends. Defoe's principal defence in this poem is that he was the victim of the state's punishment of authorship and that the pillory was the machinery by which it punished 'fancy'. It is easy to agree with Defoe, for by any modern standards his punishment was barbarous and unjustifiable. And, of course, it is true, as Defoe argues, that if 'justice' was extended to the rich and powerful in society the numbers of such cases would be too great for the state to handle. But Defoe's attempt to claim to belong to the tradition of past dissenting victims is less convincing; his offence was not at one with that of the protestant martyrs who went before him.

If modern standards of behaviour and legality are applied to Defoe's case, it can be argued that his highly personal attacks on others would be treated as libels and he would have been challenged in the courts by those defamed. Admittedly, Defoe lived at a time of vicious personal attacks by journalists, but even by contemporary standards he was not 'slow in coming forward'.

In delivering the poem to the mob surrounding the pillory, Defoe bravely challenged them. Did they, he asks, really know what was happening? Well, perhaps they did not, but then, perhaps they did. Those who knew what the Sheriff's men found when they rifled through his personal documents, the letters and lampoons, might well have thought, 'God almighty, he was really asking for it!'

If this is so, why such serious misjudgements by Defoe?[132] There was a kind of conceit here. Defoe saw his action as a last throw of the dice, a vain attempt to retain influence as the ground shifted beneath him. Was it more than a misjudgement? Was it a breaking point? Perhaps he could not bear the stress any longer. Recklessly, he plunged on. Action was the only way he could escape from unbearable tension and fear. He could not avoid making these terrible mistakes.

Chapter 17

Harley's Man

...at last I was very handsomely attack'd by a Person of Honour...he gave me Money so often...that I had seldom so little as seven or eight hundred pounds a year from him.

Roxana, of Lord H.
Roxana
Daniel Defoe 1724.

Daniel Defoe was rescued from prison by Lord Robert Harley and was indebted to him for both protection and money for eight years or as Defoe/*Roxana* tells readers 'I held this wicked Scene of Life for eight years.' This period of time was between 1704-1705 and 1712-1713; that is the period between Defoe's release from prison in 1704 and regular propaganda work for Harley, and the ending of payments from the Glass Commission and closure of the *Review* in 1712 and 1713 respectively.

Defoe must have thought that he was condemned to rot in Newgate Prison for lack of funds to pay the court fine, legal expenses and the recognizance levied on him for his good behaviour over the next seven years. In reality that fear was ended after six months when Harley came forward with administration monies to pay for his court costs and to buy off Defoe's immediate pressing creditors.

Defoe's financial position was seriously undermined during his incarceration. It is thought that his brother in law, Robert Davies, had tried to help him out at the Tilbury pantile factory but if so his efforts had not saved it. There is no evidence that any new sales had been won in the period, debt had accumulated, staff and creditors were overdue, and rent to his landlords Ghiselyn, Mauresco and Stamper of £1,050 had been incurred. Backscheider demonstrates that a number of substantial creditors launched claims against him in the courts and he was hard-pressed to deal with them. Defoe claimed to Harley that he had lost some £3,000 during his imprisonment and that this sum had bankrupted him once again, but there is no way of knowing whether that was true. If true, numerous new creditors would have been added to the old. These creditors would have sought him out. Subterfuge and government protection were needed to avoid them.

What is not known is that Defoe lost his home in Tilbury, the Manor House of East Gubyons, in his effort to get out of prison. In 1704, Earl Robert Bedingfield, the London Sheriff charged with obtaining appropriate recognisances, had the lease of the Manor House put into his name. A release enabled the lease to be transferred back in a year's time. The release no longer survives. The deed states that the Manor House was recently in the possession of Thomas King. I believe that this Thomas King was Defoe's brother. There was only one other Thomas King living in Tilbury at the time and he was a yeoman farmer.[223]

There was always an emotional cost for precipitating a failure, however he might shrug it off. He would have had feelings of despair at the closure of his premises at Freeman's Yard following his bankruptcy in 1692 and now, once more, at the loss of his Tilbury establishment.

Defoe's rescue from prison by his powerful friend, Lord Harley, a member of the government and the Speaker of the House of Commons, was not accidental. It did not arise as written by Defoe. Biographers usually account for Harley's interest in rescuing Defoe by asserting that he was keen to gain Defoe as a propagandist in his cause and to prevent his use by the Whigs. Defoe wrote about it and his rescuer in *An Appeal to Honour and Justice*. He writes 'a Message was brought me [in prison] from a person of Honour, who, till that time, I never had the least acquaintance with, or knowledge of... by word of mouth thus: Pray ask that Gentleman, what I can do for him?' Defoe replied in Biblical terms. According to Defoe, four months later, Harley having nudged the Earl of Nottingham to one side and then out of the government entirely, represented his case to the Queen, who gave his legal wife Mary Tuffley a thousand pounds, and Harley paid a further

---

[223] ERO. D/DC 23/633-644 Deeds concerning the Manor of Gobyons.

£1,000 to Defoe to take care of his immediate creditors.

Defoe's account as interpreted by others is not strictly accurate. Existing biographical accounts omit other considerations. It is important to get the record straight because Defoe's relationship with Robert Harley is crucial to the understanding of the next ten years of his life. Harley was not a stranger to Defoe. It is likely that they were collaborators from 1698 when Defoe with a sound reading of likely future political events asked William Patterson to give him a formal introduction. Defoe had written to Patterson in April,1703 asking him to intercede with Harley on his behalf and Patterson passed on the letter to Harley in May. Harley had sent a man to see Defoe in prison – but seemingly nothing followed from it. Harley had to bide his time for political events to take their course. When safe to intervene he did so.

I have drawn attention to a hostile pamphlet, entitled the *Welsh Monster*, written anonymously in 1708. This writer accused Harley of collaborating with Defoe to write *Legion's Memorial* in 1701 to the public knowledge of leading Whigs and in a concerted political campaign with them. This writer suggests that the two of them were conducting a homosexual relationship and that Robert Harley was a sodomite.[134] If any of this is true, and a reading of the original pamphlet is compelling in its allegations, it is not likely that Harley was entirely innocent of the stratagems that put Defoe into prison and the pillory. Once Defoe was imprisoned, Harley had no option but to wait for the right moment to get him out.

The issue of Harley's sexual behaviour is difficult to resolve. Some readers will think that the raising of it is unfair to both men. In my work on Jonathan Swift I suggested that there was a sexual link between Harley and Swift as a kind of pre-condition to Harley using him as a propagandist. Swift was adamant that he did not receive money from Harley although it was offered. There is absolutely no question that Defoe received a great deal of money. Harley provided him with a stream of money for the next ten years. By Defoe's own admission there was never a year when he received less than £400.

What has not been appreciated is that Defoe received a sum of at least £150 a year from his position as accountant to the Glass Commission for thirteen years after the tax was dropped and the Commission defunct. It was Harley who signed off the final accounts in 1712 when his hold on power was weakening. Similarly Defoe's editorship of the *Review* in the period 1703-1713, was subsidised by Harley.

The evidence suggests that Defoe sought to replace William III, with an alternative 'father figure' and chose Robert Harley as his patron and 'protector'. In this, Defoe chose well. Robert Harley had impeccable credentials coming from a family of good standing, a devout puritan background, and an education in a dissenting academy. Early in his parliamentary career he was a supporter of the revolution and its principles and in the early Stuart parliaments he was Whiggish. He made himself a master of the constitution and became a 'party manager' with acute skills. In William III's parliaments he supported impeachment in the secret Partition Treaties, which was enough to get him elected as Speaker of the House of Commons. He held the office of the Principal Secretary of State from time to time for almost ten years, shifting skilfully with every change in party fortunes. Coming from the centre-left, as do many parliamentary leaders, he was able to carry the consciences of the left while retaining the votes of the Tory right with whom he shared his instincts. But in the end no one believed him, for as was said of the Duke of Wellington, 'He had sat so long on the fence that the iron had bitten deep into his soul.'

Robert Harley was a genial soul who loved the arts and artists, conversation, good food and fine wines. He created for himself a wonderful library which is now an adornment of the British Library. He retained the friendship of a wide variety of friends over a long and controversial career because of his good nature. He was invariably a better judge of men and events than his enemies. These qualities infuriated the hard-working mediocrities who waited for their turn to climb the greasy pole.

There were difficulties for Harley in using Defoe. On 16 May, 1704 Defoe wrote to Harley, stating, 'I impatiently Wait to receive your

Ordrs'. When it pleased Harley, he replied, but his responses are not extant. A pattern was established in their relationship. The surviving letters from Defoe to Harley are numerous but his replies are scarce. Later, Defoe was to complain that his letters were never answered, but in 1704 they must have elicited some response, for what Defoe did was to arrange, with Harley's financial support, the establishment of his news-sheet, the *Review*. For nine years, the *Review* was to be Defoe's mouthpiece and a medium through which Harley sought to influence the electorate.

A surviving letter from Defoe to Harley sets out in detail what Defoe would like Harley to do. He saw him as a supreme leader ruling through an inner cabinet and winning the enthusiastic support of the country.[224] After all, if one was to replace the sceptre with the sword there was little point in using half measures.

Harley endeavoured to conceal his correspondence with Defoe. Until the autumn of 1706, and then some times later, Defoe signed his letters with a symbol, or on occasions with the initials of a pseudonym, 'Alexander Goldsmith'. On their receipt Harley often, but not always, tore off the bottom of the final page to remove the signature. Sometimes letters from Harley to Defoe were addressed for his collection at a coffee house.[225]

It was important for Harley to keep Defoe out of London. His concern was not primarily the need to gather political intelligence but to avoid the risk of Defoe's arrest. It was open to any political foe to buy up a debt from one of Defoe's creditors and to keep him in gaol in the hope of gaining information about the administration. After some months had elapsed, in the autumn of 1704 and again in 1705, Defoe set out on journeys throughout England to establish a network of contacts drawn mainly from a dissenting background. These contacts became a source of intelligence and information on local affairs and on the principal political issues of the day and a means of distributing the *Review*.

---

[224] H.14.
[225] H. 7.

These visits and Defoe's comments appear in Healey's collection of Harley's correspondence. They show the identity of some of the people who received Defoe and others who sought to embarrass and pull him down. In July, 1704 the Mayor of Weymouth attempted to prosecute Defoe for plotting against the government and in September Hugh Stafford, justice of the peace at Pynes, Devonshire, issued a warrant for his arrest. Defoe requested Harley to provide him with a letter of authority stating that he was acting on government business and Harley, somewhat reluctantly, gave him one.[226]

Defoe's mind and resolve were not weakened by the pillory and imprisonment, but he was a changed man with a weakened social standing even among dissenters.. Realistically, what had gone was the hope of high office, yet he retained it as a possibility. What existed of his dissenting beliefs would have virtually disappeared, although dissenters remained as his audience. He went on performing for them but he recognised that it was his addiction to dissent, among other reasons, that had led him to the pillory. In the end, and whatever the support he had received from some individuals, his friends and supporters had been unable to save him from public ignominy.

From this point Defoe felt that although he was of the dissenting brethren he was no longer part of them. In modern terms, he had lost the membership of a club and many of the loyalties associated with membership. The price had been too high. He still attended the games, but only when he chose to do so. They remained his team and he was hugely proud of them and wanted them to win, but there was no fever in or because of it.

For many the ignominy and physical stress of the pillory and imprisonment would have been overwhelming, but not for Defoe. He believed, as was common in his times, that victory (in this instance the survival of great trials) was evidence of the righteousness of one's cause. God's providence and grace had been demonstrated in his favour once again. While Defoe believed that God had saved him, it was preferable to help oneself. What was required was 'protection'. When

---

[226] H. 37.

coming from a humble birth, a powerful protector was needed. Out of the darkness of Newgate came the great light of Harley, a public figure and member of the administration, who was to be 'the Foundation of all [Defoe's] further Concern in publick Affairs'.

Defoe tells his readers that Harley was from this point (1704 until Harley's fall in 1714) a patron such as William III had been. Defoe suggested to his readers that a righteous patron should be given allegiance and loyalty. In this respect Defoe had the need for an idealised father figure. He accepted authority, gave dogged devotion and, when the tasks were defined for him, and performed to the best of his considerable abilities. Actually, however, he was rebellious, wayward and impulsive. He did his own thing and while the withdrawal or suspension of payment could draw him back to his duties it did not prevent him straying for excitement or reward.

There was far more to his relationship with Harley than fealty. Harley was extravagantly generous and indulgent to Defoe, way beyond any reasonable measure of value. Defoe had bought protection on a large scale and immunity from prosecution so long as he served his master. The terms of Defoe's sentence in 1703 included a provision that he should not publish any more works. The breach of this condition could throw him back to prison. Others believed it could too and they were anxious to achieve it. There were serious challenges to Defoe. On his travels in 1705, Defoe was accompanied by young men. They were not heralded by Defoe but just appeared and disappeared without any explanation, to be replaced by others; sometimes they were paid for by Harley.

Confident of the protection of his patron, Defoe wrote prolifically. Some of these writings had nothing to do with the administration but others were paid for by Harley and Defoe accounted for his actions to him. The first weekly number of the *Review* appeared on 17 February, 1703. It was to be Defoe's mouthpiece for over ten years. At first it was published once a week, but it became a twice weekly publication with a *Little Review* appearing at the weekends and a special advice section, the *Scandalous Club*, was published separately.

Whether Defoe would have chosen to dabble in the new market for political journalism without Harley's money (which he always denied he was receiving) is open to question. It was not much money compared with the other sums given to him by Harley, probably no more than £200 per year, and from this had to be deducted the printing and distribution costs, but it was enough.

Defoe continued to pay the most persistent of his creditors and he had families to support. The *Review's* direct revenue came from various sources: it retailed at a penny per copy, it took advertisements, and from time to time there was money for Defoe writing in support of the mighty or in favour of particular legislation.

The *Scandalous Club* became a separate publication in September, 1704. In this way Defoe could gossip about personalities and deal with personal problems separate from the serious issues of the day. The *Scandalous Club* became a sort of 'agony aunt' and the first of its kind. At the outset the *Review*, unlike its competitors, was not a newspaper or mere news-sheet, but a journal of opinion on the political matters of the day. It appeared under a strange title:

A REVIEW
OF THE
Affairs of FRANCE
AND OF ALL
EUROPE,
As Influenc'd by that NATION,
BEING
Historical Observations, on the Publick Transactions of the
WORLD; Purg'd from the Errors and Partiality of
News-Writers, and Petty-Statesmen of all Sides.
WITH AN
Entertaining Part in every Sheet,
BEING
ADVICE from the Scandal. CLUB,
To the Curious Enquirers: in Answer to Letters sent them

For that Purpose.

The *Review* announced that it had the objective of providing an impartial account of the affairs of France based on an understanding of its history and culture. Initially, the *Scandalous Club* existed to provide a means of attacking the criticisms and accounts of other journals and newspapers and to rebut their criticisms. The issue was raised in the minds of some of whether Defoe was being paid by the French. Godolphin, who was committed to pressing the war with France to a satisfactory conclusion, wrote to Harley asking for the reasons for Defoe's editorial line.

Concentration on France might have been no more than Defoe executing Harley's positioning of himself closer to the feelings of country Tories who were opposed to the war on the grounds of its necessity and expense. However, Defoe's enemies supposed he was being paid through the French Embassy in London for taking a pro-French line. But whatever it was, it came to an end with Marlborough's victory at Blenheim, which was greeted with enthusiasm in the *Review* and in Defoe's *Hymn to Victory*.[135]

From the outset the *Review* sought to take a high intellectual and impartial stand. It was a position that his rivals and enemies were not willing to cede nor one that they felt obliged to acknowledge. They scorned it on a variety of grounds: Defoe's supposed limited education, his unprincipled character, which they maintained was common knowledge, and his poor grammar and Latin. It was a pretension of the time that a gentleman's discourse should include Latin. Defoe's Latin was elementary and he could be caught out in error, and when he placed his prose in the context of a classical world, he rendered himself risible to those whose scholarship had included ancient Greek and Roman studies.

However comic or pretentious Defoe was made to appear, he had several overwhelming advantages over his rivals: his efforts to succeed despite a difficult life made him quick-witted in his reactions; he anticipated problems in advance, and adapted his writing to the possibilities of criticism; and, furthermore, where his opponents were talented and accomplished, Defoe opposed them with the prose of a wayward genius.

Almost from the start Defoe was willing to write for his competitors. James Sutherland has speculated that when Tutchin was in trouble Defoe wrote some issues of his *Observators*, and Furbank and Owens argue for Defoe's involvement in *Master Mercury* in 1704. For a modern freelance journalist, plying for hire is usual (although consistency is still a professional necessity) but in Defoe's partisan times it was seen as unprincipled and an apostasy. Anecdotally, it was said of Defoe at the time that as he wrote his regular column or pamphlet he had on the other side of his desk their written refutations.

The ability to articulate many sides of the same question can be seen as an attractive intellectual quality stimulated by the teaching of rhetoric and the encouragement of debate. In Defoe, however, there were psychological and behavioural reasons for him not sticking to any particular viewpoint. His propensity to trim his sails made almost any change of direction possible and was infuriating to many of his readers. There is fear in this. Trimming was accompanied by an awareness that the desire and necessity to provoke would result in a threatening reaction. Defoe released himself from this personal dilemma through the use of satire and personation. In *The Shortest Way* Defoe's use of satire had already led to personal disaster but setbacks did not result in him abandoning it. The reader of the *Review* would have observed Defoe developing a number of voices for himself and for Mr Review. Through the *Scandalous Club* he articulates other voices: he gave space to sounds of the real and imagined lives of his readers who wrote to him about their problems.

In the *Review*, Defoe often approaches a subject from an unexpected or paradoxical angle which invites thought but which does not always convince. Some readers found this practice annoying and felt that it trivialised their beliefs and values.

The *Review* would have been entertaining for all those readers who loved paradox and satire. Defoe was producing a news-sheet that, for the first time, displayed human foibles and dilemmas in a regular journalistic format. His readers must have been vastly amused by the problems of their fellow readers and perhaps better informed about the solutions to their problems.

Imprisonment, release, notoriety and protection unleashed in Defoe a flood of words. Over the next two years, and excluding the *Review*, Defoe wrote and published over three hundred thousand words. Even after allowance is made for works which can no longer be ascribed to him with any confidence, his energy was astounding. This output included two important works that were not overtly political and which presaged fictional works to come. It is thought probable that in 1704 he wrote about the great storm which had hit the country in November 1703, and in 1705 he wrote a curious work, *The Consolidator*. The first work displays Defoe's art of spinning fiction and drama from fact, the second work, something of his curious state of mind at the time.

The weather in 1703, even for long-suffering Britons, was awful. Heavy rain and strong winds had battered the British Isles for most of the year. From pulpits up and down the country clergymen warned their parishioners that this weather was caused by the prosecution of unwarranted wars and a turning away from God. For Defoe, storms and winds were acts of God visited upon an unworthy flock: 'Part of the Works of God by Nature'. By observation, however, it was apparent that the British Isles had more than its fair share of bad weather. Did this mean that Britons were more sinful and wayward than the citizens of other countries? Probably not, thought Defoe, but others thought so, and their beliefs and superstitions could be played upon. Preachers used the opportunity to denounce sin from their pulpits and, caught up in the excitement of the moment, Defoe knew there was money to be made in describing the great event.

Defoe appears to have started work on writing about the storm soon after its occurrence in November, 1703. He may have been responsible for even earlier works on the storm, the satirical *Layman's Sermon*, for example, and the poetic *Essay on the Late Storm* which appeared alongside *The Storm* in the summer of 1704. It is said that Defoe placed advertisements in both the *Daily Courant* and the *London Gazette* in which he requested that first-hand observations of the storm be sent to him via one of his regular publishers near Stationers Hall on Ludgate Hill. The wording of the advertisement is identical to an earlier advertisement in the Athenian.

These claims for Defoe's authorship are fraught with the problems of ascription that beset Defoe scholars. Furbank and Owens think it no more than probable that he wrote *The Storm*, and the evidence for his authorship of the other two works is no more than circumstantial. Defoe is not mentioned by name in any advertisement seeking experiences of the storm and it is not at all clear whether the accounts he used were his correspondents or his own inventions. A great deal of material entered into the public domain and Defoe and many other writers scrambled for the use of it. Defoe was accused by his competitors of plagiarism and the use of unacknowledged sources, and his attempts to incorporate within his narrative a scientific explanation of the causes of the high winds was subject to scorn for its lack of learning.

All this was par for the course in the emerging journalism of the time. What Defoe might have said in his defence, but could not, was that what distinguished his account from those of others was the power of his imagination. Defoe, among others, claimed that the accounts he was giving were strictly factual and that he would give no other, but even a casual reading of *The Storm* shows that they were not and, reluctantly, Defoe admits as much in the text.

Today we can see the work for what it was: high quality journalism which engaged with the storm and its effects on those who suffered it. It was spoilt only by Defoe's need to share the pretentiousness of the times. The careful and punctilious among his readers would have been offended by it, but the rest of the reading public must have loved it. With the benefit of hindsight, *The Storm*, if in any way it is ascribed to Defoe, can be seen as the harbinger of his fiction. The writing was non-political; he created character and a multitude of voices, incident, and atmosphere; and he invented whenever it was necessary for the engagement of imagination.

The Consolidator was written and published by Defoe in 1705. A political satire, it is what might be expected of him at this time. Defoe used satire to attack parliamentary proceedings, that would tack a ban on occasional conformity to a finance bill in November, 1704. In this fantasy the Chinese succeeded in landing on the moon to find the happenings there not only to be strange but very like those in England. The theme of lunar fantasy, and the related invention of the 'mad man', was to be used later by Defoe in the *Review*. One version of Mr Review was that he dealt in the plain truth and those who disagreed were either living in a fantasy world of their own or were mad.

In addition to what is described here, Defoe was busy with other writing in 1705. He was desperate to make money and writing was a means of doing so. It was becoming respectable to be a professional writer and the activity could be combined with other and more serious activities. It was possible at this time to bridge different worlds: statesmen wrote pamphlets; the poor could become rich through trade; riches could buy land estates, titles, public office or a place in parliament; and talent or genius could gain social advancement.

These ambitions were not Defoe's alone and those who mocked him for his pretensions may have harboured similar desires themselves. Even the disgrace of the pillory could be presented as a victory for principle; Defoe could be cast as a martyr in a long line of martyrs who could, according to religious and political beliefs, be admired. Defoe could maintain that he had betrayed neither the good cause nor the mighty men who had engaged his pen for political reasons. Within the government, whose patronage Defoe sought, he was seen as competent: as a man who could reach a voting public with effective prose and who was capable of confounding and exposing political opponents.

The triennial elections had ushered in an atmosphere of constant electioneering from 1695. Factions struggled to obtain tactical advantage. Defoe had come to occupy a place that has always existed in partisan politics: he was a man who could find out what was happening and what was being plotted by political enemies. To do this he had to assume a role for which he was ideally prepared: the role of the double agent, a man needed by both sides who, even as they were being reported on, needed the contact in order to play their necessary but dangerous game of double bluff. Such a man is never loved. Those people who were less successful than Defoe at 'double bluff', or unsuited for it and less talented, cried foul in the abusive language of the time. They were right to do so from their own points of view. Defoe's genius in fulfilling the role would have persuaded him to continue to believe that much of the world he sought as a young man was still within his reach.

Defoe knew that in a socially hierarchical world he was above the Grub Street hacks and superior in talent to his nearest journalistic rivals. What was needed now, if his dreams were to be realised, was to raise his act. He set out to do it. From around 1700 he changed his name from Foe to De Foe. In 1702 he purchased a coat of arms[136] (first used on the cover of *True Collections* in 1703) which, it was said, he displayed on the side of a coach. So far as it can be ascertained, Defoe's right to bear these arms of ancient and distinguished lineage (other than the payment of a fee) was not substantiated in any way that is recoverable to the enquirer – although such a claim could have been true![227]

To establish his reputation as a political philosopher, he published a poem in heroic couplets in twelve volumes entitled *Jure Divino*. In this poem he attempted to set out the basis of his political thought. To add gravitas, he provided a flattering portrait of himself on the cover, depicted by a fashionable painter, John Tavernier. Even as he dressed up for his portrait he complained to Harley about his difficulties in maintaining a fashionable appearance and stated that he thought of himself as becoming shabby. Whatever reservations anyone might have of the authenticity and originality of earlier Defoe political pamphlets *Jure Divino* demands to be taken seriously as a statement of Defoe's own political opinions. Of course, it can be argued that he was influenced by Puffendorf and Locke and it is known from the record of his library in 1731 that he possessed works by these authors, but in a

---

[227] See Attachment 7 . The Cavalier: Defoe's Elder Brother.

general sense all political statements are influenced by some other writer.

Subscriptions to *Jure Divino* were first sought in an advertisement in the *Review* in September, 1705 at a price of half a crown but when it finally appeared in July, 1706 the price had been raised to fifteen shillings, which left room for a pirated edition at five shillings. In the poem Defoe argues that God had permitted man to be lord of himself and that his first duty was self-love. He argues against political tyranny and asserts that those who do not fight it are fools with no proper respect for the liberty God had given them. Defoe asserts as a secondary argument that liberty of the subject is to be found in the possession of property and in respect for the rights of property holders. Tyranny can appear in many forms and many societies suffered from it. Undue respect for custom, 'the Bastard of Antiquity', assists the tyrant who takes advantage of old allegiances to make his subjects swear oaths which, when examined, are shown to be irrational. The divine right theory of monarchy is likened to popish image-worship and ridiculed, as is the fallacy of the hereditary right to rule. This argument enables Defoe to praise the English constitution, King William and the reign of Queen Anne.

Jure Divino is a poem of more than three hundred pages in length and it may have been started as early as 1701. Taken together with *The Succession to the Crown of England Considered* (1701), *Legion's Memorial* (1701) and the *Original Power of the Collective Body of the People of England* (1702), it may be considered as a statement of Defoe's political position in relation to the constitutional settlement ground out in England between the 1688 accession of William and Mary and the Hanoverian succession of 1715.

In the *Original Power of the Collective Body of the People of England*, Defoe contests the doctrine of the sovereignty of parliament, monarch and Houses of Lords and Commons acting together, on the grounds of the 'original power' of the people of England to govern themselves. In this he is, knowingly or otherwise, following Locke's Second Treatise and asserting a social contract between the people and the rulers of the time. If the governors the people have deputed to act for them betray their power, the people have the right to overthrow them even if they have to seek the assistance of a foreign army in order to do so.

Defoe's assertion begs two important questions: Who are the people? And who is to decide on what amounts to a betrayal? As expressed in *Jure Divino*, the original rights are not embodied in all people but in male freeholders alone, the other inhabitants of the country being regarded as 'Sojourners', who were to be subject to 'such Laws as the Freeholders impose upon them'.

William Payne has shown from an examination of those participating that the electorate in the triennial elections amounted to no more than ten per cent of the male population. This being so, the electorate was broadly in line with Defoe's definition of the people. Why then should not the electorate be the judge of the policies to be pursued by parliament? And should not a general parliamentary election be the chosen method for changing policies if the people disapproved of them? Of course, the franchise and the conduct of the elections were corrupt by modern standards, and to be fair to Defoe's arguments he spoke out about the need for reform, but that is not to say that imperfect general elections were ineffective in bringing parliaments to account and in limiting the exercise of power by them.

While Defoe could protect himself against the charge that he was a Leveller by limiting his definition to male property holders, he was wide open to the allegation of encouraging mob rule. The logic of *Legion's Memorial* and Defoe's support for the Kentish Petitioners was that parliament should bow to the demands of petitioners acting in the name of 'all the good people of England', whose name was Legion and who were many. It is a feature of a mob, or of those who are Legion, that many of its company would fail to meet Defoe's definition of the people who were entitled to bring rulers to account. However, it can be asserted that Defoe was far-seeing, for it is an issue today whether a universal human right to representation and freedom under the law should be regarded as a right of others to overthrow tyrannical governments.

A constant irritation to High Church spokesmen was the exaggeration by dissenters of their numbers and hence the importance of their grievances. Charles Leslie, a principal propagandist of the High Church, took on the Dissenters in an uncompromising way in a pamphlet entitled *New Association* in 1702 in which he argued that what the Dissenters sought was to rekindle rebellion and that 'if they were now as Considerable as they would make themselves: then Government is in the greater Danger, and have the more Reason to Begin with them, to take power out of their hands in Time... they must have All or None'.

It is easy to demonstrate that in the period 1701–1705 Defoe's constitutional arguments were inconsistent and troubling to the public peace, but it is difficult to demonstrate the reasons for their contradictions. For example, in *Legion's Memorial*, one of the main complaints expressed is the slowness of the government to give 'vigorous resistance to the growing power of France'; but in *The Present State of Jacobitism Considered* (1701), *Reasons Against a War with France* (1701), and in the *Review* in 1705, Defoe argued a contrary viewpoint, that the danger of France was over-stated. When, in 1702, at the instigation of King William, a committee of the House of Commons began to consider the problem of the protestant succession, Defoe seemed not to consider the matter with any seriousness. In *The Succession to the Crown of England Considered*, 1701, as has been argued here in an earlier chapter, he advocated bizarrely the claims of the Earl of Dalkeith, Monmouth's son, as the only candidate that would suit the Scots. The conclusion of the committee's deliberations led to the Act of Settlement, 1702 which, with hindsight, can be seen as securing the protestant succession. Defoe greeted this building block of the post-1688 settlement with total silence.

It is difficult not to conclude that Defoe's opinions were where his purse was: that he was urging the cases of those who paid him. In the earlier period his commitment was to King William, for whom he wrote for money and who he admired as a man, a statesman and a protestant. King William was hurt by the Act of Settlement in that it limited his powers and enhanced those of parliament. Thus Defoe could not welcome publicly the securing of the protestant succession, in which he undoubtedly believed. In the latter period, and in the early days of the *Review*, Defoe was in thrall to Harley, his paymaster: as that master of political tacking changed direction, so did Defoe.

It might be the case that Defoe supported the Jacobite cause but couldn't do so in public. He might have had the belief that family connections would lead to preferment should the Pretender succeed.[228]

None of this needs occasion surprise or indignation unless one wishes Defoe to be cast in the role of supporting revolutionary principles, values and their practical application; principles which did not exist then in the form in which they are now cast.

---

[228] See Attachment 7. The Cavalier: Defoe's Elder Brother.

Chapter 18

Return to Crusoe's Island

Through his long and immensely prolific life ...Defoe was constantly dressing up the works of his imagination as 'true' and 'faithful' accounts.

Foreword to *King of the Pyrates*, 2001
Peter Ackroyd

The *Farther Adventures of Robinson Crusoe*, 1720 is widely held to be an unsuccessful sequel to *Robinson Crusoe* written quickly by Defoe to 'cash in' on the its commercial success. It is nothing of the kind. The account given is a description of an actual journey back to *Crusoe's* island, 'Brazil', and on to Madagascar for the dual purpose of slave trading and the purchase, at knockdown prices, of diamonds and gold and silver coins from those of Captain Avery's pirates still on the island.

Defoe was writing of an audacious crime he committed and of which he was immensely proud. He needed to protect himself from detection, prosecution and execution while telling people about it. He did tell of it. There is a necessary confusion in his tale. As Ackroyd correctly tells his readers, Defoe needed to protest that his works were 'true' and 'faithful' accounts' but on the other hand he had to disguise his authorship both in the telling of it and in keeping his identity a secret. Cultural historians with a need to find reasons for Defoe's protestations that his writings were 'true and faithful 'accounts' explain that his intent in these protestations was to distinguish his fictions from Romances.

Despite all Defoe's efforts to conceal his early life there were many people who knew something of his personal history and some who knew a lot. Charles Gildon, who emerged as a robust critic of Defoe, seems to come into the latter category and his vigorous and biting attack upon Defoe has been much discussed by critics. It is sometimes said that 'you need a thief to catch a thief'. Gildon belonged to the category of the despicable living on his wits and Defoe was hard-pressed to defend himself.

Defoe had worked on the composition of *Robinson Crusoe* for at least seven years. He had to write the work into a genre of travel tales of adventurers exploring foreign places and exotic surroundings and castaway narratives, particularly those of Alexander Selkirk and Robert Knox, that had gained public acceptance and appeal. Into this genre Defoe sought successfully to pour the events of his own life without revealing place, time and person. He borrowed extensively from others and disguised himself by embellishment and invention.

Gildon's charge against Defoe was that *Robinson Crusoe* was a disguised account of Defoe's own disreputable life. In essence Defoe admitted the charge. In the Preface to *Serious Reflections* he wrote that 'there is a Man alive, and well known too, the Actions of whose Life are the just Subject of these Volumes, and to whom all or most Part of the Story most directly alludes…and to this I set my name.'[229] He signs his retort in the name of Robinson Crusoe. Defoe added that 'the Story, although Allegorical, is also Historical; and that it is the beautiful Representation of a Life of unexampled Misfortune, and of a Variety not to be met with in the World, sincerely adopted for the common Good of Mankind.'

Given that Defoe admits Gildon's charge, it is an issue for the modern reader to distinguish between autobiographical detail and invention. In our times bias works in reverse to Defoe's anxiety to avoid the accusation of writing 'romances' in favour of fiction. Consequently, today Defoe's admission is thought facetious by literary critics who argue that he could not possibly have meant it. For example, Evan Davis, in a recent introduction to the Broadway edition of *Robinson Crusoe*, expresses a widespread conviction when he writes, 'It would be a mistake to read *Crusoe* as an allegory in any

---

[229] Defoe, Daniel. *Serious Reflections, During the Life and Surprising Adventures of Robinson*, 1722.

usual sense of the word. *Crusoe* is not a disguised Defoe.'[230] In contrast it is the point of my thesis, perhaps the whole of my point here, that although Defoe's works are undoubtedly fictions and fantastical works of the imagination they are also strongly autobiographical.

I appreciate that in reading this work of mine many patient readers may have reached a point of perplexity. Such a reader will have accepted some part of the factual basis of my narrative. However, it will seem incredible. How can *Robinson Crusoe* be a biographical account of Defoe's own life? It is a very reasonable hesitation. To provide a further explanation I offer at this point a proof of the assertion that Defoe is both allegorically, in the 'usual meaning of the word', and literally speaking, *Robinson Crusoe*.

Defoe's *Crusoe* states, 'When I came to *England,* [and echoing *Colonel* Jack and *Captain Singleton*], I was as perfect a Stranger to all the World, as if I had never been known there…I went down afterwards [an undisclosed time afterwards] into Yorkshire; but my Father was dead, and my mother extinct [a fine distinction]. Later he adds the following:

> I took my two Nephews, the Children of one of my Brothers into my Care: The eldest having something of his own, I bred up as a Gentleman, and gave him an Addition to his Estate, after my Decease; the other *I put out to a Captain of a Ship*; and after five years, finding him a sensible bold enterprising young Fellow I put him into a good Ship and sent him to Sea: *And this young Fellow afterwards drew me in, as old as I was to farther Adventures my self.* (Italics mine) [231] The words in italics are virtually identical to those used in *Farther Adventures*. *Crusoe*/ Defoe does not give his nephew a ship but permits him to be captain of one in his, Defoe's, ship.

In *Farther Adventures* the nephew said to have enticed *Crusoe* to

[230] Ed. Evan R Davis. Daniel, Defoe. *Robinson Crusoe,* (1719-1722. Broadview Press, 2010), 13.
[231] *Robinson Crusoe,* 303.

return to his island is Defoe's nephew, his sister Mary's son, Francis King. The explanation I give of *Crusoe's*/Defoe's journey becomes possible once the reader accepts that Defoe had a sister Mary and brother Thomas who used their mother's surname of King and secondly that Defoe was born in 1644.

On December 1, 1705 (that is when Defoe was sixty-one years of age) a man called Francis King, a cooper, going on a sea voyage to the East Indies in a ship called the *Aurangezebe*, left all his worldly possessions to his 'beloved father Thomas King' an innkeeper of Colchester.[232] There was at the time only one innkeeper of that name in Colchester. When this Thomas King died in 1717 he bequeathed his considerable wealth to his sister Mary King (Defoe's sister).[233] His will reveals that he owned the Queens Head Inn in Aldham, Colchester, which at this time was in the parish of St Leonard's (where Defoe was in care as a child). This inn exists as a public house today and I have had lunch there on several occasions. When you stand in the car park to the rear you see to the right land leased by Defoe from the Corporation of Colchester in 1722. To the left, and within easy walking distance, is the village of Great Tey and land that was farmed by Defoe's neighbour the Quaker Richard Simmonds.[234] I have written earlier that Defoe describes marrying Mary Norton, Richard Simmons daughter (her mother was also called Mary Norton), in *Colonel Jack*.[235] I have established already a link between Defoe and Mary Norton in *Beyond Belief.*[236] It had already been known when I wrote this book that Mary Norton had lent Defoe the sum of £200 to pay arrears of rent on the land he leased from the Corporation of Colchester.[237] She produced two surviving children by him: Sophia and Benjamin Norton. I have suggested that she makes an appearance as the Quaker Friend in *Roxana* and is to be found in *Family Instructor* and *Religious Courtship*.

---

[232] ERO. D/ABW80/43. Will of Francis Kinge, Colchester, cooper. See Illustration.
[233] ERO. D/ABW82/132. Will of Thomas King. See Illustration.
[234] *Beyond Belief*, 100 for documentary evidence.
[235] *Colonel Jack*, 278.
[236] *Beyond Belief*, 100.
[237] Wright, Thomas. Facsimile of signatures, 287.

The name of the ship, *Aurangezebe*, is a reference to the Grand Mogul of India made famous by Captain Avery, the only notorious and celebrated pirate to escape capture and punishment, and who Defoe personated in *King of the Pyrates*. In 1695 Avery captured the Grand Mogul ship *Ganj-Sawaii* and made off with a huge fortune which he was successful in hiding. It has been described as 'the single richest pirate crime in history'. Among the riches was a vast collection of valuable diamonds. Avery sought refuge in the Bahamas where it is thought that he bribed the Governor Nicholas Trott. A huge reward was offered by the East India Company but Avery was tipped off and made an escape from with one hundred and thirteen members of his crew. Initially Avery and many of the crew were said to have settled in Madagascar and later when Avery fled the island it was said that many men remained there.

I maintain that the *Aurangezebe* was owned by Defoe and is the ship 'bought' by Defoe/*Crusoe* at some time after his return to England in 1680-1682. There were no central registers for the ownership of ships in the early eighteenth century. There was enormous interest among pirates everywhere in finding the Treasure. This ship *Aurangezebe* has form. It is named in *A General History of the Pyrates* in the Chapter on Captain Bowen as encountering Captain Green's boat the *Worcester* in 1703; and thus the crew were witness to the truth of Green's defence against a charge of piracy which led to his trial in Edinburgh and public execution. [238]

In the *Farther Adventures of Robinson Crusoe* Defoe describes the events leading to the voyage back to his island and I quote.[239]

Anyone would think that after thirty five years affliction [that is in my account his thirty-sixth year, 1644-1680, and his return to England], seven years of peace and enjoyment in the fullness of all things [his marriage to Mary Tuffley until his bankruptcy, 1684-1691] experience of every state of middle life [1684 to 1705 when he was aged forty to sixty

[238] Ed. Schonhorn , Manuel. Defoe, Daniel. *A General History of the Pyrates*, (1724-1728. Dover Publications), 199, 456.
[239] *Farther Adventures*, 12.

years] I might, at 61 years of age [1705, the date of Francis King's will], settle down'. He refers, I conjecture, to Mary Norton. In 1705 Mary Tuffley and Defoe were leading entirely separate lives, the children had been split up between them, and Defoe was living when it suited him to do so in a house in Hackney. Defoe/*Crusoe* had become a farmer. He was comfortable and better off and enjoyed his life. Defoe had been living in Tilbury, Essex where he worked a brick and pantile works and at some time occupied East Gubyons Manor House. The Earl of Beddingfield ended this phase of his life. His nephew, (Francis King) came to him with a project of carrying him thither to his colony on his way to the East Indies. He said, 'and now Uncle, if you will go to sea with me, I will engage to land you upon your old habitations in the island for we are to touch at the Brazils'.

I suggest that it is usually wise to assume that any Defoe account will shift the burden of suggestion or decision on to others so that he is not directly in the firing line for acts of dubious morality. I believe that the initiative for this voyage lay with Defoe. Following his imprisonment for Seditious Libel in 1703, his financial position was dire. Although he was earning money he remained unable to pay off his debts as they arose. His capital had been lost. He must have considered whether there was something he could do that would recover his position. It would need to be highly audacious and successful to make the required difference. In this account I believe that the suggestion for such a voyage came from Defoe to his nephew. The ship was not owned by Francis King but by Defoe. Further evidence of this is provided by an affidavit mentioned in a pamphlet on the trial of Captain Green which names the commander of the *Aurangezebe* in 1703 as a Stephen Grandell.[240]

The narrative account Defoe gives in *Farther Adventures* is implausible and inconsistent. By general consent *Crusoe's* island is in the Caribbean. Brazil is not, of course, an island and was a Portuguese colony. You do not normally travel from Britain to the East Indies via Brazil. I argue here that Brazil is *Crusoe's* imagined island.

Defoe's nephew uses the plural when he talks of his uncle visiting

---

[240] See page 239.

his old habitations in the Brasils. He states, 'and now Uncle, if you go to sea with me, I will engage to land you upon your old habitations'. What does he mean? When the Portuguese first colonised Brazil they named it the *Island of the True Cross*. In Irish mythology, the Irish got there first and it is claimed by them that the name Brazil was taken from Gaelic. According to the Irish myth there were two islands. The second was shrouded in mist and could be seen only once every seven years. More literally, and almost certainly the more realistic explanation, is that the term, 'Brazils' refers to north and south Brazil. The Dutch relinquished ownership of the north, known as New Holland, and which contained the headquarters of the Dutch West India Company, to Portugal in August, 1661 a mere two years before, in my chronology, that Defoe arrived in All Saints Bay in the south.

In *Robinson Crusoe*, *Crusoe* had two habitations. After he had been in the south for some time he made his way north which he preferred to the south for he 'found many pleasant Savannah's, or Meadows; plain, smooth, and cover'd with Grass and on the rising Parts of them next to the higher Grounds a great deal of Tobacco'. He built a bowyer there and split his time between north and south. He expresses a secret Kind of Pleasure in his discovery of the north where he felt 'that [He] was King and Lord of all this Country indefeasibly, and had a Right of Possession'.

Defoe's occupation and subsequent purchase of a plantation in All Saints Bay arose from restraint and forced occupation. He never possessed land there as 'an indefeasible right'. It may well be the case that the Portuguese victory over the Dutch opened up opportunities to settle in the north and to claim virgin territory. However, as befits a pioneer, his territory in the north was always smaller and scantier than that in the south.

In *Farther Adventures*, *Crusoe's* nephew could not give his uncle any guarantee of a return from the voyage out, an outcome that proved difficult for Defoe to explain to readers. *Crusoe* made a will. He left his estate to the children, and placed it wholly with, 'the widow', with a sufficient maintenance for herself. Defoe does not introduce the reader to 'the widow'.

A complicated stratagem was designed to enable *Crusoe* to be dropped off at his island and to make his own way home. The ship they were to set sail in was to contain the frame of a sloop and the passengers included five carpenters who could assemble this sloop for the journey home. However, although this clumsy contrivance enables Defoe to deal with the obvious narrative difficulty of how he would get off his island, it is not, in his narrative, what happened.

According to Defoe, the ship left for the East Indies in January, 1693 (1705-1706) in my chronology), a short time after Francis King made his will. They went first to Ireland where they landed in Galway. They stayed there for twenty-two days taking in food and other provisions including household utensils. The ship was heavily armed and carried a hundred muskets, and fusees, pistols swords, cutlasses and cannons and a great deal of ammunition. According to *A General History of the Pyrates*, Captain Avery was in Ireland at this time and in desperate need of money.

Fifteen days out on their journey, they encountered sixty-four people escaping from a burning shop in small boats. What was to be done with them? It was agreed to take these migrants back to Newfoundland from where they had come at the risk of the ship running out of provisions. But the ship did not land in Newfoundland. The passengers were put into a barque which took them on to their destination. A barque is a three or four mast ship. In all this Defoe narrates the story as if he is in charge of the boat although, in his narrative, his nephew was the Captain. Of course, as the owner of the *Aurangezebe*, Defoe/*Crusoe* was its Master.

This is a most unlikely story and it falls apart on only a cursory examination. My understanding of the voyage and the 'encounter at sea' is as follows. Francis King and his crew on the *Aurangezebe* were running slaves. They needed orders for them from planters and were proposing to collect or capture slaves in Madagascar. Defoe was essential to this trip because he had contacts with the sugar planters in Brazil, who had an insatiable need for slaves. To finance the trip the boat took on migrants in Ireland who paid for their passage to New England; but these migrants had been duped and they were dumped at the first opportunity.

Defoe had a different objective to that of Francis King. He wished to contact members of Avery's crew living on Madagascar or their agents and buy valuable diamonds from them on the cheap, or even for nothing, and possibly a promise to obtain a General Pardon to enable them to return to England. The *Aurangezebe*, as a cargo vessel, needed to be fitted out to receive slaves hence the employment of five carpenters.

Defoe/*Crusoe* tells of a visit to his 'island'. If Defoe had actually made this visit it would have been to the place where he had started a settlement in northern Brazil. In *Robinson Crusoe* Defoe tells the reader that he had sold what was left of his interest in the original plantation in the south.[241] I have argued that he was not in the 'good favour' of the authorities in San Salvador and it would not have been wise for him to spend much time there.

As recounted, *Crusoe* was keen to find out what had happened on his island since he returned to England 25 years before. The settlement remained poorly populated. It is not easy from his historical account to calculate the population and its mix between English, Spanish and the South American indigenous population; but it seems to have had a population of 50-100 people all of whom had come to recognise *Crusoe's* authority to govern despite the passing of time. (Some forty years in real time).

On realistic grounds, it is difficult to believe this account. Defoe's narrative feeds into the contemporary philosophic interest in the nature of society and the authority of kingship. It seeks to satisfy the widespread public interest in alterity, cannibalism and tales of foreign adventure. *Crusoe* states that he 'had an undoubted Right [by Conquest] to govern and dispose of [them] absolutely as he thought fit'. If he did have such a right his rag-bag gathering of Spanish, English and native American subjects could not possibly have been worth the trouble of asserting his authority. His experience of exile in Brazil equipped him to tell of culturally mixed societies earning their living from working the land and of the beneficent and accommodating Roman Catholic dominion over them.

---

[241] *Robinson Crusoe*, 284.

If *Crusoe* did stop off at his 'island' his motive, apart from curiosity, would have been the making of money; utensils, building materials and guns could be sold to the planters in return for provisioning the ship. I think it more likely that Defoe's stay on his 'island' was short and that at the earliest possible moment the ship continued its voyage to Madagascar with both uncle and nephew on board. The ship sailed along the coast of Brazil and stopped off in All Saints Bay in southern Brazil where it re-provisioned again and, I conjecture, took orders for slaves. Uncle and nephew may have received a part payment for the slaves.

The ship fully modified to take on slaves then proceeded to Madagascar. To the outside observer the ship was an ordinary cargo vessel. It may have disguised its true name. Great care must have been taken to determine exactly where to anchor. If challenged it would appear to be a normal trading vessel laden with food and general provisions to sell on the island. When a raiding party was put ashore in Madagascar it was by long-boat and surreptitiously. The crew put ashore encountered resistance from the natives and life was lost. The crew took bloody reprisals. *Crusoe*/Defoe was uneasy and critical of this for the simple reason that he needed to stay for some time in Madagascar in order to contact the right people and to bargain for diamonds.

The duality of purpose between uncle and nephew is revealed in the narrative. The ship was obliged to leave immediately for the feeding of crew and slaves during a long journey was a problem. There was a need to keep slave fatalities down to a minimum. Francis King may have become aware that agents might have spotted them and to have informed the Dutch administration. At any moment a Dutch warship might hove over the horizon. All would be lost. Defoe was left in Madagascar seeking diamonds and needed to buy a boat to carry him away from the island. There would have been no chance of the *Aurangezebe* being able to resist a Dutch warship; it would simply have been blown apart by superior gun power and all would have been lost. His nephew had left him English goods, a thousand pieces of eight and a letter of credit. *Crusoe* does not tell the reader what he had done to earn this money. He does tell the reader that he succeeded in buying diamonds at a bargain price in Madagascar and that later on the way home he fenced some of them in Hamburg. Defoe may have had to switch his diamonds for others less immediately recognisable in England as coming from the original act of piracy by Avery.[242]

Later in the narrative, when *Crusoe* tells the reader 'he was in Siam', he is warned that he had been spotted. An English sailor recently embarked on the island warns him that the East India Company knew he was there and unless he departed immediately he was in imminent danger of being captured by men who would arrive at night in five fully loaded longboats; and, if captured, he would be hanged for being a pirate. He leaves. After further adventures, which I maintain were imaginary, he arrives back in England. Crusoe tells the reader that he was able to sell his produce for £3,475 including about £600 of diamonds,

It is my belief that the documentary proof I offer in this chapter is 'point, set and match' to the thesis that Defoe was indeed born in 1644. However, I am aware that at this point in my narrative, it might be argued that there are a number of weighty and problematic objections to my interpretation of *Farther Adventures*. A number of very well-informed and thoughtful readers will be incredulous. How can it possibly have been as I have described? As I understand it, these readers will have three main objections. I discuss them as follows.

Defoe's Relationship with Francis King.

Francis King was the son of Mary King, Defoe's sister and not the son of Thomas King as this narrative of mine might be read to mean. He was, however, Defoe's nephew. Thomas King was a 'father' in the kinship sense of the word: that is the senior male in the immediate King family of which he was a member. I have suggested that Mary King had multiple marriages as stated in *Moll Flanders* and *Captain*

---

[242] Hamburg-Hull was a widely used route for European immigrants to England.

Singleton. As a reading of *Robinson Crusoe* would suggest, she was married twice in Yorkshire. After living for a time in Hull she moved to York. *Crusoe* suggests that her third husband was named Robinson and her fourth was a retired German merchant named Kreutzer. I have no record of the birth of Francis because I have not found a way to establish or confirm the names of Mary's husbands. In 1702 Francis King married the daughter of Mary Lawrence and they had a home in St James Parish, Colchester where many members of Defoe's wider King family lived.

However, and fortunately for this narrative, there is further, and highly dramatic, evidence of the relationship between Francis King and Defoe. In 1716 a Francis King, described as a merchant of Hull, sued John Morphew, one of Defoe's printers, for a report in *Mecurius Politicus* for September, 1716. Morphew was found guilty in March, 1718. The Grand Jury found King 'an Injur'd Innocente'. Defoe claimed he did not write the remarks in *Mercurius Politicus* to which Francis King objected but no one believed him. In correspondence with De la Faye, Defoe admits he was involved and expressed his anxiety that he would get caught up in the prosecution of it even though judgement had been entered for Francis King against the printer.

Healey tells his readers that Defoe was commenting upon the trial of two seamen, Thomas Barron and Edward Bourne. The accusation made against the two men was that they had confronted Francis King and a printer called Jackson a few miles outside York and demanded three and half pence. Not unreasonably Defoe had written in *Mercurius Politicus*, 'Three halfpence is a very small sum to be hanged for, and he must be a very hard fellow that swore it as a robbery.' However, it is difficult to explain the reasons for Defoe writing about the incident at all. Did Defoe put these two men up to it with the intention of preventing the publication of material damaging to him?

These men were prosecuted in the York Assizes Court. There are no extant records of the trial. However, from various affidavits presented to the Kings Bench it can be deduced that the two men put up a robust defence; but despite it they were found guilty and publicly executed.

People in York were highly indignant and thought it 'a put up job'. On one occasion Francis King was surrounded in York by a mob shouting and denouncing him and was obliged to flee to a nearby inn for refuge. By raising the issue in *Mecurius Politicus* Defoe is implying something was very wrong but he does not elucidate. The implication of Defoe's argument, and one assumed in the High Court, was that *no robbery took place* and King had bribed the Judges in York to give a cruel and unjust verdict to silence these men.

In his letter to De la Faye, Defoe claimed the benefit of his 'Capitulation' which protected him from his past crimes or in Defoe's actual words when 'all former mistakes of mine were forgiven'.[243] Healey suggests that this shows that the Capitulation took place between September, and December 1716, that is immediately after the trial of Thomas Barron and Edward Bourne.

My research reveals that Mary King, Francis King's wife, continued with efforts to support her husband. She submitted an affidavit to the Kings Bench dated 14 June, 1718, that is ten days after the date of Defoe's letter to De la Faye, claiming expenses of £150. She had gone to London to meet lawyers acting for Morphew and had demanded money. She was offered £20 and a public apology.

The Kings Bench found Morphew guilty and fined him a mere 13 shillings. On payment of the fine he was free to continue with his printing business.[244] It seems highly likely that there was an intervention by the government determining this leniency. Applebee's reported on Nov. 19 that John Morphew 'a noted publisher of books & pamphlets had died the day before at his house near Stationer's Hall'. From Nov. 20 Morphew's advertisements for his publications ceased.[245]

What was it about this case that so agitated Defoe? In particular what was the dispute with Francis King about? Francis King may have

---

[243] H. 456.

[244] NA. Kings Bench, 29/377 Controlment Rolls, Folios 10 and 28. For Mary King's affidavit 1/1.

[245] *Applebee's Original Weekly Journal*, London, Nov. 1720.

had a family grievance arising from the will of Thomas King. Did Defoe, perhaps for revenge against King for 'deserting' him in Madagascar, contrive to cheat him? Or was he motivated by the fear of a publication that threatened his life? The legal affidavits presented to the King's Bench show that Francis King was 'down on his luck' and needed money. I cannot venture too far into the issues and controversies here but I would point out that Francis King was in a position to blackmail Defoe, as were other members of the crew of the *Aurangezebe*. Would a publication threaten not only Defoe but two men, Barron and Bourne, who might have been involved with Defoe's journey to Madagascar as members of the crew of the *Aurangezebe*? In contriving with others to procure diamonds in Madagascar, Defoe was knowingly dealing in stolen goods – Avery's stolen goods. This was a capital offence punishable by a grisly execution. Defoe would have been very, very frightened if that were the case.

This legal dispute throws light on a major Defoe biographical controversy. Did Defoe sell out to the Whig administration in 1716 and become the 'Corrector General of the Press', in words used by Novak, and for his immediate profit?[246] Or did De la Faye's knowledge of Defoe's criminal escapade put him in a position to blackmail him into cooperating with the Whig administration? Or perhaps did both of these possibilities apply?

Captain Avery escaped capture and punishment but the case against him remained open. In the preface to *Moll Flanders*, Defoe writes, 'My True Name is so well-known in the Records, or Registers at Newgate, and in the Old-Baily, and there are things of such Consequence still depending there, relating to my particular Conduct, that it is not to be expected that I should set my Name, or that of my Family to this Work; perhaps after my Death it may be better known; at present it would not be proper, no, not tho' *a general Pardon should be issued even without Exceptions and Reserve of Persons or Crimes.*'

This is a very emphatic statement for *Moll's* supposed petty crimes. Could Defoe be referring to Avery's diamonds?

---

[246] Novak, 490.

2. Did Defoe have time to make the trip?

Clearly, the account given so far indicates that the *Farther Adventures* is a good deal more than pure fiction. But was it in practice possible for Defoe to make such a journey. The distance from London to Brazil by ship is 7,000 nautical miles. Today a yacht travelling this route could expect to average 140-160 nautical miles every twenty-four hours so giving a time of forty-five days to make the journey.[247] Assuming a reasonable length of 'stay on the island' to conduct business the entire journey might be expected to last four months. It might have taken time to put this voyage together after the making of Francis King's will on 1 December, 1705, as *Crusoe's* account suggests. To be present on the voyage would then have required Defoe to be abroad for at least five months in the eight month period from December, 1705 to July, 1706, the date of publication of *Jure Divino*.

There are three main ways of testing whether this was possible. First, there is Defoe's correspondence, in particular his letters to Harley for whom he was working at the time. Is there evidence of regular letter writing in this period that could only have been possible by Defoe's presence in England? Secondly, there are his regular contributions to the *Review*. Were there contributions that could only have been made if Defoe was present in England? Thirdly, what Defoe works were published in the period and did the publication of any one of them necessitate his presence in England?

There is a gap in the correspondence dates given by Healey. In November, 1705 Defoe writes to Harley about the Coventry Parliamentary By-election. Defoe made promises to repeat his account in the *Review* (29 December and 11 April, 1706) but he never did. His next letter to Harley is dated by Healey as '?April 1706.'[248]

The issue of the *Review* is more troublesome to my narrative. Ultimately it is necessary to argue that Defoe was not always able to write every word of every copy of the *Review* and, consequently, that

---

[247] Information from Travis Yates, Sirius Sailing Inc., who specialise in yachting voyages.
[248] H. 46.

he relied on others to assist him. I have no evidence of this but it does seem almost incontrovertible to me that he must have relied on others from time to time.

McVeagh[249]writes, 'It may strike the modern reader as all but incredible that he [Defoe] still managed throughout the year [1706] not only to publish the *Review* three times a week but to sustain its unrivalled ability to surprise, persuade and entertain.' McVeagh points out that one method used by Defoe was to repeat material and double it up with a publication. He points out that in the period Jan-March, 1706 Defoe concentrates on bankruptcy and in the period April-August, 1706 he deals with the public state of the nation. If Defoe was being helped by other writers in the production of the *Review* it would be easy enough for them to recycle material Defoe had left with them. For example, *Remarks on the Bill to Prevent Frauds Committed by Bankrupts* was published in April, 1706 and referred to in the *Review* on 26 March, 1706. It is interesting, and perhaps relevant, that Defoe did not seek relief for himself under the Bill until August 1706. Similarly there was a long delay in the publication of *Jure Divino*.

Taking all these factors into consideration I think it entirely possible that Defoe was abroad in the period December, 1705 to April, 1706 as he describes in *Farther Adventures*.

There is a postscript to this story. Max Novak writes of a hostile and sarcastic description of Defoe given anonymously in 1707 as follows. 'One thing Daniel, I want to know, that is, whether you keep up your Beau habit, your long Wig with Tossels the End of it, and your blew Cloak? As also whether you have left your old Wont, of holding out your little Finger to show your Diamond Ring?'[250]

3. Did Defoe know Avery?

I believe that Defoe did know Avery and that he was the Friend that came to see him in Bideford. Readers will know that one of the first books Defoe wrote in his great outburst of fiction in 1718-1724

[249] McVeagh. John, *Review*, Pickering and Chatto, London, 2004.
[250] Quoted by Novak, 318.

was his apologia for Captain Avery in *King of the Pyrates*. In this work he was at pains to diminish the value of Avery's wealth and to 'throw cold water' over his notoriety. In my account here I rely on the highly detailed treatment of Avery given by Defoe in *A General History of the Pyrates* published in 1724. I am familiar with the controversy on whether Defoe wrote the *General History* and the arguments advanced against his authorship. However, I regard the factual account I have given here to be a powerful proof that Defoe was the author. Clearly, he is the author of the chapters on Bowen and Avery. It is comparatively straight forward to demonstrate that no one but Defoe could have written about the *Aurangezebe*'s encounter with the *Worcester*. The argument runs as follows.

1. A man called Captain Green and the crew of his ship the *Worcester* were arrested when their ship came into the Firth of Forth in Scotland in March, 1705 and charged with boarding a Scottish ship named the *Speedy Return* off the coast of Malabar some time in the period March-May, 1703. The exact time and place of the alleged piracy was never established and the *Speedy Return* was never recovered. The evidence was extremely flimsy and the trial politically motivated. Early in April, 1705 some of the crew of the *Speedy Return*, who had escaped the piracy and returned to London, offered to give evidence showing the innocence of Captain Green.

2. In the *General History* a description is given of the capture of the *Speedy Return*. The piracy is attributed to Captain Bowen. The author of the section on *Captain Bowen* gives a detailed account of the meeting up of the *Worcester* with the *Aurangzebe* in 1703 off the coast of Ajango. Over a period of time the Worcester gave water to the *Aurangezebe*. Thus the crews of both boats had an opportunity to share information about their movements. At this time the *Aurangezebe* was owned by Defoe.

3. Direct knowledge of the details of the meeting between the two ships was limited to the crews of the Worcester and the *Aurangezebe*. Some of the crew of the *Worcester* were arrested. Three men, including Green, were executed others released and subsequently scattered. It is

extremely unlikely that any of the survivors would have the skills, or motivation, to write a coherent account such as given in the *General History*. However, it is highly likely that Francis King or others aboard the *Aurangezebe* would have given Defoe a good verbal account.

4. It follows then that only Defoe could have written this detailed account in the *General History* and that he was the author of the section on Captain Bowen.

5. I believe that it follows also that Defoe is the probable author of other parts of the *General History*, most likely the whole of it, and, in particular, of the section on Captain Avery.

6. Defoe writes a highly detailed and authoritative account of Captain Avery and his exploits in the *General History*.[251] After his escape with the diamonds, Defoe states that Avery went to Boston in America. There he deceived most of his crew and sailed away without them with the bulk of the treasure. Avery made his way to Ireland where he left some of the remaining crew and from there to Bideford in north Devon. Some of his crew made their way to Madagascar with their share of the booty.

Avery had been told by a Friend that there were some persons, Bristol merchants, who might take over the diamonds and sell them for him so avoiding arousing suspicion of their origin. The Friend had approached these merchants on Avery's behalf and they had visited him in Bideford. Reluctantly he agreed to pass over to them his 'Effects', consisting of Diamonds and some Vessels of Gold in return for a small down payment and a promise of a regular income. He changed his name and lived at Bideford, 'Without making any figure, and therefore there was no great Notice taken of him; yet [he] let one or two of his Relations know where he was.' Soon the regular payments ceased he went privately to Bristol to plead his case and to demand that the agreement be honoured. He was shocked by threats to reveal him to the authorities and returned immediately to Ireland. After a while, and being desperate, he resolved to go back to England and force the issue

---

[251] *A General History of the Pyrates*, 49-62.

with the Bristol merchants. He worked his passage back to Plymouth and walked the long journey to Bideford, where he fell sick and died.

Could Defoe have been not only the Friend who acted on Avery's part with the Bristol merchants but one of the Relatives who came into knowledge of his lodgings in Bideford? Did Defoe travel to Bideford and then to Bristol? I consider these issues in Chapter 27, *A General History of the Pyrates*. I am also able to prove, using this new biographical material, that Defoe wrote extensively about Captain Avery and from an earlier date that has been supposed and that he was the author of other related works: These additional works are: *The Life and Adventures of Captain Avery, the Famous Pyrate*, 1709; a play, *the Successful Pyrate*, 1713; *A Letter from Scotland*, 1705; *The Tryal of Captain Green*, 1705;. *Observations: made in England on the Trial of Captain Green, and the Speech at his Death*, 1705; and *Mists Closet Broke Open; on Several Letters Intercepted, in which Are Contained Some Old Truths New Told*, 1728.

The Autobiographical Content of

Selected Works

Chapter 19

Defoe's Written Work: Introduction

If any one reads my story pleases to make the same just reflections which I acknowledge I ought to have made, he will reap the benefits of my misfortunes...the history of men's lives may be many ways made useful and instructing to those who read them, if moral and religious reflections are made by those that write them.

Colonel Jack
Daniel Defoe, 1722

If I were to write that my work is concerned with the truth behind Defoe's fiction every literary critic would welcome it. What objective could be more helpful? However, this is not all I am doing. In order to establish the truth of Defoe's early life, I have had to dispute the biographical information used by literary critics in their interpretation of Defoe's writings in the 23 years since the publication of Paula Backscheider's interesting and informative biographical work. I maintain and seek to demonstrate that all Defoe's fictions, and some part of his non-fiction, are based on embellished accounts of actual happenings in his life, strange or unexpected as it may seem to the reader and critic. I recognise that in doing this, I shall not please every reader.

I hold it to be true that there is hardly *any* character in a major Defoe work that is purely fictional in the usual meaning of the word. Defoe is writing about real people in his life, at a distance from all the information required to identify them, but often in an astonishingly frank manner. Defoe's work may be judged purely on its literary merits by established conventions; however, as a biographer, I welcome Defoe's written works as a rich source of information about the life he led. I recognise the need to justify my approach by reference to literary conventions.

I am aware that there has always been tension between literary criticism and biography and a constant need for negotiation. Biography can be regarded as conservative in that it 'celebrates' a known life of the past whereas the cultural images which post modernism project are seen by literary critics to offer greater insight into the meaning of a text.

Many literary critics would agree with John Carey when he wrote:

> Deconstruction has popularised the idea that what an author actually means in a text is not discoverable, or anyway not provable, so readers not only can but must construct the meaning of a text as they go along. Roland Barthes has pronounced that the author is dead and the reader is free. If so there is not much point in worrying about authors. [252]

It is generally accepted today that the best approach to an understanding of Defoe's fiction – or for that matter any literary critical subject – is through cultural and language studies. What has taken root is the thought that through the adoption of a set of practices it is possible to locate texts precisely within a broad range of cultural trends and thus identify the purposes of specific discourses.

It is generally understood that the fiction of Richardson opened up two hundred golden years of the novel to, say, D H Lawrence. At the conclusion of this period Lawrence was able to write, 'Trust the tale'. In this he meant that even if an author insists on telling you the meaning of a story he is unable to do so. He does not understand it: and the true meaning must always elude him. [253]

Not so commonly understood is that around the time of the emergence of the novel Samuel Johnson ushered in a revival of Georgian interest in biography. It was very clear to him that as a form biography was in conflict with fiction. He wrote about his extraordinary *Life of Richard Savage*:

> It may be reasonably imagined that others may have the same Design but it is not credible that they can obtain the

---

[252] Carey, John. 'Literary Biographies', *English Review*, 1/1 (Sept.1990), 11.
[253] Lawrence, D.H., *Studies in Classic American Literature*, London, 1924, 9.

same Materials, it must be expected that they will supply from Invention the want of Intelligence...they will publish only a Novel filled with romantick Adventures and imaginary Amours.[254]

Readers will have noticed that I date the golden period of the novel with Richardson, who came after Defoe. This is deliberate on my part. Defoe and his female counterpart Eliza Haywood lived in a period of literary transition where the novel and biography began to move in separate but not immediately distinguishable directions: they mixed both forms with a fine lack of distinction. This being so, and accepting that literary and biographical expressions of the meaning of a Defoe work are inter-textual, both forms are necessary to an adequate understanding of it. It is not sufficient in interpreting Defoe's work to rely on the belief that although as an author he is there (at best a truism) he is to be found only in the subtext. I go further by maintaining that in a Defoe work the autobiographical is more often than not the story itself.

It follows in this argument that a defective chronology of Defoe's life that omits the first 36 years of his life and puts 20 years of political, historical, and religious criticism in its place, no matter how interesting it is, produces a flawed interpretation of his work; and in reverse, a better grasp of the detail of Defoe's life will enrich any understanding of it.

An understanding that Defoe lived 56 years of his life in the seventeenth century, shifts interpretations of his fiction to the conventions of the picaresque and the spiritual account. Both Max Novak and G.A.Starr have suggested that Defoe writes into the seventeenth century tradition of spiritual biography best exemplified by Bunyan's *Pilgrim's Progress* and *Grace Abounding*. I have written that Defoe's fiction shows him with his head in the eighteenth century and early capitalism, where the profit motive and the pursuit of wealth appears as a norm, but his heart, or as Defoe might think and feel it, his

---

[254] Johnson, Samuel. *Life of Savage*, (1744 ed .Clarence Tracy from the first edition), Oxford University Press, 1971.

soul, was in the seventeenth century. It was difficult for any writer to shake himself free from the all-embracing demands of religion throughout the eighteenth century.

Defoe's fiction lacks two essential ingredients of the realistic novel that was to follow him. First his writing is episodic and careless of linear time. Although Defoe invariably writes in the first person and the past tense he finds it difficult to mediate his stories. He leaves characters of seeming importance high and dry or abruptly removes them. Secondly, his work lacks any use of irony except in very special definitions of the term. The narrative effect of these deficiencies is that Defoe leaves the reader with unresolved moral dilemmas about the nature of man, the effects of original sin, and the problems of redemption.

Defoe is an unreliable narrator. His fiction is replete with narrative tricks and devices. He displaces emotions and behaviour onto others to deflect any possible criticism, tells half-truths and gives specious evidence. We can see from his very many affidavits lodged in various courts of law that he possessed arts of obfuscation. Defoe was a talented investigative journalist; but even in the exercise of these skills he confounds the basic rules. All journalists need them. A good journalist reports on what happened, to whom, where and when, and clearly identifies the public interest. On the other hand, and I think to his credit, in his work Defoe demonstrates a brutal awareness of his own complexities and shortcomings.

Makikalli and Muller, writing in 2012, have questioned Defoe's competencies as a writer of fiction. They quote a number of literary commentators who have criticised Defoe. For example, Ian Watt who expressed the view that Defoe had difficulty in controlling his material; Michael Boardman, who believed that Defoe did not always understand what he was doing; and G.A.Starr, who argues pithily that Defoe was neither 'overly concerned with maintaining the boundaries of genre' nor 'primarily concerned with pushing those boundaries either.' [255] I suggest

---

[255] Makikalli, Aino and Muller, Andreas. *Positioning Daniel Defoe's Non-fiction: Fiction Form, Function, Genre*, Cambridge University Press, 2010.

that the truth of Defoe's literary competency is simpler than these critics suggest. As Defoe was always writing about his own complex life, he simply got on with his story as best he could.

It is not part of my argument that the autobiographical in Defoe's works can be interpreted and portrayed literally. Defoe gives embellished and fantastical accounts of his life. It is my belief, however, that in his fiction Defoe is recounting the life he lived as he understood it. Given the secrecy with which Defoe lived his life, these accounts are clues to the truth of it. I accept, of course, that as this is my view I should be willing to find acceptable evidence that proves the theses I put forward. Often, and more usually than my critics are prepared to admit, there is good documentary evidence to support the propositions I advance. It is necessary sometimes to conjecture. All biographical accounts confront the problems involved in doing so. The truthfulness of a conjecture should be judged on its merits. Where strong documentary evidence supports a conjecture it is possible to accept it, especially when it falls within a structure and pattern of events or behaviour.

It is possible to argue that biographical accounts of Defoe's life that are influenced by his fiction can be construed falsely and unfairly to him. He is often portrayed as a rogue living on the verges of criminality and an unreliable friend to everyone and every value. It is not a fair or balanced portrait: the truth of it is far more complex. I do not recognise it. For example, Defoe's fiction shows him careless and callous towards his many fictional children in an age of cruelty towards them. It is my considered view, and to the contrary, that Defoe did his best to ease his own children's way in the world. He seems to have thought that he could have done more. What parent does not have these feelings? In reality, as I have argued here, he looked after them all, provided for their everyday care, furthered their education and provided for their futures in his lifetime.

I believe that Mikikalli and Muller, and their contributors, turn away from fiction to non-fiction in the hope that better order can be established. It is certainly true that Defoe's non-fiction presents the critic with different problems. Defoe uses his skills as an investigative journalist to write into many genres: fictional accounts of actual events, such as the *Storm* and *Journal of the Plague Year*; criminal biography, in *A True and Genuine Account of the Life and Actions of the Late Jonathan Wild*; conduct books, such as *Family Instructor* and *Religious Courtship*; piracy, such as *A General History of the Pyrates* and *King of the Pyrates*; travel stories and guides, of which *Captain Singleton* and *Atlas Maritimus are* examples; spiritual and magical accounts, say the *Political History of the Devil*; and so on, for there are others. However, the common denominator of all these works is that they would have little interest to most readers today but for the fact that they were written by Defoe.

While writing into these genres, Defoe brings to them his own uniqueness. It is widely recognised that he does. Max Novak writes of *Religious Courtship* that the work is 'more novel than conduct book' and [but] 'its experiences seems to strike some personal notes.' I agree with Novak. Defoe is writing about his own family life. It is helpful to establish which families he is writing about, for he had several, and to what and to whom he refers when raising and discussing issues.

Chapter 20

Robinson Crusoe

The Life and Strange Surprising Adventures of Robinson Crusoe of York, Mariner: Who lived Eight and Twenty Years all alone in an un-inhabited Island on the Coast of America, near the Mouth of the Gewat River of Oroonoque.

Title Page of First Edition of Robinson Crusoe
Daniel Defoe. 1719

Robinson Crusoe is acknowledged to be Defoe's literary masterpiece. It has been said that if he had written nothing else he would have been remembered for this single book and without it no one would have thought it worthwhile to write his biography. By general literary consent *Crusoe* meets most of the requirements of a literary classic. The story of *Crusoe's* shipwreck and his long stay on a desert island can now be read in almost every language in over seven hundred different versions.

Defoe describes his fictional works as 'Personal Histories or Memoirs'. It is usually commented on this assertion that he was seeking to distance himself from the act of writing fiction or 'Romances'; acts thought disreputable by reading elites, although not by the reading public. Describing his work in this way invited critical attack on the grounds that Defoe was hiding a disreputable life and claiming a religious belief and a wish to redeem that was untrue, blasphemous and inconsistent with public knowledge of the life he led.

Earlier I discuss Defoe's reactions to fierce criticism from Charles Gildon. In summary, Defoe maintained his position by affirming, in the name of *Crusoe* that he was writing a 'just history of fact' and of forced Confinement, which in my real History is represented by a confined Retreat in an Island; and 'tis as reasonable to represent one kind of Imprisonment by another, as it is to represent any Thing that really exists by that which exists not. The Story of my fright with something on my Bed, was Word for Word a History of what happened, and indeed all those Things received very little Alteration, except what necessarily attends removing the Scene from one Place to another.' In signing the Preface to *Serious Reflections* in the name of Robinson Crusoe, Defoe is admitting that he is 'truly' writing about his own life.

Defoe's defence is sound in literary terms and for all creative writers. It has the virtue of being true. He is telling the reader that his story of 'imprisonment' and 'confinement' is real to life and the events he describes are not the result of incarceration on an island as such but is in another place. I believe that the 'other place' is Brazil as my earlier examination of *Farther Adventures* reveals.

As a work of art, *Robinson Crusoe* is over-determined: that is, it can be read logically in almost any one of vastly different, often multiple, sometimes complex, usually contradictory, interpretive readings. Not many people have argued that the book is autobiography because in the conventional account of his life the chronology cannot be made to fit. Other and more persuasive readings have been advanced.

To my understanding, and historically, the number of ways of reading *Crusoe* can be reduced to seven. On one level the work is a 'novel of romantic adventure.' This is the most common reading today. It is seen as a simple story of a man marooned on a desert island and his attempts to survive and escape. It is an all-male challenge as there are no women on *Crusoe's* island, at least if reading is limited to the first volume. Considered in this way the book has lost its appeal as a unique account of survival. From a different, and bowdlerised, point of view it is a children's adventure story. For political economists and sociologists, *Crusoe* is an archetype of homo economicus, a man who reduces everything to book keeping. Perceptively, G.A. Starr regards the book as a late example of spiritual autobiography and a secular version of John Bunyan's *Grace Abounding*. Related to Starr's *Crusoe* is the popular eighteenth century interest in the nature of man and the predicament of being cast out by society, of being cast away. Samuel Johnson defined a castaway as a person lost or deserted by Providence.

There were many eighteenth century tales of foreign adventures involving some form of incarceration on an island. Clearly there is a case for the book as an island story in the tradition of Shakespeare's *Tempest*. And last, but not least, it is a European story of imperial colonisation and exploitation.

The bald statement that *Robinson Crusoe* is the story of Defoe's enforced state of exile from England for part of the period 1662-1680 naturally raises issues of determination and literary consequence. If his early life, that is to 1680 when he was 36 years of age, was not in London and if his upbringing was vastly different to that supposed for him previously, how do these differences impact on interpretive readings of *Crusoe* - if at all?

In an earlier chapter I show that the *Farther Adventures* is an account of an actual voyage Defoe undertook in 1705/6 in the ship *Aurangezebe* captained by his nephew Francis King who is described as a 'Hull merchant resident in York.' In the description quoted above, Defoe makes a similar claim: Robinson Crusoe is 'a merchant from Hull'. *Crusoe*/Defoe gives details about his relatives there consistent with my discovery of the relatives found there on his mother's side of the family.

However, the interpreter of Defoe's fiction needs to proceed with caution. Defoe writes in *Robinson Crusoe* that he was born in 1632, embarked on his voyage in 1651-1652 (the actual date is not given) landed on his island in 1659, left the island in 1687 and returned to London in 1688 after 29 years of isolation on his desert island. Following Aitken's maxim that to find the actual date of an historical event in Defoe's fiction the reader should add 27 years, some biographers have suggested that the subsequent birth date, 1659, is evidence that Defoe was born in that year. In so doing, of course, they are accepting the autobiographical in Defoe's fiction.

All Aitken is really suggesting to readers is that Defoe had difficulty in hiding dates: there is no golden rule. There are other ways of regarding *Crusoe's* dates. In 1651-1652 by *Crusoe's* account he was about 18 years of age when he left England. In *Colonel Jack* and

Memoirs of a Cavalier the narrators were 17-18. In *Captain Singleton* there is no precise date. However, readers are told that *Singleton's* first voyage in home waters was at the age of 12, an age and date consistent with my narrative here, and as the voyage out occurs quite soon afterwards in the narrative, it can be assumed that the date of departure was also in his youth. All these voyages out were to result in similar disasters: capture, and periods of restraint against the narrators will, three by Portuguese authorities and involving southern Brazil and one following a forced journey to Virginia.

It follows from the proof offered in Chapter 18, *Return to Crusoe's Island*, that *Robinson Crusoe* is a real-life account of Defoe's exile from England as he states it is; but in real-life it was not started in the way *Crusoe* suggests. Of the four accounts of the voyage out offered by Defoe, all published in the period 1719-1722, only one can be corroborated - the account of the 'Grand Tour' in 1662 in *Memoirs of a Cavalier*. The date and circumstances of this Tour, as I have explained, can be verified in the links between Defoe and two of his companions, Robert Spencer, second Earl of Sunderland and William Penn. [256]

Was Defoe/*Crusoe* really exiled for 28 or 29 years? As I have suggested, Defoe may have regarded himself as in Exile as a Huguenot from his birth. Adding twenty-eight years to that would take him to 1672-1673. At this date Crusoe was not living under constraint and could have returned to England. He chose not to do so. More likely I suggest is that Defoe needed to distinguish his account from other stories of isolation on islands, by a really long stay. 'Gosh, really, was he on an island for 29 years?' However, as 29 years is a common period in Defoe's usage of time, it may have a meaning that has eluded me.

Literary speculation is rife on the sources Defoe used to select an island. Derek Walcott using co-ordinates given by *Crusoe* places him in Tobago.[257] English critics tend to the theory that Defoe borrowed

---

[256] See Chapter 5.
[257] Walcott, Derek. *Pantomime and Remembrance*, New York: Farrar, Straus and Giroux, 1980.

material from Alexander Selkirk who was cast ashore at his own request on one of the three Juan Fernandez islands off the coast of Chile. American academics tend to favour Robert Knox's account of his stay on the island of Ceylon in *Historical Recollections* as Defoe's island. Katherine Franck, in a spirited account, draws reader's attention to Knox. She argues that is clear that Defoe owned a copy of *Historical Recollections* because it was listed in the auction sale catalogue of his books in 1731 after his death.[258] More persuasively Frank shows that in *Captain Singleton* Defoe borrows text word by word from *Historical Recollections* and uses imagery from Knox's description of the white man in Africa – assumed by me to be an allegorical Captain Avery. This is undeniable. However, Defoe borrowed extensively from other authors in many works without acknowledgement. It is not a great crime: all creative writers are 'great thieves' and after all, there are a limited number of plots. In *Captain Singleton* Defoe states explicitly that Ceylon was not his island.

Defoe and Knox never met. When Knox published his memoirs, *Autobiography*,[259] in 1701 he made no mention of Defoe. In contrast, Thomas Wright offered a proof that Defoe met Selkirk in 1712. I rounded out and strengthened that proof in *Beyond Belief.* [260] Wright offers an interesting and convincing speculation that following the purchase of Selkirk's notes in Bristol, Defoe spent time in Halifax where he started work on writing *Robinson Crusoe*. I have offered a proof that Defoe met Nettleton in Halifax around this time, that he was an old friend of Defoe's, and that the conversations between these two friends was written up by Nettleton in his essay, *A Treatise on Virtue and Happiness.* [261]

Consequently, I conclude that Selkirk sold Defoe more than his notes. He 'sold' him the notion, or strengthened an existing conviction,

---

[258] Heidenreich, Helmut. *The Libraries of Daniel Defoe and Philips Farewell*, Berlin, 1970, 198.
[259] Knox, Robert. *Autobiography*, (1681 ed. J.H. Paulusz, Dehwila, Sri Lanka, 1989).
[260] *Beyond Belief*, 189-190, n.300.
[261] BL. 8407.e.18. Nettleton, Thomas. *A Treaty on Virtue and Happiness. in a Letter to a Clergyman*, London, 1729.

that writing a memoir or history of his stay in Brazil and the subsequent adventures beyond the period of constraint could best be narrated in an 'island-life' setting. It took Defoe seven years to produce and publish his composition, *Robinson Crusoe*. I think that I should make it quite clear at this point that in my opinion Defoe turned dross into silk. Nothing that I write here should be construed as a kind of foray to diminish Defoe's authorship of *Robinson Crusoe*. It is a wonderful work of the imagination; but it is a work of Defoe's imagination.

Defoe achieved more than he could ever have envisioned. I agree with V.S Naipaul when he wrote:

> Robinson Crusoe, in its essential myth-making middle-part, is an aspect of the same fantasy [the heroic legend of an untouched complete world]. It is a dream of being the first man in the world, of watching the first crop grow. Not only a dream of innocence: it is a dream of being suddenly, just as one is, in unquestionable control of the physical world, of possessing the first gun that had been fired there since the creation of the world. It is the dream of total power.[262]

What did Defoe's actual experience in Brazil bring to *Robinson Crusoe*? The elements of Defoe's exile in Brazil, and subsequent trading along the trans-Atlantic route as a merchant and slave trader, brought many of the cardinal features of *Crusoe's* experience: Solitude, Retirements from the world (isolation), Strange Notions, Apparitions, Dreams, Visitations and Man Friday [s]. In the end, or so Defoe tells his readers, it brought Repentance. Defoe maintained also that:

> in a 'Life of Wonders' he experienced, 'continu'd Storms, fought with the worst kind of Savages and Man-eaters, [experienced] unaccountable surprising Incidents, fed by Miracles...all Manner of Violences and Oppressions... injurious Reproaches, contempt of Men... In a Word, there's not a Circumstance in the imaginary Story but has its just

---

[262] Naipaul, V.S. 'Essay. 'Columbus and Crusoe', 1967. Quoted by John Thieme. *Post Colonial Subtexts: writing back to the canon*, Continuum, London and New York, 2001.

Allusion to a real Story, and chimes Part for Part, and Step
for Step with the inimitable Life of *Robinson Crusoe*

When allowance is made for hype, the promotion of a book to
readers hungry for accounts of strange foreign adventures, it is easy to
agree. Of course, Defoe had such experiences.

In *Crusoe* Defoe gives tells the reader an account of his stay in
Brazil but he does not recount anything much about his day to day
experiences, the persons who were important to him, and the day to
day conditions he experienced. The reader must imagine them
virtually unaided. However, in *Colonel Jack* he tells something of a
life lived on a Virginian plantation. From this account something
more can be said about *Crusoe*. In 'Virginia', Defoe's living
experience was of unremitting daily labour alongside slaves and
contract labourers. *Colonel Jack* succeeded in ingratiating himself
with the plantation owner so that he could assume a supervisory role
and performed his duties as one until he had demonstrated to the
owner that he was reliable. The living conditions must have been
highly primitive. And this is how it was for *Crusoe* in Brazil. As time
passed in both Virginia and Brazil the narrator's living conditions
improved.

It seems to me to be likely, and understandable, that Defoe was
permitted early on in his stay in Brazil to choose a plot of land and to
try to work it. When Defoe came into money some two years later he
was able to buy tools and use slave labour. He would have been told
that the countryside around him was waiting for someone to claim it
and that he could build something for himself. This virgin land could,
with hard work, become his territory, his kingdom, for no one else at
this time was there to challenge him. At first, *Crusoe*, until 'the ink
ran dry', kept a journal record and marked the passing of each day.
Crusoe's practice of record keeping is often discussed. I understand it
to be akin to a prisoner isolated in a cell without reference to a
calendar ticking off the days to his release on a cell wall. For *Crusoe*
release would come once the period of constraint had been counted.
Beyond this period, once money had been raised, he could work his

own plantation in agreement with his 'keeper' and presumably to the 'keeper's' profit.

As Defoe/*Crusoe* gained a measure of freedom, and the capital and labour bought in London, he was able to build up his Castle, and develop other shelters including one in the north of his island. The natural conditions encouraged the development of sugar and tobacco plantations. He kept goats and milked them and grew rice and corn and ground it into bread. He became settled in his world and with his regular daily routines. He built himself a boat and voyaged along the coast between his northern and southern domains.

Defoe was not without human contact in Brazil, there were other planters, slaves and contract workers, but for much of the time he would have been completely isolated. Living this way was dangerous for there was either no, or inadequate, civil authority, particularly in the north. Native invaders from neighbouring islands and from the northern Spanish controlled territories could land by boat along any part of an extensive coast line and some of these natives were rumoured to be cannibals. *Crusoe* observed boats landing from a secure position on a hill and he studied and tracked their habits. He concluded that their ins and outs were on the tide, that they sought only water and provisions, and that provided he kept out of sight they would not be a threat to him. As *Crusoe* recounts his story he is somewhat over-optimistic; these invaders thought nothing of bringing captives to the island to eat them.

A typical reader of *Robinson Crusoe* remembers two events in his life on the island. First, and most dramatic, was the discovery of a footprint on the sand and his subsequent encounter with Man Friday; and secondly, *Crusoe's* 'religious conversion.'

The Foot Print and Man Friday

When Crusoe had been on his island for about 22 years he found a footprint on the sand. It was not his. He was thunderstruck. If there was one print there must be others for the intruder could not have made his way onto the island on his own. He retired to his shelter and spent several days and nights in a state of anxiety. When he ventured forth he There were no other intruders. As time passed he felt more secure. The reader shares his anxiety for the same reason: fear of the unknown. Among readers this footprint is associated with Friday but it is more than two years later when *Crusoe's* stay was in its twenty-fifth year that he encountered Friday fleeing from two cannibals on the beach. *Crusoe* shot and killed one of these intruders, and Friday cut off the head of the other with *Crusoe's* sword.

It might have been thought that *Crusoe* would have welcomed Friday as a companion after years of isolation but the very first step taken by them both was for Friday to recognise and swear fealty to *Crusoe* so establishing a relationship of master to servant.

Defoe describes Friday. It is the longest and most intimate portrait of another person given by Defoe in any of his writings. He wrote in a well-punctuated and poetic form:

> He was a comely handsome fellow, perfectly well made; with straight strong limbs, not too large; tall and well shap'd, and as I reckon, about twenty-six Years of Age. He had a very good Countenance, not a fierce and surly Aspect; but seem'd to have something very manly in his Face, and yet he had all the Sweetness and Softness of an *European* in his Countenance too, especially when he smil'd. His Hair was long and black, not curl'd like Wool; his forehead very high, and large, and a great Vivacity and Sharpness in his Eyes. The Colour of his Skin was not quite black, but very tawny; and yet not of an ugly yellow nauseous tawny, as the *Brasilians*, and *Virginians*, and other nations of *America* are; but of a bright kind of olive Colour, that had in it something very agreeable; tho' not very easy to describe. His face was round and plump; his nose small, not flat like the Negroes, a very good mouth, thin lips, and fine Teeth well set, and white as Ivory.

I would define this description as erotic. Hans Turley writes, 'I see the desire exhibited by *Crusoe* toward Friday as distinct from the usually uncomplicated master/slave dichotomy that critics tend to observe…he is an essential part of Crusoe's life.' Turley contrasts the affectionate farewell to Friday following his death in *Farther Adventures* to the terse dismissal of his wife's death. In this I think Turley is wrong. Defoe often uses a death to remove a character from the narrative. In this instance Mary Tuffley, the wife referred to by *Crusoe*, had not died other than in the sense of being 'dead' to Defoe.

Hans Turley is on stronger ground when he refers to 'Humphrey Richardson's pornographic and amusing novel, *The Secret Life of Robinson Crusoe*. In this novel *Crusoe* has rough sex with Friday and he is acting out, what Turley believes is implicit in *Crusoe's* character; 'a sexual desire made manifest by its very silence in Defoe's novels.'

An unasked question in Defoe biography is just how many Friday's are there in Defoe's fiction: that is how many black boys are mentioned? In *Crusoe* there are three: an un-named boy bought in London when Defoe came into money as described earlier in *Robinson Crusoe*; the slave Xury, who was willing to give his own life for *Crusoe*; and Man Friday. There are two others in his fiction: Mouchat in *Colonel Jack*, and the black boy Toby in *Religious Courtship*, acquired by Defoe from a ship's captain from Barbados most probably, I conjecture, Captain Edward Singleton.

It is not possible to maintain that all these black boys are fictional. I am able to demonstrate later that Defoe names Friday after his neighbour John Friday. If any black boy is Man Friday, that is if Friday is not a fictional composite, it is Toby. It was quite common for adventurers to Africa and the Americas to return to England with black slaves. Defoe almost certainly encountered Admiral Penn's black servants in London in 1660-1662. In Brazil the relationships 'Richardson' describes were commonplace. No biographer is a party to Defoe's relationships with black boys. I conjecture that these relationships were sexual but I cannot prove that they were.

Religious Conversion

A spiritual biography must end in repentance. Crusoe had brought a bible onto his island, a present from the kindly Captain on his return from London. Once he was settled he thought often about the nature of God's Providence and his punishment. As he settled he came to believe that God had been kind. Here he was with a sufficiency which met his daily needs and a routine that occupied his time. He was almost happy. But he didn't stay that way for very long as his mind turned to ending his exile on the island.

It is to be expected that a man in *Crusoe's* predicament would suffer. Prolonged loneliness with the threat of attacks by strangers would be expected to produce a hallucinatory frame of mind: extreme anxieties, sleeplessness, visions and inexplicable spiritual manifestations. It can be argued that it is part of Defoe's writing ambition to re-create these terrors for his readers.

There are other explanations. It is the genius of another writer, and physician, Freud, that holds the key to a richer understanding. In an earlier chapter I suggest that some of the effects on Defoe of the death of his father, and the loss of his mother were harmful to him. I suggest that as a result of these disasters Defoe failed to make a trouble free transition to adulthood. It would have been far better psychologically not to have been born at all: the womb had been abandoned without reward. A return to the womb was of course impossible but womb substitutes were numerous: houses, shelters, caves, prison cells, ships and islands. All these womb-like places were subject to external threat: discovery, the pillory, execution, shipwreck – and savages who might engulf you entirely in the act of eating you. However, in reality every person must escape from the womb, and the greatest disaster to the embryonic child would be not to be born at all.

Leo Abse in his psychoanalytical study of Defoe[263] quotes Ferenczi. He described the weaning process following a birth as showing that a baby emerges from the period of harmless oral eroticism, sucking, into a cannibalistic stage; it develops within the mouth instruments for biting with which it would fain eat up, as it were, the beloved mother, compelling her eventually to wean it. In the seventeenth century the weaning process was longer than it is today. In a normal loving and prolonged relationship with the mother the baby passes from a pre-ambivalent oral phase to a second stage, a sadistic one, the oral-

---

[263] Abse, 51.

cannibalistic phase. Abse suggests that Defoe never experienced this transition. *Crusoe's*/Defoe's preoccupation with the fate of being devoured by cannibals evokes a psychological nightmare rather than a reality.

If the reader follows the drift of Freudian analysis, Defoe's relationship to a father he could not remember is central to an understanding of his need for redemption. Defoe gives *Crusoe* a nightmare (which in the Preface to *Serious Reflections* Defoe insists is his own). He writes:

> I had this terrible dream I thought that I was sitting on the ground when the storm blew after the earthquake, and that I saw a man descend from a great black cloud, in a bright flame of fire, and light upon the ground ...I could just bear to look towards him...He was no sooner landed upon the earth but he moved toward me with a long spear or weapon in his hand to kill me...I heard a voice so terrible that it is impossible to express the terror of it; all that I can say I understood was this: 'Seeing all these things have not brought thee to repentance, now thou shalt die. At which words I thought he lifted up the spear that was in his hands to kill me.'

The imagery of the dream is important to an understanding of it. *Crusoe* is on the ground, as a small child might be, he is small and the threatening man tall and 'falling from the sky towards him'. The man has judged *Crusoe* for un-stated crimes. These crimes are so terrible that without repentance he must be killed. He is to be killed by a spear, a Freudian penis symbol.

It is a matter of speculation as to whether Defoe could ever hold to his aspiration to repent the errors and sins of his life. It was Freud's achievement to demonstrate that the traumas that haunt and hamper adults are all experienced in early childhood. Much though Defoe might have wished to live a blameless life there was no real possibility that he could. I believe he tried many times and failed on each occasion. Defoe has the honesty to admit these things. For example,

Crusoe sets out to teach Friday English and to make a Christian of him. Ruefully, he comments that Friday became a better Christian than him.

It has become common practice to adopt a cultural approach to the interpretation of dreams in the Early Modern period. What, it might be argued, can the dream-content of a Viennese woman at the turn of the nineteenth century have in common with the dreams of a seventeenth century merchant? Any interpretation of a dream is welcome and there is much to be learnt from a discussion of it. The more the merrier. However, my own belief is the Freud's *Interpretation of Dreams* provides the yardstick against which all other theories are best measured. Defoe's interest in apparitions and the spirit world was life-long. Late in his life he was prolific in writing about these subjects.

As all readers know, *Crusoe* saved Friday's father from the cannibals and others were indebted to him for their lives. *Crusoe* believed that he held land on his island as a right of possession. It was his kingdom. Those that owed their lives to him became his subjects on the ground of his inheritance of the territory and the fact that he protected them. On his return to England he tells readers that he sold his lands in the south. I have conjectured, in Chapter 18, that he retained his plantation in the north. In *Farther Adventures*, 25 years later, *Crusoe* tells readers that his kingship was still recognised by its inhabitants.

There are important conclusions to be drawn from my readings of *Robinson Crusoe* and *Farther Adventures of Robinson Crusoe*. It is not possible to hold on to existing accounts without the recognition of the events of Defoe's early life from 1644-1680. It follows also that previous readings of *Robinson Crusoe* fail to convince because they use false chronology and biographical material. I do not think that these accounts can be reconciled with the portrait of Defoe presented in earlier biographical accounts. There are no childhood traumas conjured-up in them.

Chapter 21

Moll Flanders

Moll Flanders is suspiciously like her author even in matters where we would expect striking and obvious differences.

Ian Watt
The Rise of the Novel, 1957

It is unusual for a man to write two successful fictions in the guise of a woman. It is not unreasonable to seek to find a reason for it. I assert that Defoe was bi-sexual and a cross-dresser: that is, he enjoyed dressing-up and behaving as a woman. Defoe had passionate relationships with men. Some of these relationships were extremely important in the conduct of his life; some men he regarded as trophies. Defoe was proud to tell of his exploits and in the recounting of them he released some of the excitement of these sexual encounters. Defoe sought to write about these relationships without giving himself or others away. Public disclosure of homosexual activities was unwise throughout his life and, in particular, in 1700-1730. In this period there was a public reaction against sodomy and men were arrested and publicly executed. There was no better way for Defoe to write about his sexuality, while hiding his identity, than writing as a woman.

Very few readers will thank me for the reading of *Moll Flanders* I give here. It is usual to summarise the book as 'the story of the notorious life and ultimate repentance of a woman [Moll Flanders] who lived for much of her adult life as a whore and a thief'.[264] Readers enjoy the story of *Moll Flanders*, warm to her personally, and become involved in her fate. They like her. I like her.

For the last five decades *Moll's* story has been read as an illustration of the unfair treatment of women in a male-dominated and unequal society where women were exploited. As Defoe writes his tale, it can

---

[264] Blewett, David. Introduction, Defoe, Daniel. *Moll Flanders,* Penguin Classics, 1972.

be seen that the opportunities open to women were unfairly limited and that often they had to resort to thievery and prostitution to make their way in life. However, that honest judgement does not explain *Moll Flanders*. The reader suspects that *Moll* gets excited by her escapades: she is 'naughty with it'. *Moll* goes from one disaster to another and finishes in Newgate under threat of death; but in the spirit of a narrative made reality by Hollywood films there is a happy ending. *Moll* experiences a spiritual awakening, 'a rebirth of the soul that leads to her to repentance and happiness'.

It is 'raining on the party', spoiling the fun, for me to suggest an entirely new and troublesome reading of a familiar and well-liked book. Hastily, I point out that others have had the same suspicions and reservations. To complete the quotation above by Ian Watt, previous readings have ignored the obvious. Watt's work has held its place in required reading in literary studies of the 'rise of the novel' for fifty-five years.[265] He writes:

The facts show that she [*Moll*] is a woman and a criminal, for example, but neither of these two roles determines her personality as Defoe has drawn it. ...the essence of her character is, to one reader at least, essentially masculine...she seems fundamentally untouched by her criminal background...and ...displays many of the attitudes of a virtuous and public minded citizen...Moll Flanders...is not noticeably affected either by her sex, by her criminal pursuits, or indeed by any of the objective factors which might have been expected to set her apart from her author; on the other hand, she shares with Defoe...many of the traits that might have been expected to set her aside from her author...and many of the character traits that are usually regarded as middle-class. She is obsessed with gentility ...she has by osmosis, picked up the vocabulary and attitudes of a tradesman. Like Robinson Crusoe, she has, by some process of osmosis, a restless, amoral, and strenuous individualism and it is surely more reasonable to assume that, [Defoe's] identification with Moll Flanders was so complete that, despite a few feminine traits, he created a personality that was in essence his own.

[265] Watt, Ian. *The Rise of the Novel*, 1957, Pimlico Press, 2000, 93-134.

I am inclined to write 'just so' to Watt; but it is not quite that. In writing as a woman Defoe had embarked on something more difficult than Watt imagined. Defoe is not writing merely about his own life but of that of his sister Mary. He identifies with her 'feminine traits' and intermixes and hides his own sexual adventures by displacement onto Mary in a most ingenious manner. The 'feminine traits' that Ian Watt recognises owe much of their origin to Mary but also, and mostly, to Defoe.

It is essential for any biographer, or literary critic, to appreciate the narrative structure of *Moll Flanders*. As is common in Defoe's fiction the book splits into two main parts: the first is the story of *Moll's* early life, her upbringing, relationship with her brother, having children, and her relationships with other men. In real life this period ends with Defoe embarking on the European Grand Tour in July, 1662 when he was in his eighteenth year and *Moll*/Mary in her seventeenth. The second part describes *Moll's* delinquent behaviour, her life as a petty thief, her punishment and imprisonment, removal to America and subsequent redemption and return to England.

Mary (*Moll*) King's chronology is provided in this book. It is possible to divide the first part into five segments each of which is ended by a 'death' of a 'husband'. These are not sequential nor are they uninterrupted. Defoe is hard-pressed, as the narrator, to relate or inter-lock his accounts. The second part is mainly concerned with *Moll's* criminal behaviour which leads to incarceration in Newgate prison, transportation, re-union with a 'son' and subsequent return to England and redemption. The reader of this work of mine will understand immediately at this point that these descriptions of criminal activity are remarkably similar to those described in *Colonel Jack*, *Captain Singleton* and *Memoirs of a Cavalier* and that I ascribe these characteristics to Defoe.

I maintain that *Moll Flanders* is first, an embellished account of Daniel Defoe's, and his sister Mary (*Moll*) King's, upbringing in Colchester and Tilbury in the period 1647-1662; secondly, it discusses Defoe's early life as a petty thief.; and thirdly, the book provides information about *Moll*/Mary's first two marriages, also described in *Captain Singleton*, together with embellished accounts of a number of Defoe's passionate involvements with men.

Defoe succeeds in his autobiographical account by writing *Moll's* story into a genre of fictional rogue biographies involving women thieves, some of whom he may have encountered in London and in Newgate. It is a successful endeavour that has been aided and abetted by cultural historians and literary critics. Defoe attempts to show how his sister resolved the conflicts in her life by achieving bourgeois marriages, four in number, which freed her from incest with her brother and supported and changed her life for the better. The relationship with her brother, Defoe, is disguised by reference to him as a 'husband'. The other nine passionate relationships ascribed to *Moll*/Mary are hidden accounts of Defoe's relationships with men. Ultimately the book draws upon, and writes into, the puritan tradition of spiritual biography.

Defoe's task in writing *Moll Flanders* was 'heroic'. I admire him greatly for doing it. There are practical difficulties for a man writing as a women but eager to write into the tale his own adventures. It might be said that Defoe could not possibly succeed. As Ian Watt describes, Defoe makes mistakes in doing this. When these mistakes are pointed out to new readers, or readers willing to look at the work afresh, they are really rather obvious.

The Authors Claim

I start by following Defoe's advice 'in the beginning' by posing the question of how he succeeds in establishing the identity of the author. Defoe writes in the Frontispiece to the original production and the opening paragraphs of his narrative as follows:

> [Moll Flanders] was Born in Newgate, and during a life of contin'd Variety for three score Years, beside her Childhood, was twelve Year a *Whore*, five times a Wife (whereof once to her own Brother), Twelve Year a *Thief*, Eight Year a Transported *Felon* in Virginia, at last grew Rich liv'd *Honest* and died a P*enitent*. Written from her own MEMORANDUM.

And:

> The Author is here supposed to be writing her Own History...she gives the Reasons why she thinks fit to Conceal her true Name...When a woman debauched from her Youth...[gives] an Account of all vicious practices ...an Author must be hard put to it to wrap it up...

And further:

> My TRUE Name is so well known in the Records, or Registers at Newgate and in the Old Baily, and there are some things of such Consequence still depending there, relating to my particular Conduct, that it is not to be expected I should set my Name, or the Account of my Family to this work; perhaps after my Death it may be better known; at present it would not be proper, no, not tho' a general Pardon should be issued, even without Exceptions and reserve of Persons or Crimes. It is enough to tell you, that as some of my worst Comrades, who are out of the Way of doing me Harm, having gone out of the World by the Steps and the String[266] as I often expected to go,...knew me ...so you may give me leave to speak myself under that name [Moll Flanders] til I dare own who I have been, as well as who I am.

It is rewarding to examine this apologia closely and to bear in mind in doing so that Defoe is psychologically impelled to 'sail as close to the wind as possible'; but from my narrative it is clear that these descriptions of *Moll* apply to Defoe and thus much of the narrative could have been written without reference to *Moll* at all.

1. Mary's Age at the Time of Writing Moll Flanders

The age of consent for sexual intercourse for a girl, and hence of marriage, was twelve. A boy reached adult maturity at fourteen years. Mary Foe was born on March 4, 1645.[267] If, following Defoe's

---

[266] The ladder and the rope of the gallows.
[267] NRO. Etton Parish Records.

narrative in the Frontispiece and elsewhere, three score years plus twelve are added to Mary's date of birth we get a date of 1717 and if Defoe was using his own birth date, 1716. It follows, therefore, that the date of writing *Moll Flanders* or composing the beginnings would have been, 1716-1717. Readers will readily understand that you do not arrive at that date using a year of birth for Defoe of 1659/1660.

2. Whore, Prostitute, Thief or Blameless?

It is possible to read *Robinson Crusoe* and *Captain Singleton*, as I do, and to conclude that Mary King was married legally on four occasions, twice in London in the 1660's and twice in Yorkshire in the 1690's. She 'married' her brother, Defoe, in 1658-1661 and, if Defoe as the narrator is to be believed, she had two children by him. Arguably, at least one of the infants may have survived. Defoe accuses his sister in *Moll* of having relationships with thirteen men. Five of these are in 'marriages' which leaves eight others. Whore is a word of abuse used for a person living 'loose' and perhaps taking money from other people for sex when it suited. A modern girl would not think *Moll's* sexual encounters to be very remarkable or reprehensible and it is difficult for readers today to be shocked.

Defoe's life mirrors his sister's as displayed in *Moll*. The evidence that Defoe had four marriages is very strong indeed. In my reading of Defoe's fiction he is persistent in claiming that he had incest with his sister and hence had 'married' her. It follows then that like *Moll* Defoe had five 'marriages'. They all produced children who stand as evidence of them. I have argued that Defoe's first church marriage to Jone Reade, which ended tragically with her death, probably produced a surviving child. These thoughts raise the possibility that Defoe while using his sister's personae, and actual life experiences, is also and perhaps mainly reminiscing about his own life.

In the period 1650-1660, normal conventions for marriage and relationships were being questioned by Quakers who challenged authoritarian paternal authority. Coggeshall, where Mary would have spent time,[268] was a centre of early Quakerism. Quakers were accused of promiscuous behaviour; of adultery within families and sexual relations outside them. This idealistic behaviour did not make these early Quakers prostitutes in the general meaning of the term, that is, a person who debases himself, or herself, for money as a livelihood. .

Essential to *Moll's* story is that she travelled to Virginia and South Carolina with her brother on two occasions at an interval of 20 years; and that she stayed in Virginia after the first visit for eight years. In my narrative readings, these journeys are actual real-life visits and took place in 1682 and 1700.

Was Mary (Moll) King blameless? Who *is* blameless? I expect Mary lived a life in which she made many mistakes and found herself in difficulties on many an occasion. In mentions of her in *Captain Singleton*, Defoe gives an impression of Mary/*Moll* being a good-hearted woman who was generous and loving to her brother. Of course, Defoe is writing into a genre of 'romances' of fictional rogue biographies of the time and titillating the reading public with sensational stories and accounts of condemned criminals on the verge of a public death. Defoe was familiar with this world and writing into it was straightforward for him. But still, if Mary loved and cared for him, to pillory her in the way he did in *Moll Flanders* was, to say the least, something of an unkind act albeit she was dead by the date of publication of the book in 1722.

3. The Records, or Registers of Newgate, and the Old Baily?

Defoe gives contradictory reasons for not disclosing his authorship to the reader. First he writes 'so you may give me leave to speak myself under that name [Moll Flanders] till I dare own who I have been as well as who I am.' Secondly, and later, he writes passionately and emphatically, 'after my death it may be better known...it would not be proper, no, not tho' a General Pardon should be issued, even without Exceptions and Reserve of Persons.'

---

[268] Dale, *Annals of Coggeshall.*

It is puzzling. As written, *Moll's* crimes are petty thieving. In the early eighteenth century, a General Pardon, that was extended to all, or a category of persons, for petty crimes was possible; but one embracing all the crimes Moll confesses to have committed would have been difficult to construct. Defoe in 1716, could have been referring to his discussions with the Whig administration for his own 'Exception' for 'past mistakes'. As discussed earlier, Defoe's 'Capitulation' was agreed with the Whig administration in the period March-October, 1716. This time is consistent with the period 1716-1717 for the writing of the preliminaries to *Moll Flanders*. It was in this year that it was first sorely tested by Francis King as described in Chapter 18. Mary King was alive in 1717 for her brother Thomas King left her his entire estate.[269]

Typically, Defoe presents the interpreter of his work with a conundrum. What is the meaning of the words, 'till I dare own who I have been, as well as who I am.' He can only mean that the person he is now is different from the person he was in the past. If in the past Defoe/*Moll* had led a disreputable life he is claiming that he was reputable at the time of writing.

4. Which Foe child was born in Newgate Prison?

If any Foe child was born in Newgate Prison it would have been Thomas, as I have argued earlier. *Moll* tells readers that there were various oral accounts she had heard about her mother's fate and she did not know the truth of it but that the one common theme was that 'she pleaded her belly' and was transported.[270]

5. Choice of Name

Moll states that she called herself Mrs Flanders.[271] It has been speculated that Defoe selected this name because he knew that in common parlance Flemish women in London were associated with prostitution. In the eighteenth century it is said many of the Flemish

---

[269] ERO. Will of Thomas Kinge.
[270] *Moll Flanders*, 48.
[271] *Moll Flanders*, 43.

women migrating to London were prostitutes.[272] As *Moll* is presented to readers by Defoe she is not a prostitute.

There are other possible explanations for the use of Moll Flanders as a description. First there is his family origin in Flanders and the recognition of, and use of 'Flanders', in Colchester, at the time of Defoe's upbringing – and now.[273] Defoe's mother Ellene was a member of the Lawrence clan in Colchester, in particular, that of the Mayor Thomas Lawrence, who had had a home there in 1647. Ellene was imprisoned for stealing lace. Colchester and its surrounding areas were associated with the Huguenot migration of Flemish weavers and Coggeshall for the production of lace. In *Moll's* story the nurse introduced *Moll* to the trade of 'working on lace' and the mending of clothes. She continued in this trade even when she was taken into the household of one of the Lawrence families. In colloquial terms, the locals may have dubbed a textile worker as a 'Mrs Flanders'. The name may have been spoken in Defoe's presence. If it were to be assumed that the narrative in *Moll Flanders* is of Defoe's life alone, it can be assumed that it was Defoe who was put to work repairing clothes by a Church Poor Law Overseer as explained earlier in my narrative.

Secondly, and related to the first, there is the plasticity in the use of the term 'a Moll' at the time. As now, a Moll was the term for a 'loose woman' whose sexual favours were readily available to men; but the word Moll was also understood as a reference to a sodomite who attended, or even organised, a Molly House. I have produced evidence that Defoe did attend Molly Houses in the 1720's. He referred to the threat of prosecution in *Conjugal Lewdness*.[274]

Part 1. Defoe's/ Mary's /Moll's/ Upbringing and Relationships

In Essex

In earlier chapters I have written extensively about Defoe's upbringing in Essex and of the importance of this to his biography as a whole.

[272] *Moll Flanders*, 108, n.92.
[273] The surname Flanders is used in Essex today.
[274] *Beyond Belief*, 258-261, 267-270.

Although it is untrue, it will be argued by some about this work of mine that it lacks sufficient documentary evidence to prove the propositions I advance without a reasonable doubt; that there are too many conjectures and suppositions. This will be rich coming, as it will be, from scholars who have pinned their faith on conjectures. However, this thought prompts me to do something unusual. I shall not be repeating all the documentary sources quoted in the first part of this book; but I have highlighted, in what follows, the major assertions in this work where documentary evidence is advanced for Defoe's early experiences in Essex. I give a rating of two stars where, in my opinion, the evidence in itself is beyond doubt and a single star where it points to a highly probable conclusion. I project some of this material to Defoe's death in 1731. I invite the reader to compare the weight of this evidence with the 'conventional' account. The 'conventional account' cannot offer a single documented fact for the period 1660-1680. I accept, of course that there are issues to be discussed and I do this in appendices to this work

I concentrate on what is known now about the time spent by Defoe and his family in Essex as it bears on *Moll Flanders*. Defoe and possibly his sister Mary (*Moll*) were taken into the care of the Colchester Corporation, in the Parish of St Leonard's, Lexden, in 1647 ** when Defoe was three years of age** and his sister two years**. They remained in this care until 1658 when Defoe was fourteen years of age (1647/8-1658, that is ten years).* Under existing Poor Laws it is unlikely that care would have been granted to the children or a Pass accepted by the Corporation of Colchester without a family link, that is evidence of the birth of the child in Colchester, or residency of the children's family in Colchester, or the direct intervention of a powerful person acceptable to the Corporation.** It would have been open to Defoe's grandmother, Rose, and his mother Ellene to give proof of residency if, as I believe, they were born in Colchester to a Lawrence family related to Alderman Thomas Lawrence.* All the five Lawrence's who became Mayors of Colchester in the period 1643 to 1722 were direct descendants of Alderman Thomas Lawrence.** It is inconceivable that, given the likelihood of twenty to thirty percent of

Colchester's children living rough in Colchester, ** that the Mayor and his relatives would have taken a close interest in the Foe children/*Moll*. A couple of foundlings would not have attracted the attention of the Mayor and other bourgeois and apparently related, Colchester families Both Mary and Defoe were taken into the household of a Lawrence family (there were many), ** probably John and Anne Lawrence in East Tilbury * but possibly another Lawrence family, until Defoe embarked on the Grand Tour in 1662.** Some two years afterwards Mary/*Moll* moved to London where she married the first of two husbands. It can be deduced from a reading of *Captain Singleton* that she married twice and had two children. In 1681 she was re-united with Defoe, the Captain in Molls account, and went with him to America where she stayed for eight years.* In 1699 Mary accompanied Defoe to America where she was re-united with his 'son' by Jone Reede, called Humphrey in his fiction.* They had travelled there in order to claim an inheritance from her 'mother' (Jone Reede's mother). She travelled to South Carolina to claim her inheritance. She returned to England in 1702.*

Defoe was probably in Tilbury soon after he returned to England in 1680. When Defoe described himself as in the Country in 1681 he was most probably in Essex.** No biographer or commentator on Defoe's life has ever been able to prove that he was resident in any part of the country in England other than Essex except for a very limited period of time. ** A possible exception to this is that he rented property in Hackney and Stoke Newington between 1705 and his death in 1731. These places were sometimes referred to as being in the Country. He was resident in Tilbury from the early 1680's to 1703 the date of his imprisonment.** In the period 1705-1717 he had residency at his brothers Inn, the Queens Head, Aldham.* In the period 1722-1731 he leased land in Colchester abutting the Queens Head in Fordham, Essex.** I assume that as he was living at the inn with his 'common law' wife Mary Norton with their children Benjamin Norton** and Sophia**, and Defoe's son Daniel by Elisabeth Sammens.** The association between Mary Norton has been proved: by Essex Quaker marriages, and her fathers will,** the children she produced by Defoe, and in particular Benjamin Norton; ** and Coggeshall, where Mary Norton was brought up and her father was a member of a trading association,** or Great Tey where Benjamin Norton was resident and married.**

While I describe Coggeshall as a small town, in reality, in the 1660's, it was no more than a significant village where all the residents knew and encountered everyone else continuously. I suggest that Penn, Robert Spencer and Defoe met in Coggeshall and London in the period 1660-1662.* As university students at Oxford, these two young men of Defoe's age, gave robust support to John Owen over the form and place of religious worship and attended services held by him in various homes in Oxford in 1660. They were as a consequence drummed out of Oxford colleges to the disgust of their parents ** Owen was the vicar of the parish church in Coggeshall in 1655** and would have made friends there. ** Nathanial Lawrence and Thomas Lawrence had homes in Coggeshall.** Thomas became a Republican MP** in 1646 and Nathaniel fought in the siege of Colchester in the same year.* Owen was Chaplain to the Republican army in 1648** Coggeshall was a centre of the Quaker resurgence in England**. It is likely that William Penn visited Coggeshall accompanied by Sunderland for the two abandoned their homes following expulsion from Oxford and accompanied each other on journeys throughout England where Quakers and other religious dissenters were concentrated. ** It was the practice of Penn and Fox to stay at the homes of fellow Quakers or sympathisers when they paid visits to a place. ** It is then entirely possible that Defoe and Mary (Moll) met Sunderland in or around Colchester or in London in the way described in *Moll Flanders*.**

Defoe's son Benjamin Norton had a known residency in Colchester until and after Defoe's death in 1731.** Benjamin Norton was Defoe's legitimate heir. ** When all these years are added together Defoe lived in, had residency in, or worked in Essex for some 63 years. His children Hannah, Benjamin Norton and Daniel had a known association with Colchester between c. 1690 -1735. **

When these asterisks are considered as a whole it can be seen that the documentary evidence supporting the evidential basis of my autobiographical reading of *Moll Flanders* is strong. I have listed thirty-six asterisks of which twenty-six come into the two star category. Behind each assertion there is additional documentary evidence and persuasive conjecture (as I have defined earlier in this work) that taken together is either conclusive or strongly supportive to the reading I give of the autobiographical basis of Part 1 of *Moll Flanders*. I regard the sheer volume and weight of this evidence as, statistically speaking, conclusive; and that this being so, there is no reasonable basis for disbelief in it.

Relationships

Moll Flanders gathers in momentum and vicarious excitement when *Moll*'s narrative moves into descriptions of her passionate relationships, her affairs and 'marriages.' The question arises as to whose sexual relationships they are: *Moll's*, Mary's or Defoe's. Theoretically, Defoe might have fantasised about men and created the characters of *Moll* and *Roxana* in order to do this: that is to say these characters are purely fictional. Biographical evidence suggests otherwise. If in reality they are Defoe's gay relationships, as I maintain they are, they were illegal and best kept secret. If Defoe and others have kept them secret there would be no documentary evidence. The enquirer must then resort to anonymous pamphlets that rely on insinuations and random allusions. There is some of this material. There are various descriptions of Defoe's appearance from people who met him and who wrote about it. This material is commented upon in Appendix 6. Commentators refer to Defoe's 'beauish' appearance.

However, Defoe is concerned about the 'the truth' of his life and is helpful to enquiring readers. He decided to write about his sexual preferences by personation of women in *Moll Flanders* and *Roxana*. He does this, I believe, for two main reasons: he needed to flaunt his sexuality in the way he dressed and by cross-dressing. Secondly, and for several complex reasons, Defoe wished his fiction to be authentic. In the desire to be 'true to himself' Defoe leaves a paper trail; it is possible to deduce the identity of some of the men involved and to guess who others might be from the information he and others gave.

Husbands and Lovers

In a chart to this work I set out the names, and approximate dates, of men I believe were involved sexually with Defoe. I have hesitated before doing this. I think it wrong morally to advance suggestions such as these on inadequate evidence. If this debate were to be conducted on the rules of evidence prevailing in an English Court of Law, I could not assert these suggestions unless the defendant had argued that his past conduct was unimpeachable. This would 'open the door' to allegations that he was other than he pretended to be.

Many biographers have argued that Defoe's conduct was always or usually honest and straightforward. I take the view that those who have asserted a good character should not complain: those 'who throw stones in glasshouses' have no grounds for objection. However, I choose to limit my proof to two of these relationships for practical reasons.

1. The Gentleman Who Came to Bath: Sir John Clerk.

The Gentleman who came to Bath to meet *Moll*/Defoe was Sir John Clerk. He came all the way from Edinburgh. The encounter does not come as a complete surprise or 'magic itself' without precedent. It has been long known that Defoe had a relationship with Sir John Clerk in the period c.1702 to 1712 and a recent work of mine provides a proof that the relationship was sexual. Sir John Clerk's *Journal* dates and describes a visit to Bath together with the revelation of his emotions in doing so. The details of the visit can be compared with the description given by Defoe in *Moll Flanders* of her stay in Bath.[275] Literary critics tend to write of *Moll's* account of the meeting in Bath that it is an event dis-connected from his narrative; that is, it comes out of nothing and goes nowhere. No critic has been in any doubt that it involved intimacy, sex and the giving of money by the Gentleman to *Moll*.

I have set out a proof in *Beyond Belief.*[276] Some literary critics have

---

[275] *Moll Flanders*, 156-169.
[276] *Beyond Belief,* 214-216.

commentated that it is not believable. When examined this disbelief is seen to be mere incredulity. What could possibly constitute a proof that could satisfy such critics? Obviously, I did not witness the meeting in Bath; nor is it likely, given that the act of homosexuality was illegal, that anyone could be expected to find the encounter mentioned in correspondence or documented in any way. Confronted with this difficulty I have offered an arithmetical proof of probability. I have improved it as a result of various exchanges with academics.

The background and preliminaries to the encounter are crucial and are documented. I repeat my gratitude to Paula Backscheider for the acumen of her account of the Scottish Commissioners in London in 1706 and the early negotiations on the proposed Act of Union between Scotland and England; and in particular drawing attention to the correspondence between John Clerk and his father.[277] In this correspondence Clerk writes favourably of Defoe and tells his father that Defoe is in favour of the Union and will becoming to Edinburgh. Defoe had been quick to make contact with the Commissioners and the negotiations did result in the subsequent sending of Defoe to Edinburgh by Harley as an agent and propagandist in the Union cause.

Backscheider hazards the information that Clerk was young, handsome and intelligent and known to be 'a pretty young man'. It might have been added that he was prodigiously rich, extremely well-read, highly literate, powerfully placed in Scottish political life with a firm grip on economic realities and open to opportunities to make money. The Scottish Parliament was to appoint Clerk to make a Report on the consequences of a Union prior to any commitment to it and to make recommendations. Subsequently, Clerk was to become Baron to the Exchequer for many years.

It is my belief that Defoe's polemical balance in various pamphlets on Captain Green's trial in Edinburgh in 1705 and his relationship with Clerk was a major factor in persuading Harley, and perhaps a reluctant Queen Anne, bruised by Defoe's act of Seditious Libel, to appoint Defoe as an agent. Defoe stayed close to Clerk throughout the process

[277] Backscheider, 208.

of steering the Union Bill through the Scottish Parliament.

Homosexuality was a common practice among the Scottish aristocracy and ruling political class in the seventeenth and eighteenth centuries. The patronage system in government and the arts encouraged it. Care needs to be taken in the use of gender terms. I use the word homosexuality in the context of pre-modern views of effeminacy, manliness, sodomy and pederasty as experienced socially in the interplay between sex, politics and the arts. In a previous work on Swift I suggested that he discovered to his surprise and repugnance that patronage often required sexual activity between patron and recipient.

Defoe was back in England from Scotland by the end of 1707. In 1708 he contrived to persuade Godolphin to let him return to Scotland in a governmental role. In 1709 Defoe was back in England but in Edinburgh in the late autumn for the Edinburgh seasonal celebrations. At this time he entered his son Benjamin Norton into Edinburgh University. Defoe had developed extensive business interests with the assistance of the Clerk's and in his absence John Russell acted as his agent.[278] Defoe stayed many times in the Clerk family home and enjoyed Clerk family patronage. Clerk's father became a collector of Defoe's written works. Defoe must have thought that he might settle in Scotland. However, with the reinstatement of Harley as first minister in 1710 Defoe decided not to do so and returned to England. He paid his last visit to Scotland in 1712.

Clerk would have interested Defoe for many reasons. He had much to say about Europe, where he had travelled extensively, and he was the author of many philosophical treatises and other written works. However, it is almost always true of Defoe's relationships with men of influence that his interest in them was self-seeking. The Clerk family gave him an entrée to Scottish political affairs and happenings and thus Defoe became an important conduit of them to Godolphin and Harley.

Moll provides the reader with some background information. Moll writes about coming back into the country after eight years. Bastian

---

[278] Backscheider, 240.

suggests that Defoe was out of the country and in Scotland in 1702 when he was seeking to avoid arrest. Eight years would date the encounter in 1710. The relations with the Gentleman continued for 2 years and he bought Moll an apartment in Hammersmith, London. This apartment is featured in *Colonel Jack* where it becomes a centre of a Defoe family crisis. I date this crisis as 1712 when it is known that Defoe became ill. Defoe's last visit to Scotland was in 1712.

Bath is noted for its hot springs which are thought from Roman times to have medicinal value. In the *Tour* Defoe describes the activities at the baths where both sexes could meet for their entertainment. He writes, that the town [Bath] 'is taken up in raffing, gaming visiting, and in a word, all sorts of gallantry and levity'.'[279]

Moll has prefaced her account of the visit by stating that: 'I had spent the first Season [in Edinburgh] well enough, for tho' I had Contracted some Acquaintance with a Gentleman who came to Bath for his Diversion, yet I had entered into no *felonious Treaty*, as it might be call'd'. [sex] Moll said she was waiting for a ship to arrive in Bristol and that as it became a long wait she had run out of money.

The elements of Moll's account of the visit is as follows: the gentleman had singled him out in the previous winter season; he came down again in the spring season with another gentleman and two servants, and he was a man of Honour and of Virtue as well as a great Estate. Before anything happened between them he paid *Moll* £200 pounds; the gentleman was ill but she looked after him; they had sex together and the gentleman paid another £50. He stayed in this state for 5 weeks, 15 miles from Bath. Defoe (and presumably *Moll*) went to Bristol; he then went to London.

Clerk gives a full and striking account of his visit. In July, 1710 he decided to go from his home in Edinburgh to Bath, for health reasons. The essential details of his visit taken from his *Journal* are as follows. He 'fell ill of a great cold' in April 1710 and resolved to 'take a journey into England the length of Bath against the advice of his physicians'.

---

[279] *Tour*, 359-360.

On that journey the cold had abated a little. He had left his new wife, who had recently given birth to a son, in a state of anguish and was doubtful 'if ever I should see her again'. He travelled with two agreeable gentlemen friends, and he was driven to travel by 'some secret and irresistible impulse.' He became ill again. He stayed in Bath for some weeks and during his stay he made an excursion to Bristol where he visited his good friend and Brother [a Masonic description] Mr Baron Scroop. He then went to London.

The congruence of these two accounts is remarkably close. It contains at least ten identical elements and no discordances. This being so I regard it to be arithmetically probable that the two men, Defoe and Clerk, met in Bath at this time and that therefore Moll's description of the meeting between Moll and the gentleman in Bath is of one and the same event.

Did Sir John Clerk pay Defoe £250 for sex? Was *Moll*, as Defoe suggests behaving as a whore or as a prostitute? I don't think so. As written it was mainly a commercial matter. Defoe makes it clear in the text that *Moll* was relying on cargo shipped to Bristol. In speaking to her Gentleman, at the prompting of her Landlady, *Moll*/Defoe says: I stood off very boldly. [from receiving money] I told him that tho' my Cargo of Tobacco was damaged, yet that it was not quite lost.' What on earth would *Moll* have been doing in shipping tobacco? For Defoe as a merchant, it is probable; but for *Moll*, as a penniless 'whore', it is not.

The language used in *Moll's*/Defoe's account is highly suggestive of an affectionate, admiring and long-term relationship. It is possible that it lasted longer than I claimed originally and, perhaps it was of ten years duration, 1702-1712. Defoe/*Moll* explains that the relationship lasted another two years [Defoe went to Scotland for the last time two years later]. Defoe states that the gentleman 'went three times to London in that time, and once he stayed there for four months'. It seems that the relationship ended in a legal arrangement of some kind. In 1712-1714 Defoe became ill and thought he was dying. It is pure conjecture but might Defoe have suffered a psycho-sexual breakdown of some kind?

2. Moll's Lancashire Husband

Moll's Lancashire Husband, thought by some critics as being her best-loved husband, is James Logan, William Penn's secretary and representative in America. This relationship is described in an earlier chapter and in *Alien Come Home.* I do not wish to repeat this material here. I identify that this marriage is by a 'gay ceremony' of the kind performed in a Molly House and I have pointed out that Defoe described his private treaty marriage to Mary Norton by using some of the imagery of a 'gay marriage'. I attempted in *Beyond Belief,* for the first time in Defoe biography, to describe Defoe's knowledge of and involvement in, cross-dressing, 'drag parties' and Molly Houses.[280] I return to this subject in the chapter, on *Roxana.*

This link with James Logan is part of a thesis that William Penn, who employed Logan, was a close friend of Defoe from their youth 1658-1662 until Penn's death in 1718, that is a period of sixty years. The religious beliefs of Jone Reade, Defoe's first wife is unknown, but as she travelled to Barbados as a religious migrant from South Carolina in 1672, it is possible that she was a Quaker. Mary Norton, Defoe's second or third wife, was a Quaker. In *Alien Come Home* I comment on Defoe's Quaker connections in Stoke Newington. I comment also on the thread of Defoe's involvement with South Carolina.

It is open to a critic of the themes I advance, in particular that of Defoe's sexuality, to assert that they exist only as acts of Defoe's imagination. However, such an argument does not run far for there is a mountain of evidence of his real life passions and sexual predilections. I suggest to the reader that if he is persuaded of the truth of any of the examples I give that he should credence to them all.

America

In *Moll's* tale she travels with her Captain/brother/husband to America on two occasions. I date these journeys as 1682 the date of William Penn's first visit to Pennsylvania and 1700-1702, Penn's second and last visit. In his fiction Defoe writes about visiting Barbados, Virginia,

---

[280] *Beyond Belief.* 81, 102, 205, 210, 236. 239-240, 267.

Maryland, Kentucky and South Carolina.

Moll's/Mary's first visit to Virginia in 1682 is described by Defoe as a decision to settle there. The *Captain* 'husband', her brother Defoe, had decided to return to Virginia where he had two plantations. He persuades *Moll*/Mary to come with him. The *Captain* tells *Moll* that his plantations provided him with a handsome income and that she would enjoy a much higher standard of living there than in England where life had become difficult for her. *Moll*, as the story is narrated, is mercenary in her consideration of the proposal. She was told that her *Captain*/brother had a very good house. His 'mother' lived there with one sister, which was all the relatives he had, but would move out so that [she] *Moll* would have the house to herself. As Defoe narrates his story this 'mother' had been imprisoned in Newgate. When *Moll* hears the 'mother' speak of this, and somewhat illogically, she comes into an understanding that this woman must be her mother also and, therefore, she had been committing incest with her brother the Captain. This knowledge unsettled her. The 'mother' suggested, thinking it more appropriate, that *Moll* should occupy a separate room from her brother. She decides that she could not live with her brother any more, and that she wanted to stay in Virginia and seek a more normal relationship with some other man. Her brother was greatly upset and returned to England. After eight years *Moll* returned to England.

The second visit to Virginia in 1700-1702 enables the reader to establish the 'truth'. I conjecture that in 1682 Defoe persuaded his sister to settle in South Carolina and to take care of a child born to Jone Reade in Barbados in 1681. She was to go first to Virginia where the Read family had a plantation and live there for a while with Jo Reade's mother and a sister, either of Jone's or of the mother. After a while mother and sister would move out. They did. The entire family including *Moll*/Mary then moved to Virginia. As Jone Reade had moved from South Carolina to Barbados as a religious migrant it is possible that the family were being persecuted for their religious beliefs in South Carolina. If the mother in law had been branded this might have been because of her religious beliefs in South Carolina and not because of imprisonment in Newgate. She may have been a Quaker. At the earlier of the dates, the *Captain's* two plantations were in South Carolina (yet to be claimed by Mary) and Virginia. Before embarking for Virginia in 1700, Defoe may have been allocated additional land by Penn and Logan. The usual conditions for new settler's allocated land in New England was that they should invest in the necessary tools and implements needed to work the land. The first action taken by the *Captain* and *Moll* on arrival in Virginia was to buy the tools and other necessities that would enable a plantation to be worked.

Defoe gives a highly convoluted account of his second visit. He starts the narrative by a meeting between the Lancashire Husband and Moll in Newgate and their subsequent voyage to Virginia. It is immediately clear to a questioning reader that the ship was not a prisoner transport vessel but an ordinary passenger ship. At Gravesend, the London customs boundary, they were let ashore. Gravesend is directly opposite Tilbury in Gravesend Reach. It was but a short river crossing to Tilbury wharf. From the Tilbury jetty, still visible today at low tide, it was a 100 metre walk to the Ferry House Inn and a ten minute walk to Defoe's brickhouse. When Defoe writes, 'staid all Night, lay at the House where we Supp'd in the morning with [beer, Wine, and Fowles] he is either teasing the reader or forgetting his fictional duty for he is describing the Ferry House Inn. [281]

The only relatives *Moll*/Mary had in Virginia, or so she believed, were a Father, Mother, a sister or aunt in law, and a 'son' fictionalised as Humphrey. It was *Moll* who looked for and found the plantation where she believed her 'mother' lived for she had been there before. She discovered an Old Man and his son, both called Humphrey. Moll was told by a local person that the mother of this family was 'dead'. This is how *Moll* described her family connections:

> I immediately knew that this was no Body else but my own
> Son, by that father she shewed me, who was my own
> Brother after about twenty years absence [1682-1702]'. [The
> local who gave *Moll*/Mary this information continued by

---

[281] Now trading as the World's End public house.

telling her a very odd Tale circulating among the Neighbours where this Gentleman formerly lived that] this man when he was a young Man, fell in Love with a young Lady there [in England]…and Married her…her Circumstances being poor he brought her over hither to her Mother, who was then living. He lived there several years.

In interpreting this narrative it is necessary to realise that when *Moll* talks of a mother she refers to 'a step mother', that is to Defoe's step mother by his marriage to Jone Reade, and the Old Gentleman was then her brother's/Defoe's step father. Humphrey was *Moll*/Mary's nephew and only her 'son' by virtue of accepting the responsibility for bringing him up. This family had lived in another place [I suggest South Carolina] before coming to Virginia. The mother in law had been grateful to *Moll* for taking responsibility for bringing up the child for eight years [before returning to England] and had left her a property/or cash in South Carolina that had to be claimed quickly before other relatives got their hands on it. Presumably they may have argued that as it was impossible for them to contact *Moll* the cash or property set aside for her would not, or ever could be, claimed

It is important for the commentator to recognise that seventeenth century family law gave a father absolute rights over his child and, therefore, it was up to him and not to anyone else to claim the child as his own. A father was legally responsible for any decision about the care and upbringing of a child.

Moll continues:

I began to go into the Circumstances of the Family [with a local person]…and how the Old Gentlewoman, her mother had promis'd me very solemnly, that when she died she would do something for me, and leave it so, as that without its being in the Power of her Son, *my Brother* and *Husband* to prevent it: She told me she did not exactly know how it was order'd but she had been told by my mother that she had left a sum of money, and had tyed her Plantation for the Payment of it, to be made good to the Daughter, if ever she be heard of in England, or elsewhere; and that the Trust was left with this Son, who was the person that we saw with the Father.

Humphrey, the son, confirmed the arrangement and said that he would facilitate the execution of his mother's wish.

I believe that this 'the other place' where this gift should be claimed was in South Carolina. *Moll* and her brother/husband proceeded to take possession of another plantation in Virginia for which I conjecture *Moll*/Mary and her brother had bought the tools and provisions as required of religious settlers on their arrival in Virginia. They were led to this plantation by a friendly *Quaker* (italics mine). After taking possession of the new settlement *Moll* and her *Captain*/Husband made their way to South Carolina to claim *Moll's* inheritance.

This is a highly convoluted explanation required by Defoe's highly convoluted narrative. It may well be the case, given Defoe's ingenuity, that he contrived to retain the settlement in South Carolina. In the opening chapter to this work I mention Mrs Brooke's belief that Benjamin Norton Defoe, Defoe's legitimate heir, had gone to America in the late 1720's when both he and his father were in dire financial straits. George Chalmers, the earliest of Defoe's biographers, believed that Defoe had relations in America. Defoe's vigorous and persuasive advocacy of the religious and constitutional rights of settlers in South Carolina remains unexplained. It is straightforward at this point to state the obvious: Defoe had married a South Carolina religious dissenter, her family probably owned property in South Carolina, a son of this marriage in Barbados to Jone Reade survived the death of his mother, this child was 'owned' by Defoe, he persuaded his sister to go to South Carolina and help to bring up the child and this is what she did.

Crime

Mary's gradual descent into crime captures the imagination and sympathy of readers. Defoe lived through a period of notorious women thieves some of whom he may have met. There is no doubt in my mind that Defoe was drawing upon the real world in writing about *Moll's* crimes. However, Defoe as the narrator is disinclined to call *Moll's* crimes delinquent. Eventually *Moll* plucks up the courage to come clean. She says, 'in a little time, by the help of Confederates I grew as impudent a thief, and as dextrous as ever Moll Cutpurse was, tho' if Fame does not belie her, not half so handsome.' [282]

Defoe lived in an age of anxiety about crime. Whether or not there was more crime is a matter of controversy. There is little statistical support for the claim. However, it is a truism that at a time of great material acquisitiveness, and even greater poverty, there would be great anxiety at all levels of society. The enriched merchant classes in London displayed their growing wealth. The vast inequalities in its distribution alienated many of the poor. In London in the early eighteenth century, primitive criminal justice and penal systems were unable to deal with crime; honest citizens were in an uproar and demanded severe sentences, the breaking up of gangs, and civic action to change matters for the better. All those who lived at the edge were conscious that they made desperate mistakes at the risk of an untimely death; there were over two hundred crimes for which a person might be executed.

Defoe's own attitude to crime is ambivalent and ambiguous. All his literary creations indulge in crime. What *Moll* tells her readers is strikingly similar to the behaviour of *Captain Singleton*, *Colonel Jack* and the narrator of *Memoirs of a Cavalier*. Their early delinquent behaviour and their reasoning and justification for it could be switched from one fiction to another without any reader noticing the change. The reader of them all is bound to pose the question of whether the common denominator, that is the writer Daniel Defoe, is the real culprit.

I choose three examples from *Moll's* criminal activities in order to show that the incidents described are repeated elsewhere in Defoe's fictions.

Robbing a Little Girl

A memorable incident in *Moll Flanders* is the theft of a necklace from a young girl. Defoe writes:

---

[282] Anecdotally, it is argued that Moll Cutpurse would not usually have been considered handsome: she was thought to be a lesbian and a pimp.

There was a pretty young child …going home, all alone, and my Prompter, like a true Devil, set me upon this innocent Creature; I talked to it [the child] and it pratl'd to me again…I led it [into an alley] that goes into Bartholomew Close…the Child said that was not its way home…I said I'll show you… the Child had a little Necklace on of Gold Beads, and I had my eye on it …and took off her Neckless and the Child never felt it…Here the Devil put me upon killing the Child in the dark Alley, that it might not Cry… But I turn'd round to another Passage and bade it go back [and then passed through in a maze of named streets] mixing with Crowd of People usually passing there, it was not possible to have been found out…[The fault was] the Vanity of the Mother to have her Child look fine…a Maid set to take care of it taken up…with some Fellow…I did the Child no harm.

Bastian has pointed out that this incident is mentioned in two other Defoe works.[283] To Bastian's list I would add the stealing of a child in *Captain Singleton*. I regard the recollection of it by Defoe to be potentially sinister. For Defoe it is a traumatic recall of an actual event. Defoe attributed the thought that he robbed the child and might have killed her to the Devil. Form requires Defoe to de-personalise the Child by the use of 'it'. Robbing her was not his fault. The people to be blamed were the child's Mother, the child being a victim of her vanity, and the nurse.

Stealing a Horse

Moll was asked by a Gentleman's servant to mind a horse outside a tavern. She decides to steal the horse and walks off with it very soberly. Not knowing what to do with the horse, *Moll* decided to leave in at another inn with a note. Defoe describes the theft as 'Robbery and No Robbery'. The theft is entirely meaningless in *Moll's* narrative. The account is very similar to that of the theft of a horse in *Colonel Jack* and to a real-life allegation that Defoe had actually stolen a horse. It

---

[283] Bastian, 4, note 111.

does appear extremely unlikely that a woman would first be asked to look after a horse and, secondly, that she would not have been challenged by someone if she stole it.

Disguise and Personation

In the restricted areas of the City of London *Moll* became known as a notorious thief. To avoid recognition she sometimes dressed as a fine lady, on other occasions as a Widow-woman or Beggar and then to 'Dress …up in Mens Cloths, and to put herself into a new kind of Practice.'

The issues of secrecy and disguise run through Defoe's entire life as I understand it and as I describe it in this work and in others. There are many causes for this behaviour and I do not wish to simplify them except for one assertion: throughout his adult life Defoe personated himself as a woman and taken singly and together the evidence of cross-dressing is very strong. I quote several occasions when he did so in this work. It was not easy for a man to put on women's clothes in the early eighteenth century and not surprisingly Moll is not persuasive in her passing-off. *Moll* confesses that it proved difficult to be 'so dextrous at these things [what things the reader might enquire] in a Dress so contrary to Nature'. She decided to stop the practice. Defoe leaves us with the impression that when Moll gets taken to bed in these clothes she is fearful that a partner would find out that her sex was other than he/she had supposed.

Newgate

In *Moll's* narrative she finishes up in Newgate, found guilty of a crime, sentenced to death and then successful in pleas to convert the death sentence to transportation. This is fiction. However, the reader knows that Defoe himself did spend time in Newgate and was able to write from this experience. *Moll* describes her incarceration as follows:

O! I had been sent to any Place in the World, and not to Newgate, I should have thought myself happy…how did the harden'd Wretches that were there before me Triumph over me? What! Mrs Flanders come to Newgate at last? What *Mrs Mary* [italics mine], Mrs. Molly and after that plain Moll Flanders…and sure I had Money in my Pocket, tho' they had none. [284]

Defoe seems to imply that his heroine started out in life as a Mary, became a Moll and then dubbed herself as Mrs Flanders. Nowhere else in *Moll's* account does Defoe tell the reader that she is a Mary.

---

[284] *Moll Flanders*, 351.

Chapter 22

Colonel Jack

I believe my case is the case of the most wicked part of the world, viz., that to be reduced to necessity is to be wicked; for necessity is not only a temptation to be wicked; for necessity...is such a temptation as human nature is not empowered to resist.

Colonel Jack
Daniel Defoe, 1722

Commentators have found it difficult to categorise *Colonel Jack*. To some it belongs to a group of fiction which can be described as 'stories of travel and adventure', to others it belongs to 'dressed up tales of crime', to me it is a valuable autobiographical account of Defoe's early life. It is entirely possible, of course, to think it to be all three.

I maintain that the book is an account of Defoe's travels across Europe and to North America but not quite in the form or at the time generally assumed by other biographers. The best general account of Defoe's travels in Europe is that provided by Frank Bastian, in particular his account of Defoe's connections and activities in Spain and Portugal.[285] Unfortunately, Bastian was 15-16 years too late in his chronology: it affects the accuracy of his narrative. Cultural historians have had great fun in numerous lectures and conference speeches on 'Defoe's geography'; but while they are often right about place, an inadequate biographical understanding limits the deductions they can draw.

It is true also that the book provides 'dressed up tales of crime'. The version of the book I am using devotes over 100 out of 347 pages, that is 29 percent of the whole book, to a panoply of crimes committed over 2 years when Defoe, by my chronology, was 16 to 18 years of age. On further examination it can be deduced that Defoe is not conforming to linear time and some of these crimes were committed at later dates.

---

[285] Bastian, 67.

These later crimes imply a sophisticated understanding of commercial and financial transactions and instruments. We know from chronicled legal cases discussed by Backscheider,[286] and in an earlier work of mine,[287] that Defoe practiced some of these deceptions and determined individuals pursued him in the courts. I shall defer discussion of Defoe's 'criminal mentality' to another chapter except to assert the following: Defoe sought to limit his crimes, wherever and whenever he thought it prudent, to actions that did not imperil his life and liberty; and, in particular, he avoided acting as part of a gang or conspiracy, that is, he maintains that he acted alone in the pursuit of a necessary self-interest.

Leslie Stephen, writing with a measure of Victorian prurience, stated the following, 'We (who we wonder is we?) do not imagine that *Roxana, Colonel Jack* and *Captain Singleton* can fairly claim any higher interest than that which belongs to the ordinary police report, given with infinite fullness and vivacity of detail.'[288] Pshaw, to that is a modern retort: that is what makes them so interesting!

In the body of my work I discuss many of the autobiographical aspects of *Colonel Jack* and I do not want to repeat them here. I believe it will be most helpful to readers to limit discussion to the principal autobiographical issues raised in and by the work.

Who Were The Three Jacks?

In *Colonel Jack* the narrator does not tell the reader how he came to be looked after by a nurse. *Colonel Jack* tells his readers that his Father was dead and that he never knew a Mother. Elsewhere, he narrates that his mother came from a considerable stock and his father had put aside some money for his care. This nurse had a son called John, the narrator was called John and later another boy, also called John joined them. To distinguish them one from another the narrator was called Colonel, the elder boy Captain and the younger Major. The narrator explains that in Goodman Fields, London where they were

[286] Backscheider, 33.
[287] *Beyond Belief*, 85-91.
[288] *Colonel Jack*, vi.

brought up, John's were normally called Jack's and so they became known as the three Jack's.

The use of the description Jack is open to multifarious explanations: it can mean anyone and no one as in Jack of all trades, denote union as in the Union Jack and is a common term for a sailor. At this time there was a link in common usage with the monarchy and later with Jacobitism

These three Jacks were Defoe, Robert Spencer, the future Second Earl of Sunderland, and William Penn. A general proof that these three youthful 'cavaliers' embarked on the Grand Tour together in July, 1662 is given in Chapter 5. Autobiographically, Defoe gives several clues to their identity. He writes of the elder, 'Captain Jack was the elder of us all by a whole year; he was only Jack for some years …till he came to preferment *by the merit of his birth* (italics mine)… I was almost ten years old, the Captain eleven the Major about eight when the good woman my nurse died…[and] we three Jacks were let out in the world. We rambled about the three of us together…'

The date of birth of Robert Spencer was September 5, 1641. He was plain Robert Spencer until he succeeded to the title of Second Earl of Sunderland in September, 1662. William Penn was born October 14, 1644. When Defoe writes of Spencer being a year older than him, he is at least two years out; when he writes of Penn being less that a year younger he is nearer: both were born in 1644.[289] In this manner of living (venturing forth together) they went on for two years but after a while Spencer went off on his own. The ages used by Defoe are not accidental. In *Moll Flanders*, *Moll* writes that she was taken into the care of a family for a period of one year when 10 years of age. *Colonel Jack* states that at 10 years of age his nurse died. I do not think she did. Defoe is using a familiar narrative device of killing off a character when of no further use to his narrative. Once established as a petty thief

---

[289] There is a possibility that Defoe was born to a mother other than Ellene and baptised late.

in London, *Colonel Jack* tells the reader that he was in his fifteenth year. I have maintained that the three Jacks were out and about in London over two years in 1660-1662 and most frequently when Penn and Spencer were drummed out of Oxford University towards the end 1660. In this period Defoe would have been sixteen to seventeen years of age.

Colonel Jack describes the Major/*Penn* as follows:

> [he] was a merry, facetious, pleasant boy, had a good share of wit...was full of jests, and good humour...something of a gentleman...true manly courage, feared nothing, and could look death in the face...was the most generous and compassionate creature alive...had native principles of gallantry...talked very well... wrote very good sense and very handsome language...

This is how *Captain Singleton* describes William the Quaker from Pennsylvania. The similarities between the two descriptions are obvious and striking:

> We had one very merry fellow here, a Quaker...we took out of a ship bound from Pennsylvania to Barbados ...He was a comic fellow indeed, a man of very good sense...very good humoured and pleasant in his conversation, and a bold stout, a brave fellow too, as any we had among us.

Crime

The petty crimes that are committed in *Colonel Jack* might well be described as 'normal' youthful delinquency bordering on serious crime. Perhaps, the best known example of this type of crime is found in *Moll Flanders* at the stage of her story when she resorts to crime. I quote as follows:

> ...it happened in a crowd, at a meeting house where I was in great danger of being taken...I had full hold of her watch, I found it would not go...I let it go and cried out...giving the impression that there was certainly pickpockets about...I had very good clothes on, and a gold watch by my side...the

other gentlewoman cried out, 'A Pickpocket.' too, for somebody had tried to pull her watch away…a little further in the crowd …a young fellow was seized…very opportunely for my case.

This Defoe description is widely admired as a convincing, indeed compelling, description. It is not usually remarked that it would be unlikely for gentlewomen to wear gold watches in such a crowd although gentlemen with an appetite for display might well do so: and then *Moll* did not succeed in pulling a watch! The emphasis of *Moll's* narrative is on technique. It is a guide to newcomers – and a warning. Be good at it or suffer the consequences.

Tales of pickpockets appear in several Defoe fictions. In *Memoirs of a Cavalier*, for example, Defoe writes:

We stayed at Amiens for one day… [outside] the great church we saw a crowd of people gazing at a mountebank …[who] had a great trade…the people raised a cry 'Larron, larron (in English, 'Thief, thief').' [One of] two English gentleman and a Scotchman [Penn, Spencer and William Crawford, Earl of Crawford], travellers as we were…caught him. [The man ran away, was seized and brought] to the gentleman …[when he saw the man he] told them it was not the same man. This was the first French trick, I had the opportunity of seeing; but I was told they have a great many more as dextrous as this.

The subsequent accounts of crime in London do not involve either Penn or Spencer. In *Colonel Jack* the Captain, Robert Spencer, absents himself from these and does not reappear in the narrative until the end of the London adventures.[290] Nor is it clear that either of them were involved in petty theft. In real life Spencer had begun to make the first of three forays into Europe. Major Jack, William Penn, appears to have given the *Colonel* money for clothes and eating out in the style of a gentleman. Crimes of significance are first executed by the *Colonel* in

---

[290] In the period 1661-1663 Spencer made three trips to the Continent.

consort with other delinquents until the appearance of Will. In *Beyond Belief* I suggest that the character of Will is based on Defoe's cousin, William Foe, who was living in London at the time.[291] In the flight from London the *Colonel* is accompanied by Captain Jack. In this the narrative follows the account given in *Memoirs of a Cavalier*. Penn having being called home by his father after the duel which killed a man in Paris, Spencer and Defoe travelled on to southern France.

There is no easy way to describe the crimes the *Colonel* narrates. Ostensibly, Will and the *Colonel* succeed in robbing eminent goldsmiths of valuable bills of exchange, and gold and diamonds, and then persuading the victims to buy them back for a fraction of their value. Samuel Holt Monck pointed out that some of the victims are real people but he does not comment on their inclusion.[292] Those personages who are named explicitly are: Sir Stephen Evans, a Governor of the Hudson Bay company, 1700-1712; Sir John Cullum, thought to be a Quaker mariner by Bastian [293]but more probably Sir John Cullum, Baronet, whose son John was a vicar at Bury St Edmunds where Defoe stayed for a time; Sir Henry Furness, Baronet of Walder, whose oyster dredging at Whitstable would have been known by Defoe; Sir Charles Duncome, 1648-1711, an MP and Lord Mayor of the City of London, a goldsmith, who on his death was dubbed 'the richest commoner in England'; Sir Francis Child, 1642-1713, another goldsmith, and the Mayor of London in 1698/9; and Sir John Sweetapple and Sir Jonathan Loxham, London goldsmiths.

Several of the many Defoe conundrums are involved in an understanding of Defoe's audacious naming of these men. Did he/*Colonel Jack* really rob them or is it purely fictional? Is it not a malapropism to phrase such an issue in this way? After the granting of Defoe's Exception in 1716 he could have named these men with temerity because he could not be tried for his previous mistakes (crimes). In any event they were all dead by 1722, the publication date

---

[291] *Beyond Belief*, 23.
[292] Defoe, Daniel. *Colonel Jack*, Oxford University Press, 1989, n.52.
[293] Bastian, 29.

of *Colonel Jack*. Did he name these men because he wished as the author, even given that the book was published anonymously, to proclaim his ability to hoodwink seriously rich and prestigious men? Or is Defoe alluding to another crime: the receiving and fencing of Avery's diamonds after 1705? Is Defoe boasting that even these well-respected and rich men were willing to receive stolen goods for a fraction of their true value and so make money out of Defoe's amazing exploits in Madagascar? The reader can make his own choice. However, my own view these mentions are a kind of boasting and an assertion of moral equality. These men were among the most wealthy and successful in the City of London. Defoe was asserting that rich and powerful though they were, none were above doing deals for 'stolen' goods.

Colonel Jack's Marriages

Hamish Hamilton in their Note to the 1947 edition of *Colonel Jack* write about his marriages as follows:

> [They are] four successive and unfortunate marriages. Out of these marital experiences come some of the most dryly amusing passages in the book. Wife Number One having run up debts and deserted him sends a bully to demand money from him on her behalf, and here the Colonel candidly shows himself less dauntless that his title would suggest. Then there is Wife Number Two in Italy with whom 'in an unusual height of good humour he consents to be married.' And Number Three, a melancholy widow met in the Canterbury coach, who protests to being invited to dine, that has stolen her appetite. Nevertheless, 'in order to treat her handsomely, but not extravagantly, I provided what the house afforded, which was a couple of partridges and a very good dish of stewed oysters; they brought us up afterwards a neats's tongue, and a ham, that was almost quite cut down, but we ate none of it, for the other was fully enough for us both, and the maid made her supper of the oysters we had left, which were enough.' ...Wife Number Three takes to

drink and dies, and so comes Number Four, a sweet creature called Moggy, to whom the Colonel with economical generosity presents his late wife's wardrobe. Moggy also dies and the Colonel goes back to Virginia where like Moll Flanders, he meets his first and now repentant spouse with whom he is happily re-united.

In a following Chart, I list Defoe's four marriages and numerous children. Defoe's Number One wife, as described here, is clearly Mary Tuffley, Number 3 Elisabeth Sammens, and .Number Four, Mary Norton. However, there is no mention elsewhere in Defoe's works, revealed or obscured, of Number Two. In *Beyond Belief* I conjecture that the 'Italian wife' was a man. I suggest that the reader resists the instinct to be judgemental. Mary Tuffley was a 'wronged' woman but well able to look after herself, while Mary Norton experienced a long family life with Defoe in what, on the face of it, was a happy marriage. As for his sister Mary, like Defoe 'she lived a life of infinite variety' and so far as is known, or can be reasonably conjectured, she did not die of boredom.

Defoe in the Americas

In his fiction Defoe inter-mixes Virginia and Brazil to describe the same experiences. In Chapter 18, Return to Crusoe's Island, I believe I offer a definitive proof that *Crusoe*/Defoe was not a castaway on an island but condemned to spend time under constraint in Brazil. In *Colonel Jack* and *Moll Flanders* the fictional heroes spend time in Virginia and South Carolina. I have carefully examined all the available evidence that Defoe and his sister Mary were there too. Further research is needed to substantiate Defoe's visits and the property he owned; but it is clear to me that Defoe was there.

My narrative shows that after his period of constraint in Brazil and throughout the 1670's Defoe traded along the trans-Atlantic routes between Africa, the Caribbean islands, in particular Barbados, and North America. Defoe's fiction strongly suggests that he was an active slave trader and that for this he got into difficulties with the Portuguese authorities in Brazil. I believe that this caused him to move his activities along the coast to Chile, where he fattened cattle as he did in Tilbury, to Barbados and the New World.

In the period 1680-1682 Defoe was undecided on where and how to live. He was in the money. As his wealth had been acquired in the Americas partly from land he must have considered very seriously indeed whether he should settle there. The alienated Portuguese authorities made it impossible for him stay in Brazil but there was nothing for him to fear in Virginia.

Following his return to England in 1680 he may well have found it to be too problematic to make money from trade much as he wished to do so. The effects of the Navigation Acts made it difficult for him to trade with the English colonies in the New World. In *Robinson Crusoe* Defoe tells the reader that he had sold his plantation in southern Brazil. There was nothing to stop him buying land in Virginia and elsewhere. I believe also that William Penn helped him to settle on land in Virginia. In 1700 when Defoe travelled to Virginia with his sister he claimed everything it was possible for him to own: land there allocated to him by Penn, and a property in South Carolina acquired by him on the death of his wife Jone Reade.

Each step forward in building wealth was accompanied by a step back. Some of Defoe's creditors, men who had been pleased to lend him money, knew something of his wealth because Defoe flaunted it by conspicuous consumption - or so it seemed to them. Wealth brought friends but it sharpened the resolve of his enemies.

Chapter 23

Captain Singleton

Containing an Account of his being set on Shore in the Island of Madagascar... His great deliverances from the barbarous Natives and Wild Beasts... Of his meeting with an Englishman, a Citizen of London among the Indians ...the great Riches he acquired, and his voyage home to England

Title Page
Captain Singleton
Daniel Defoe 1720

Defoe published *Captain Singleton* in 1720 shortly after *Robinson Crusoe*. Critics have noted that Defoe's first known foray into fiction, which came as a rush in the five year period 1719-1724, concentrates on pirate adventures for which there was a public appetite. It is possible to argue that piracy is fore-grounded in *Captain Singleton* if not its guiding trope.[294] The structure of the book is questionable. It divides into two distinct halves: the first part is an account of *Singleton's* transition from childhood and seaman to pirate, and his adventures in far off places; the second part is an autobiographical account of how he turns his life around and works a passage back to England. Most critics believe that the book is a relative failure as a narrative because Defoe is unable to handle its fragmentary structure. However, the overwhelming virtue of the book for me is that it provides an embellished account of an important period of Defoe's life.

There is a difficulty from the very beginning. The book is narrated in the first person past tense and purports to be an account of the adventures of a *Captain Singleton* but he is never mentioned by name in the entire book. This simple fact has to my knowledge never been stated by any literary critic before. Defoe sets out to tell us as little as possible about his origins. He writes, 'As it is usual for great

---

[294] Turley, Hans. *Rum, Sodomy and the Lash: Piracy, Sexuality and Masculine Identity*, NewYork University Press, 1999.

persons…to insist upon their originals, I shall do the same, though I can look but a little into my pedigree.' The narrator tells the reader that he was kidnapped as a small child, disposed of to a beggar, moved on to the care of others, taken into the care of a parish, came under the control of a ship' s master and put to sea at the age of twelve. The first ship's crew was characterised by 'Thieving, lying, swearing, forswearing, joined to the most abominable lewdness…I was exactly fitted for their society…I had no sense of virtue upon me…when I was a child about eight or nine years old; nay, I was preparing and growing up apace to be wicked as anybody could be, or perhaps ever was.'

From this beginning *Singleton* drifts into piracy. Defoe tells the reader that after various adventures, he fell into the company of 'some masters of mischief' who proposed an act of piracy. When asked to join in Defoe writes that 'I told him, yes, with all my heart; for I did not care where I went, having nothing to lose…I, without the least hesitation came immediately into this wicked conspiracy…and being well prepared for all manner of roguery, bold, desperate (I mean myself) without the least checks of conscience for what I might do…' Defoe added to his credentials by associating himself in his narrative with two of the best known pirates of his age, Kidd and Avery.

The nearest Defoe gets to naming his narrator arrives well into the book. *Singleton* takes part in a mutiny that failed and was put ashore somewhere in Africa with a group of fellow conspirators. At a crucial stage of their survival, *Singleton* assumes leadership in fighting off savages. Defoe writes, 'From that day forward they would call me nothing but Seignior Capitano; but I told them I would not be called seignior. 'Well then', said the gunner, who spoke good English, 'you shall be called Captain Bob'; and so they gave me my title ever after.' I believe it to be mistaken to assume that Bob was *Singleton's* name or a diminutive of one. Such a phrase was used to denote a temporary or makeshift state not a Christian name; that is in the sense of 'in the absence of the real thing we shall make use of what is to hand.'

Captain Edward Singleton and William Penn

Defoe's intention in seeking to avoid identifying Singleton, is to protect both his own identity for actions, real or fictional, that he describes; and to disguise that of Captain Edward Singleton, a sugar surveyor and merchant from Barbados; and lastly, but not least, William Penn, the Quaker from Pennsylvania, the 'Citizen of London among the Indians.' Notwithstanding the secrecy of these relationships there are in real-life discoverable links between the three people.

Captain Singleton

Captain Edward (Bob) Singleton was a sugar surveyor and merchant in Barbados. Parish records in Barbados for the sixteenth and seventeenth centuries are poor. The only Singleton families that I could find there from a local search were in the Parish of St James, immediately north of Bridgetown where Defoe married Jone Read. It is a distance of one mile from the port to the Parish. There is a distinct possibility that Singleton was a native of Barbados. For a period of time, c.1695-1706 he was resident in London but he returned to Barbados. In the 1670's and especially in 1680-1683, I believe that Defoe encountered both Singleton and Penn there. In *Captain Singleton* Defoe describes Barbados as a 'staging post, that is a convenient place to replenish a ship between Brazil and New England. William the Quaker from Pennsylvania was captured when his sloop was boarded by *Singleton*. Subsequently, the Quaker agreed to join him. There is no mention in this encounter that William was a Citizen of London as described on the title page. Penn's negotiations with the Indians, as mentioned in the title page, are well-documented in numerous biographies of him. In *Alien Come Home* I established links between Captain Edward Singleton and William Penn.[295] The principal and undeniable link is that Penn appointed Singleton his unofficial representative in Barbados in 1701 without telling his official representative there. It is possible that Singleton was either a Quaker or sympathetic to Quakers. He was named as an executor in two Caribbean wills, one of which, the will of Jonas Langford, was that of a wealthy sugar plantation owner in Antigua. Jonas Langford was also a pioneer Quaker preacher. The will was proved on November 18, 1705. Singleton was described as resident

---

[295] *Alien Come Home*, 95 n.27.

in London. The second will was that of William Boswell, a Bridgetown merchant, proved on April 19, 1705. No residence was given.[296]

There are several links between Defoe and Captain Edward Singleton. First, of course, is the fact Defoe filched his name for fictional purposes. Secondly, and of considerable interest, is that in 1696 Singleton was arrested and charged with the illegal importation of goods in London. The customs details describe Singleton as a government sugar surveyor. The release warrant reads as follows:

Offender: Edward Singleton

Charge: Corruption/non-payment of fine

Petition of Edward Singleton prisoner in Fleet shewing that he was kept 7 months in a messengers custody on the information of one Paine of delivering French goods to Young Bromefield but that at his trial Joseph Beverton an officer [of the Customs] procured another person to swear against him on whose single evidence he was fined 100l and is now in the Fleet; therefore praying a discharge and release.

Young Bromefield may have been Sir Edward Bromefield, second baronet, the son of Sir Edward Bromefield, snr., Lord Mayor of London in 1636 and a merchant. [297]

The issue of delivering goods to London via France, sometimes a necessity when vessels were driven into French ports by stormy weather, is discussed by Penn in his correspondence. In order to circumvent the Navigation Acts Defoe used a French agent in London, most probably a man named Du Foe. If Singleton was working for either Defoe, Penn or Singleton at the time any of these three men might have paid Singleton's fine.

Singleton may have been grateful to Defoe for getting him out of the Fleet. Around the late 1690's, when Defoe was resident in Tilbury, *Family Instructor* mentions the 'gift' of a slave boy, Toby, from a

---

[296] Journal of the Barbados, Museum and Historical Society, XL:193, Jonas Langford (a Quaker of Antigua) and RB6/37/ 530. William Boswell, St. Michael's, Barbados, November, 1712.

[297] *Chronological List of aldermen*, 1660-1650, Temp. Henry III, 1912. Lee. *Payments List of Baronets*, 1912.

Barbadian sea captain.

Penn, Defoe and Civil Society

In *Alien Come Home* I revealed for the first time the length and depth of Defoe's relationship with William Penn that started in Essex and London when both were 16 to 18 years of age and which lasted to Penn's death in 1718, a period of 58 years. It is not an easy to describe their friendship for they shared a desire to keep it secret. An understanding of it is not greatly helped either by past biographical endeavours; Penn's life has not, for the most part, been blessed by attempts to describe the man and his place in the society in which he acted out his life. As with Defoe, the tendency of authors and readers to deify biographical subjects in the period 1960-1990 obscures their subjects.

The two men had more in common than is recognised even in the most immediately noticeable of characteristics. They were both revolutionary in intent with a desire to tear down the old and put something better in its place. Englishmen of the time had not had the 'world turned upside down' for nothing. Penn and Robert Spencer had been drummed out of Oxford colleges for refusing to turn the clock back in religious matters; they were at war with the old. Both Penn and Defoe were modish. When Penn returned to England in August 1664 after his European adventures, particularly in France, his neighbour Mrs Pepys described him as 'a most modish person, grown a fine gentleman'. Samuel Pepys, less impressed, and perhaps resistant to his wife's impressions of other men, for she was certainly a person of independent mind, observed 'but a great deal, if not too much of the variety of the French garb, and affected manner of speech and gait.' They were radical, bold, brave and resolute – but prudent with a shared sense of thanatos. Penn as a young man did not behave well. Lastly, they were fluent and articulate in speech and word.

The conversations between William the Quaker and *Captain Singleton* took place between Penn and Defoe in the period 1680-1682. Initially I believed that all these conversations, and I believe there were many, took place on one occasion when the two men met in Barbados. I still believe that they met on the island but I now conjecture that they were in touch frequently in 1680-1683. The two men had many problems and opportunities in common. The principal common problem was that of the difficulties confronting law-abiding merchants from attacks by Caribbean pirates. How could they legitimately defend themselves? The awarding of proprietary status for Penn's North American territories was only sustainable in the long run if he could demonstrate that he could protect the legitimate activities of settlers at sea. In William the Quaker's discussions with Singleton he had to disrupt conversations on three occasions for diplomatic missions that were successful in gaining a new understanding among various countries and territories of their responsibilities to police the seas.

William Penn was a compassionate man and 'Singleton' was in a state of distress. As Defoe narrates his story Singleton had several acute problems that he and William could not resolve. He had made a great deal of money but what could he do with his riches? Would it possible to return to England with his wealth and make a new life? Would God permit them both to have the use of so much wealth? William's practical advice was that as this wealth could not be given back it was their duty to use it wisely.

Singleton had judged himself to be 'a thief. A rogue, by my calling: I am a pirate and a murderer, and ought to be hanged'. If this statement is taken at its face value then William is also guilty of piratical acts. I do not accept this statement to be true on its face value; but I believe it is true that the two men had common problems of protecting cargoes at sea and that they committed questionable deeds.

Edward Singleton suggests as much in his correspondence. He provides a graphic account of a fleet of merchant ships under his captaincy losing ships in a storm, being attacked by French warships and seeking refuge in a French port. Valuable cargo was lost. Penn states that the ships and cargo were insured but the insurer broke - as they often did.

It is I think probable that Defoe was a 'wanted' man by the Portuguese authorities in Brazil. He suggests as much in *Captain*

Singleton. He was forced by his fear of prosecution to shift the centres of his commercial activity north to Chile, Barbados and North America. In these places he could not settle easily. He was not part of any civil society and in a sense he was an outcast.

In Brazil, Defoe had by his own efforts and ingenuity become a respected citizen. He belonged. But by his own actions he had cast that security adrift on the high seas by illegal slave trading. He had in his own language gone from one situation to another without thought of future consequences. He was adrift without roots in any one place, without family, and a citizen of no country. He had cast adrift the restraints of all society as if he were a pirate. In the words of Sir Edward Coke, as quoted by William Blackstone, he had become Hostis Humani Generis. He had renounced all the benefits of society and government, and reduced himself to a state of nature; by declaring war against all mankind, with the consequence that all mankind must declare war against him.

Singleton confesses that in the dire conditions he found himself, 'it pleased God to make *William the Quaker everything to me* [italics mine]...I told him the perplexity of my mind, and under what terrible temptations of the devil I had been; that I must shoot myself, for I could not support the weight and terror that was upon me.

The impulse to commit suicide has been commented upon in Abse's psychoanalytical study of Defoe.[298]My own preference for a reading of Defoe/*Singleton's* distress, following Durkheim's ground-breaking study, is to view suicide from a sociological point of view. Several of Durkheim's analytical categories apply to Defoe: the egotistic category reflects a prolonged sense of not belonging, a weakening of the ties that integrate an individual into society; in the altruistic form, the individual becomes overwhelmed by a group's goals and beliefs; and in the anomic form, a person suffers moral confusion and lack of social direction. Controversially, Durkheim stresses that suicide rates are greater among Protestants than Roman Catholics. Recently commentators have argued that while Defoe is steadfast in opposing

[298] Abse, 158.

Roman Catholicism as an institution, that there are many examples in his writing of a far more sympathetic understanding of the virtues of the practice of suicide among Roman Catholics.

Defoe does not tell us everything about his state of mind in the period 1680-1682; but, through *Singleton*, he does tell the reader that it took two years to change from one state of being to another. This is not the only mention of a 2 year transition period. There is a transition point between the first part of *Captain Singleton* and the second. *Singleton* returns to England. This is how Hans Turley describes the disappointment of his attempt to resettle:

Singleton is embarrassed by the way he frittered away his fortune in England: 'the rest Merits to be conceal'd with Blushes, for it was spent in all Kinds of Folly and Wickedness.' Prudent investments such as buying property or marrying well ought to be just as profitable when he returns 'home' to England, 'But…he does not fit in…He is an outsider; former friends are now spoilers who take advantage of his wealth and naiveté.' They let him know that he has 'nothing to expect farther than I might command it by the force of my money'. His undermined identity precludes allegiance with or affection for his homeland. *Singleton* wholeheartedly embraces the pirate way.[299]

Defoe was torn between two ways of conducting his life. As I read his state of mind, in 1680-1682 he chose to build his fortune and conduct a family life away from England where he had never truly belonged. His decision was not sustainable for the cruellest of reasons.

Defoe places William Penn at the centre of these disasters. Defoe/*Singleton's* dialogue with Penn takes place in Barbados for good reasons. In 1681 Defoe married Jone Reade on the island and most probably, although I can only conjecture, found himself with a child following her death. Such a happening would be deeply traumatic in itself but for Defoe it would have been terrifying. Emotionally it would have activated his own childhood terrors: the traumas of the 'disappearance' of his mother and the death of his father. He would

---

[299] Turley, 109-117.

have identified with the child. How could he abandon it in circumstances that he, deep in his own psyche, had suffered himself? Was he to 'cast away' his child?

In *Captain Singleton*, *Moll Flanders* and *Colonel Jack*, Defoe 'fictionalises' the solutions to the central difficulties of his life in 1680-1682. He solves his problems in a highly ingenious way, and explains them with inventiveness. I have outlined the actions *Singleton* took in an earlier chapter but I develop it more pithily here. Defoe/*Singleton* persuaded William to send his 'impoverished' sister bills of exchange for £5,000 to enable her to move to a 'safe house'. The reader will know that in *Moll Flanders* the *Captain*/Defoe takes the money back. I am arguing that Defoe persuaded his sister to settle in Virginia on plantations he owned, and which he may have bought in the 2 years *Singleton* tells the reader was needed before he could settle back in England. The un-stated purpose was that he wished to create a family establishment with his sister to take care of his son by Jone Reade. The *Captain* needed to be a part owner of a ship and so to be in a position to import goods to England in conformity with the Navigation Acts. He succeeded in getting Mary to Virginia for a reunion with his son only to find that she rejected him for a normal family life. I think it believable that confronted with a re-enactment of the circumstances of his own loss of a mother and father that Defoe became distraught and suicidal.

Defoe could not have survived his transgressive and highly dangerous life without the compassionate support of William Penn. In effect Penn became Defoe's spiritual mentor. The agreement reached between the two men was far-reaching. They were to behave as brothers and always help each other. In essence, William Penn became Defoe's spiritual mentor and life-long friend. Defoe pledged that he would never reveal anything of the way Penn had saved him from a rootless and highly dangerous life, except to his sister; while Penn committed himself to reveal nothing of his relationship to Defoe. In particular the truth of it all should never be spoken or written about in public; and when in public they should speak in a foreign tongue.

There are several obvious reasons for the agreement. There is an implied assumption that in passing themselves off as foreigners (applicable in particular to Defoe) they would not in their trading habits have been thought to have infringed the Navigation Acts, and neither could be held to have committed piratical acts. Penn may have had qualms about supporting an incestuous relationship between Defoe and his sister Mary although there would have been relief - and perhaps Penn's influence in the decision - to abandon an incestuous relationship. Subsequently Penn may have used his influence with Sunderland to assist Defoe to emerge as a leading Whig polemicist; while in return Defoe committed himself to the defence and promotion of Quaker issues such as opposition to the Test and Corporation Acts.

A 'leopard does not change its spots'. Defoe remained a transgressor but he was able to modify his behaviour, he read more widely, thought more deeply, and sought a better social place. Arguably, but for Penn's friendship and constancy this would not have been possible; and it would appear to be true that without Penn's assistance at this crucial time the man known now as Daniel Defoe would 'never have existed'.

Chapter 24

Roxana:
The Fortunate Mistress

That unhappy Girl...Broke in upon all our measures...she brought me to the brink of Destruction...have tru'd me out at last...if Amy had not by the violence of her Passion ...put a Stop to her...

Roxana
Daniel Defoe, 1724

Whereas *Moll Flanders* is mainly an account of Defoe's early life from humble beginnings, *Roxana* is an account of his later life when money was able to buy him social position. Like *Moll* the book is a personation rooted in the reality of a life with many achievements but, in the end, a sense of failure amidst the mounting complexities of his life - and despair.

It is easy to imagine it otherwise and to seek other formative influences on the work. Most literary and cultural accounts assume that *Roxana* is a woman of modest beginnings who becomes a high-class courtesan. She can be understood as a composite of the excesses of the Court of Charles II, with its French mistresses, George 1's German mistresses, and popular actresses of the day. The title page offers the prospect of a saucy read, a salacious history and a mix of true-life scandal. However, those who read it as a romance with a dash of didactic morality are in for a disappointment.

David Blewett in a perceptive introduction to the version of the book I am using writes as follows:[300]

Roxana is the story of the moral deterioration and ultimate defeat [it displays] the psychological turmoil of a woman who wilfully chooses a glamorous but immoral life of a courtesan over the honourable but duller life of a married woman... she sacrifices personal integrity for

---

[300] Blewett, David. Ed *Roxana*, (1722. Penguin Classics, 1987), 9-25.

worldly opinion. *Roxana* is [Defoe's] only tragedy. As the novel advances Roxana becomes more and more mentally ill...[and finally] gives way entirely...*Roxana* is ruined because her immoderate vanity and ambition can only be satisfied at the expense of the love and trust which she desperately needs. Her life is her punishment and her story Defoe's expression of his tragic vision of the human lot.

What Blewett does, which is what every cultural historian attempts to do, is to embed his interpretation into the social structure of England in the early eighteenth century with its acquisitiveness and greed, inequality and poverty and the exploitation of women, together with a dash of didactic moralising.

However, whatever the social construct of *Roxana's* life, Defoe is telling a story of his own life in the period 1683-1723. Defoe starts *Roxana's* story with a birth in 1683. This is the date which marks Defoe's re-settlement in London and marriage to Mary Tuffley. He ends the story in late 1723, on the eve of its publication. It would be wise for the reader to take account of the notion that all biography is but a dream of someone's life. Defoe was better able than me to fantasise his life. I suggest that the contrast is not between the bourgeois Dutch merchant and a Prince as Defoe describes his choice but between dull respectability and material and sexual adventure.

We owe to Freud the knowledge that dreams are inherently unreliable. Freud provides a methodology for interpreting them and a toolkit to assist any dreamer interested in understanding his own dreams. No reader should approach a biographer's dream of someone's life without such a toolkit; especially when that person is a creative writer. Freud stresses that the memory of the content of a dream is condensed and fragmentary but by various techniques the pieces can be remembered and put together as a whole; they express wish-fulfilment, moments of shame and troubling traumatic events. Their reliability can be tested.

In my discussion of *Roxana* I was tempted to delete her name and substitute the name of the author, Defoe: it would have made better sense. But reason prevailed. However, I suggest that the reader try it from time to time. It does not always work because of the variety of ways Defoe displaces himself onto other characters and the issue of agency, so important in considering the character and role of Amy, *Roxana's* alter ego.

The book can be divided chronologically by subject as follows.

Marriage, Family and Business Failure, 1683-1692

Roxana is of Huguenot descent her family having come from Poitiers[301] as religious refugees – as Defoe's grandfather Daniel Foe did. She married, began to raise children while her husband ran a business – as Defoe did. Eight years after her marriage the husband's business failed, that is 8 years after Defoe's marriage in 1684 being 1692. Defoe went bankrupt in this year. After 4 years her husband had inherited money from his 'father' and this gave him some respite. He began to use a horse and carriage. Defoe did this but at a slightly later date so far as is known. My conjecture is that Defoe would stable his horse and carriage at the Ferry Inn, East Tilbury, a short distance from his brick house. It may well be that he borrowed a dray-horse to get him from the inn to his house a ten minute walk away. John Lawrence, whose family, I conjecture, took Defoe in at his age of 14 that is in 1655-1658, died in 1688. This date coincided exactly with *Roxana's* statement that her father in law died 4 years into her marriage and left her husband some money. Unfortunately, there is no extant will to substantiate this conjecture.

The business failed for lack of professionalism and attention to detail and despite *Roxana*/Mary Tuffley using some of her marriage portion. *Roxana* dumped 5 children with relatives. These children were probably 4 girls, Maria, Henrietta, Hannah, and Martha. The boy, described by *Roxana* as born in another Parish, I believe to be Daniel. The charitable old man who responded to a request that he take care of the children was probably Samuel Tuffley, Defoe's father in law, and the aunt who took them in would be Joan Tuffley. It is assumed in various biographical accounts, without evidence, that the Tuffley's did

---

[301] There are Defoe family histories in Poitiers in all the many versions of the name.

take care of the children. Not all the children were Mary Tuffley's – Daniel was a son by Elisabeth Sammens and Maria and Henrietta daughters by another man I dub 'Sir Charles', as he is described in *Religious Courtship*. I do not believe that Defoe 'dumped the children' in quite the way described in *Roxana*. He would have thought he had no alternative to letting the children go to someone who could look after them. The husband fled. Not in real life to Paris but, more prosaically, to Tilbury.

Lodgings with the Sammens, 1692-1705

When in London Defoe lodged with Nathaniel and Elisabeth Sammens. According to *Roxana* he/she lived rent free for a year. It has been known for some time that the Sammens gave Defoe a lodging between 1692 and 1705. In his time Defoe's association with the Sammens created malicious gossip.[302] What has been unknown until my work *Beyond Belief* in 2006 was the nature of the relationships. Amy's agency can be put to one side. There are 3 adults involved, Nathaniel Sammens is the landlord and he permits Defoe to have sex with his wife Elisabeth. Consequently, Elisabeth had a son by Defoe that I believe was Daniel. Defoe, as the narrator, writes that he was a 'charming Child who did very well'. However, later the reader is told that although she (*Roxana*) had promised to support the *child at a distance*, (italics mine) she had never cared for it. This statement suggests that Defoe at some time cared for Daniel at some distance away. I suggest and describe in a later chapter, *Religious Courtship*, that this other place was in Essex with Mary Norton. There was one other child, Sarah, of this union. Daniel was taken back into a family establishment with his father, Elisabeth Sammens and Sarah, as discussed in an earlier chapter, by 1696.

Fame, Riches and Social Status: 1692-1703

The third chronological phase in *Roxana's* story spans the period 1692-1703. It requires very careful analysis and my narrative raises controversial conclusions. The principal difficulty for the biographer is

---

[302] *The Welsh Monster.*

to determine the aspects of this phase of Defoe's life that are fantastical works of the imagination and what parts are real.

The difficulties of interpreting Defoe's narratives are illustrated by his involvement with a courtesan in Naples when he was 18 years of age. Defoe attributed it to the *Cavalier* in *Memoirs of a Cavalier.*

> At a certain town in Italy…I was *prevailed upon* rather than tempted, by la Courtezan. If I should describe the Woman *I must give a very mean Character of my own Virtue* to say I was allured by any but a Woman of extraordinary Figure; her Face, Shape, Mein and Dress, I may without Vanity, say, were the finest I ever saw. When I had Admittance into her Apartments, the Riches and Magnificence of them astonished me, the Cupboard of Cabinet of Plate, the Jewels, the Tapestry, and every Thing in Proportion, made me question whether I was not in the Chamber of some Lady of the best Quality…her Conversation…was exceeding agreeable, she sung to her Lute and danced as fine as ever I saw, and thus diverted me two Hours before any Thing else was discussed of: - but the vicious Part came on the Stage, I blush to relate the Confusion I was in, and when she made a certain Motion by which I understand she might be made use of, either as a Lady or as--- [whore?] I was quite thunderstruck, all the vicious support of my Thoughts vanished, their place filled me with Horror, and I was all over Disorder and Distraction…I confess that I had a strong Inclination to visit her again… I happened to meet this Lady coming out of the Church…The End of my relating this Story is answered in describing the Manner of their Address, [Seigniors} without bringing my self *to Confessions; if I did any Thing I have some Reason to be ashamed of, it may be a less Crime to conceal it than expose it.* (Italics mine). [303]

Bastian thinks that this confrontation gave Defoe/the *Cavalier* the idea for *Roxana*. He may well be right. As it stands, however, I find the

[303] *Memoirs of a Cavalier*, 30.

usual interpretation of the encounter improbable. The *Cavalier* was solicited by a prostitute. He knowingly enters her apartment. He is astonished by its luxury and opulence. There is an unanswered question of how she acquired this wealth. When he was offered the usual services he is struck with horror, 'Distracted' and 'Disordered'. Nevertheless he contrives to meet the Lady again. He tells the reader, 'If I did anything I have some reason to be ashamed of, it may be a less crime to conceal it than expose it.' Congress with a prostitute freely entered into would not have been a crime. I suggest to the reader that Defoe was admiring a particularly successful act of cross-dressing. He was being importuned by a man.

It is my contention that an understanding of Defoe's sexuality is crucial to any interpretation of his literature. The reader has a number of options. He can regard the work as pure fiction and conclude that Defoe, as the author, is tapping into the cultural obsessions of his time, in particular of the making of money and the aggregation of fortunes. Secondly, the work might be considered as a work of fiction augmented by Defoe's actual experiences. Thirdly, and it is my position, Defoe is writing embellished and disguised accounts of his own experience. This experience led him to a detailed understanding of deviant sexuality and practices at Molly Houses.

For example, what did Defoe mean when *Roxana* writes of her Prince- and to whom she might be considered a Princess? *Roxana* uses the term Man-Woman to describe herself. This is a third gender definition used by sodomites. Its meaning in the common parlance of the time is a man who acts as a woman while being acceptable to men. I have argued in an earlier chapter that Defoe's gender identification falls within this third gender categorisation. Sodomites had developed a unified subculture with its own slang. When *Roxana* longs to be a 'princess', she uses a slang term common to this culture.

Roxana is confronted with a choice of husband: either with a Dutch merchant who was to become a Baronet, or her Prince. The term Princess butch was in the Molly House slang of the time. It was first mentioned in a published work in James Dalton's *Narrative*, 1727 but it was in currency long before. The term denoted a butch man who preferred other men. The term became more universally known in 1732 with the trial brought to court by a Princess Sarafina, who is commonly described as the first drag queen.

In his imagination Defoe dreamt of becoming a baronet for services to William III. It could be argued that this was not a ridiculous notion. Persons of modest background could achieve social advantages if they performed services to the Court. Under Charles II common people, regardless of gender, obtained the highest positions in the land by 'selling themselves' to kings and courtiers. Good connections were vital. The accession to the throne of William III presented Defoe with opportunities to get near to the Court. With the assistance of Sir Thomas Neale and Sir Dalby Thomas, Defoe won himself the appointment of Treasurer to the Glass Commission and valuable contracts for his brickworks at Tilbury. Talking through Amy, Defoe maintains that he/she had slept over a hundred times with a Gentleman at the Court. Amy confesses that 'she lov'd the fellow so much'.

There is ample evidence to show the besotted nature of Defoe's attraction to William III. Defoe/ *Roxana* forms passionate relationships with two men. One of these is called a Prince. Roxana goes on a foreign trip with him. She describes the Prince's wife as 'The Best Lady in the World'. [304] This kind and gentle lady knew that her husband had affairs with others but she tolerated them. The Princess had been pregnant three times without producing a child. William's wife Mary was supposed to have been pregnant three times without producing a child. One pregnancy was aborted, but there are doubts about the other two children, although these doubts were not shared with the general public.[305]

I assume two things about this account: Defoe/*Roxana* did not go on a foreign tour with William III and the account is a fantastical dream in which she did.

Roxana moves to London. She tells her readers that:

[304] *Roxana*, 211-212.
[305] Van der Zee, Henry and Barbara. *William and Mary,* MacMillan, London, 1973.

I was rich, beautiful and agreeable and not yet old; I had known something of the influence I had upon the Fancies of Men, even of the highest Rank; I never forgot that the Prince of de—had said with an Extasie, that I was the finest woman in France; I knew I could make a Figure in London, and how well I could grace that Figure; I was not at a loss how to behave, and nothing less than of being Mistress to the King.

Elsewhere in her account *Roxana* admits to being in her fifties at this stage of her life: that is, in Defoe's life around 1700.

Roxana establishes herself in Pall Mall in a rich and opulent apartment. She 'walk'd sometimes in the Mall' and followed the nobility in walks along Pall Mall and rides in her own coach and horses. She tells the reader 'that seeing Liberty seemed to be the Men's Property …[she] would be a Man-Woman.' It is known about Defoe that around this time, 1700, that it was remarked by others that he was attempting to cut a figure with a change in his name to Defoe and adopting a coat of arms emblazoned on a carriage.

Roxana began to operate in a new sphere. She observes that the 'Courtiers …were as wicked as any-body in reason could desire them…and that a Woman who had anything agreeable in her appearance could never want Followers.' She began to organise balls at which 'fine gentlemen came masked as in Masquerade… and played cards and danced with Ladies'. She believed that the king came and that she might have danced with him. At these balls and by popular demand, *Roxana* wore her Turkish dress and danced to general acclaim. This behaviour, that Bastian refers to in his narrative as quoted above, was Defoe's aping of the 'man-woman' in Naples.

At such a party Defoe claims for *Roxana* that she danced with the Duke of Monmouth [long since dead although she may have intended the description to fit his son] and with a Lord H. who made her a substantial private offer and who had talked to her of love. *Roxana* responds that this was 'a point so ridiculous to me without the main thing, I mean the money, that I had no patience to hear him make so long a Story of it…' This Lord was obliged to consider a financial arrangement worth five hundred pounds a year 'yet he gave me money so often, and in such large Parcels, that I had seldom as little as seven or eight hundred pounds a year and occasional other payments.'

The only person who fits this description in Defoe's life is Lord Robert Harley. I have dated their collaboration as starting in 1699. I have accepted the account of Defoe's delivery of *Legions Memorial* to Harley dressed as a woman in 1701 as commented upon in an earlier chapter. I believe that Defoe's association with Harley included some sexual element but it is difficult to be certain about what it was.[306] In my book on Swift I maintain that Harley sought sex from him in return for patronage.[307]

There are a number of realistic objections. Whether Defoe organised such parties is questionable. On the other hand there is good evidence that Defoe cross-dressed. Taken overall I maintain that *Roxana's* descriptions are most probably fantasies. They are certainly fantastical. Freud discusses daytime fantasies in his *Interpretation of Dreams*.[308] According to Freud day-dreams share a large number of their properties with night-dreams. Like night-dreams they are wish-fulfilments but based to a greater extent on impressions of infantile experiences. There is an important difference between the two: day-dreaming is never confused with reality. If then Defoe is acting-out in his literature, and in particular in *Moll Flanders* and *Roxana*, a desire to be regarded as a Man-Woman in day-dreams, he is likely to respond with his sense of reality during waking hours. In other words, it is probable, or at least more probable than in night dreams, that he acted out fantasies in real life.

Blackmail, 1716-1724, and Beyond

Some time in the period 1716-1718 Defoe was being blackmailed by the family of John White a tenant of a house Defoe owned in Church Lane, Stoke Newington for misdemeanours involving his son, also called John. This young boy was said to be a pupil of Henry Baker's.

[306] *Beyond Belief*, 272-278.
[307] Martin, John. *The Man Himself: A Life of Jonathan Swift*.
[308] Freud, Sigmund. *Interpretation of Dreams*, Oxford University Press, 1999.

A long, intricate and well-documented proof is provided in *Beyond Belief*.[309] This proof cross references to *Conjugal Lewdness* [310]and Defoe's correspondence towards the end of his life, much commentated upon by biographers, [311] to the baptism records of John White, jnr and his sister Elisabeth,[312] and to their fathers will.[313]

In *Roxana's* story, the reader discovers that Defoe is concerned about the progress being made by eight of his children. Of these children *only seven were known to be his or Mary Tuffley's* and living in England in 1716: Maria was married and living in Dorset; Henrietta, Hannah and Sophia were living in Stoke Newington; Benjamin Norton and Daniel, living in Tilbury; and Sarah living with her mother Elisabeth Sammens in Spittalfields, London. Amy, on *Roxana's* bidding, went searching for Sarah and for an unaccounted for ' son'.

Amy went first to the *Weavers House* in Spittalfields (where the Sammens lived). A neighbour informed her that a daughter (Sarah) had been taken into service by a Lady elsewhere in London. The son was easily found. He was working as an apprentice in a menial trade. Amy set out to transform his life by changing his apprenticeship to a more respectable trade and for paying for his education, even if this transformative process was to cost ten thousand pounds (nine hundred thousand pounds in current money value)! In realistic terms this was a ridiculous sum of money.

This boy had a sister who also sought money. When denied this, she came seeking her 'mother'/*Roxana*/Defoe at the Quakers House, (that is, Mary Norton's house in Essex). This girl states that she knew everything *Roxana* had been up to in London; she wished her claim as a daughter to be accepted by *Roxana*; and asserted that she should be looked after by her mother. The knowledge that this girl was hunting him around the country threw *Roxana* into a dreadful state of anxiety and fear. She authorised Amy to deal with this troublesome girl and the

---

[309] *Beyond Belief*, 267-275.
[310] Defoe, Daniel. *Conjugal Lewdness*, 1729.
[311] Novak, 697-702. Backscheider, 495, 500-503, 526-529, 595, 610.
[312] *Beyond Belief*, 267- 270, 277-279.
[313] *Beyond Belief*, 269, 277-279.

reader is left with the distinct possibility that Amy had murdered her.

In her discussion with the Quaker (Mary Norton), the 'daughter' remarked that she 'came in hopes of a Discovery in my great Affair which you know of'. However, *Roxana* had not told the Quaker anything of his difficulties with the White family. The 'daughter' stated that she would return in two or three day's time. *Roxana*/Defoe gives an explanation of the Quaker's ignorance of her/his secret life:

> I put my Affairs in a Posture that I might go to *Holland*, I open'd up all my Affairs to my dear trusty Friend the QUAKER. and placed her, in Matters of Trust, in the room of Amy, and with a heavy, bleeding Heart for my poor Girl, I embarked with my Spouse...I must put in a Caution, however, here, as I did not let my Friend the QUAKER into any Part of the Secret History of my former Life nor did I commit The Grand Resrv'd of all to her that I was really the Girl's Mother and the Lady *Roxana*; there was no need of That Part being expos'd; and it was always a Maxim with me, That Secret's shoul'd never be open'd without evident Utility...for tho' she lov'd me very sincerely...yet she would not Lye for me....

Roxana tasked the Quaker with receiving Money, Interest, Rents and the like. But Defoe/*Roxana* stated, 'But there fell out a great Difficulty here, which I knew not how to get over; and this was, how to convey the usual Supply, or Provision and Money, to the uncle and the other Sister... [Samuel and Mary Tuffley] but how to direct her to manage them, was the Great Difficulty.' Defoe is indicating that it was the payment of money that was needed to resolve the challenge from the daughter and that he would be hard pressed to deal with it.

The girl who came looking for Defoe/ *Roxana* was Elisabeth White the daughter of his Stoke Newington tenant John White. Defoe tells readers something of the reasons for this girl's pursuit of him in his strange work *Conjugal Lewdness*, published in 1729. Defoe ends this work by giving his readers a peculiar and striking warning. He writes that he has not been able to find words [All the words?] to describe certain vile and perhaps unheard of practices. The Crime he wished to reprove could not [be exposed] because special language was needed to understand it: Defoe writes, 'The Dialect these people talk is a great part of the Crime; and as it not [to be used to reprove them] I talk to the dark and reprove by Allegory and Metaphor.'

Defoe continues by issuing something of a threat or a pre-emptive strike to head-off a criminal prosecution. He tells the outside world of readers that, 'If these people do not heed his words then they could expect no mercy. If they cannot [mend their ways] let them expect no Quarter…My next attack will be personal …I may come to Black Lists, Histories of Facts, Registers of Time and of Surname.' Dalton, in his *Narratives*, writes that dignitaries attending Molly Houses were often the target of blackmailers. Lists of people attending could be bought. Blackmailers followed people home and could obtain their names by speaking to their neighbours.

Defoe recounts the story of the 'marriage' of a sixty-five year old woman (Defoe) to a ten year old boy (John White, jnr) This Old lady has two nieces (Sophia and Hannah) who slight and neglect him. They think they will inherit her/Defoe's estate and in particular the house they are living in (Defoe's residence in Church Lane, Newington) but they are mistaken in this. The Old Lady/ Defoe decided to retire into the country (Colchester). The nieces employed other relatives to intercede on their behalf. The Old Lady visits her tenant (John White, in Church Lane)). She met the White family in their home. Present were John White and his wife Elisabeth, John White jnr and his sister Elizabeth. Defoe told the White family that he had decided to give his two nieces £100 each and thus he was able to dispose of other assets. To the astonishment of the White family, the Old Lady/Defoe made them an offer to 'marry' John White jnr. The Old Lady explains, she will put him to school and afterwards put him to Prentice at London in a good trade and give him one hundred pounds and 'that I shall be dead before he will be out of his Time; and selling part of the Estate he will have a good stock to be set up with, and then when he is re-married will make a good Jointure for a Wife.' This proposal is similar to the account Amy gives of her meeting with the missing son in *Roxana*. Perhaps, Defoe had neglected part of the bargain he struck with John White and had to move quickly at a later date to appease him.

Defoe writes that the 'The tenant was distast'd' by the proposal.' John White was a prudent and calculating man. He believed that something more should be done for the nieces. As a 'man of the world' he was aware that wills could be put aside However, Defoe writes that the Old Lady/Defoe was adamant on that point and would not be moved. Defoe writes, 'After some difficulties which the Old Tenant started, for he didn't come willingly into it, no not to the last, it was however agreed on, and she was married to the Boy.'

If this text is approached by a cultural historian, perhaps one lacking biographical skills, this 'marriage' of an Old Lady to a young boy might be considered to be a folk tale. Defoe goes on to tell the reader that everything worked out well: the Old Lady lived to the ripe old age of one hundred and forty having developed an entirely new set of teeth; and the boy reached his normal, that is biblical, life span of seventy years. However, against the plausibility of that reading are inescapable facts of Defoe's life. Defoe believed in shunamitism. The Old Lady's story is part of an argument, a belief by Defoe, that a man could prolong his life by sleeping with much younger people whether or not he had sex with them.

In recounting this tale Defoe makes a mistake. John White tells his wife that the proposal made by the Old Lady/Defoe would 'take away all the Scandal that he was before concerned about [that is before the proposal] on her account'. The reader is left with a question - what scandal?

Into this story comes Henry Baker. It is said that Henry Baker entered Defoe's life when he sought him out in Stoke Newington in 1724. Baker specialised in teaching deaf children by a method he kept secret. In his papers Baker states that he was instructing a ten year old son of John White, who was deaf, on three days a week. In his spare time he established contact with people in Stoke Newington's coffee houses.[314] Defoe, he states, sought him out.

Much of what is known about Baker's story comes from edited papers and copied letters given by the Baker family to Thomas Wright, the biographer. Wright made the grievous mistake not to see any originals. He was content with copies of a selection of letters written out by the Baker family. Thus Baker's account cannot be relied upon. Wright received the material they wished him to receive. Not a single word deleterious to the reputation of Henry Baker was published. It is almost certainly wrong. John White junior's date of birth is in 1708 and so he would have been ten years of age in 1718: that is, six years earlier than Defoe suggests. There is no evidence either that John White jnr was deaf. As Amy/Defoe was able to conduct a sensible conversation with him at a much later date, it does seem highly unlikely.

Henry Baker had, by his own account, a very difficult upbringing: he was abused by his father and slept rough in the street before being taken into local parish care. He was placed with John Parker a Pall Mall bookseller as a Charity Child. He stayed there for thirteen years between 1707 and 1720, Defoe knew most of London's booksellers and it possible that he might have had contact with Baker when he was in the care of the bookseller. It is notable also that Defoe places his 'drag party' in Pall Mall.

I find this particular story difficult to narrate. I have no wish to offend my readers. Defoe's meeting with the Whites must have come between 1708, when John White became his tenant, and 1718 when John White, jnr was ten years old. The arrangement must have been necessitated by the White family having evidence about Defoe's sexual practices. This scandal affected the White family. It may have been related to group sex involving local people at 'drag' parties and local Molly Houses. These activities included Henry Baker. It is my belief that Defoe attended local Newington version(s) of Molly Houses held in people's homes. If he was accompanied by Baker or John White jnr this would amount to a local scandal. If Baker and John White jnr

[314] Potter, George. Henry Baker, F.R.S. (1698-1774) *Modern Philology*, 29, 1932.

attended a 'drag party' in Pall Mall it would have been regarded as scandalous in Stoke Newington. The person who came looking for Defoe in Essex was Elisabeth White, John White, jnr's sister. *Roxana* can be read to support the contention that Elisabeth White was the person who witnessed Defoe/*Roxana* dancing at a Pall Mall party. She claimed to have done so. [315]

John White, snr concluded that Defoe should be bled dry in his lifetime and not left to the vagaries of inheritance law and the legal claims of relatives. He may have known that Defoe never owned the freehold or a head lease of his large house in Stoke Newington. Defoe did succeed in negotiating a new lease but there was little value in it. Defoe gave Henry Baker a charge worth four hundred pounds against his leasehold interest. On Defoe's death the charge gave Baker a claim against the house. He decided to occupy it before Defoe's death.

John White died in 1732. His will is discussed in *Beyond Belief*. He left his son the huge sum of £7,500 (six hundred and fifty thousand pounds in current money value) leeched from Defoe over fourteen years. Defoe fled from his house and family by end 1729 and died in a desperate state eighteen months later.

Elisabeth White got her reward. Her father bequeathed her one hundred pounds and her son three hundred pounds because 'I have already advanced them and provided for them.' He sought to prevent her claiming against his Estate and making a damaging fuss. His will reads that 'If they (William Smith, his son in law, and his daughter Elisabeth) shall not comply with the will but shall contravert or take any course in law or in Equity or otherwise and shall use any other part of my personall Estate then I doe declare that the aforesaid devises of three hundred pounds to their sonn John Lewis Smith and one hundred pounds to my said sonn in law William Smith and his wife shall be void and shall goe and be paid to and amongst the children of my said sonn John White.'

It would have needed the threat of a horrible death to force the ingenious Defoe to pay over these huge sums over so long a period of time.

---

[315] *Beyond Belief,* 246.

Chapter 25

The Life and Actions
of
Jonathan Wild

*I had occasion to wait upon Mr Jonathan...I came again and again [but] it being only
a silver-hilted sword...there was no coming at it.*

The Life and Actions of Jonathan Wild
Daniel Defoe, 1725

William Lee, a Defoe biographer, writing in 1869,[316] advanced the theory
that from about 1720 Defoe entered into an agreement with Ambrose
Appleby, the printer-owner of *Applebee's Journal*, to provide essays,
articles and letters. These contributions were to be written anonymously or
under pen-names. Lee asserts that from 1724 Defoe widened his role with
the *Journal* and became an Applebee crime reporter. He argues that
Applebee and his staff were given access to the prisoners in Newgate to
obtain confessions and that as a result the *Journal* was able to print
accounts by prisoners of their crimes and their dying speeches. When in
the prison the reporters were dubbed 'Applebee's Men'.

Lee widens his appeal to his readers by a series of anecdotes that are
irresistible to modern biographers. Furbank and Owens brusquely
dismiss the link between Applebee and Defoe. They maintain that Lee
was not able to produce any hard evidence for these claims and that they
rested entirely on his judgement of the stylistic characteristics of letters,
articles, and pamphlets. While admitting that Lee's conclusions might be
correct, although they doubted it, Furbank and Owens accused him of
being the victim of his own rhetoric.[317]

The idea that Defoe was an original pioneer in the writing of

---

[316] Lee, William. Daniel Defoe: *His Life and hitherto Unknown Writings*, 3 Vols.,
London , Hotten, 1869.
[317] Furbank and Owens. *The Canonisation of Daniel Defoe*, 62-68, n. 29.

criminal biographies is not that easily cast asunder. Richard Holmes, a much respected English biographer, has recently looked at the evidence and concluded that Defoe was probably the author of one of the criminal biographies attributed to him by Lee: *The True and Genuine Account* of *the Life of Jonathan Wilde* published anonymously by Applebee in 1725; and possibly a contributor or sole author of two biographies of John Sheppard: *The History of the Remarkable Life of John Sheppard* and A *Narrative of all the Robberies and Escapes of John Sheppard* , both published anonymously by Applebee in 1724.[318]

Holmes needs to admit an interest. He has been studying and advancing a history of biography in the English speaking world and has enlisted Defoe as a pioneer of criminal histories or biographies. This literary genre has particular appeal to 'Anglo-Saxons'. In England today interest in criminals and their crimes has become a popular cultural obsession. Holmes makes the legitimate claim that in the early eighteenth-century criminal biographies fed into a number of rich traditional literary forms: folk tales, ballads and popular journalism. Defoe must have been aware that he could gain access to prisoners in London gaols and there is some evidence over a long period of time that he concerned himself with criminals. Lee believes that Defoe gained access to prisoners in Newgate by posing as, or being, an Applebee man, and that he involved himself in real-life confessions. Criminal confessions had been published and sold in pamphlet form on the streets of London since the early seventeenth century.

There are a number of distinct reasons for Defoe becoming engaged in this particular journalistic trade late in his life. First, there were political and sociological reasons. The so-called Black Act, 1723, increased the number of capital offences to more than two hundred and a person found stealing even a trivial item from a private house could be executed. While the law reached into the upper echelons of society, it was generally believed that the rich could always buy themselves a release or a pardon. Writers such as Gay and Defoe saw the criminal justice system as a mirror image of a corrupt political society that was

---

[318] Ed. Holmes, Richard. *Defoe on Sheppard and Wilde,* Harper Perennial, 2004.

to be made more odious under Walpole. Gay said as much in the *Beggars Opera.*

Secondly, there was human empathy. The circumstances of Defoe's life had led him into crime. Defoe shared the feelings of anxiety, excitement, audacity and ruthlessness he described in Wild and Sheppard. Defoe lived his life in constant fear of being caught-out at any time. He believed that he might be unmasked by a vengeful society. He placed himself time and again in desperately difficult situations. Danger excited him. While he may not have chosen to live on the edge of disaster, in practice the decisions he made led him there. Once there, Defoe always contrived escapes. He admired the escapology of others.

Thirdly, there are literary considerations. It is not a trivial, or marginal, matter for admirers of Defoe whether or not he wrote these admirable biographies of Wild and Sheppard. Holmes is right to point out that the works he attributes to Defoe are fine examples of that genre. Defoe's skill in writing contributed in some ways to invention of the genre of criminal biography. Much fiction that has been ascribed to Defoe has been questioned. The criminal biographies attributed to him by Holmes go someway to correcting the record. Defoe's authorship of them, if sustainable, establishes beyond peradventure that Defoe was a distinguished biographer.

Fourthly, and in my opinion, Furbank and Owens are wrong to dismiss any judgement of the quality of the writing as evidence in favour of Defoe's authorship. They disparage William Lee for doing this but it is not as easy to ignore Richard Holmes. Like Lee, Holmes relies on internal evidence to make his claims. Holmes argues that *The True and Genuine Account* is a highly controlled and well-written book. It focuses on Wild alone. I believe that this omission of other criminals in this account is significant in Defoe's actual history. Holmes believes that the writing of such a book would have been beyond the reach of any of Applebee's hacks; that is, it incorporates the skills of a practiced writer of considerable experience. Holmes regards the *History* as too crude to be wholly attributed to Defoe, but believes that the occasional flashes of brilliance might arise from Defoe editing the work. He regards the *Narrative* as brilliantly written in the first person. He makes the point that the writer's point of view in the *Narrative* is ambiguous, and that the reader's admiration for Sheppard, which is instinctive, is always qualified by another narrative judgement – that Sheppard might well be thought to be brutish and stupid and best put out of harms way.

Fifthly, there are distinct and definable psychological reasons for Defoe's authorship arising from his birth and early life as I have described it in this work. I emphasise, that unlike clinical psychologists, I do not believe that these early experiences determine Defoe's adult life. However, it is my opinion that it pre-conditioned his life and, other things being equal, strongly influenced it. We might expect from an understanding of the theories of psychological clinicians to expect that the behavioural traits of childhood will continue to influence a subject's adult life.

The view I advance here is that Defoe was probably the author of both *The True Account,* and the *Narrative*. It will be obvious to the reader that it is open to anyone to demonstrate a link between Defoe and Applebee by a single proof that he wrote a particular letter, essay or book. It would follow from a proof of any one criminal history that there would be a distinct possibility that Defoe wrote another.

The Crime Scene

Jonathan Wild (1683-1725) was born in Wolverhampton as the eldest child in a poor family. He came to London in 1702 where he worked as a servant. He came to the notice of a wider public when, like Defoe, he was gaoled for debt in March, 1710. He spent two years in a debtor's prison in the City of London. He was released in 1712. While in prison he was given its *liberty*, the freedom to leave the prison at night to find known criminals who could be captured. He received a reward for each criminal he captured. In this way he became popular with the warders who gained financially from the arrests. While outside the prison, Wild struck up a relationship with a well-known prostitute Mary Molineaux. In 1712, Wild was released from the prison under an Act of Parliament for the relief of insolvent debtors

Wild started a business as a fence of stolen goods and a thief-taker. The Government offered forty pounds for each thief. Around 1713 Wild started a business with Charles Hitchen who had obtained the position of the City's Under Marshall for the payment of £700, in effect he became the City's Chief Policeman. In 1713 Hitchen got into trouble for abuse of his office. Something is known about Hitchen's corrupt practices because of a confession he made in 1713 when he was accused of corruption. Hitchen paid bribes to get prisoners out of gaol, some of whom he arrested and for which he received a fee for their capture. He was highly indiscreet. It was known that he was 'gay' and demanded free sex in Molly Houses on threat of arrest. Hitchen was known also for selling sex with young children. In 1714, Hitchen was restored to his official office but Wild split from him to run his own business. The two thief-takers became bitter rivals. In 1718 the two men entered into a turf war. Both accused the other, in competing pamphlets, of nefarious conduct. The effect of this mutual blackening did neither man any good. The public, although deeply concerned with crime, lost confidence in both of them. John Sheppard came to his grisly end in 1724. Wild was convicted of the minor crime of stealing lace and hung in May, 1725. Hitchen survived until 1727. He was targeted by the Society for the Reformation of Manners and went on trial for sodomy. Found guilty he was fined twenty-pounds, put in the pillory and spent six months in gaol. The public beat him up in the pillory. This beating may have contributed to his death in 1727 shortly after his release from prison.

Defoe acquired a lease on his substantial property in Church Lane, Stoke Newington in August, 1714. In his letter to Henry Baker dated 12 August, 1730, Defoe writes that he was sorry Henry Baker was debarred from seeing him and that he no longer had 'a lodging in London nor have I that place in the Old Baily'. The reason for someone, or some circumstance, preventing Baker from visiting Defoe, is not clear. The assumption in Defoe's letter is that Baker knew of the place in the Old Baily. Wild's office was in the Blue Boar Tavern run by Mrs Seagoe at Little Old Bailey. Defoe's lodging would then have been a very short distance, a 'stones throw away', from Wild's place of work. It is reasonable to assume, therefore, that in the period 1717-1725 Defoe would have encountered Jonathan Wild. There is no known direct link between Hitchen and Defoe. However, Defoe might have encountered him in a Molly House.

A True and Genuine Account

Defoe as the Narrator

The narrator of *A True and Genuine Account* had met Wild on several occasions over some period of time. Defoe tells the reader that 'I had occasion to ...wait upon Mr Jonathan with a crown in my hand...I came again and again [but] it being only a silver-hilted sword there was no coming at it.' According to Defoe, he had made a down payment for the recovery of a lost article.

In an every-day understanding, a sword denoted chivalry, courage and determination but in Freud's work it is a phallic symbol. Freud regards the sword blade as masculine but the sheath as feminine. A sword without a sheath is, therefore, a masculine symbol. Both Defoe and Wild customarily carried a sword. Wild has been described as a short brutal man while Defoe is described by others as beauish. Every reader will be familiar with the scene in Shakespeare's, *Hamlet*, when Hamlet confronts his mother with a sword and conducts a conversation with her which is commonly interpreted by critics as displaying Hamlet's desire to bed his mother.

The narrator's account includes two characteristics that I maintain to be Defoe's. First, Defoe in his account of meetings with Wild does not describe him. Defoe seeks to diminish Wild by referring to him as Mr Jonathan: that is, he is not confronted with a powerful assailant but by a childlike figure. Secondly, the account is repetitious and unfruitful. Despite coming back time and again there is no resolution to the narrator's problem. This suggests that the encounter has something of the acting out of a trauma, of a past event for which there is no resolution. Defoe, as with Hamlet, has lost his father but, alas, has not been rewarded.

In the gender fantasy world that Defoe occupied at the time he considered himself to be a 'man-woman' thus he might have imagined that if he could not achieve what he was seeking from Wild by appearing before him in his usual persona, a beauish man, he might resolve matters by posing as a woman. This is what he does. The narrator introduces the reader to a Lady of his acquaintance. This Lady is 'seeking the recovery of a gold watch with trinkets and some diamonds about the watch'. She offers Wild the considerable sum of twenty guineas (eighteen hundred pounds in current values) for their recovery and in the end pays much more. It is a usual Defoe narrative device to replace his identity with another when writing about himself.

Richard Holmes when describing this encounter, and not unreasonably given his biographical knowledge, supposes that this Lady might be a female from his family establishment in Stoke Newington. However, this assumption lacks credibility. There are obvious unanswered questions. Would Defoe have knowingly exposed a family member to an encounter with Wild? How would this notional person own and then lose possession of a valuable gold watch in the first place? Nothing is known. It might be supposed that the notion that Defoe could cross-dress is even more unlikely. However, in this work I have presented evidence that was a cross-dresser. Readers might use the index to remind themselves of this evidence.

Knowledge of Wild's Business.

The reader of *A True History* becomes aware that Defoe had a detailed understanding of Wild's business. A great deal of the first half of the book is devoted to the ingenious ways in which Wild organised the fencing of stolen property. At the risk of being disagreeable to some of my readers, I need to stress that it was not only Defoe's fictional characters that fenced stolen goods. Defoe was an artist in the activity. Some of the descriptions of Wild's activities are familiar to readers from other Defoe fictional accounts, in particular *Colonel Jack*. William Lee supported the whimsical notion that Defoe had written such works to encourage the reform of the criminals described there.

In particular Defoe had a clear understanding of the consequences for Wild and Hitchen of changes to the law which made the receiving of stolen goods to be a felony. Wild and Hitchen had to diversify into other crimes: burglary, blackmail and the exploitation of children. Defoe had a respect for Wild's flexibility and organisational powers, the brutality with which he conducted his business, and his success in making changes to his criminal activities.

The reader is right also to recognise that in *Colonel Jack* and *Moll Flanders* the narrators had to change the nature of their crimes as their notoriety became known and the law changed around them. When Defoe writes of Wild, that late in his audacious and daring career, he turned to the exploitation of a 'young generation of thieves and corrupting the poor children of London', his accusations are sexual. The language is as specific as Defoe allows himself when he writes, 'many a boy he has picked up in the street to breed them up to thieving and to ripen them for the devil'.

A critic who supposes that *A True History* was written by one of Applebee's hacks fails in both his biographical knowledge of Defoe and the masterly way the book is written. Defoe was uniquely qualified by his experiences to write this book and the nature of Defoe's early life, with its tragic loss of both parents, is stamped on its narrative.

It is my belief that both Defoe and Henry Baker were involved in the exploitation of children at this time and that they attended Molly Houses. These suppositions cannot be proved. However, there are a number of powerful conjectures, some of which I have drawn upon, that show it to be possible if not probable.

A Narrative of all the Problems and Escapes of John Sheppard, 1724

The *Narrative* is a brilliant biographical account of John Sheppard's life as a burglar and thief. His exploits, capture, imprisonment, and amazing escapes captivated a London audience. He became a celebrity. I agree with Furbank and Owens that there is no hard evidence that Defoe wrote the *Narrative*. I do not wish to fall into sin. It could not be a proof as such that if Defoe is shown to be the author of *A Genuine History* that ipso facto he must be the author of *A Narrative*. However,

I do think it follows that if the link with Applebee is established, as I maintain it is, that it becomes a possibility that he did write it.

Unlike the *True History*, I cannot point to Defoe identifying himself in the *Narrative*; that is, there is no internal evidence that, to my own mind at least, is conclusive. I am, therefore, in the same position in considering the text as William Lee or William Trent. The problem confronting me is the issue of 'How can we know him?'

1. The First Person

A normal reporting style would be to write in a mix of person: a combination of a narrator steering the subject and quotes seemingly in the subject's voice. The *Narrative* is written in the usual Defoe practice of a first person narrative. It is not easy to write biography of this kind in this way.

2. Anxiety and Preservation

Robinson Crusoe is characterised by anxiety about psychic preservation in the face of an unstable experience, and 'the recourse to enclosure and barricade'.[319] To assess his position *Crusoe* resorts not to forms of mobility but to these refuges. The pattern of Sheppard's behaviour is similar. When he escaped Sheppard immediately committed another crime, usually of a capital nature, and was consequently returned to the enclosed space of the prison.

In common judgement this behaviour would be regarded as stupid. However, Abse suggests that it is traumatic. He relates this behaviour to the concept of the birth trauma. Under the Chapter title of 'The birth traumas of Sheppard, Wild and Defoe' Abse writes as follows:

> For all of us there is one travail, replete with anxiety, that is inescapable; being born is the trauma we are all fated to endure. Freud considered that it was the act of being born, when the biological helplessness for the infant is proclaimed, when the inner world of the womb is replaced by an unknown external environment, when the organism is

---

[319] See Ermath, Elisabeth. *Realism and Consensus in the English Novel*, Princeton University Press, 1981, 96.

flooded by amounts of excitation beyond its capacity to master, that induces what Freud named as 'primary anxiety'. Freud maintains that this event is the common root of all anxieties that affect us later in life.' [320]

Abse continues:

Defoe lingers over every detail of Sheppard's life obstacle courses, recounts the ingenious methods used by him to defy all locks and bolts, with the whole adventure taking more a than nine hours and in total darkness. It is a thrilling tale.

Nothing is known about the circumstances of Sheppard's birth. But something is known now about Defoe's. Abse might have remarked that when the rite of passage from babyhood to adulthood is denied, as it was in Defoe's life, the fear and 'anxiety of leaving the womb' is heightened. This fear is accompanied by a desire to return to the womb. Such a desire can be fulfilled by enclosed spaces: homes, sheltered refuges, caves, ships, islands and prison cells.

Freud writes that the source of all human anxiety is the birth trauma. It follows, therefore, that when anxiety is extreme, a person may seek to return to the safety of the womb, an act that is impossible. In the absence of a womb to return to, the subject is left in a state of extreme anxiety and will need to seek a substitute. Otto Rank writes, '...when we leave a child alone in a dark room the stimulus it experiences is as a return to the womb...this stimulus is similar to sitting in a small room, travelling...sitting in a small cabin in a car or train.'[321] However, none of these substitutes is a womb and the cycle of mounting anxiety, relief, escape and re-capture is repeated. The behaviour is compulsive.

For all the many reasons I have advanced here for the possible involvement of Defoe in the sharing and recording of exchanges with Sheppard and in writing about them, I conclude that Defoe did write the *Narrative*; he was there (the prison), he had the incentive to do so, and he possessed the necessary skills. It is mistaken to argue that Defoe did

[320] Abse, 167, notes 7 and 8.
[321] Rank, Otto. *The Trauma of Birth*, Martino Publishing, 2010, 11.

not need money at the time. He was being bled dry by a resourceful blackmailer and needed every penny he could get his hands on.

In the terminology used by Furbank and Owens, it is probable that Defoe wrote *A True Account* and possible that he wrote the *Narrative*.

Chapter 26

A Journal of the Plague Year
and
Due Preparations for the Plague

His [Defoe's] novels are too much like novels to seem like novels; they read like real life.

Journal of the Plague Year
Daniel Defoe, 1722
Introduction by Antony Burgess

Daniel Defoe wrote two works on the Great Plague of London, 1665, published at around the same time in 1722, that is, 57 years after the event. The *Journal* is incomparably the better of the two. These works describe the terrifying visitation of bubonic plague. They are fictional accounts of actual historical events. They do not stand in isolation from any literary genre. Defoe is writing into over two thousand years of literary accounts of cities under siege: from Homer's *Iliad*, and the siege of Troy, to Albert Camus's *La Peste* in recent times. Camus recognised a debt to Defoe in his work.

It might be argued that this work proves that my central assertion, that all Defoe's fiction consists of embellished accounts of his own life, is wrong. Perhaps, Antony Burgess is correct when he writes about the book, 'In reality it is a rather cunning work of art, a confidence trick of the imagination.' I think he is right: but I am not wrong. Defoe is at the centre of this book and it cannot be interpreted adequately without placing him there.

In earlier chapters I have written about Defoe's character predispositions arising from a troubled childhood. I have suggested that womb–like enclosed spaces are of particular interest and concern for him. These spaces offer safety, for example as portrayed in *Robinson Crusoe*, but prolonged tenure is dangerous also. Ships offer an escape. However, passage on the high seas could result in tragedy: pirates and storms were ever present dangers. Refuge on an island offered forms of escape but were not necessarily sufficient or a lasting solution: babies must escape the womb to survive and develop; an island could be invaded by other beings, cannibals, who could consume you entirely.

Defoe lived out the fantasies of birth and renewal in real life. I have suggested that the account of three men seeking to escape plague-ridden London is a acting out of an unsuccessful attempt to join the Monmouth Rebellion. In itself it illustrates both the necessity to leave and the dangers of any attempt to do so.

Defoe writes incessantly in the *Journal* of the effects of the shutting up of plague affected families in their houses. Rationally, he recognises that this enclosure condemned many healthy people to catch the plague from their affected relatives. In individual instances healthy people enclosed themselves in this way; sometimes this would succeed, and in others fail, in avoiding contamination.

In Defoe's account of the great storm in *The Storm*, 1704, Defoe listened to, or took account of, sermons delivered from many a pulpit that propagated the doctrine that disastrous storms were God's punishment for sinful behaviour. While emotionally affected, Defoe recognised that there were other and more rational, explanations for storms and diseases: after all a good man could be destroyed by the plague and a dishonest man unaffected.

The *Journal* is narrated by HF, Defoe's Uncle Henry, and as described by Defoe, was a Citizen of London 'who continued all the while in London'. HF tells the reader that he lived in Aldgate, identifies his trade as that of saddler, and states that his principal reason for staying was to look after his business and family establishment. HF tells the reader that he had a brother, recently returned from Portugal, who urged him to leave the capital. He 'had already sent his wife and two children into Bedfordshire'. These children are Elisabeth and Mary Foe for whom there are extant baptism records. In an earlier chapter I write at length about this passage and I shall not repeat it here other than to state that there is one categorical conclusion that can be drawn from this statement: it is virtually inescapable that there is no son, no

Daniel Defoe. James Foe did not have a biological son. Some biographers have reached this conviction[322] from a reading of the passage while others realise that there needs to be some revision to descriptions of Defoe's family links.[323]

When Defoe makes biographical references, they usually turn out, when they can be checked, to be true. However, there is often confusion about family terms and, within the Foe family kin, the identity of the person alluded to is often difficult to establish. For example, in *Due Preparations* Defoe writes of 'Two brothers and a sister, the children of one pious and serious mother a widow [who lived together in one house in the City] in London during the Plague.' One brother was 'near forty' and the sister (the youngest) nineteen. In 1665 Henry Foe was in his thirty eighth year and Mary Foe (King), his niece, was in her twentieth year. The brother aged twenty-six could not be James Foe for he was aged thirty-five, and as the reader knows he had left London, but it could be John Lee, Henry Foe's apprentice who married Mary Lawrence, a kinswoman of the Foe family. Mary Foe, Defoe's sister, had moved to London by 1665. Thus, and it is not at all untypical of merchant households of the time, Henry Foe's substantial family establishment would have included a 'brother', John Lee, and a 'sister', Mary Foe (King).

Such a conjecture is of importance to the creative origins of the narrative of the *Journal*. Defoe was abroad in 1662-1680 and Henry Foe died in 1675. He could not have told Defoe anything about the Great Plague, 1665 unless in a letter. Bastian suggests that Henry Foe might have been an examiner responsible for collecting weekly parish records of the dead. It is possible that he did but there is no evidence of it. It is not a necessary condition to this account that Henry Foe possessed detailed records. These parish records were publicly available. Access to them was possible in 1722 and today. Novak writes helpfully that Defoe may 'have been contemplating these compositions [the two works] for many years. References to the Great

---

[322] Sheldon, Rogers. *Notes and Queries.*
[323] Bastian, 3, note 8.

Plague of 1665 are scattered throughout his early writings, and in the *Review* he suggested that he collected the bills of mortality published during that time.' [324] It may have taken Defoe many years to obtain 'a full set'. HF may have kept a Journal. If so this material would have passed to James Foe who inherited Henry Foe's papers in 1675.

More persuasive to me is the thought that the Defoe drew upon the numerous tales told by neighbour to neighbour and within their families. Defoe would have started with his relatives and kin, Mary Foe and John Lee. Being an investigative reporter of genius, Defoe would then have tapped into the commonwealth of human experiences of the plague, much as he did in preparation of *The Storm*.

Defoe seeks to be authentic by drawing upon the actualities of his life. This was difficult for him. In many accounts he is involved in contradictions because of the need to add twenty- eight years to an actual date, the time *Crusoe* claims for his Exile in *Robinson Crusoe*. In *Due Preparations* he gets into such a difficulty. Defoe describes two brothers, one who was a widower with two children (James Foe?) and the other an Elder Son who was a bachelor (Henry Foe was a bachelor and an Elder brother) and a young sister, (I suggest Defoe's sister Mary). Defoe introduces the reader to an Old Lady, a widower who lives outside London but who comes to London to visit her sons. Rose Foe (King) was a widowed mother to the two brothers. Defoe writes that this Old Lady had two or three younger children who lived with her. Rose King had three children by other marriages, two sons and one daughter. Defoe's description of the sons as being about nineteen and twenty years of age is consistent with what is known about Rose Foe's children.[325]

The Old Lady urged upon her relatives, whenever she came to London, to make Due Preparations for the Great Plague which, she states, she did twenty-nine years before. This would place the date of these conversations with her 'family' as 1693-1694. Rose King was most likely dead before this date.

---

[324] Novak, 603.
[325] See Chart.

However, in her conversation she states something very different. She says that 'in the year 1625 when I was newly married and settled in the world, and we were full of mirth as you are now, and on a sudden the distemper broke out, and all our smiles were lamentations and tears'. This account is consistent with what is known of Rose Foe's life in Etton and Peakirk and Glinton, Northamptonshire that I have written about earlier. The first baptism record of the marriage of Rose to Daniel Foe's grandfather was the year 1625.[326]

The Plague visited the Diocese of Peterborough on numerous occasions throughout the period 1620-1630. It was the subject of furious debate among clerics and resulted in actions to purify acts of worship and to root out religious dissent in the Diocese. In the south-east corner of St Stephen's, Etton graveyard there is a mass grave of victims of the plague; that is on the very doorstep of the farmhouse occupied by Rose and Daniel Foe. There is no DNA evidence to date the find. However, the Old Lady dates the plague there as 1625 when she was 'newly into her marriage' with Defoe's grandfather. There is no extant Parish record of Rose's marriage to Daniel Foe, the grandfather. Consequently, although the evidence demonstrates that the Old Lady was Rose Foe it is impossible to date her conversations with her family as Defoe seeks to do. The absurdity of the dates he uses is demonstrated by actual dates. In 1693-1694 the Old Lady, Rose Foe, if we are to believe the narrative would have been approaching 100 years of age and her Elder Son 65 years of age. Henry Foe died in 1675 at the age of 47 years. Rose was widowed from her third husband Thomas King in 1658. If born in c.1597-1607 she would have been 58 or 68 in 1665. There is no extant record of her death.

The sources for Defoe's two works are clarified by this biographical material. Both oral and written sources are important. Obviously on Defoe's return to London in 1680 memories of the Great Plague and subsequent Great Fire of London were all about him. Defoe developed a comprehensive knowledge of the streets known now as the West End and City of London because of the life-style he adopted and the

---

[326] See Chart.

lodgings he occupied. Fifteen years after these two calamitous events evidence of their effects and the human accounts of the experiences Defoe recounts were everywhere to be found. Re-building had begun and had made good progress but much remained to be done. Defoe would have heard much from his relatives, in particular his sister Mary if, as I surmise, she was in London at the time; and surely, although his Uncle Henry had been dead five years before Defoe's return, from other members of his family establishment.

An additional and rather obvious source of information on plague to Defoe was his direct and indirect experience of the effects of the plague on trade. It is important to recognise that the plague was universal in its incidence; originating in the Levant it was spread to Europe mainly by rats carried by ships. For some time, 40 years, Defoe was collecting and delivering merchandise to ports throughout the trans-Atlantic trading routes. My account in this work demonstrates that he was the captain and master of some of the vessels involved in the trade. There must have been many occasions when a vessel of his was barred entry into a port and some occasions when it was prudent not to enter a plague stricken territory.

In *Due Preparations* Defoe writes of the way authorities dealt with the plague in France, and, in particular, Marseilles. In 1720-1721 Marseilles experienced a bad attack of the plague. It is often commented that Defoe from the awareness of this outbreak was opportunistic in recognising the fear aroused in London that the plague might spread once again to the capital. The reader will understand that I have emphasised that Defoe's trading experience and knowledge of French ports was considerable.

There are two memorable passages in the two works that show Defoe's knowledge of the refuge offered by ships. In *Due Preparations*, [327]a family take refuge in a ship that sails along the Thames to Woolwich, Deptford, Greenwich and Bugsby's Hole. This was a journey of some 12 nautical miles from Defoe's home(s) in Tilbury in 1660-1705. Secondly there is a memorable and moving

---

[327] *Due Preparations*, 89.

passage in the *Journal*. I have written about this passage at length in *Beyond Belief.*[328] Defoe writes in a passage of great warmth and feeling of a poor waterman who sits outside his house where there is infection but whose inhabitants he continues to support. 'Why, says he, if they may be said to live, for my wife and one of my children are visited, but I do not come at them.' And with that word I saw the tears run very plentifully down his face: and so did mine too I assure you...I do not abandon them from want... I had happened on a man that was no hypocrite; but a serious, religious, good man ...in such a condition as he was in, he should be able to say his family did not want.' The waterman says, 'I seldom come on shore here, and I came only to call on my wife and hear how my family do, and give them a little money.' I turned away from the man...for indeed, I could no more refrain from tears than he had a family to bind him to attendance, which I had not.

I do not believe that this passage is to be explained purely in fictional terms although it may be, for I can only conjecture. Nor do I believe that the narrators tears (Defoe's) are crocodile tears. Defoe may have met such a man reminiscing about his experiences with the plague; the emotion may be Defoe's for surely he must have grieved that in periods of misfortune he had not been able to support his family as he would have wished. However, I accept that this drawing upon self-experience is what creative writers would normally do.

Notwithstanding this admission, there are many other passages in these works that are episodic accounts, or intellectual pre-occupations, of Defoe's own life. Defoe raises an issue of honesty. Clearly the plague gave people opportunities to be dishonest. Families had abandoned their homes and possessions. Although houses were boarded up it was a simple task to burgle them. Some property was abandoned where it lay. To take it involved risks of disease. Defoe writes about going to a post office where two men are talking and seeing close by a purse on the ground. He writes:

In the middle of the yard lay a small leather purse with two keys hanging at it, with money in it. I asked how long it had lain there [to be

[328] *Beyond Belief*, 97, n. 137.

told for an hour]... they had not meddled with it, because they did not know if the person might come to look for it... I had no ...need of money, nor was the sum so big that I had any inclination to meddle with it. [the post man did his best to de-contaminate the purse and abstract the money from it] ... I observed that the few people who were spared were very careful of themselves at that time when the distress was so exceeding great.

Defoe's narrator is telling the reader that the act of stealing the money was a matter of expediency: from a moral point of view the act of theft was relative to him. If there had been a lot of money he might have taken the risk of stealing it, if presumably he could do so unnoticed. A poor man would have been justified in taking the risk of catching a disease in picking up the purse. As most men were prudent they did not steal.

However, the happening of the Great Plague was an act of God. Sin had carried men into acts displeasing to God. But for Defoe 'whatever the cause there was for it, [the plague] it could be observed that all manner of wickedness [remained] among us.'

Chapter 27

A General History
of the Pyrates
and
Related Works

I got passage on board one Captain Guillaume, a New England Captain, whose owner was one Mr Johnson, a merchant living at Hackney, near London.

King of the Pyrates
Daniel Defoe, 1719

It is a common opinion that *A General History of the* Pyrates, 1724-1728, is the most comprehensive account of the exploits and villainies of the most celebrated pirates of Defoe's time. There is no consensus on the authorship. The title page was ascribed to a Captain Charles Johnson. This is widely thought to be a pseudonym although 'it is known' that a contemporary playwright of the name Charles Johnson wrote about pirates. In Chapter 1, Captain Avery, the narrator (ostensibly Charles Johnson), writes without any irony, comment or a backward glance, that 'a play was writ upon him (Avery) called, the *Successful Pyrate*'. [329] Un-remarked upon by the narrator of the *General History* was the short biography of Captain Avery published in 1709 and also attributed to Charles Johnson.[330]

In Chapter 18, I offer a definitive proof that Daniel Defoe wrote *A General History*. However, as the authorship of the *General History* was not the main purpose of the chapter I set out the proof more precisely and comprehensively here. Before I do this, and not out of any bibliographical passion or expertise, I set out the main elements of the authorial controversy.

Defoe as the Author

[329] BL. G19416(7). A play *The Successful Pyrate*, 1712.
[330] BL.162120. *The Life and Adventures of Captain Avery, the Famous Pyrate*, 1709.

There are two existing candidates. The claim that Defoe was the author was first made by Professor John Robert Moore in 1932.[331] He had been mulling over the issues for some years. Moore based his ascription on a series of contextual similarities in works now ascribed and non-ascribed to Defoe. Moore maintained that the *General History* was reliable in its information though 'interspersed with a good many passages of historical fiction and with some unrestrained romance.'

This claim has been criticised by Furbank and Owens.[332] I am surprised to have stumbled on the truth of the controversy and to have concluded that Moore's instincts, and I would not put it higher than that, were right in respect of the *General History*. I agree with Furbank and Owens that Moore's bibliographical methods, with their reliance on stylistic similarities between different works, and an alarming degree of circular reasoning, is unsound and leaves a good deal to be desired; but in this instance his instincts lead him to the right conclusion.

Correcting the chronology of Defoe's life, and sound biographical detail, enhances the analysis Moore attempted. I comment on the five main reasons given by Furbank and Owens for disbelief in Moore's ascription.

Contrasts between the *General History* and *King of the Pyrates*

Furbank and Owens point out that the account of Captain Avery in the *General History* is greatly different in matter of fact and tone from another Defoe work on Avery, the *King of the Pyrates*. Readers of my narrative will understand the reasons for these differences. In 1719, Defoe felt that he needed to josh about Avery and render his account fabulous because he was near in time to the enormity of Avery's exploits and his own involvement in fencing some of his diamonds. He was being dismissive of Avery and seeking to persuade others 'to calm down' about him.

A criticism I would make of Furbank & Owens is that despite their

---

[331] Moore, John Robert. *Defoe in the Pillory*, 126.
[332] *The Canonisation of Daniel Defoe*, 104-121.

perceptive reading of Defoe's character they fail to appreciate the full extent of his polemical ability to look in more than one direction at the same. It was said colloquially of Defoe – and I believe it to be true- that as he was writing a polemical pamphlet or opinion he had on the opposite side of his desk his refutation of it. This saying understates Defoe's abilities: if he chose to do it he could have lined-up any number of refutations or contrary points of view. It is necessary also to take both the time and purpose of writing into account.

Secondly, there are difficulties in the 'conventional account' of Defoe's early life in explaining his comprehensive and detailed knowledge of piracy and pirates and all things naval. Schonhorn and Moore suggest that Defoe may have acquired such knowledge from meetings with Woodes Rogers and Selkirk and they point out that he was a voracious reader of many written works about pirates and their adventures. Furthermore, it can be appreciated now that Furbank and Owens are wrong in stating that there is no proof that he met pirates. I have offered proof that he did so in this work. From this narrative the reader will understand that Defoe's eighteen years experience of trading between Africa, South America and New England gave him considerable knowledge of pirates and piracy. He must have encountered numerous pirates some of whom he wrote about in the *General History*. Once back in England, Defoe was adept at tracking the lives of seamen many of whom washed up in British ports.

Thirdly, Furbank and Owens express doubt that Defoe could have gained information from a friendship with Bowrey, the principal owner of the *Worcester*, in particular from meetings requested by Bowrey in 1708. As I explain in Chapter 18, Defoe's ship the *Aurangezebe* encountered the *Worcester* as described in the Chapter on Captain Bowen in the *General History*. Defoe can be expected to have had a detailed understanding of the encounter from discussions with his crew and, in particular, his nephew Francis King, Captain of the *Aurangezebe* in 1705 - although not in 1703. Defoe was not, therefore, dependent on Bowrey for information as Moore believed and Furbank and Owens thought necessary. The crew of the *Worcester* could not help an enquirer very much as they had either been executed or had fled to remote places to avoid arrest and thought it advisable to keep quiet after Green's trial.

Captain Green and the *Worcester*

The trial of Captain Green and his crew excited great public interest. In Edinburgh the East Indies Company, for whom Green had worked, was blamed for the failure of the Darien Project for which Defoe had shown an enthusiasm in contacts with William Patterson since 1698. The British Library has 33 extant pamphlets written anonymously about the trial of Captain Green and the crew of the *Worcester*. The English administration had started the process of bribing the Scottish aristocracy into accepting Union. In his *History of the Union*, 1707, Defoe described the tumult over the trial as one of six matters obstructing progress in establishing it. When Defoe's intense sense of personal involvement in the trial is added to the mix, he might have been expected to have written one or more of these pamphlets. Critical attention has centred on two: *The Tryal of Captain Green and his crew for Piracy, Robbery and Murder*,[333] Anderson, Edinburgh, 1705, and *A Letter from Scotland to a Friend in London.* [334] To these I have added another, *Observations made in England, on the trial of Captain Green, and the Speech at his Death*, London, 1705 published by J.W.[335]

Furbank and Owens consider that neither of the first two pamphlets is likely to be Defoe's because they differ in their approach and sympathies, and also because he had written contrary views elsewhere. For example, Defoe had adopted a cautious line on the Edinburgh trial in the *Review* dated 26 April, 1705 stating that the Scottish authorities had acted with due process. However, *A Letter from Scotland* is a belligerent attack on the Scottish authorities. A flip answer to the apparent contradiction is another day, another master and a different audience. However, to be more considered, in this instance Furbank and Owens

---

[333] Anon. *The Tryal of Captain Green and his crew for Piracy, Robbery and Murder*, Anderson, Edinburgh, 1705.
[334] Anon. *A Letter From Scotland*, Anderson, Edinburgh, 1705.
[335] Anon. *Observations: Made in England, on the Trial of Captain Green, and the Speech of his death*, Reprinted by J.W., 1705.

seem not to have understood the passions and complex political issues raised by the trial and that it was a quickly moving affair of great public interest and conflicting passions in both London and Edinburgh at various stages of the drama. In 1705 Defoe was writing at the behest of the English administration and, in particular Harley, but in *a Letter from Scotland* he is stating his own opinions.

Obervations is a carefully constructed work that argues readers should trust due process and 'the St James Privy' because there were reasons to suspect that things were not quite right. The author points out that 'If Captain Drummond [in command of the *Speedy Return*] was alive, Captain Green was Innocent.' He points out a number of anomalies and raises a carefully constructed viewpoint that not all the 'Affidavits and declarations' and information from the East India company were available at the time of the trial and concludes, 'I take the Case to be plainly this: Captain Green did in general deny all Piracy at his death. I suspend my judgement.' It is worth stating again that no ship was named as the victim of piracy in the trial.

The arguments in this pamphlet, and in particular the telling point about unused evidence, are fully consistent with Defoe's knowledge, not generally shared, of 'the truth of the matter', the review by the Queens Privy Council, and Defoe's article in the *Review*. As Defoe was writing in support of the English administration in London in this pamphlet, and being paid for it, there is no good reason to suppose that he did not write it. I do not see why it would be supposed otherwise.

The Scottish ruling elites, bribed by the English administration, needed to calm the tumult and desire for revenge in Edinburgh for the alleged perfidies of the East India Company. *The Tryal of Captain Green* served this purpose. Given Defoe's subsequent close relationship with and use of the Edinburgh printer Anderson, it seems probable that this pamphlet was also written by Defoe

The argument in *Observations* about missing evidence and the importance of locating Captain Drummond is repeated in *A Letter from Scotland*. I have no doubt whatsoever that Defoe is the author. The author/Defoe cleverly dates this Letter 1 May, 1705, that is after the execution of Captain Green, although not so cleverly, the pamphlet itself is dated 20 April, that is before it. He states his reasons for publication as, 'Requittal for the many Scandalous Relations and Reflections published in the Flying-Post.' 'The Friend' [who may in reality have been one, for example, Sir John Clerk] states, 'Pursuant to the frequent Promises I lately made you, I now at last send a Narrative of the Proceedings against the Ship *Worcester*, and her crew.'

The pamphlet sets out in robust but diplomatic ways the numerous contradictions of the trial. It is interesting in itself; but it is distinguished by the inclusion of an affidavit of Captain Steven Grandell, Mariner, described as the Commander of the *Aurangezebe* and Henry Walter the second mate. It is dated Martii ((March) and drawn up by a man called Smith. It is not signed. In essence the affidavit sets out an account of the meeting-up of the *Aurangezebe* with the *Worcester* and the taking in of water as described at length in *A General History* and is consistent with affidavits presented at the trial, in particular that of Antonio Francisco. The narrator/ Friend/ Defoe, states his opinion that if the affidavit had been presented at the trial the charges against Green would not have been sustainable.

The inclusion of an unsigned draft of an affidavit dated March, 1705 invites many questions. It might be wondered that if the affidavit existed in March, and was known of by the 'Friend' in Edinburgh, why was it not presented at the trial? There is no mention in trial records anywhere of this affidavit. To my knowledge, no other pamphlet written on the trial includes an account of the meeting of the *Aurangezebe* and the *Worcester*. The only written accounts of the meeting of the two ships are to be found in the *General History* and the anonymous pamphlet *A Letter from Scotland* which I attribute to Defoe. Defoe could write both these accounts because he was the owner of the *Aurangezebe* and could talk to the crew. Defoe could have supplemented his understanding of the complete story by the discussions with Bowrey, the owner of the *Speedy Return*, in 1708 as discussed by Furbank and Owens and mentioned above.

One thing is certain: Nathaniel Mist, 17 years later, would not have known of the encounter between the *Worcester* and the *Aurangezebe* without reading the pamphlet and even then he would not have been able to amplify the account as subsequently recounted in the *General History*. No one knows Mist's whereabouts in 1705 or whether he had any chance to read the pamphlet. It seems unlikely. Let me be clear. If it is accepted that Defoe is the author of the Chapter on Captain Bowen in the *General History*, by virtue of unique information about the encounter between the *Aurangezebe* and the *Worcester*, he must also be the author of *A Letter from Scotland* and *Observations*.

I have made a case for the belief that Defoe committed the audacious crime of obtaining and fencing some of Avery's diamonds and gold and silver coins and had escaped undetected. Almost any man in this circumstance would really wish to celebrate the crime and be recognised, as a sort of celebrity, for 'pulling it off'. One vicarious way of doing this would be to write about it. Defoe did write about it in the *General History* eighteen years after the event; but would he have waited that long to celebrate? Fearful though he must have been about any publicity, might he not have written something further and earlier about Avery?

At this point in my argument I wish to distinguish between the creation of chain reasoning based around issues of style and language, a practice that has caused difficulties in Defoe bibliography, and ipso facto reasoning based on provable fact. It is ipso facto reasoning that if Defoe is the author of the *General History* by virtue of a unique set of facts that it is probable that the use of these facts elsewhere in another and anonymous publication might be thought to indicate Defoe's authorship. I think he did write about Avery before 1719 and more than once. Furthermore, I believe a strong case can be made for Defoe using the pseudonym Captain Charles Johnson. There was a playwright named Charles Johnson but no real-life Captain Charles Johnson. It is entirely understandable that many commentators have confused the two.

Other Related Works

It is my assertion following the proof that Defoe wrote the *General History* that he was the author of other works about Avery: in particular, *The Life and Adventures of Captain Avery, the Famous Pyrate*, 1709; the *Successful Pyrate*: a play, 1712; *Mists Closet Broke Open: on Several Letters Intercepted, in which Are Contained Some Old Truths New Told*, 1728, and that he was the Editor and a partial contributor to *Robert Drury's Journal*, 1728. I comment on them below.

The Life and Adventures of Captain Avery, the Famous Pyrate, 1709 and *The Successful Pyrate, a play,* 1712. [336]

The version of the works I am using has a helpful introduction by Joel Baer. He makes an implicit assumption that the two written works were written by the same man and draws parallels between them. His analysis is convincing. It has long been supposed that the play was written by Charles Johnson the poet and playwright (1679-1745) a tavern keeper who wrote 27 works in his lifetime and succeeded in gaining the enmity of both John Gay and Alexander Pope. There is no evidence that this Charles Johnson ever wrote a biography or had any inclination or incentive to do so. On the other hand there are many reasons for Defoe to do so.

Joel Baer makes the point that there were marked tendencies in public life (and in particular in the arts) to condemn the rich and powerful in society for their greed, corruption and acquisitiveness by equating them with the courage and ambition and boldness of pirates and thieves (in particular, the writings of Fielding, and Gay). Defoe shared these attitudes. In the *Review* dated 18 October, 1707 Defoe reproduces the main reasons for Reducing the Pyrates at Madagascar. He writes that 'doing business with pyrates is doing business as usual'. Baer shows that Defoe/ Charles Johnson uses the same language as the author of *The Life and Adventures* and refers to the same sources. In particular both are aware of the offer made on behalf of the pyrates that was discussed by the Privy Council.[337]

---

[336] BL.WP 2367a. Ed. Joel Baer. Augustan Re-print Society, William Andrews Clark Memorial Library, University of California, Los Angeles, 1980: Long Title, (*raised from Cabin –Boy, to a King now in Possession of Madagascar*).
[337] NRA. Calendar of State Papers. Privy Council and Council of Trade and Plantations, Colonial

Defoe as the writer of *A General History* observes:

A Play was writ upon him called the Successful Pirate; and these Accounts obtained such belief (of their power and threat to trade), that several Schemes were offered to the Council for fitting out a Squadron to take him; while others were offering his Companions an Act of Grace, and inviting him to *England, with all their Treasure*, [italic mine] lest his growing Greatness might hinder the Trade of *Europe* to the *East- Indies*.

In *King of the Pyrates* Defoe wrote:

> If the absurdity in the former relations [accounts] of this matter is that of the making of an offer of I know not how many millions to the late Queen, for Captain Avery's pardon, with a petition to the Queen, and her Majesty's negative answer...the history of Captain Avery [can be] set in a fairer light, the end is answered.

These fabulous and romantic accounts were created in part by Defoe. *The Successful Pyrate* suggests that Avery was living in Madagascar with 15,000 men and forty warships. Defoe knew at the time of writing that Avery had died penniless in Bideford three years before. And in the words of Woodes Rogers in 1712, 'those miserable Wretches , who had made so much Noise in the World were now dwindled to between 60-70 , most of them very poor and despicable, even to the Natives.'[338]

I believe that the true story is that Defoe 'upped the anti'. When it suited him he emphasised the potential hazard to shipping of so great a power in Madagascar. What better then but to negotiate away the hazard. The Privy Council demurred to provide a pardon which would have benefited Defoe. Such a pardon would have tended to diminish his own offence. In addition Defoe might have struck a bargain with the pirates in Madagascar. He might have agreed with them that they would give him additional diamonds if he was able to get them back to

Series, American and West Indies, 1708-1709, X1X, 340, 345.
[338] Woodes Rogers. *A Crusing Voyage Round the World*, (London), 1712.

England with a Pardon. The Privy Council was having none of it. They argued solemnly that it was wrong to negotiate with pirates, and that they had found the information it had been given them by Defoe to be unreliable.

As to authorship, I suggest that Defoe wrote the *Life and Adventures* and contributed to the *Successful Pyrate* as a script was converted to the demands of a play.

Mists Closet Broke Open: on Several Letters Intercepted, in which Are Contained Some Old Truths New Told, 1728.[339]

Original copies of this 16 page pamphlet are scarce. The British Library believes that there are only two originals in British Libraries. I refer in my comments to their digital copy *which is acknowledged to be Defoe's work*. I reproduce the front page as an Illustration in this work.

Mist Closet Broke Open is organised as fifteen fictional letters. Nine of these are written by miscellaneous persons, whose names are poorly disguised, and six from Mist, five of which can be identified but one which seems to read Mist to Mist. One letter is from Captain Johnson to Mist and another from Mist to Johnson. Thus the author is implying a link. Identifiable names are: Bolingbroke, Henry St John, an exile in France; Richard D'Anvers, a French cleric; the Bishop of Rochester; and Robert Benson, 1st Baron Bingley and former Chancellor of the Exchequer.[340] Letters to Mist originated in France, Spain, and Rome (the home and centre of the Pretender's Court).

At a first reading the pamphlet is drivel. It reads as a disorganised ramble through political and religious aphorisms which while meaningful when considered separately lack a cohesive whole. However, when considered more carefully there is meaning. The letters assume some commonality of experience and mutual sympathy. Caleb and D'anvers are descriptions that assume that Mist and Defoe share common values and experiences: exile, persecution for common beliefs and courage in following a chosen path. Caleb is a reference to one of

[339] BL. Digital Copy described as ** Defoe 30. 728. A10M2.
[340] Alternatively, William Benson, a Whig writer, who sought to embarrass Defoe and caused his imprisonment.

two leaders with the courage to lead the Israelites into the Promised Land as recounted in the Book of Numbers; while Roan assumes that two men are acting in utmost good faith. There is an implication that the two men shared a sympathy for the Jacobite cause. [341]

These values of good faith and principled positions are best illustrated by random quotations.

1. Many men are so proud that they know not their own Fathers.
2. There is no treachery at Court because there are no secrets.
3. The fairest field for a roaming head is the sea. (Johnson, Sea Captain)
4. The pursuit of the vainglorious 'are upon Terms of quitting their country's Allegiance to be made free of Denison's of England.' (Captain Johnson)
5. The shortest Cut to the Riches of the Indies, is by contempt.
6. Few dare to write the true News of the Chamber. The Devil is a perfect Courtier.
7. We must make all Time an Occasion of Amendment because the Devil makes it an Occasion to tempt.

These words were written in the same year as an update to *A General History of* the *Pyrates* and two years after the *Political History of the Devil* and *A System of Magic*. It is entirely obvious that the words were written by Defoe.

Robert Drury's Journal

The controversy about the authorship of *A General History* feeds naturally into the issue of whether Defoe or Robert Drury wrote *Robert Drury's Journal*. Arthur Secord points out that Richard Temple in research for his book on Captain Green and the *Worcester* Affair

---

[341] See Attachment 7. The Cavalier: Defoe's Elder Brother.

³⁴²'had to draw upon Drury's *Journal* to help explain the fate of Captain Robert Drummond and the innocence of Captain Green and his crew…who were commonly supposed to have murdered Drummond and pirated his ship.'

Furbank and Owens maintain that Defoe took no part in the production of *Robert Drury's Journal*. They over-egg their argument for even Arthur Secord, whose patient and systematic research over many years authenticated both Robert Drury and his tale of incarceration on Madagascar, does not claim this. The real issue is did Defoe write sufficient of the published account for he, or others on his behalf, to claim that he was the author?

The *Journal* and the *General History* have several sea Captains in common: for example, Captain Drummond, Captain Thomas White, Captain David Williams, John Pro and Captain William Mackett. Secord makes a number of interesting comments about Mackett. He points out that Drury's return to his island in 1717 was on White's ship and that White was a friend of Mackett. He suggests that Mackett was alive and well in London as late as 1728-1729 and highly regarded by the East India Company. He suggests that Defoe could not have used Mackett's name in the *General History* without permission. Thus Defoe could easily have discussed the *Journal* with Mackett. Defoe would have known also of the arrival in London in March, 1705 of two escapees from Drummond's *Speedy Return*, Israel Phippany and Peter Freeland. These two men arrived in Portsmouth on the *Raper* with a survivor of the *Degrave* and deposed on 31 March, 1705 that the *Speedy Return* had not been harmed or seen by the *Worcester* and that Captain Drummond was alive on Madagascar.

I believe it is possible that Defoe wrote and edited parts of the *Journal*. The preface of the original printed version of *Robert Drury's Journal* indicates that Drury had been helped by a 'transcriber' and that the story as printed had been to an undetermined but substantial degree modified by him. This conclusion is supported by stylometric analysis

---

³⁴² Secord, Arthur W. *Robert Drury's Journal and Other Studies*, Kessinger, Legacy Reprints, University of Illinois Press, 1961.

conducted by Professor Irving Rothman that concluded that Defoe wrote parts of the book.

Among the publishers listed is Old Tom's Coffee House, in Birchin Lane, Stoke Newington, London. There was at the time several Old Tom coffee houses. It was said that the Old Tom in Convent Garden was a venue for 'whores', in Defoe's use of the word, and popular with the capital's literati. This coffee house was owned by a Tom King and his wife Mary. On Tom King's death in 1739 the venue changed its name to Moll Flanders!

Arne Bialuschewski and Nathaniel Mist

Where does this analysis of Defoe works leave the bibliographical controversy on the authorship of *A General History of the Pyrates*? Arne Bialuschewski of the University of Trent has produced a seemingly simple and persuasive argument that the *General History* was written by Nathaniel Mist the Jacobite printer, former sailor and proprietor of the *Weekly Journal*.[343] However, on further consideration and taking new chronological information into account his proof can be seen as a 'house built on sand'.

Defoe worked for Mist over the eight year period 1716-1724. Bialuschewski argues that the two men were not in touch with each other after 1720. However, most commentators question this assumption. It was Mist's practice to employ gifted polemical writers such as Defoe. At this time Defoe was working for the Whig administration and attempting, so he says, to moderate the provocative Jacobite stance of the *Journal*. The relationship between the two men was troublesome and complex and their reactions to each other were rumbustious. Defoe complained in correspondence with *Applebee's Journal* that he often had fights with Mist. There were rumours of a duel.

Bialuschewski's position is that Moore's ascription of the work to Defoe in 1932 does not rely on any direct evidence and that none exists, a fact admitted by Schonhorn in his edited version of the book in 1972 and 1999. Bialuschewski believes that he offers a better set of

---

[343] Bialuschewski, Arne. *Bibliographical Society of America*. Vol.198 (2004), 21-38.

conjectures and that these prove that the printer Nathanial Mist wrote the work.

In his argument Bialuschewski assumes that Mist had special knowledge of piracy from his merchant sailing experience in the Caribbean. He relies on two documentary facts: the first edition of the *General History* was printed by Charles Rivington, one of Mist's regular printers, whose premises were close to Mist's office; and secondly, that the book was first registered at the Stationery Office in Mist's name. It cannot be denied that Mist undertook the responsibility of getting the *General History* into print and to the public. It is equally clear that Defoe could not take the risk of acknowledging his authorship for fear of prosecution for his own nefarious 'piratical deeds'. The two men were natural collaborators: Defoe wrote and Mist printed and distributed the book.

There are several major difficulties with Bialuschewski's thesis. First, it is not clear who Mist was. The name is a pseudonym. No one knows where he was born, in what name and where. Consequently, although he may well have been a seaman, or even a pirate, no one can be certain of his background and experience. As I have explained, it is not probable that his knowledge of pirates was superior to Defoe's.

Secondly, there is a problem in explaining Mist's literary competence and writing skills. Did Mist really have the ability to write such a complex work? Bialuschewski argues that, contrary to the opinion of others, Mist did have the literary and writing skills to write the *General History*. Max Novak, who has seen some of Mist's correspondence, maintains that Mist was semi-literate.[344] Pat Rogers concluded that Mist did not write anything in the *Journal* or elsewhere.[345] Bialuschewski produces evidence that he could write reasonable copy. He believes that in 1728 when exiled abroad Mist, who was a Jacobite, sent long accounts of various public matters to James Edgar, the Pretender's private secretary in Rome, using the

[344] Novak, 501-505.
[345] Rogers, Pat. *Papers of the Bibliographical Society of America*, 2010, 10 (3), 299-331.

aliases of Luden, Ravell or Stonehouse.[346] Mist could have been the originator and writer of these documents. However, he may have continued the lifetime practice of passing off the work of others as his own. While some credence must be given to the correspondence, it does not alter my view that Mist had as much chance of writing a complex book such as the *General History* as 'the man on the moon.'

Thirdly, Bialuschewski seeks to provide documentary evidence. He quotes the 'anonymous' pamphlet entitled *Mist's Closet Broke Open: or Several Letters Intercepted, in which Are Contained Some Old Truths New Told*. The author associates Mist with Captain Johnson. In particular, Bialuschewski is interested in a fictional letter from Mist to Johnson entitled 'Sea-news from Captain Johnson to Mist.' He mentions also an undated letter by De La Faye which seems to indicate that Lord Townshend was seeking the whereabouts of Mist.[347] Bialuschewski does not consider the possibility that Defoe might have been the anonymous author. However, it is common to describe the work as written by Defoe. In the Illustration I give of the manuscript, the original of which is kept by the Boston Public Library, an archivist has assumed that he did. I assume that Defoe wrote it. I think that there is good internal evidence as set out above to support a claim that Defoe did so. As I have pointed out, Defoe was familiar with the name of Charles Johnson. I maintain that he used the name first in 1709 and repeated it in 1709, 1712, 1724 and 1728. He refers to the Avery play in the Introduction of the *General History*.

Fourthly, Bialuschewski has the problem of explaining when Mist could have written the book. He suggests that he may have started the book when in prison in 1721 and on the assumption that he enjoyed 'the liberties' of being there.

Confronted with these difficulties, it is argued by protagonists of the theory, changing direction, that Mist did write the *General History* but with the assistance of someone else. If someone else was needed, it

---

[346] Bialuschewski,, Arne.
[347] 'Anon.'/Daniel Defoe, *Mist's Closet Broke Open: or Several Letters Intercepted, in which Are Contained Some Old Truths New Told,* 1728.

might have been Daniel Defoe who would have been the right man for the job. After all, at certain times Defoe might have been found occupying the adjacent desk.

However, if it is supposed that Daniel Defoe was the prime mover in the matter he would hardly have needed Mist's help. Mist could not in any way be regarded as a co-author in any real sense of the word. The two men used each other. Defoe had to maintain the secrecy of an authorial pseudonym because of his very real fear of retaliation by pirates with a grudges against him, and a possible trial and grisly execution were his Capitulation with the Whigs, that pardoned him from crimes committed before 1716, to be weakened or scrapped by a new administration

The proof I offer that Defoe was the author of the *General History* at the very least the major part, and most probably in its entirety, is based on the conclusion that only Defoe could have written the chapters on Captain Avery and Captain Bowen. Theoretically, that is within the framework of a proof, it would remain possible that other people might have written some or all of the other chapters. I think it unlikely. It is more likely that the whole is written by Defoe. This is a conclusion influenced partly by style but not mainly so. Defoe was an investigative reporter of genius. He relied on others for material but wrote up the accounts himself. He knew where to look for intelligence, from whom, and how to verify the information he obtained. The proof I offer here is based partly on documents but also on conjecture.

In Chapter 18 I provide a documented proof that Defoe's *Farther Adventures of Robinson Crusoe* is an account of a journey he made to Brazil and Madagascar in 1705/1706 in a ship he owned named the *Aurangezebe*. .This ship was captained by his nephew Francis King. As explained, *A General History of the Pirates* includes a description of an encounter between this ship and the *Worcester* in 1703. It follows from this that Defoe was uniquely well-placed to write about the incident recorded in the *General History* in the chapter devoted to Captain Bowen.

I do not wish to repeat the proof here. However, in order to help readers I list some issues requiring due diligence by them.

1. When Was Daniel Defoe Born?

This proof breaks down very quickly, is hardly one at all, unless the reader accepts that the Daniel Defoe I am writing about was baptised Daniel Foe in Etton in 1644 and brought up in the way I have suggested. For example, Defoe describes *Crusoe* as 'sixty one years of age' when he made the trip known as *Farther Adventures*, that is in 1705/1706 when Defoe was 61 and the decision to make it was taken in conversation with his nephew. His nephew made a will referring to the *Aurangezebe*. It is dated 1705 and sworn in Colchester, Essex, not Cripplegate, London or Stoke Newington.

2. The Trip to Brazil and Madagascar, 1705/1706

Are you, at the end of this proof, satisfied that there was a relationship between Francis King and Defoe and that the trip to Madagascar described in *Farther Adventures* took place in 1705/1706?

3. Madagascar

Do you think it probable then that Defoe was put ashore on the island of Madagascar in the way described in *Farther Adventures* and as interpreted in the narrative here. Literally, could he have done this? Arne Bialuschewski believes that any ship approaching Madagascar would have been spotted and recorded by the Dutch authorities, intercepted and blown out the water. In general this must be right. However, Defoe must have known this and taken the necessary precautions: landing where his presence was least likely to be noticed, perhaps changing the name of the *Aurangezebe* when approaching the island, and leaving Madagascar as fast as possible. All this was well within the knowledge and ingenuity of Defoe.

4. The Account in 'Captain Bowen' in the *General History*

Do you think it probable, or even possible, that someone other than Defoe could have described in such detail the encounter between the *Worcester* and the *Aurangezebe* as set out in the *General History*?

Avery

5. Do you think it to be probable or likely that Defoe had been in touch with Avery as described in the *General History* in the guise of a Friend, that Defoe obtained diamonds from some of Avery's men, and that subsequently he fenced them in circumstances similar to Defoe's description in *Farther Adventures*? [348]

6. Defoe's 'Capitulation' and the Law-suit of Francis King.

Do you accept that the Francis King who sued Defoe in 1718 was Defoe's nephew and that this case was a major factor in Defoe's willingness to agree an immunity with the Whig administration in 1716?

The answer to these questions will determine a logical basis for accepting or challenging my proof. As in all proofs, the issues that require consideration are immutable.

7. Defoe as Captain Charles Johnson?

Did Defoe, as he often does, leave a clue or give a hint to the identity of the elusive Captain Johnson credited with the authorship of *A General History*? How did the author come to be given the name of Captain Charles Johnson? Defoe can be given the last word on the subject as he often tries to have it. In *King of the Pyrates*, as quoted above, he writes:

I got passage on board one Captain Guillaume, a New England Captain, whose owner was one Mr Johnson, a merchant with a house in Hackney.

An 'interpretation' of these seemingly superfluous words might consider the following:

1. For Guillaume read William; perhaps, William Penn?
2. The use of a French version of the name William avoids any association with William Penn
3. It is Defoe, the owner, who was a merchant living in Hackney.

---

[348] Defoe may have been in touch with Avery in 1704. See letter from Robert Davis, a Defoe relative and associate. Enclosure dated 25 September, 1704 in a letter to Harley: HMC, 29 Portland MSS, v.350-1 which describes lifting silver nougats off the Cornwall coast.

4. As the owner was British, there was no breach of the Navigation Acts.

In 1709, Defoe became Johnson. He was still using the pseudonym in 1728 some 19 years later.

Chapter 28

Family Instructor and Religious Courtship

The merchant [in Religious Courtship] was Defoe himself, the three daughters were his own three daughters, for whose edification...the book was written.

The Life of Daniel Defoe
Thomas Wright, 1879

Defoe writes about his family life with Mary Norton and their children in Colchester and his family establishment in Stoke Newington with three of his daughters in two works: *Family Instructor*, written in three parts in 1715, 1718 and 1727,[349] and *Religious Courtship* written in 1722.[350] These accounts are in the form of conduct books, a genre largely created in Defoe's own time. Conduct books concentrated on relationships within families, between husband and wife and parents and children. Defoe entered into a crowded field and his two works are not the finest examples of their kind available to his contemporaries. They are extant now, and possess the interest they do, because they were written by and about Defoe. In this account I consider all three parts of *Family Instructor*.

Academic critics have sought explanations for Defoe writing these works in generalisations about the influences upon him of cultural trends and political events; and in reverse, because of what they believe these works might tell them about Defoe's thoughts on those events. There is an interest also in how these works fit into the Defoe canon.

For example, Novak writes: 'The passage of the Schism Act [1713], with its resemblance to the revocation of the Edict of Nantes, seemed destined to destroy the Dissenters. Defoe saw the Dissenters as

---

[349] Defoe, Daniel. *Family Instructor*, parts 1 and 2 (1715 and 1718. Brightly and Childs, 1816).
[350] BL. MO/20286. Defoe, Daniel. *Religious Courtship*, 1722.

embattled, and he hoped that from the difficulties and sufferings they experienced would come a new dedication to religious faith.'

Novak describes these two works as being *novellas* and suggests that they mark a development stage in the evolution of Defoe's writing; a transition from journalism to the writing of fiction.[351]Others have followed Novak in stressing that the enactment of the Schism Act was a direct influence on Defoe's *Family Instructor*. Irving Rothman, a Defoe academic, who has tended in latter years to specialise in Defoe's non-fiction, has made an organised attempt to describe this influence.[352]

There are several misunderstandings. First, in 1713, Defoe was not particularly concerned with the effects of the Schism Act; and nor, since 1704, and his release from prison, was he agitated by the disadvantageous position of dissenters in society. The evidence for this is to be found in Defoe's correspondence with Harley and in his own published words.

This misunderstanding arises from confusion about the nature of Defoe's political and religious dissent. I have suggested in this work, and elsewhere, that Defoe was not a dissenter in the English sense of the word; he was centred in the Huguenot tradition of dissent. Defoe wrote to Harley in 1704 that he did not need to do anything for dissenters. He argued that 'tis not necessary in the present juncture to restore the Dissenters to offices... [that he was persuaded to the view] that freedom to the Dissenters is the directest method to lessen their numbers and bring them at last into the Church [and that] some small mismanagement among the Dissenters [that is dirty tricks] by useful agents [Perhaps himself?] might be useful to settle the general temper'.[353]

The Schism Act abolished nonconformist academies in December, 1713. *Religious Courtship* was written nine years later. Defoe went even further than his indifference to their fate in his written work. He

[351] Novak 483-489.
[352] Rothman, Irving."Defoe's *The Family Instructor*. A Response to the Schism Act", *Papers of the Bibliographical Society of America*, 74, 205.
[353] H.14 and 15.

wrote and published a pamphlet entitled, *A Letter to the Dissenters*. In this pamphlet Defoe criticised both dissenters and Whigs. He pointed out that it was against the law for dissenters to have their own schools. It might be argued that Defoe was merely obeying his master Harley and that he didn't mean these words. Commentators must be a little careful in jumping to such a conclusion as it is easy from that position to argue that Defoe never, or only rarely, believed in the truth of what he wrote. Such a conclusion would be unfair to him.

Secondly, some critics advance the thought that Defoe would have jumped to the defence of dissenting academies because he was educated in one, the Newington Academy for Dissenters, some forty years earlier. However, this assumption is false. Defoe had no special attachment to the academies. He was not educated in an academy (see Appendix 4 to this work) and did not send his sons to one.

Even if it was supposed that Defoe was Harley's man in 1713 some consideration must be given to the idea that a man's political and social views change through time. Harley would have had no difficulty, and neither would Defoe, in explaining that what he believed in the seventeenth century was not applicable to the situation in the country many years later. Unlike Defoe, Harley was educated at a dissenting academy. Of course, in a very general sense Defoe remained interested in the political events in his later years and in cultural changes. He was finely tuned to them.

Other and more pressing matters influenced the writing of these two works and preoccupied his thoughts in the period 1715-1727: his own complex family life. In *Serious Reflections of Robinson Crusoe* Defoe had written that he had 'heard of a man' [an expression commentators normally interpret as a Defoe ruse to avoid identification] upon some extraordinary disgust which he took at the unsuitable conversation of some of his nearest relations, whose society he could not avoid, resolved never to speak any more [to them?] … only one daughter …kept with him till, being very sick, he broke his silence. Both Chadwick in 1759[354] and Wright in 1894[355] believed that Defoe had

---

[354] Chadwick, *The Life and Times of Daniel Defoe*, John Russell, 1859.

separated from Mary Tuffley early in their marriage and that they were not reconciled until 1712/1714 when it is known from Defoe's own writing that he was sick.[356] I am alone among recent Defoe biographers in agreeing with them.

It is my belief that in 1715 when Defoe published *Family Instructor* he had not lived with Mary Tuffley for twenty-nine years that is from circa 1686. Wright points out that this is the period of silence Defoe attributes to *Crusoe*. Defoe married Mary Tuffley in January, 1684. If this period of twenty-nine years is actual time, Defoe could not have been the biological father to all of Mary Tuffley's children unless he conceived them in silence. I have argued earlier that he was father to only two of her children: Mary who died young and Hannah who lived a normal life span and who was faithful to Defoe as her father until his death in 1731.

At the start of the calendar year 1714, Mary Tuffley was living with her brother Samuel Tuffley and three daughters: Hannah, Henrietta and Maria. I agree with Backscheider when she writes that by October, 1714 Maria had married Henry Langley and lived with him in Wimborne, Dortsetshire. This being so, by end 1714 the two children living with Samuel Tuffley were Hannah and Henrietta.

I have offered documentary evidence that by the 1690's, Defoe was living with Mary Norton, first in Tilbury and subsequently in Colchester. I have suggested, from an interpretation of *Colonel Jack*, that Defoe did not *recognise* Maria and Henrietta as his daughters. By 1715 Defoe tells his readers through *Colonel Jack* that he had 5 children by Mary Norton of whom only 2, Benjamin Norton and Sophia, survived childhood. In addition living with them in Colchester was Defoe's son Daniel by Elisabeth Sammens.

If it is generally accepted that Defoe is writing about his family life in *Family Instructor* and *Religious Courtship*, it follows that he is going to give his readers important and interesting information about his family. Defoe does not disappoint. Although he doesn't name family members and truncates real time for narrative reasons he gives a

[355] Wright, 24.
[356] *An Appeal to Honour and Justice*, 1715.

remarkable description, in embellished form, of his family life over 25 years or more. He does this in a self-deprecatory manner with frank and disarming insight into how other family members viewed his life.

At the time of writing the *Family Instructor* Defoe's family life was entering a phase of upheaval and disturbance. Defoe discusses this upheaval in *Colonel Jack*. There were two causes for family discussion and agitation. The Tuffley children were without the protection of a father at a critical period of their lives. Whomsoever, was the father of Maria and Henrietta, it is apparent that he was either dead or otherwise no longer on the scene. Secondly, Samuel Tuffley, Mary's brother, was aware that on his death, as things stood, it was Defoe as the legal husband who would be able to inherit his considerable wealth. He recognised that he needed a legally tight will that would protect his sister Mary on his death against any legal challenge by Defoe or any other of his wives and sons.

Samuel Tuffley made his will in October 1714 and it was proved in August 1725. In the will Samuel left the vast bulk of his estate in trust for his sister with the words, to 'his dear sister Mary Defoe, the wife of Daniel Defoe and for and to her, disposing and appointments absolutely and independent of her husband, or any claim or demand by, from, or under him by right of marriage or otherwise might have or made to the same.'[357]

Samuel Tuffley appears to have been a sensible man. He was anxious to ensure that following the death of Mary's male partner, his sister and her progeny were looked after following his death. He was aware that the possession of his wealth by his sister made her vulnerable to a Defoe legal challenge to his will. A compromise solution was needed because Defoe, as a legal husband to Mary Tuffley, had an arguable cause in any court of law at the time to contest his will. In the period 1712-1714 a family meeting was held to discuss the future of 'the family' in a Westminster, London property.[358] I conjecture that at this meeting a bargain was struck between the Tuffley

---

[357] NRA. Prob. 11/604/383 Will of Samuel Tuffley, 1714.
[358] *Beyond Belief*, 216.

family and Defoe. This agreement gave Defoe a lease of a substantial property in Stoke Newington on certain conditions: that he drop any claim against the Tuffley estate, that Mary Tuffley and her daughters be permitted to live in the property, and Defoe be allowed to bring his daughter Sophia with him.

Mary Tuffley made her will on 5 July, 1731 shortly after the death of Daniel Defoe. Biographers have found it puzzling. Mary Tuffley left the sum of £1 only to each of Defoe's children by other women: Benjamin Norton, Daniel and Sophia. Benjamin received a gold watch. I have suggested that this watch was left in Mary's care by James Foe on his death in 1707. She divided her considerable estate between her daughters Hannah, Maria and Henrietta: the first being a daughter by Defoe, and the other two girls by an unknown man or men. It is inconceivable that Samuel and Mary Tuffley could have left these wills without prior agreement with Defoe: without such an agreement, Defoe would have succeeded in a legal challenge to Samuel Tuffley's will and, following his death, Benjamin Defoe, as Defoe's eldest son and legal heir, would have had the legal right to challenge it.[359]

The law on marriage contracts in the early eighteenth century was complex. It was weighted in favour of legal husbands. Defoe had a good understanding of the law on dowries and marriage contracts and others have pointed it out.[360] For example, Robert Clark writes that, 'Defoe had an acute understanding of marriage contracts...he was always ready to point out where a legal situation was insufficient...the inequalities of the marriage contract are lodged in the general law of a patriarchal society that gives the husband total control...' [361]

Samuel Tuffley's will, and the Westminster family meeting, provide the background to Defoe's description of his family relationships. The first part of the *Family Instructor* describes relationships within *one* family while the second part describes the 'goings on' of *two* families. Beyond 1714 Defoe maintained both these families, one in Colchester

---

[359] NRA. Prob. 11/604/383.
[360] *Beyond Belief,* 61, 65-66, 286 n. 68, 293 n.188.
[361] Introduction to *Roxana*, Everyman, J.M.Dent, 1998.

and the other in Stoke Newington. His Colchester family entered a period of uncertainty and his Stoke Newington family a time of hope. *Family Instructor* and *Religious Courtship* demonstrate the trials and tribulations of a process of change.

First, in *Family Instructor* Defoe identifies the Mother as a Quaker, inadvertently or not, when he addresses her in the Quaker fashion as 'thee'. Living with Defoe and Mary Norton were two Elder brothers, Benjamin Norton named after his mother, and Daniel, his son by Elisabeth Sammens; an Elder daughter, Sophia; and, or so it seems, two younger children. These children, Thomas and Jacky are described in *Family Instructor* but not in *Religious Courtship*. The two children who survived were Benjamin Norton and Sophia. Thomas and Jacky, together with Martha, may be Mary Norton's children who died in childhood.

Secondly, Defoe provides sufficient information to enable the reader to identify these children. The narrator explains that one Elder brother was intended 'for the practice of the law' so identifying him as Benjamin Norton. Benjamin was entered at the Inner Temple on 29 August 1715 as the 'son and legitimate heir of Daniel Defoe of Stoke Newington', where he met Dudley Ryder who thought ill of him.[362].Defoe had moved into the Stoke Newington property in August 1714.

Defoe describes his second Elder son as his 'uncle's eldest son, by a former wife', and that an old lady, mother in law to him, had lodgings in Westminster. This statement is truly convoluted. I assume he means Elisabeth Sammens. While this second son, Daniel, complies with his parents wishes the other Elder son, is scornful. He says, 'What, must I forsake all my mirth and good company and turn hermit in my young day? Not go the park! Not see a play! Be as demure as a Quaker and set up for a saint!' Benjamin must have felt that as he was on the verge of an escape to London, a place where he could enjoy himself with no parental control, that there was no need to bother about changing his ways.

---

[362] Ryder, Dudley. *The Diaries of Dudley Ryder*, 1715-1716 (ed. William Mathews, London, Methuen, London, 1739). *Beyond Belief*, 94.

At first the Elder daughter, Sophia, objects robustly to her Mother seeking to change her behaviour, to being hit, and her book romances burnt; but she changed her mind. Sophia spent ten weeks at the home of an aunt. She had got 'leave of her Father to stay with her aunt', described as a pious dissenter. On her return she remarked:

> I thought I was in heaven there to what I am at home; everything was so sober, so pretty, so grave, and yet so cheerful, so pleasant, so innocently merry...the young ladies obliged to be down stairs half an hour after nine in the morning , ready dressed. Then my uncle calls to prayers, and soon they all go away to the Church [so identifying himself as an Anglican] or to the Meeting House but whichever it is, they are almost sure to meet together after the sermon, sometimes at the very door, and the children and servants no one stirs from home. In the evening my Uncle calls them altogether, reads to them in some good book, and then sings psalms, and goes to prayer; when that is over they go to supper, then they spend an hour or two in the most pleasant discourse imaginable; it is always about something religious.

The Mother in Defoe's narration refuses to join in communal prayers: but then, as a Quaker, she had no belief in that form of worship.

The Mother's objections to her children's behaviour was to their practices of playing cards all night, going to theatres, wearing patches, reading foolish romances, singing popular songs, taking God's name in vain and going for walks on a Sunday instead of attending a church or meeting house. This form of behaviour was unacceptable in the house of their uncle and aunt and they were particularly obnoxious to Quakers.

Arguably, the uncle and aunt referred to were Mary and Samuel Tuffley, for the use of such terms in describing them are well within Defoe's definition of family relationships. It is important for me to stress the looseness of the family terms used at the time. If this is so, it is evidence that following the rupture of Mary Tuffley's relationship with

Defoe, and perhaps the death of the 'other man' who had taken Defoe's place, the 'family' had taken refuge with Samuel Tuffley.

This knowledge, and Sophia's description of their household, suggests that Sophia was on trial there: if there were no objections to her behaviour by Mary and Samuel Tuffley they might agree to her living with them and 'her cousins'. It is understandable also that Wilson's description of Henrietta and Maria as being regarded as committed and earnest members of the Church in Wimborne, where they settled, was as a result of their upbringing in Samuel Tuffley's household. [363]

This information suggests also that the mother may have been motivated in her rebuke of Sophia by apprehension that her daughter would 'let her down' at the Tuffley's and by implication that she, Mary Norton, would be criticised as an inadequate mother. Such a conclusion is supported by Defoe's narrative for later when the daughter had moved permanently to her aunt's new home, the aunt came visiting. It appears that she came often. In reality this might not be true. The mother was concerned that her daughter might be behaving badly in her new family. She was reassured by the aunt that once when she was thought to have gone out without permission she was found walking 'in the lime-tree walk behind our house'. This is close to the description given by Henry Baker when he visited the Stoke Newington property.

When the aunt was asked by the mother for the reason for her visit at a particular time, the aunt explains that she was worried about her son. The mother exclaims that she (the aunt) had no son. She received the reply 'not my son but my husband's, that is Benjamin Norton the mother's son by Defoe and Mary Tuffley's legal husband. At this time, the 1720's, there was good cause to be worried about Benjamin who could not earn a living as journalist and who was supporting a large family.

Defoe's account of the exchanges between the mother, himself and the children could be read to Mary Norton's detriment. She uses crude language, is forthright to her children, and rude to the father. Her

[363] Wilson, 645.

language is simple and she is portrayed as dogmatic. You might assume that there would be no future for the marriage: religious differences would be too divisive. However, this is not so. Defoe continued to have a close relationship with Mary Norton until the end of his life. In 1714 this relationship was to change; but not his feelings for her.

Quakers to Defoe were true friends. Although he could not emulate their behaviour he had a healthy and deep respect for the differences between their behaviour and his own. He and Mary Norton had a private treaty marriage for approaching forty years. In *Colonel Jack* and *Roxana* Defoe tells readers something about her. From *Colonel Jack* readers learn that she was a loving and serious woman who got on well with his children. In the conversation at the Quakers House in *Roxana*, Defoe tells readers that she was scrupulously honest and could never tell a lie. This made it difficult for Defoe to tell her some unpalatable things about his life because were she to be asked about them by others she would tell the truth. However, Mary had a good understanding in general of his activities in London and disliked what she knew. The exchanges between the two of them are blunt. Mary is under no illusions about her husband: she does not think him truly religious and saved, and claimed that she knew where he was going to end up in the next life.

Defoe takes it all in good spirit. After the move to London he stresses time and again in his fiction that he had given Mary Norton considerable sums of money to cover household expenses. When Defoe writes about marriage and money it is wise to conclude that there must have been long periods of time when they received nothing at all from him; but it does appear that, in general, he did his very best for his family. Mary Norton had many relatives in Tilbury, Colchester, Coggeshall and Great Tey where she lived with Defoe. She could be sure that they would look after her in his absence.

In *Family Instructor* Defoe introduces readers to a young son Thomas whose simple questions about the meaning of God and subsequent religious faith brought his parents back together. Defoe devises a very grisly fate for Benjamin Norton. He enlists in the army, loses a leg, drifts into despair and dies. For Defoe this represents what will happen to a person who leads a dissolute life without Repentance. Novak writes, and I agree with him, 'Defoe relies almost entirely on a broad definition of Repentance as the key to all belief.' For a Christian, Novak argues, 'to repent meant a full recognition of past sins , or the nature of original sin, and a thorough belief that such an awareness brought with it a sense of salvation.'[364] It might be objected that such a belief expressed by Defoe was something of a 'cop out': sin, confess, repent and commit the next sin and so on. In a deeper sense Defoe is telling readers that although he loved his son he accepted that he behaved foolishly and learnt little from his mistakes; he made errors in his life that would bring him down. From what is known about Benjamin's life it can be deduced that he was a foolish and impetuous person who did bring poverty upon himself. Nevertheless his parents loved him. Benjamin adopted his mother's name: he was sometimes described as Mr Norton and always as Benjamin Norton. This seems to imply that not only was he seeking to distinguish himself from his father (perhaps at his request) but that he loved his mother and she him.

Every Defoe biographer knows that Sophia did live in Stoke Newington with her father. In *Conjugal Lewdness*, Defoe (in the fictional guise of an Old Lady) made proposals for future payments to John White, his tenant in Stoke Newington who was blackmailing him. The Old Lady (Defoe) told John White that he had two nieces at his home in Stoke Newington who expected to inherit from him. These nieces would be Hannah (the aunt's daughter and hence a niece of some kind) and Sophia. Sophia came into the possession of Defoe's house and Hannah inherited a share of what was left of Defoe's 'estate' in Colchester.

Backscheider expresses the thought that when in 1725 Defoe wrote to John Ward his farm manager to tell him that the death of a relative gave him 'a considerable estate' he was over optimistic. However, Hannah, an unmarried daughter in Defoe's care and dependant upon

---

[364] Novak, 485.

him, did inherit property from her mother. Defoe was probably right in law to consider his daughter's property as his own.[365]

Something is told the reader of the character and beliefs of Mary Tuffley in *Family Instructor*. The aunt (Mary Tuffley) expresses a number of common sense opinions that show her to be conventional but straightforward. In *Colonel Jack*, Defoe expresses regard for Mary Tuffley. He thought her right to expect maintenance for her children by him, and he expressed the opinion that he had always had a regard for her. From this account Mary does not appear to 'deranged' or unreasonable as Defoe remarks elsewhere. Defoe had been unable to sustain his marriage to Mary Tuffley but he did sincerely regret its loss. Something is learnt also about Sophia. She emerges from various exchanges as a lively, difficult and determined girl who was eager to take her chances in life. Henry Baker was taking on a lot when he married her.

Daniel, the other Elder son, appears as a ghost at the table. After Defoe's death Daniel continued to live in Colchester where at least he had the support of a loving 'step-mother'. In *Roxana* Defoe confesses that he did not really love him.[366] Later, in the last throes of his life, Defoe describes Daniel as ungrateful. It would appear from the limited knowledge of Daniel that he did achieve something reasonable and rewarding from his life. In 1729 Daniel may have had the means to help his father but chose not to do so. Children always know more about the nature and extent of their parents love for them than their parents are willing to admit.

In 1715 Defoe kept a black boy slave called Toby. In a series of equivocal exchanges the reader is told that this boy is about 14 years old and that he had been given to the young son Jacky by a friendly sea-captain from Barbados. Jacky believes that Toby can be beaten and seeks his Father's help in doing so. Toby tells Jacky about the life of black slaves in Barbados and that black people were not allowed to be Christians. They had to be work very hard all day and they were beaten

---

[365] Backscheider, 497.
[366] *Roxana*, 84.

if they attended church. Jacky says, 'So they won't let them know God, because they shall not be free mans, is that the reason Toby? They are very cruel.' In this exchange the father agrees with Jacky in wanting to have Toby baptised but the mother scolds the father for talking in this way and states that, 'You'll put into his head to be baptised and then he will run away.' In an exchange with the father the mother says, 'Why need you care where any body goes? You know well enough where you are going.'

Toby stands in a long line of 'fictional' black slave boys owned by Defoe. I do not believe for one moment that he was given to Toby as a present. It was far more likely that he was sold to Defoe by Captain Edward Singleton who was William Penn's representative in Barbados in the early 1700's. The wording of Defoe's text suggests a payment. The life I reveal for Defoe shows that he visited and in some sense lived in Barbados, off and on, for several years and was married there. He certainly knew how slaves were treated on the island. However, the account he gives of slavery from Toby and the thought he expresses that baptism would set him free in Barbados or England is wrong. In Barbados at this time whether or not a slave could be baptised and allowed to attend church on a Sunday depended on the owner. Quakers, who were numerous on the island, and some Anglicans, permitted their slaves to be baptised and attend church. The main objection of planters to church attendance was that they lost the use of slave labour on a Sunday. In England a slave could not be made free by baptism or running away. Slaves had no civic rights in England until the nineteenth century.

Slaves were kept by many people in England in the early eighteenth century. They were acquired as trophies on foreign travels. Pepys tells readers that his neighbour Admiral Penn kept black slaves in their family home in London. Both William Penn and Defoe believed that black slaves had souls and they should be treated well on humanitarian and utilitarian grounds. Defoe kept young black slaves for less straightforward reasons. Black boy slaves might be though acquiescent in the practice of shunamitism.

In the eighteenth century disputes about slaves in England were dealt with as property issues. The notion that a slave could be freed in England was fallacious. While the courts ruled in 1772 that the state of slavery did not exist in England the rulings were ignored. Slaves were bought and sold. A slave could be sold back to his place of origin to work on a plantation. Defoe in common with most owners of slaves made much of the 'old saw' that when offered their freedom slaves opted invariably for servitude. As a slave could not gain any civil rights in England the contention was always an empty one. The wrongs of slavery were not redeemable. What might have happened to Toby? Was he sold on when he had out-lived his utility to the family?

Religious Courtship, 1722.

A conclusion that can be drawn from *Family Instructor* is that the two families had contact with each other. This conclusion is strengthened by a reading of *Religious Courtship*. The full title of this work on first publication was *Religious Courtship: Being Historical Discourses on the Necessity of Marrying Religious Husbands and Wives only. As also of Husbands and Wives being of the same Opinions in Religion with one another*. This conduct book was written about Defoe's family life from 1714 to 1722 the date of its publication

The long title is carefully worded. In *Family Instructor* Defoe reveals that he considered both Mary Norton and himself to be devout Christians. However, they did have differences about how best to bring up children. As a sober minded Quaker, Mary believed in a life of seriousness, polite demeanour and decorousness. Defoe found it difficult to share her views on how best to bring up and discipline their children. The resulting tensions influenced, I believe, the last sentence of the title: that is, that it is best if husband and wife have the same religious opinions.

Primarily, I limit the discussion of the book here to its biographical implications. However, I think it reasonable to explore what was meant by Defoe, and those who engage with him in this work, when they talk of religious belief and conviction. In any discussion today on religious belief and religious values consideration would be given to distinctions between faith, worship, and moral and ethical behaviour. In the early seventeenth century emphasis was placed on the outward signs of the good life: on piety, quietism, prayer and regular attendance at a church or meeting house. Since the Enlightenment the emphasis of discussion has been on openness, genuine debate and a man's actual behaviour: 'by your deeds shall you be judged'. Earlier in this book I point to the conversations recorded by Nettleton, the discoverer of immunisation, with Defoe where Nettleton's defence of the Enlightenment is contrasted with Defoe's religiosity. This is a comparison very much to Nettleton's advantage.[367] I point out that to my knowledge Defoe was not a member of any church and that there is no evidence of any regular attendance at church, other that his interest in listening to sermons early in the 1680's, that has ever been advanced. Defoe's family did not consider him to be a religious man. In *Religious Courtship*, Defoe is described by his daughters as 'not a religious man'. By this they meant that he did not go to church or join in family prayers.

The question arises as to what Defoe really means by his interminable pre-occupation with religious niceties? I suggest that he is talking about behaviour. Defoe draws a distinction between the appearance of things, of being a 'religious believer', and actual practice or behaviour. This distinction troubled him throughout his life. He was aware from his own life that it was better, at least for him, to conceal real feelings behind an outward conformity.

Part 1 of the book describes the youngest child (Sophia) as being approached by a rich young gentleman, a merchant who is indifferent to religion. Sophia is unwilling to marry anyone who lacks religious conviction. Initially, the Father is understanding of the daughter's refusal of this suitor but later he becomes angry and attempts to insist that she marry him. It is suggested that the suitor's intentions are honourable. He becomes sad and reflective, reads religious writings and becomes a believer so making a marriage more possible. Sophia continues to have doubts. The suitor decides that after studying religion he should become a Christian. He approaches the daughter again and

---

[367] Nettleton, Thomas, Dr. *Some Thoughts Concerning Virtue.*

was accepted. They were free to marry. There is no knowledge of any suitor other than Henry Baker, the man she was ultimately to marry. In an earlier chapter I argue that Henry Baker met Sophia much earlier than had previously been supposed. If the suitor described in *Religious Courtship* is based on Baker it is proof in itself for this assertion as the book was written in 1722. Baker entered into a very long courtship of her. There came a stage in this courtship when Defoe was insisting that Sophia marry Henry Baker and Baker showed a determination to pressurise Defoe on the dowry terms. Correspondence between Defoe, Henry Baker and Sophia was censured by the Baker family so making it impossible to determine Sophia's real feelings. It is my belief that for a long time she refused Henry Baker because she did not like him. I have suggested that the reason for Sophia's dislike was her knowledge of his sexual behaviour. These negotiations were unresolved when Defoe wrote *Religious Courtship* and thus it is reasonable to assume that Defoe hoped his daughter would become reconciled to the marriage.

Hannah, the Elder daughter, acted as an intermediary between Defoe and Sophia. She urged Sophia not to be too dogmatic about the matter and not to make her father angry. She advised Sophia not to be judgemental as the suitor might turn out to be a good man and, if she loved him and was understanding, that he might change his attitude to religion. This was inconsistent of Hannah for in respect of her own choices in life she was adamant that she did not wish to marry. Her argument against marriage was that no man could be relied upon. Even when a man professed to be religious and attended church regularly he might behave badly for men at that time got up to all kinds of disagreeable and immoral practices. While daughters should pay proper regard to a father's wishes, Hannah argued that she should not be forced to marry against her will.

Hannah remained a spinster. However, there is anecdotal evidence in Colchester that she became involved with the Rev William Smithies, Rector of St. Michael's, Mile End to the north of Colchester who it is thought had been a good friend of Defoe's. Rumour has it that Hannah occupied a house in Mile End owned by Smithies. Mile End is mentioned in *Moll Flanders*. There is no documentary evidence to support a conjecture that they had an arrangement of some kind. If she did have one it could be commented that she was showing a preference for a religious man of considerable wealth. Evidence of the relationship between Defoe and Hannah suggests that whatever his reservations Defoe looked after her. He settled South Sea stock in her name and gave her co-ownership of the lease of his Colchester farm.

Defoe's relationship with Henrietta is discussed in Part II. It raises different issues. The second daughter expresses the opinion that 'she would not trouble herself, when it came to her turn, whatever the religion of a gentleman, or whether he had any religion or none, if she had but a good settlement.' She encounters a rich merchant from Italy who visits Defoe in Stoke Newington where 'he had an opportunity to see the two maiden daughters; for the youngest who had been married some time, was gone into Hampshire to her country-seat with her husband'. The daughter who married and settled in Hampshire was Maria who lived her early married life there. Thus the two daughters the merchant met were Henrietta and Hannah. The merchant took a fancy to the younger daughter, Henrietta.

Defoe describes this gentleman as follows:

> A very agreeable person, perfectly well-bred, having lived abroad, and seen a great deal of the world. He was also a man of excellent parts and sense, talked admirably well, almost to every thing that came in his way, spoke several languages, and in short was not only, but much of a gentleman; and all this to be added, that he was very sober, grave, and oftentimes, as occasion offered, his discourse upon religious affairs discovered him to be very serious and religious.

He was also very rich. Henrietta found him to be very agreeable but her elder sister warned her that as he was brought up in a Roman Catholic country she would be wise to discover whether he was one. Her father, Defoe, assured her that having been brought up in a Roman

Catholic country he was bound to have Romish and other foreign ways but that she should not worry about it.

However, when he died suddenly after eight years of marriage it became apparent that he was a Roman Catholic because in his will he appointed a tutor whose task was to bring up two sons of the marriage in the Roman Catholic religion.

This revelation came as a shock to Henrietta. However, it is difficult to comprehend what the fuss was really about. He had been an excellent husband and had left his wife and children with the means to lead a good life. The Father was reproachful. He stated that he suspected it all along and had reason to suppose it. He had given groundless assurances. The Father's neglect was not surprising to the other two sisters. In an earlier discussion Sophia says to Hannah, 'Dear sister, have not you and I often lamented the loss of a religious family, even in our own father? the want of religious conversation, the want of a father to teach, instruct, inform and explain religious things to us.'

Henrietta had a similar thought for Defoe writes that she 'did take one step to leave a sad example of a father perfectly unconcerned about the religious settlement of his children, and making the good of their souls no part of his care'. She had said to her Father, 'I hope you have good grounds to be satisfied, sir, for I depend upon you, sir, for everything...he is a Protestant, sir, is he not?' He answered, 'Protestant, child, yes, yes, he was always a Protestant, all the while I traded with him; I have an account of it from several people you may be sure he is a Protestant, I dare say he is.'

The narrative reveals that Mary Tuffley's second husband was not a religious man but kind and agreeable nevertheless. Defoe describes a conversation between a brother and a sister (I suggest Defoe and Mary Tuffley) about this husband, a 'Sir Charles'. He is further discussed by the Elder and Younger sisters (Hannah and Sophia). 'Sir Charles' is also introduced in *Family Instructor*. This man is described as being in situ for 25 years. I believe that this is the man who came looking for Defoe in *Colonel Jack* in the early 1690's demanding payment for the upkeep of Hannah. This would be consistent with a relationship of 25 years. If Sir Charles had died shortly before the publication of *Religious Courtship* in 1722 he might well have been the man seeking-out Defoe in the early to mid 1690's.

In *Family Instructor* and *Religious Courtship* Defoe is self-deprecatory. He shows readers that those who knew him best, or more accurately, those members of his family who judged him in a domestic context, recognised him to be being irreligious and dishonest. But that is not all they knew. Defoe lived a most difficult life. He wished to be loved and respected, as all men do, but recognised that many of his instincts and desires undermined him. He was capable of generous acts. His difficult childhood motivated him to do his best for his children and all those that recognised, loved and admired him for his many talents - and some for the man he was. Clearly he knew himself extraordinarily well. At this time of his life he had few illusions. In these two conduct books he gave his family members a place in his world. He gave them a voice.

Attachments

1. Defoe Bibliography

Introduction

Defoe's bibliography is a vexed subject and I do not wish to venture far into it. I am not encouraged by the track record of the very many Defoe biographers who have attempted to engage in the art.

However, it will be among the first thoughts of academics ahead of reading my book that the account and analysis I give of Defoe's life must have the effect of undermining Defoe scholarship. It may seem to some that there will be a continuation of the process of diminution started by Furbank and Owens in their analysis of the Defoe canon.

This is not the case. It is to the contrary. A surer understanding of the chronology and circumstances of Defoe's life enables me, without trying very hard, to identify internal evidence in many works that point to, and sometimes confirms, Defoe's authorship. The evidence for various new and strengthened ascriptions is given in this book.

Ascribed to Defoe

On the basis of internal evidence, a changed chronology, a surer grasp of the circumstances of his life and a better understanding of his complex motivations, I ascribe the following ten works in their entirety to Defoe or probably by him:

1. *The Life and Adventures of Captain Avery, the Famous Pyrate*, 1709.
2. The play: *The Successful Pyrate*, 1712. (P)
3. *A General History of the Pyrates*, 1724.
4. *A Letter from Scotland to a Friend in London*, 1705.
5. *Observations on the Tryal of Captain Green and the Speech at His Death*, 1705.
6. *The Tryal of Captain Green*, 1705. (P)
7. *Mists Closet Broke Open: on Several Letters Intercepted, in which Are Contained Some Old Truths New Told*, 1728.
8. *The True and Genuine Account of the Life and Actions of the Late Jonathan Wild*, 1725.

9. *A Narrative of all the Escapes of John Sheppard*, 1724. (P)

10. *Proceedings Against Sir John Fenwick, Bar.....,* 1702 and related pamphlets from 1697. (P)

(P) stands for probable or possible.

2. I ascribe the following two works as written in part by Defoe:

11. *Robert Drury's Journal*, 1729.

12. *The History of the Remarkable Life of John Sheppard*, 1724.

3. I confirm on the basis of internal evidence that the following works are entirely written by Defoe and that the doubts raised about his authorship of them cannot be sustained:

13. *Moll Flanders*, 1722.

14. *Roxana*, 1724.

4. I do not think that Defoe is the author of the following manuscript work until a check of the handwriting and an investigation of its origins confirms that it is. I suspect that these thoughts originate with John Collins and are more accurately and securely ascribed to him.

15. *Meditations*, 1681.

5. Definition of Authorship

I suggest that further consideration be given to how much of a work must be proved to have been written by Defoe to constitute a claim of authorship. For example: *Historical Collections*, 1682. Some works, acknowledged or ascribed as being by Defoe are described as edited in their original form. I believe that it should be accepted today that some of these works are best regarded as being edited or arranged by Defoe.

5. Unfound Works

I believe that Defoe may well be the author of additional polemical pamphlets written in the 1680's some of which may be extant, discoverable and provable.

6. Reconsidered Authorship

Some works removed from the canon may be Defoe's work in whole or in part. It may be possible to draw upon the biographical evidence of this book to substantiate some of these. It is not a purpose of this work to do it. I can list a number of these works.

7. Genre and Oeuvre

The effect of the changes I suggest here is to alter the balance of Defoe's work by genre and subject. He wrote more biography, in particular of criminals and pirates, than is recognised today; and was more involved in the writing of military memoirs, most of which were edited versions of the work of others to which he added knowledge of his own; and he wrote a play. It follows from this conclusion that if literary critical judgements about Defoe are to be based on his entire oeuvre that current judgements need to be revised.

8. Defoe's Polemics

In his political journalism and polemics Defoe was 'a man for all seasons'. In a long life in which he served several masters, all of whom were adept in the arts of survival in politically turbulent times, Defoe's family allegiances and plasticity of character served him well. Defoe shifted in the wind. It is a mistake to try to fix him in generalisations and general theory. In an age of fierce partisanship, Defoe is not easily lashed to the mast of any particular political dogma.

2. Reasons for Secrecy and Deception

A Lye Does Not Consist in the Indirect Position of words, but in the Design by False Speaking to Decieve and Injure my Neighbour, So Dissembling does not Consist of Putting a Different Face Upon our Actions, but in the further Applying That Concealment to the Prejudice of the [other] Person.

Defoe to Harley

1704

It was a complicated matter being Daniel Defoe; and much time would be needed to discuss the issue of secrecy and lying with him. Everyone has something to be secret about, and one would be hard-pressed to argue that there are not times when lying is the better of two bad options. It is healthy and inevitable also that we should not disclose many happenings and aspects of our inner lives. Sometimes lying or dissembling is ethically justifiable, at times we hide from ourselves, and at all times, we repress important events in our lives and often the most profound. When this happens we may need help to establish our true feelings. In ancient times our ancestors sought out the wisdom of soothsayers and oracles to explain the puzzles of life and in modern times the rich and the sick have taken refuge in the psychiatrist's chair.

If the existence of Defoe's subterfuge is indisputable, as I believe it to be, there are a number of interpretations open to enquirers to explain it. However, any attempt to do so must take account, so far as is possible, of the discoverable facts of his life – a psychiatrist would believe it to be a necessary preliminary to any analysis. It must also be approached, in this context, from the viewpoint of one or more academic disciplines. It is what I do briefly here. Each discipline has its advantages and limitations; but when several approaches are undertaken some part of the 'truth' of Defoe's well-established secretiveness and many deceptions emerge.

Psychological

Antony Storr, an academic authority on psychoanalysis, wrote a letter to Lytton Strachey commenting on his biographical work *Elisabeth and Essex* which sets out some of the considerations, as he understood them, that arise from seeking to apply psychoanalytical theory to literature. I quote:

> You are aware of what other historians so easily overlook - that it is impossible to understand the past with certainty, because we cannot divine men's motives and the essence of their minds and so cannot interpret their actions...psychological analysis does not suffice....it breaks down because of the incompleteness of our knowledge... [However, Storr was able to add that] you have known how to trace back her [Queen Elisabeth 1st's] character to the impressions of her childhood, you have touched upon her most hidden motives with equal boldness and discretion, and it is very possible that you have succeeded in making a correct reconstruction of what actually occurred.

Leo Abse has recently subjected Defoe's life, as he understood it, to psycho-analytical enquiry from a Freudian and clinical perspective. He draws attention to Defoe's unresolved Oedipal Complex and consequent psychological problems; the acting out of its consequences in sexual identity, excessive risk taking, anxiety, and social delinquency. He also seeks to explain the reasons for Defoe denying his origins. I have touched upon these matters in earlier chapters but I add to them here to explain Defoe's overwhelming desire to hide his real life.

Oedipal Complex

It has been argued that all literary endeavours arise as a desire to act out in creative writing the problems experienced by writers as a consequence of the Oedipal Complex. Abse did not know that Defoe had no conscious memory of his parents as he had lost both them by three years of age. As a small child Defoe knew that his father had died and his mother had 'disappeared'. In Freudian terms he had 'succeeded' in getting rid of the father but failed to gain his mother.

The father figure for Defoe was Daniel Foe. Defoe had to accept the Oedipal task of claiming the power and status attached to Daniel Foe, a man he did not remember and whose estate was 'scattered to the four winds'. Defoe's father figure was too remote to be a male role model to him although his father's relatives and some of his family history were known by Defoe and could be romanticised. I believe that Defoe established a compelling fantasy about his father's inheritance that drove some of his actions. Those models most immediately available, however, were men on his mother's side of the family. As Defoe had not completed the rite of passage to his father, he appears to have sought male approval not as a man but as a woman. In seeking this assurance Defoe had a fear that he would be punished if he made bad judgements. Thus in his sexual orientation he represented the female partner in gay relationships; and in his fictions the narrator requires to be wooed by his/her sexual partners. To attract their attention Defoe needed to dress and fashion himself in a modish manner. When fully garbed as a woman in cross-dressing he could pretend to himself, and perhaps to others, that he was a woman. However, he feared that he might be found out in sexual encounters when dressed as one. This fear was accompanied by excitement as in some sense he was daring others to detect him. Defoe was unable to act out his sexuality freely in the public domain for fear of detection, prosecution, and severe legal punishment. He needed to keep these matters secret.

Melanie Klein writes that, 'Infantile anxiety situations are deflected in a work of art and in the creative impulse.'[368] Abse poses the question of why Defoe led a life of extreme anxiety. He believes that Defoe's behaviour was dictated by internal and not external necessity; that is, he had a pre-disposition from childhood. I agree with Abse on Defoe's childhood pre-dispositions but not that there were no external threats to him justifying deception. Abse, I believe, would have modified his opinion with better biographical knowledge.

Ablation

Abse suggests that Defoe ablated his early memories of origin and family background. The Oxford Concise Dictionary suggests that ablation amounts to a slicing across the entire memory of painful events. Thus to recall early events would have been for him both

---

[368] Klein, Melanie. *International Journal of Psychoanalysis*, 10 (1931).

painful and difficult giving rise to anxiety. I do not think this condition was as serious as Abse suggests. In his fictions Defoe's 'narrators' on occasions, when it suited them, do tell readers more than cursory information about beginnings.

Acting Out

It was not possible for Defoe to repress these psychological difficulties. He needed to act them out in delinquency and excessive risk taking amounting to gambling. All this activity was accompanied by extreme anxiety and the fear of punishment and death by execution. His characters always avoid the worst. All attempts to press social authority to the point of severe punishment were accompanied by extreme anxiety and a perception that he deserved to be punished. The crimes he committed, real or imaginary had to be kept secret.

Sociological

The sociological approach to Defoe's behaviour stresses the social conformity required of all citizens down the ages. Those individuals unwilling or unable to conform to those rules of restraint that are generally accepted in their societies place themselves as social outsiders. If the rules are not to be followed the social delinquent needs to build defences against the inevitable retaliation. Deviant behaviour can be categorised into two types. Conforming behaviour is simply that which obeys the rules and in ways in which others perceive as obeying them. At the other extreme, the pure deviant type of behaviour is that which both disobeys the rules and is perceived as doing so. I categorise these types below:

Types of Deviant Behaviour [369]

1. Obedient Behaviour	2. Rule-breaking Behaviour
Perceived as Deviant	Falsely accused. Pure deviant
Not perceived as Deviant	Conforming. Secret deviant

---

[369] Becker, Howard S. *Outsiders: Studies in the Sociology of Deviance*, The Free Press, 1991.

In Defoe's fictional accounts the crimes committed by his narrators fall initially into the first category but subsequently into the second. Defoe tells readers that the courts were persuaded of his narrator's good character by their respectable dress, good demeanour, and awareness of right and wrong. He was contrite but insistent that he had done nothing wrong. In *Captain Singleton* Defoe states, 'I was reputed to be 'a mighty diligent servant to my master, and very faithful. I was diligent indeed, but I was very far from honest; however, they thought me honest, which, by the way, was their very great mistake.' This being so Defoe's all-consuming secrecy is to be explained by undetected crime or put more neutrally by his persistent practice of ignoring social rules as determined by various social authorities.

Anthropological

Various studies of ancient societies confirm that all societies establish social rules for their own survival and good order. While the rules vary geographically and throughout time they are all a reflection of the desire of communities to protect their societies and are based on power relationships accepted by the majority of ruling groups. From this viewpoint morality is a means for individuals to avoid punishment at the hands of the group.[370] Biologists have argued that 'being nice' is a necessity for selection to a group. If thought 'not nice' an individual who persists is 'castaway'. These individuals become outsiders and may literally be cast out.

Defoe's Secrecy

Defoe's need to make his own rules, and to keep his violation of other and more social regulations a secret, had several causes. First they arose from the shame and humiliation of his birth and early nurture in the care of a parish. In his childhood Defoe rejected the social rules that labelled him as part of the undeserving poor. Secondly, his difficulties were added to by his sexual identity and the consequent need to keep his sexual orientation a secret from all

[370] Boem, Christopher. *Moral Origins: The Evolution of Virtue, Altruism, and Shame,* Basic
Books, May, 2012.

those to whom he did not choose to reveal it. Thirdly, the life he led involved 'necessary' crime'. Criminal acts did not end with his teenage years. They became more serious through time. Fourthly, criminal activity migrated to business crimes as a result of disobeying business rules; poor and risky decision-making caused him to trade when technically bankrupt. In Defoe's time it was a sin to do so. It was then and is now a crime in most countries. Defoe's insolvencies created numerous creditors who felt entitled to hound him into the courts. Fifthly, Defoe planned and executed very serious crimes, the disclosure of which would lead to his execution. Sixthly, Defoe may have had family allegiances to Jacobitism, that after 1706 were best kept to himself.

Minor crimes can be dismissed as the waywardness of youth. Business crimes can be discounted in various ways: bad luck, addiction to high-risk business ventures and unregulated capitalism; and sexual crimes explained by the unreasonableness of sexual discrimination. However, the audacious act of fencing Avery's stolen goods is less easily explained away. Defoe attempts to defend his actions in general terms. He believed that the distribution of wealth was indiscriminate and unfair; that the possession of capital was either an accident of wealth or the reward for corruption and possession of power. Why, was not the very existence of the East India Company, and the vast riches it gained for its investors, the greatest known act of capitalist exploitation and, yes, a form of 'piracy' in itself?

However, Defoe's re-distribution of the East India Company's 'stolen' wealth cannot be regarded as a Robin Hood act of taking money from the rich and giving it to the poor. It is best to understand Defoe's remarkable actions for what they might reasonably be held to be. Defoe carried through a criminal act with courage and superb organisation.

I do not know whether Defoe set out to deceive Captain Avery. He might have reasoned that Avery's days were limited in number and that he lacked the ability to stay ahead of the forces of law, order and human greed. Perhaps, Defoe did not realise that he had set in motion a course of events that few people would wish to experience: the pursuit of desperate and immoral men and a righteous court system. Defoe's ingenuity and talents saved him from the gallows but it did not protect him from all the consequences of his admirable audacity.

There were a host of reasons for controversial writers to seek anonymity in the early eighteenth century and scholars are well aware of them. However, that having been said, Defoe's secrecy and deception was not normal in his time – or in any age - and does require explanation by any critic who comments upon him.

To summarise, there are simple and 'off the cuff' explanations for Defoe lying about his age and origins. He needed to lie for a variety of reasons – and, in practice, it was so easy for him to do so. In the 25 year period 1706 to 1731 during which Defoe created the traceable public personae described by biographers, he lived in a state of constant fear and anxiety. Most men would have crumbled under the strain and stress but amazingly Defoe needed the danger and thrived on the pressures.

3. Further Research

Introduction

The research for this book was conducted in England in the three year period 2009-2012 and covered England, Scotland, continental Europe, Brazil, the Caribbean, and the USA. The resources available were limited. I funded the work and had no grant to assist me. While England was a good place from which to research this unknown period of Defoe's life it was not the only place where work was needed. Future work is best done in America and Brazil and preferably by others with the necessary experience of public and private sources of archived historical material in these countries.

England

There is good archived material in England dating from the seventeenth century. However, it is not perfect. I have been handicapped by significant gaps in records of births, deaths and marriages. Some of these gaps cannot be made good from other material. For example, a married women dying before her husband was not likely to have left a will except in exceptional circumstances. Consequently, further research will continue to be imperfect. Notwithstanding these problems it is possible that with diligence, persistence and time some gaps can be filled. It should be possible to provide further information on Defoe's family and kinship links on both sides of his family.

Portugal and Brazil

The Foe presence in Portugal is traceable. By sheer persistence Bastian was able to provide some information on merchant activity in Lisbon.[371] Family and land ownership can be traced back in these countries. However, much of the relevant information is in private archives and special language and research skills are required to find it. For example, I believe lists of prisoner arrivals in Bahia, Brazil from Portugal in the 1660's are extant. A skilled and experienced Brazilian researcher will be able to find them. I believe also that some seventeenth century land records exist and can be found.

---

[371] Bastian, 17, n. 39.

USA

I believe that is possible to find family records for Jone Reade's family in South Carolina, and possibly in Virginia, and Defoe's occupation of land in Maryland. Her family story is part of the history of religious persecution in that state in the seventeenth century. The Reade family may have been Quakers. I do not know whether Humphrey is the real name of Defoe's putative son by Jone Reade.

Penn maintained that the land allocated by him for settlement was always to religious refugees entitled to start a new life in New England. No doubt his motives were good. However, it was not a perfect world. I believe that Defoe was allocated land in Virginia and Maryland for settlement. If so Pennsylvania, where many of Penn's papers are to be found, is the place to start a search to find them.

Defoe, William Penn, Robert Spencer and Harley

I believe that it is possible to find out much more about the relationships between Defoe, Penn, Spencer and Harley. Defoe was an intimate of Spencer for 40 years, Penn for 55, and Harley 17 years. Much of what passed between them was never archived but some was and can be found. A handicap in finding this material is the lack of good, modern biographies. Much of what is available dates from a 40 year period 1950-1990 that although meritorious in its own terms tends to be characterised by 'a breathless hush in the close': a predisposition to limit enquiry to 'historical facts and public records' and a certain awareness of being in the presence of great men. To update these approaches and adapt them to modern tastes are considerable tasks: ten years or more of concentrated research for any of these people.

The Whig Bias

It is I contend important to free-up historical and political accounts of the Early Modern period from a bias of reading them from a Whig point of view. Of course, the passage to representative government was an undeniable part of historical accounts of English public life for over a hundred years and cannot be ignored. However, if these accounts are glued to the Whigs, a distorted representation of English political, cultural and social life will be given. In particular, Defoe is much too complicated a person to be explained teleologically by attachment to one version of history and a narrow concept of religious and political allegiance.

Jacobitism

Late in my research I stumbled into some knowledge of his father's family history.[372] This wider span of family influences embraces not only religious dissent, and support for representative government, but allegiances to other persuasions. English civil life was dominated by serious divisions on the monarchy and democratising institutions for an entire century. The Civil War, and the political and religious differences displayed in it and which motivated individuals, divided the nation. Different loyalties split, regions, counties, towns, villages and families. It is, I believe, entirely possible that they divided Defoe's loyalties. Among his relatives were Jacobites. It has long been suspected that Defoe may have had more than a sneaking sympathy for Jacobite causes (Novak's index mentions Jacobites and Jacobitism on 53 occasions). Defoe expresses sympathy for Nathaniel Mist's political loyalties in *Mists Closet Broke Open*. Further research can establish more about the nature of these allegiances.

---

[372] See Attachment 7. The Cavalier: Defoe's Elder Brother.

Charts and Lists

1. Marriages and Children

1.1. Defoe Marriages and Number of Children in Separate Families

Type	Partner	No. Born Boys	Girls	No. Surviving Childhood
1. Church	Jone Reade	1		1
2. Special Licence	Mary Tuffley	-	4	3
3. Private Treaty	Mary Norton	3	2	2
4. Private Treaty	Elisabeth Sammens	1	1	2
Totals		5	7	8

1.2. Surviving Children by Mother and Name

Mother	Surviving	Father	Not Surviving
Jone Reade	'Humphrey'	Defoe	
Mary Tuffley	Hannah	Defoe	Mary
	Maria	'Sir Charles'	
	Henrietta	'Sir Charles'	
Mary Norton	Benjamin	Defoe	Jacky
	Sophia	Defoe	Martha
			Thomas
Elisabeth Sammens	Daniel	Defoe	
	Sarah	Defoe	

1.3. Important Relationships with Men

Names	Period of Time
Thomas Neale	1692-1699
Robert Harley	1699-1712
James Logan	1698-1699
John Clerk	1702/1706-1712
Henry Baker	c.1714-7 to c.1724

2. Family Establishments

2.1 Foe Family of Etton, Northamptonshire

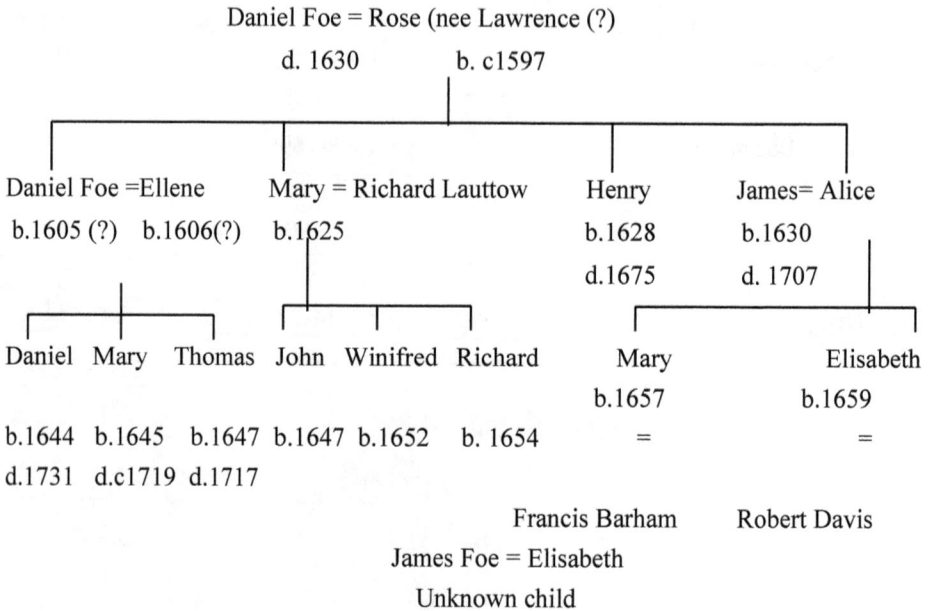

Daniel Foe = Rose (nee Lawrence (?)
d. 1630   b. c1597

Daniel Foe =Ellene   Mary = Richard Lauttow   Henry   James= Alice
b.1605 (?)   b.1606(?)   b.1625   b.1628   b.1630
                                                     d.1675   d. 1707

Daniel   Mary   Thomas   John   Winifred   Richard   Mary   Elisabeth
                                                          b.1657   b.1659

b.1644   b.1645   b.1647   b.1647   b.1652   b. 1654   =   =
d.1731   d.c1719   d.1717

                                               Francis Barham   Robert Davis
                                James Foe = Elisabeth
                                   Unknown child

Sources:

Etton Parish Records

St Giles, Cripplegate, London:

Parish Records

Wills of Daniel Foe, Henry Foe and James Foe.

2.2. Family of Thomas and Rose King, Bottlebridge, Huntingdonshire.

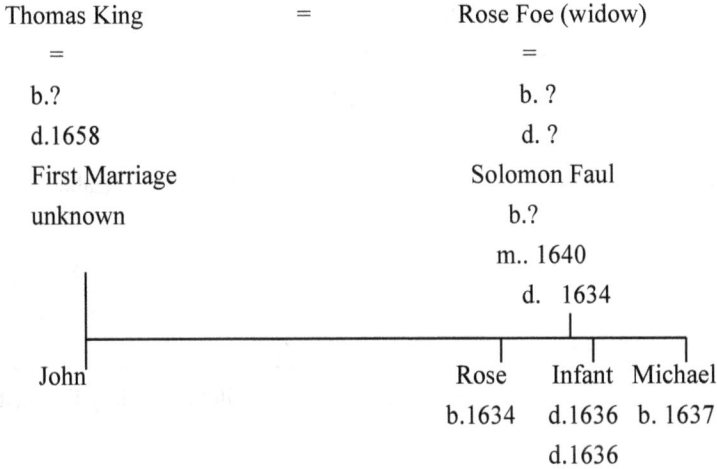

Thomas King	=	Rose Foe (widow)
=		=
b.?		b. ?
d.1658		d. ?
First Marriage		Solomon Faul
unknown		b.?
		m.. 1640
		d. 1634

John   Rose   Infant   Michael
              b.1634   d.1636   b. 1637
                          d.1636

Sources:

NA Parish Records of Peakirk and Glinton

NA. Will of Thomas King

2.3 Family of Randle Wildbore, Glinton, Northamptonshire

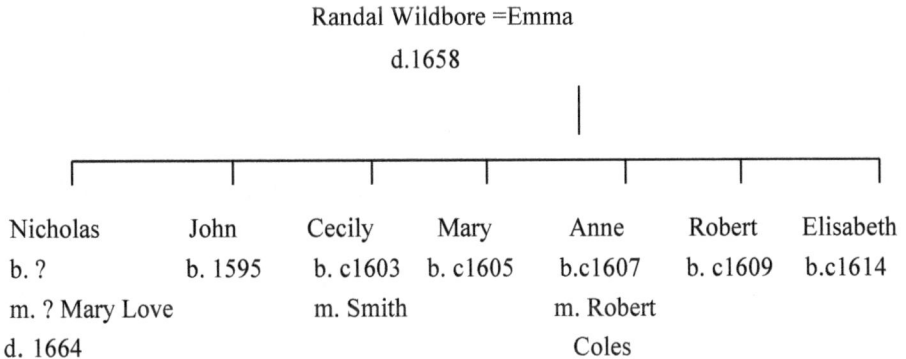

Randal Wildbore =Emma
d.1658

Nicholas	John	Cecily	Mary	Anne	Robert	Elisabeth
b. ?	b. 1595	b. c1603	b. c1605	b.c1607	b. c1609	b.c1614
m. ? Mary Love		m. Smith		m. Robert		
d. 1664				Coles		

Source: Will of Randle Wildbore

2.4. Family of Nicholas Wildbore, Braintree, Essex

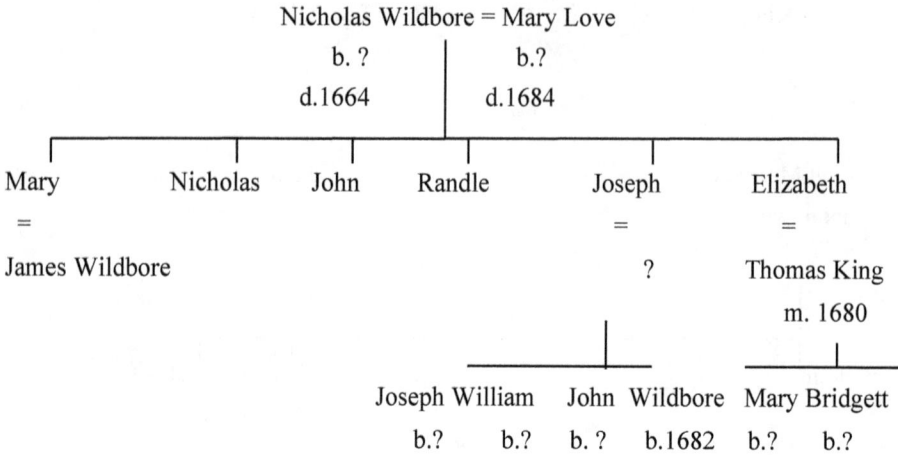

```
                    Nicholas Wildbore = Mary Love
                          b. ?              b.?
                         d.1664           d.1684
   ┌──────────┬──────────┬──────────┬──────────────┬──────────┐
  Mary      Nicholas    John     Randle         Joseph     Elizabeth
   =                                               =            =
James Wildbore                                     ?        Thomas King
                                                               m. 1680
                              ┌──────────┴──────────┐    ┌─────┴─────┐
                      Joseph William   John  Wildbore  Mary    Bridgett
                        b.?      b.?   b. ?   b.1682    b.?       b.?
```

Sources:

Will of Nicholas Wildbore

Will of Mary (Love)Wildbore

ERO. Parish Records

All Hallows, London Wall parish records for the marriage of Elizabeth Wildbore to Thomas King

At Stephens, Colman Street, London parish records for the baptism of Wildbore King

2.5. Family of Robert Wildbore, Colchester, Essex

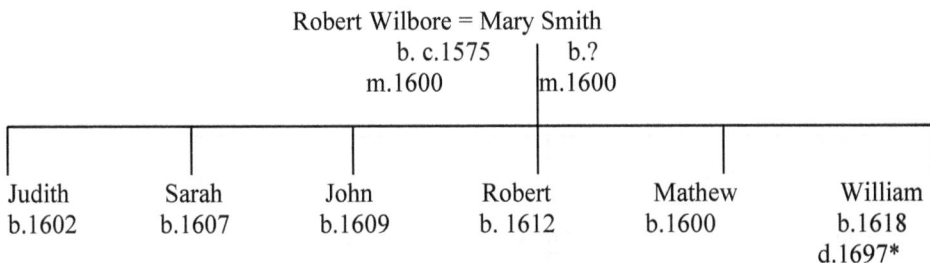

Robert Wilbore = Mary Smith
b. c.1575 | b.?
m.1600 | m.1600

Judith	Sarah	John	Robert	Mathew	William
b.1602	b.1607	b.1609	b. 1612	b.1600	b.1618
					d.1697*

Sources: ERO Parish Records of St Peter's and St Leonard's*
* Described as the Parish Clerk of this Parish who died in his 80th year.

Family of Alderman Thomas Lawrence, Colchester, Essex

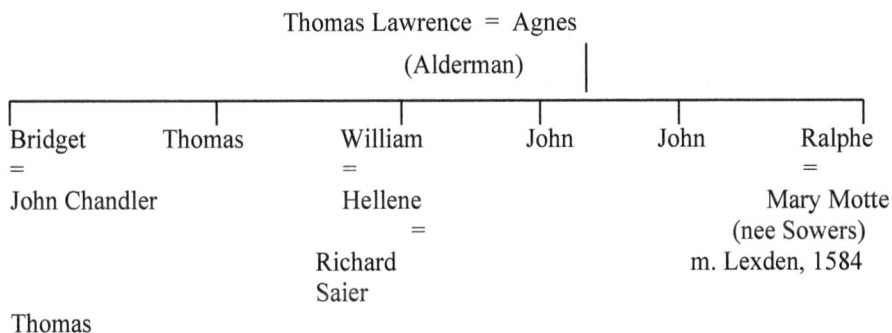

Thomas Lawrence = Agnes
(Alderman)

Bridget	Thomas	William	John	John	Ralphe
=		=			=
John Chandler		Hellene			Mary Motte
		=			(nee Sowers)
		Richard			m. Lexden, 1584
		Saier			
Thomas					

Sources: Will of Alderman Thomas Lawrence
        Will of William Lawrence
        ERO. St James,
.Colchester Parish Records

2.7. Family of William Lawrence, son of Alderman Thomas Lawrence, St James, Colchester. Essex

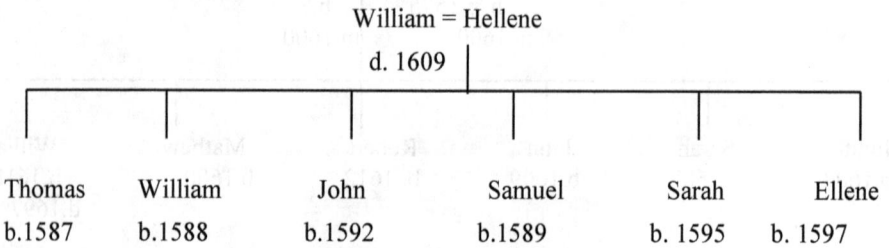

```
                    William = Hellene
                     d. 1609  |
  ┌──────┬────────┬────────┬────────┬────────┬────────┐
Thomas   William   John     Samuel   Sarah    Ellene
b.1587   b.1588   b.1592   b.1589   b. 1595  b. 1597
```

Sources: Will of William Lawrence
          ERO Parish Records

2.8. Family of Edward Lawrence, East Tilbury and Kent

John Lawrence
Captain of Tilbury Fort
d. 1557
=
Anne Giddinge

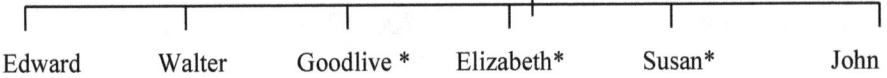

Edward	Walter	Goodlive *	Elizabeth*	Susan*	John
W. Farleigh, Kent					=
=					Ellene
Alice Cornelius					

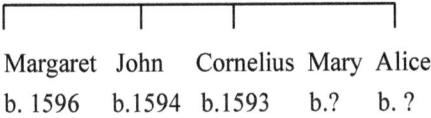

Margaret	John	Cornelius	Mary	Alice
b. 1596	b.1594	b.1593	b.?	b. ?

Alce	An.h	Wm	John	Marie	Judith	Gidd.ge	Ellene	Henry	Barbara	Alce	Oliver	Elizabeth	Thomas
1595	1596	1598	1599	1601	1603	1605	1606	1607	1610	1611	1612	1613	1616

Sources: Will of John Lawrence. Will of Edward Lawrence. Parish Records of East
Tilbury and West Farleigh

3. List of Lawrence Family Mayors of Colchester: 1625-1719

Name	Years
Edward Lawrence	1625.
James Lawrence	1706, 1711, 1713, 1719.
Nathanial Lawrence	1672, 1679, 1683, 1709.
Nathanial Lawrence, jnr	1706, 1711, 1713, 1719.
Thomas Lawrence	**1643, 1655.**

Source: Essex Record Office

Appendices

Arguments For and Against
the
Paternity of James Foe

1. The Nature of Historical Evidence

It is not for me to seek to teach anyone epistemology. However, I do wish to emphasise that readers of my narrative are invited to choose between two competing accounts of Defoe's early life. I suggest that they approach a judgement by considering the following.

1. Is there anything in either account that would seem to preclude the other? For example, the baptism record of Daniel Foe's birth would seem to preclude Defoe being the son of James Foe. In the seventeenth century the only documentary proof of a person's date, place of birth and biological parents was a record of his birth. Those readers who deny the obvious conclusion that Daniel Foe was the son of Daniel Foe and the grandson of another of the same name need to demonstrate that there were two contemporary Daniel Foe's/Defoe's in a small Etton family. I have been unable to do this and so has anyone else. Similarly, it is necessary for me, and anyone holding to my account, to be certain that there are no particulars in the entire period 1660-1731 for which the most logical explanation is that Defoe was born in 1660 to James and Alice Foe.

2. Therefore, there are two separate and related issues central to my narrative. First, I need to be able to show that Defoe was not resident in London in the period 1660 -1680 other than as a visitor and guest of his relatives and friends in 1660-1662. Defoe scholars have come up with several particulars which they believe show Daniel Defoe to be in London in the period and they are commented upon in the following appendices. Secondly, scholars have pointed out that there are events beyond the period 1660-1680 that tend to suggest that Defoe was the son of Daniel Foe. I consider these as well.

3. My work demonstrates something of the way knowledge is communicated through the ages and the nature of the proof of an historical, biographical, cultural and literary 'fact'. I do not pretend that these insights are unique to me because they are commonplace in social studies. [373]

---

[373] For example, see, Ed. Peter Howlett and Mary S Morgan. *How Well Do Facts Travel?* : *the dissemination of reliable knowledge*, Cambridge University Press, 2010.

4. While I do not wish to use ridiculous parallels, I suggest that the test of a philosophical or scientific theory is its ability to explain the phenomena it addresses. A new theory should re-place an old wherever and whenever it is demonstrated to explain more or better. For example, for some 300 years it was believed that Newtonian physics gave a complete explanation of the phenomena it sought to study. Einstein thought otherwise. If Newton were here to day he would accept the theory of relativity and seek to advance it.

5. Psychologically, it is not an easy matter to abandon or seriously modify a body of knowledge that has been relied upon for nearly three hundred years: there is a weight to it that seems to demand acquiescence. Some academics fear that changing the chronology of Defoe's narrative will diminish his reputation. However, in this instance the chronological changes I advance do not undermine his literary importance. The contrary is true. As in all new and persuasive alternative 'theories' and accounts a change in chronology opens up the possibility of new interpretations and understandings.

6. It is difficult for the average law-abiding, respectable person who admires Defoe's work to accept that Defoe was a great liar. Defoe set out to confuse people by lying about his age. It is not difficult to work out his method for doing it or the reasons for his behaviour. Lying was a character trait learnt in the struggle for survival as a young boy. It became habitual in a life of deceit. Defoe had compelling reasons for keeping silent about his origins. Beyond 1680 he lied to evade his numerous creditors and to escape identification, prosecution for piracy, the contraventions of the Navigation Acts, the handling of stolen goods - and a gruesome death. It would not have been prudent or sage for Defoe to reveal the truth of his beginnings and dubious activities. Much of Defoe's lying conveys the essence of the truth. His lying techniques were admirable but they did not always work.

7. It is not an easy matter for serious literary academics with a life-long commitment to one set of assumptions to abandon them for others. However, if it is true, that is if the balance of the evidence is decisively in favour of my narrative, as I believe it is, and if this is recognised by

individual scholars, it would be intellectually dishonest or deluded to continue to deny it.

8. A biographer of a seventeenth century man of ordinary or plebeian background cannot be expected to answer every question about him. It is especially difficult if the subject leads a secretive life. Consequently, the narrative I advance is not perfect or watertight in all respects. I cannot put right the errors of 280 years of Defoe biography entirely on my own in limited time and resources. I set out an outline of the further research needed to advance the new perspectives suggested in this work. It is for readers to decide whether this further work is done.

I do wish to emphasise that there are no other rational objections to the fact of Defoe's baptism on Dec 3, 1644 other than those discussed here. If the reader accepts that the argumentation is convincing then whatever reservations he might have should be put to one side. I appreciate that the outcome to my enquiry may be unwelcome. Many readers may wish to obfuscate at this point wishing the evidence to be otherwise and regretting a loss of the man they know to be Daniel Defoe, a person they have become accustomed to living with. This book does not limit or destroy the man known as Daniel Defoe. 'The king is dead, long live the king.'

2. Early Ascribed Works and Readings

Unfortunately it is true that any conscientious Defoe biographer, despite his best efforts to avoid it, runs into the vexed problems of attribution of works to Defoe. In particular, biographers have found problems in bridging the gap between Defoe's early life, about which very little has been written in the 'conventional account', and the 1680's when he emerged as a writer. Much has been made of Defoe's possible attendance at sermons delivered in London during 1681 by John Collins and of the attached thoughts on them written in *Meditations*. Similarly, *Historical Collections* an anonymous publication dated 1682 is also attributed to Defoe. Whether or not Defoe attended John Collins sermons or not is important to my narrative because it is difficult to explain his marriage to Jone Reade in Barbados if at the same time he was busy in London listening to John Collins. The Huntington Library has a provenance statement for the Collins sermons and *Meditations*.

John Collins Sermons

John Collins was in his day a well-known and celebrated preacher with a large Lime Street congregation. He was one of the original Pinners Hall lecturers.[374] By modern standards Collins would be thought an orthodox preacher of the Gospels but in his time he was controversial. Collins did not print any of his sermons or lectures for fear of prosecution. The enquirer is dependant, therefore, upon the notes of others. It may well be that these notes were circulated between dissenting preachers as a form of samizdat: write it out, copy it, return the original, and pass on.

The Huntington Library has a manuscript which it is claimed is Defoe's written word by word account of John Collins sermons taken while listening to them. It is suggested that the existence of these notes prove that he attended five of the six sermons given by Collins in 1681.

Max Novak wrote about the Huntington document as follows. 'On

---

[374] Backscheider, 28.

that Sunday, [20 February 1681] and on 26 March, 15 May, 12 June, 25 September and one following date, which Defoe omitted, Defoe attended and took down every word. Defoe was 'Absent in the Country' on 10 July and did not attend'. The Huntington manuscript contains a note on page 118 stating that 'There was a sermon preached between these two [that is, the June and September sermons] on ye 16th verse, which I being absent could not write.' (Signed. Daniel Defoe). The Huntington manuscript contains an undated copy of a sermon that could have been delivered on 10 July. I have reservations about the authenticity of the writing and the explanation as described above.

All the sermons in the Huntington manuscript are written in the same hand. It follows, therefore, that if the undated sermon was that of 10 July, as I believe thematically it was, Defoe could not have written down a note while listening to a sermon that he did not attend. There are a number of possible explanations. First, the handwriting might not be Defoe's. I compared the handwriting in the sermons with known examples of Defoe's writing. I found discordances which raised doubts in my mind as to the authenticity of the writing. However, I admit that although I have my doubts I am not an expert. Secondly, it is possible that Defoe attended 5 sermons, came into the possession of a copy of the missing sermon, or John Collins actual notes, copied it for himself and passed the original back to its owner. Thirdly, Defoe did not attend any of the sermons but came into the possession of copies of all 6 sermons and either passed them off as his own notes or wrote them up in his own hand with the intention of studying or using them in some publication of his own. The same reasoning applies to *Meditations*.

If he did the latter, Defoe may have set out to deceive. He would have wished to be in a position when he could have claimed that he attended the sermons. It was a Defoe technique to state partial truths. In this instance it would be along the lines of, 'Well I may not have attended them all but here are my notes.' It is known that Defoe was a prolific copier of existing manuscripts and kept notes and copies of many scripts and that he drew upon some of these in his own work entirely unacknowledged.

I have a common sense objection to the statement that Defoe 'wrote down every word of the sermons' while attending them. I use Pitman shorthand. I know that it is virtually impossible for a person using an advanced shorthand system, let alone some inferior version, to record every word of a sermon delivered in a public place? What did he use for a pen? What ink did he use? Was the lighting adequate? On what did he rest his paper? It is a simple matter to take down copies of a manuscript in a library or in the sanctity of your own home; and it is of course true that people in Defoe's time had developed skills in recording actual words spoken in a variety of public occasions including trials and parliamentary proceedings. However, a scribe recorded trial proceedings in a court room sitting at a desk, with an inkpot in front of him and a quill pen. A scribe possessed special skills, but I do not think he sought to write down every word spoken; and no doubt he could consult with others on the accuracy of his words.

A normal person speaks at a speed of 140-160 words per minute. You would need to be exceptionally skilled to write shorthand at that speed. It is known that Pepys developed his own system of shorthand. Much cannot be claimed for it. The principal editors of Bell's edition of the Diaries write, 'he used a method (mixing shorthand with heavily abbreviated longhand, and occasionally adding scrambled shorthand and full length writing)'. There is only one example, known to me, of Defoe using a similar method. Wright describes symbols and abbreviations used by Defoe in the composition of the *Compleat English Gentleman*.[375] In my judgement this does not amount to a system of shorthand. Specifically, Defoe could not have recorded a sermon delivered at 140-160 words per minute by using this method. I concluded that Defoe could not have written the sermons in the Huntingdon Library as assumed by the Library.

In practice those attending a sermon at this time or making notes at an educational establishment were able to make decent notes. In dissenting chapels a sermon was sometimes repeated. It was common practice to assist listeners on the second occasion by providing

---

[375] Wright, 376, 403

headers.[376] If abbreviations were used they would be incorporated in the notes taken. In this way a decent working copy could be obtained with the symbols and abbreviations clearly marked. A good sermon was repeatable and under the Conventical Acts could be read aloud subsequently to small numbers of people. Inevitably, the scrip became corrupted each time it was repeated.

The Huntingdon Library provenance statement indicates that the Rev. Duncan's first attempt to sell the documents was unsuccessful. It may be that there was at that time no link to Daniel Foe. It seems possible to me that the Defoe signature, which is questionable, may have been added to the manuscript to make it more sellable.

I wrote to the Huntingdon Library expressing my reservations about the documents. They conducted an enquiry into its provenance which did not include, as I had suggested, an examination of the handwriting. This enquiry decided that there were strong arguments for and against de-attribution and that it was up to scholars to decide.

Historical Collections

I have doubts also about *Historical Collections* but of a different kind. This is an unpublished autograph manuscript dated 1682, unsigned by Defoe, and purchased by the William Clark Memorial Library as 'non-ascribed' in 1951. There is no obvious reason for Defoe not wishing to sign the document if indeed he wrote it. It appears to be in Defoe's handwriting. I have suggested to the Library that they initiate a forensic examination of the writing.

The suggestion that this manuscript should be ascribed to Defoe originates with Max Novak who found it in the Clark Memorial Library.[377] This is how Novak described his discovery: '*Historical Collections* was named as one of 547 items in John Robert Moore's *Checklist of the Writings of Daniel Defoe*. Moore never saw the manuscript.' John Robert Moore and Max Novak rely on Walter

---

[376] I am indebted to the Dr Williams Library, London, who specialise in the sermons of

   dissenting ministers for this information.

[377] *The Clark Newsletter*, Fall 1981.

Wilson, *Memoirs of the Life and Times of Daniel Defoe*.[378] Wilson had heard of the manuscript from J. Duncan, the minister of a dissenting congregation at Wimborne, Dorsetshire (the source of the Notes on Collins Sermons) who appears to have come into the possession of some of Defoe's papers from either Hannah, Henrietta or Maria Defoe, all of whom were buried in Wimborne. Moore had speculated that this unseen manuscript (by either Wilson or Moore) might be a list of dates recording the remarkable events that occurred on the same day. *Historical Collections* does not do this so there is a possibility that Wilson was describing a different manuscript.

When individuals set out to deceive, especially if they have limited experience of the art, they make mistakes. I am sure that Defoe's descendents and Mr Duncan in Wimborne behaved with good if not strictly honourable intentions. It was not only the money. After all it would be important for the family to support the reputation of their most distinguished relative.

Without any evidence Max Novak has written: the introductory letter in the script to 'Clarinda', was probably to the woman he married, Mary Tuffley'. In that letter, Defoe says that he had recorded his histories without changing them in significant ways to which Novak adds the thought that 'he told stories as Defoe was always to tell stories'.

Novak and other writers have suggested that *Historical Collections* was given as a gift to Mary Tuffley as part of a courtship. An unfriendly critic, Leo Abse, has described *Historical Collections*, as an unlikely wooing gift. He writes that such a gift 'would be likely to strike fear and apprehension in a teenager, the only protected daughter of a wealthy merchant.' This is what Abse wrote:[379]

> The stories...are replete with violence: forty of them involve death and execution with the moral instruction usually accompanying the original texts expurgated; most of the tales are of ruthless heroes...men triumphing and

---

[378] Wilson, Walter.
[379] Abse, Leo, 11.

overcoming their enemies by their wit and remarkable displays of strength...

There are other and more likely explanations of the manuscript. I suggest *Historical Collections* is an example of Defoe's habit of collecting and copying the manuscripts of other people. Defoe gives a clue that this is what he had done by writing in his explanation that 'he recorded [that is he had copied the original stories] without altering them in significant ways'. It is clear. Defoe was not the author of *Historical Collections* as such but an editor. Given that he did not write them, there were many possible reasons for not publishing them under his own name. For example, if the writer of the collection of these stories was still alive, any claim by Defoe of his authorship might be challenged. Defoe waited. Thus *Historical Collections* may well fall into the category of copied manuscripts. Defoe may have written out the narratives and added to them in some minor way. The problem for a commentator is whether he did enough to claim the work as his own. Borrowing the ideas of other people is not a sin. All creative writers are great thieves in that they filch ideas and plots from others. There are a limited number of plots, after all. However, to be too bold invites legal objection.

I conclude that not much can be claimed for Defoe's authorship. On a practical level the linkage to Mary Tuffley is improbable. Mary Tuffley was 17 years of age at her marriage in January, 1684. In 1682 she would have been 15 years of age. In December, 1681 Defoe's legal wife, Jone Reade had died, and the chronology I supply here for Defoe shows that he could not have been in England until late in 1682. I have suggested that Defoe's marriage to Mary Tuffley was in some sense arranged and mercenary in motivation. He was seeking a dowry. A love gift was not likely to be something to which he gave much thought.

The Huntington Library bought these two manuscripts in good faith. The issue for Defoe scholars is to what extent these documents can be regarded as Defoe's. Clearly, neither document originated with him. The sermons originated with Collins who might also have written the *Meditations*. It can be argued that Collins is the writer to be celebrated.

A number of people would have had copies. Ownership, possession, cannot in itself become a yardstick to measure authorship. I possess a copy of *Robinson Crusoe*. Self-evidently, I am not the author. In English law copyright can be claimed if someone materially alters, selects or re-arranges material. For example, the editor of an anthology can claim copyright. Defoe added nothing to Collins sermons but might, if he wrote it, have claimed copyright for *Meditations*.

A claim to the authorship of *Historical Collections* raises different considerations. I believe this work is best ascribed to Defoe as an anthology.

3. Family, Friends and Kinship

In contrast with the evidence of the disjunctive family life of both James Foe and Daniel Defoe, biographers and commentators have persisted in assuming that they had nuclear or companionate marriages in keeping with seventeenth century social trends in family life. The authorities mostly drawn upon have been the pioneering studies of the Cambridge Population Group and the interpretive survey of Ralph Houlbrooke.[380]

The evidence has always been conflicting. Whereas Habakkuk[381] has suggested a reversion to marriages of convenience in the latter half of the seventeenth century, Laurence Stone has argued for a continuous evolution towards the nuclear family.[382] Social trends have been understood as supporting Habakkuk in that there appears to have been a surplus of unmarried women and a male reluctance to marry in the late Georgian period. Domestic servants were plentiful and cheap and sex, therefore, was freely available without the tie of a legal marriage.

Since the 1970's, however, it has become clear that new concepts are needed to understand seventeenth century family life through to the second half of the eighteenth century. Linguistic studies have resulted in new conclusions. When the language used by people living at the time, literary or otherwise, is examined, it can be seen that the predominant family form at the time was the family-household. In the language of contemporaries when they wrote about families they meant households. These households included many diverse dependants: friends, servants, apprentices and co-resident relatives.

As late as 1755 Samuel Johnson defined a family 'as those who lived in the same house'. In writing about Foe family households, I draw upon the work of the English language academics who have

---

[380] Cambridge Group for the History of Population and Social Structure, Dept. of Geography, University of Cambridge. Houlebrook, R. *The English Family*, 1450-1700, Longman, 1984.
[381] Habbakuk, H.J. *Marriage Settlements in the Eighteenth Century* , London, 1950.
[382] Stone, Laurence. *Family, Sex and Marriage in England*, 1550-1880, Penguin, Abridged Edition, 1990.

explored the family-household concept and in particular on the work of Naomi Tadmor. [383] Tadmor has advanced the theory that the family as a household is the best way to understand family life in Defoe's period. She argues that if we need to think of a typical family establishment it consisted of a male head as Father; a wife, nurse or other such person, as the female housekeeper; children, whether or not related to the father; and friends, servants, neighbours and apprentices. An example of such a family would be that of Mr B. in Samuel Richardson's *Pamela*. [384] Mr B. was a bachelor and an orphan so it follows that he is not a biological father, husband, brother or sister to anyone in his family.

In these families kin was included but in some households friendship was more important. 'Friends' might act as kin but some families included no kin and no one acting as kin. Membership of a family might be temporary and non-exclusive. People could be, and often were, members of multiple families. (The cover of Tadmor's book gives a picture of a middle aged man taking a fond farewell of a female partner with the words, 'You may expect to see me again Sunday Fortnight.')

While much of this description of family is known, literary biographers seem to have ignored it in writing about Defoe and other writers of his period. It should not be neglected in literary studies, however, because not only is it evidence of the family life of literary figures but a sure guide to how they thought and, in practice, how they behaved.

In particular it should not be ignored in accounts of Defoe's life. I have written in another work about marriage, dowries, patrimony and other domestic arrangements in Early Modern England [385] and I do not want to replicate it here. I restrict my comments to particular characteristics of Defoe's family life that biographers have had difficulty in comprehending despite the growing evidence of his

[383] Tadmor, Naomi. *Family and Friends in Eighteenth Century England: Household, Kinship and Patronage*, Cambridge University Press, 2001.
[384] Richardson, Samuel. *Pamela*, Oxford World's Classics, 2008.
[385] *Beyond Belief*, 61, 65-66, 296 n. 68, 302, n.188.

multiple marriages and domestic arrangements. I categorise them as follows:

1 Definition of Marriage

Under the Marriage Act, 1753 a marriage was defined as a promise freely given by men and women to live together and to bring up children. The Act legalised common practice.

2. Church Marriage

If this marriage was solemnised in a church it carried full inheritance rights and dowry and jointure rights.

3. Private Treaty

Many marriages were not solemnised in a church. Couples could regard themselves as married when they entered freely into an arrangement to live together and bring up children whether by ceremony or otherwise.[386] Such a marriage possessed all the legal rights of a church marriage other than inheritance or dowry rights.

4. Same-sex Marriages

In Defoe's fictions sexual relations between men are often described as 'marriages'. This usage is deeply embedded in the language of his time. There are numerous examples in a number of Defoe fictions. The best examples are in *Moll Flanders*.

3. Domestic Arrangement

A domestic arrangement falling short of an intention of permanent cohabitation, and without a specific joint responsibility for the caring of children, was not a marriage.

4. Bigamy

The Bigamy Act, 1603 made bigamy a felony punishable by death. It was defined as more than one church marriage at the same time. If one marriage was a church wedding and the other a marriage by private consent the second was not regarded as bigamous. Trials for bigamy were rare.

---

[386] See *Colonel Jack* 249, for such a ceremony.

5. Incest

Incest was common. Churches considered incest to be a sin and therefore shameful but it was not declared illegal in England until the Incest Act, 1908.

6. Children

Children were regarded as little adults and treated as such. Children were the property of their parents and in particular of the father. It was thought right to punish children severely to drive out sin. The legal age of consent for sex with children was twelve. An offence was punishable by a fine. Sex with minors was common. [387]

7. Defoe and Shunamatism

Defoe practiced shunamatism as advocated by Francis Bacon in the early seventeenth century. Shunamitism is the pseudo-scientific belief that sleeping with young people will extend life. This belief got Defoe into trouble.[388]

8. Homosexuality

In modern terminology Defoe was bisexual. Homosexual acts were illegal throughout his life and at times dangerous to him.[389]

5 Defoe's Domestic Arrangements

To my knowledge, Defoe was never a bigamist although his son Benjamin Norton was one.[390] In a Chart, I set out Defoe's wives and children to the best of my knowledge and understanding. He had two Church marriages. The first was to Jone Reade, in Barbados in May, 1681. Their marriage is recorded in the Parish Records of St. Michael's, Bridgetown. Jone died seven months into the marriage.[391] The second church marriage, by Special Licence, was to Mary Tuffley, 1684-1731, St Botolph, Aldgate, in London. There are two 'known marriages' by private consent: Elisabeth Sammens, c.1692-c.1707, and

---

[387] Read my discussion in Martin, John. *The Man Himself, a Life of Jonathan Swift.*
[388] *Beyond Belief,* 42-3.
[389] Abse, 27, 31.
[390] *Beyond Belief,* chart 2, 289.
[391] Birth in May, 1681 and death in December, 1681.

Mary Norton c.1697-1731. For some time Defoe shared a family establishment with the Sammens as described above,[392] and was mocked for it, but at another time he and Elisabeth Sammens shared a family establishment with their two children Sarah and Daniel.[393]

By my account Defoe was resident in Brazil in 1662-1680 when a young man aged nineteen to thirty-six. years of age It seems highly likely that he had a 'marriage' of some kind and that there were children. In *Farther Adventures* a dialogue between Will Atkins and his native wife suggests, if we assume it to be autobiographical in origin, that he did 'marry' but not in a church. A Roman Catholic priest officiated. Roman Catholicism was the official religion of Brazil at the time.[394]

It seems to me that a man living in the Early Modern Period who spent long periods of time in several places would settle in some way into several homes and personal relationships in which children would be produced. Defoe lived 60 years of his life, on and off, in Essex; 18 years in Brazil; and 30 years or more in London and the Home Counties. In these places he had 'wives' and children. It was usual for a person living a life like Defoe to have multiple 'marriages' and other domestic household arrangements. It was not extraordinary then and, perhaps, not so very unusual in our own fully accountable times. We have other names now.

---

[392] *Beyond Belief,* second edition, n.134, 299.
[393] *Beyond Belief,* 92.
[394] *Farther Adventures of Robinson Crusoe,* 99-106.

4. Newington Academy for Dissenters

It is widely accepted by biographers that when Defoe was 14-16 years of age his putative father, James Foe, sent him to study at the Newington Green Academy for Dissenters for four or five years of formal education in lieu of study at Oxford or Cambridge University, most probably in the period 1674-1680, and under the tutelage of Charles Morton. An assumption made here is that James Foe was a religious dissenter, in all probability a Presbyterian, and thus Defoe was barred from attending Cambridge or Oxford because of his unwillingness to take an oath of loyalty to the Crown. Readers may be surprised to learn that there is no documentary evidence that Defoe was a student at the Newington Academy in this period or for any course of study similar to that of a university education at any time. He never claimed it. Furthermore his two sons, Daniel and Benjamin, were not educated at an Academy; and in adult life Defoe *did* swear an oath of loyalty.

I invited critics of my discovery that Defoe had been born in 1644 to give me any instance or event that would place Defoe in London in the period 1660–1680 as the biological son of James Foe. A number responded. In all instances they quoted Defoe's attendance at Newington Green Academy in the 1670's. They are wrong in believing this as I shall endeavour to demonstrate.

Academic critics today are supported by the unanimous conclusion of biographers over 280 years. How can it be then that I dispute the received wisdom of successive generations of so many good scholars? Surely it has become a social fact? In an earlier work I wrote:

> It is often assumed that a fact is a fact but the life of a fact is a complex matter. Everyday experience suggests that, like gossip, facts that travel rarely remain stable and they may be perpetuated by and re-formed in myth, folk tales and victim psychology. Historical accounts reveal that 'facts' about behaviour are often invented, altered, or removed in historical accounts depending on who is telling the story,

and why. Some social scientists maintain that units of selection in culture, 'memes', are passed through the ages much as genes as units of selection in evolution. In the 'viral account' memes are regarded as strongly analogous with genes. These viral memes move from mind to mind. The consequent, invented and re-fashioned 'facts' then become part of the received wisdom at any moment of time. Although biographers do not really mean to do it, this fund of received wisdom is drawn upon, added to and embellished with each new biographical attempt.[395]

I maintain that the nature of Defoe's education is a good example of the perils of received wisdom. At its root, the problem arises because it is difficult for a modern scholar educated for many years in a good university to conclude that Defoe was largely self-taught. How could it be possible that a man with such a sophisticated conceptual understanding of the world he lived in could acquire such distinction without a higher education of some kind? But he didn't. In this appendix I suggest how the error occurred in biographical accounts.

Over the years four main reasons have been advanced for the belief that Defoe attended the Newington Green Academy and I comment on them as follows.

1. His Own Words

In 1709 Defoe wrote that he was 'first...set apart for, and then ...set apart from the Honour of that Sacred Employ [that of clergyman].[396] It is assumed from this ambiguous statement that his putative father, James Foe, decided that young Daniel at 14 years of age should enter the ministry and that the place to study theology was the Newington Green Academy for Dissenters. In contrast, I have argued that the most that can be considered as supporting the conclusion of Defoe's religious seriousness in the early 1680's is that he may have had a desire to repent his sins and obtain redemption from them. He may have listened to, or read copies, of sermons from such people as Collins

---

[395] *Beyond Belief*, vi.
[396] *Review*: 6.341, for 22 October 1709.

and Annesley. Defoe may have involved himself in religious studies and readings; and he may have considered also, or fantasised about, becoming a minister. At this time, 1680-1682, he might have had contact with Charles Morton. Defoe may have received scriptural reading lists from Morton and discussed them with him. It is possible also that Morton, Penn or some other person lent him copies of Collins sermons with the advice to copy them out and return the originals. I have no documentary evidence for these propositions but they amount to a passable conjecture.

The conviction that Defoe mentioned Charles Morton in his writings and gave public recognition to the value of the instruction he received as a pupil of his at Newington Green has been carried forward into our present time. Writing in 1989, Backscheider states, 'To the end of his life he spoke of *his* [italics mine] education there with pride, and many of his interests, abilities and opinions show the influence of Morton's school.' But that is just what he did not do – that is, attend the Academy, as Backscheider suggests, for a period of four years in the 1670's. [397]

Defoe could not have done this because he was not in London in the 1670's, James Foe was not his father, and he was too old to attend the Academy in the period 1670-1680. However, it is likely that following his return to London in 1680, Defoe did become aware of Morton's teaching methods and that he did 'admire them'.

2. James Foe's Religious Beliefs

By a series of non-sequiturs, we have the following reasoning. As Daniel Defoe was a Dissenter it is supposed that James Foe must have been one too. The Foe family of Etton baptised their children in St Stephen's the Anglican Church in the village. James Foe recorded the births of his two daughters Mary and Elisabeth at St Giles, Cripplegate in London where he lived at the time. His parish Vicar, Samuel Annesley, left St Giles following the Act of Uniformity, 1662 and set up a nonconformist meeting house at Little St Helen's in London. It is

---

[397] Backscheider, 16-22.

assumed by modern biographers that James Foe left St Giles to worship there. There is no evidence that he did. Annesley's congregation in St Giles was one of the largest in London and James Foe was a busy merchant who travelled abroad. It is unlikely that they knew much of each other or that they kept in touch as friends.

The myth of their friendship was perpetuated over a long period of time. Thomas Wright, in 1879, felt able to write as follows: [398]

> When about fourteen Defoe *was placed by his father, who intended him for the Dissenting ministry,* [italics mine] at a well-known academy at Newington Green, conducted by that polite and profound scholar, Charles Morton. Mr Morton, styled by those who did not love him 'a rank Independent' had formerly been rector of Blisland, in Cornwall, and was one of the two thousand ejected in 1662. To the goodness and learning of his tutor…Defoe pays many a tribute; and he also looks back to the liberality of his father, who spared nothing that might qualify his son to make a good scholar. [Morton]…drilled his pupils in English…Besides theological knowledge, Defoe was grounded in Latin, Greek, French, Spanish and Italian…other subjects were mathematics, natural philosophy, logic, geography, and history, especially ecclesiastical.

This passage is pure invention and without factual basis in anything it states about Defoe and James Foe.

The most ingenious account that James Foe was a Dissenter has been given by Frank Bastian in 1981. He writes: [399]

> Defoe was born in Cripplegate, London where James Foe lived and where the births of his two daughters were recorded but described as 'Not Christened' in St Giles, Cripplegate in 1657 and 1659. [By the time of Defoe's birth,

---

[398] Wright, 9.
[399] Bastian, 14-17.

Bastian argues, the Parish had reverted to an original practice of recording not births but baptisms,] ergo, [f James Foe was against baptism in 1660, Daniel Foe's birth would not have been recorded.]

However, the known facts do not support Bastian. Annesley, the Vicar of St Giles, baptised his own children. As he left the Church of England in 1662 it might be supposed that he had become something of a Presbyterian. If James Foe had followed him, he too would have been something of one. However, Presbyterians were in favour of child baptism. Bastian suggests, therefore, that in 1660 James Foe might have succumbed to supporting a fanatical sect opposed to baptism and/or Alice Foe his wife, was a Quaker and, therefore, opposed to baptism. Such presumptions are without evidential foundation. They are entirely conjectural. If they are evaluated as such they are unlikely and without conviction. Nothing is known about the life and death of Alice Foe.

Notwithstanding these difficulties, Bastian presses on. He suggests that given that Annesley was once the Vicar of St Giles he must have been a friend of the Foe family; that in manhood Defoe attended Annesley's religious services and, further, that he became a personal friend of Defoe. The evidence for these conjectures is that Defoe wrote an Elegy in praise of Annesley upon his death in 1697. The Elegy cannot be read as supporting these propositions.[400] And then in order to substantiate his point on the Foes being Presbyterian, Bastian writes, 'Whatever the truth… Defoe certainly sprang from a strongly Puritan background.' In several of the more strict interpretations of the word, Defoe was not a Puritan nor brought up as one. He was always an immigrant Huguenot at heart and as such centred in Dissent.

There is a gap of at least 10 years from Annesley's ejection from St Giles and the opening of Charles Morton's Newington Green Academy. What is being supposed is that Annesley and James Foe kept in touch throughout this period and Annesley knew sufficient about Defoe to urge his father James to send him to the Academy. These are most unlikely conjectures.

---

[400] Novak, 42.

434

When Backscheider writes that to the end of his life Defoe wrote in support of Charles Morton and the Academy she meant comments such as those in *The Compleat English Gentleman,* 1729 written some 50 years after Defoe's supposed stay at the Academy. Defoe wrote these words:

> I was once *acquainted* [italics mine] with a tutor of unquestioned reputation for learning, and who was himself a critick in the learned languages and even the oriental tongues, as the Syriac, Chaldee, Arabic and Hebrew ...[he compelled] all their pupils to learn the sciences [in English].... He taught Physicks ...Astronomy, Geography...all the parts of academical learning, except Medicine and Surgery ...And he taught in English.

Max Novak believes that Defoe had given his readers the best exposition of Morton's education that has been written.[401] However, three things are clear about the piece. First Defoe describes his subject as an *acquaintance* not a teacher; secondly, it does not refer to Defoe as a pupil of the Academy and is not, therefore, a proof that he was one; thirdly, he does not refer to Morton by name. It is possible to read the piece as proof that in 1729 Defoe admired, and had a good understanding of a system of education that could be Morton's. There is a difficulty even in this. No one to my knowledge has ever made a claim that Morton was an expert in oriental languages although, of course, as a student at Wadham College, Oxford he might have become one. Defoe may have been alluding to a tutor who taught him between the ages of fourteen to sixteen or an acquaintance made in Brazil.

Writing in 1958, John Robert Moore takes the argument that Defoe attended the Academy a stage further by pointing out to his readers that probably the character of the gunner who imparted knowledge to *Captain Singleton* in the book of that name was based on Charles Morton.[402] Defoe described his learning experience with this gunner as follows:

---

[401] Novak, 42.
[402] Moore, John Robert, 35.

The gunner was an excellent mathematician, a good scholar, and a *complete sailor*...[italics mine] finding me eager to understand and learn, he laid the foundation of a general knowledge of things in my mind, gave me just ideas of the form of the earth and of the sea, the situation of the countries, the course of the rivers, the doctrine of the seas, the motion of the stars; and in a word, taught me a kind of system of astronomy, which I afterwards improved.

The extract suggests to me that the gunner was proficient in navigation and had thought about his subject. Of course, Moore was unaware of the wealth of practical knowledge Defoe had acquired in the perils of piloting a ship on the high seas.

I have argued that Defoe was largely self-taught. There are several occasions in his fictions that suggest that this is so and the extract Moore quotes from *Captain Singleton* is one of them. A further illustration of the process is provided in *Colonel Jack*. Defoe writes that Jack came into the frame of mind 'that he might still be born for greater things...that it was honesty and virtue alone that made men rich and great, and gave them a fame as well as a figure in the world and that he had learned to read and write [and] began to love books'. *Colonel Jack* bought a collection of books of classical history, philosophy and ethics, and then came to know an excellent scholar who taught him Latin and other languages. [403]

As Defoe passed into manhood, if we follow his fictional characters, he developed a desire to learn. He seized every opportunity to acquire knowledge. When this new learning was combined with his house-education (most probably lessons in English for he lacked Latin) and his keen verbal knowledge of continental politics, arising from his intense intellectual gifts and his search for personal identity, in all probability he had achieved a good conceptual understanding of his world and of the life he led. This served him well as an education. However, there were rough edges to his knowledge that made him an object of derision to his many enemies. For those who despised him,

---

[403] *Colonel Jack*, 177.

these limitations stood as general evidence that he was not as he claimed to be. His critics thought him to be a charlatan and that they had a duty to expose him.

Throughout his adult life Defoe was criticised for a lack of education. It was supposed that he had no further education after the age of fourteen In particular his Latin was thought of a poor quality. Proficiency in Latin was regarded as the hall mark of a gentleman so, ipso facto, Defoe was not one. Furthermore Defoe's critics, and there were many, noticed something very odd about Defoe's use of Latin. As I have explained earlier in this text, he spoke a kind of vulgar or colloquial Latin that was used as common discourse in France, Italy, Spain and Portugal in the seventeenth century. Not unreasonably some critics concluded that there was more to Defoe's background than he was willing to explain.

Charles Gildon in his fierce and compelling onslaught on the literary virtues of *Robinson Crusoe* and its author reflected the uncertainties and contempt that was widely felt about Defoe's written work, his character and behaviour. He believed that *Robinson Crusoe* was a disguised and allegorical account of Defoe's own life. *Crusoe* described his education as follows, 'My Father, who was very ancient, had given me a competent Share of Learning, as far as House–Education, and a country Free-School generally goes...' Gildon had never heard of such an education by which he meant that this was not an education proper to a literary man or of a gentleman. As readers of this work will know I describe Defoe's education as being precisely as Defoe had supposed it to have been and as he described as *Crusoe's* in *Robinson Crusoe.*

Defoe was never comfortable about this type of criticism. He responded by stating the virtues of being taught in English and wrote repeatedly on the theme. If so, must have thought his critics, if this man was taught in English (and taught Latin too) at an Institute where else could he have acquired the knowledge other than at a Dissenting Academy?

2. The Special Role of Samuel Annesley

These accounts by previous biographers give a special role to Samuel

Annesley. They were conscious that it would add force to the conjecture that Defoe sought a religious education at the age of fourteen at Newington Green Academy if Annesley was seen to be playing a special role. Annesley must be the missing link and the driving force that propelled Defoe into the Academy. There is no evidence for this theory but by the linking of non sequiturs an argument has been constructed.

It is said that James Foe was a member of Annesley's Meeting House in St Helens; Annesley and James Foe were good friends; Annesley knew the young Defoe and recognised his potential; that as an adult Defoe knew Annesley through his friend John Dunton, who was married to one of Annesley's daughters; and that Defoe was a personal friend of both Dunton and Samuel Annesley.

Frank Bastian expresses these thoughts as follows: 'Dunton had married a daughter of the Rev Samuel Annesley, whose meeting house at Little St Helens, was attended by Defoe...*whether or not the Foes had been regular members of his congregation since his ejection in 1662.*' (italics mine) Dunton wrote in 1707 that Defoe was 'a great admirer and consistent Hearer of my Reverend Father in Law Dr Annesley.'[404] Backscheider quotes several remarks made by Dunton in support of Defoe and his writing. Dunton wrote that Defoe's 'thoughts on any Subject are always *Surprising, New,* and *Singular*'.[405]

However, dates are important and critical in these accounts. The particulars referred to in these accounts relate to events in the period 1680-1697. There is no piece of information that could arguably be taken as a fact and, ipso facto, that could be concluded as convincing when considered in a broader context. There is nothing in them that could amount to a supportable conviction that Annesley and James Foe were friends and that they kept in touch with each other in the 1670's It does seem plausible that Defoe attended some of Annesley's sermons in the period 1680-1697 but his Ode to Annesley upon his death in 1697 is evidence of respect rather than friendship. It is most unlikely,

[404] Dunton, John. *Impeachment*, 1704.
[405] Backscheider, 178-180, n.32.

therefore, that Annesley could have been a driving force impelling Defoe into the Newington Academy in 1674-1679.

3. The Boy Genius

John Robert Moore was aware that something more was needed. After all, the natural route for Daniel Foe, if a child of James Foe, was an apprenticeship into trade, the route taken by James and his brother Henry. How then was Defoe picked out for a different kind of education in the ways of the world? Moore suggests that perhaps this boy possessed a mysterious religiosity and others 'mistook his religious zeal for the mysterious 'call' to preach the gospel' and further that 'Annesley (who it is said had great influence in the selection of candidates for the ministry) had recognised something of the boy's abilities and *had urged* (italics mine) that he be trained to the ministry.' This is fantasy and pure and unconvincing conjecture as I have sought to explain.[406]

4. Nudges and Winks

It might be thought odd, and not unreasonably, that if Defoe had attended the Newington Green Academy for Dissenters, and was proud of it, that he failed to answer his critics by saying so. He might have written along the following lines: 'Yes, indeed I did have a further education. I attended the Newington Green Academy for Dissenters in 1674-1679 and was given a fine education, with lessons in English, by that distinguished scholar Charles Morton.' Why not, why did he not declare it? There was no danger of prosecution. Charles Morton had died in America in 1695 and the Academies had become respectable before the Schism Act, 1713 which brought them to an end. Defoe would have been safe from any criticism because it would have been clear that although he had a higher education he had been taught in English. By making such a remark, Defoe could have enlisted the support of his contemporaries alive that day, who could have vouched for it. Those academics that persist at this point of my narrative in believing that Defoe attended the Newington Green Academy might be

---

[406] Moore, John Robert, 32.

asked the perfectly fair question as to why he did not say so clearly and explicitly.

Instead of such a frank response, Defoe sought to counter his critics by offering them a series of hints, nudges, and sly allusions. If these statements are taken seriously it might reasonably be assumed from them that Defoe was suggesting to his critics that he had a relationship of some kind with Charles Morton and, in particular that Morton had assisted him in theological studies and, on some occasion, poetry. These subjects were necessary accoutrements for a gentleman wishing to engage in political and religious discourse.

4. Contemporary Evidence

It would have been compelling evidence of attendance if Defoe had been able to name a contemporary. It can be argued that Defoe came close to doing this. For example, in *The Present State of the Parties in Great Britain*, 1712, when he names Samuel Wesley as being taught by the same person as him.[407] I believe that the words of this pamphlet are proof in themselves to some that Defoe attended the Newington Green Academy of Dissenters in 1675-79. Specifically Defoe wrote that he and Samuel Wesley had been taught poetry by the same scholar. It was known at the time that Wesley had spent time at the Newington Academy and so, ipso facto, had Defoe. Morton did not have a reputation for teaching poetry.

However, on examination this statement cannot be relied upon. It is suggested that the mention of Samuel Wesley by name as a fellow scholar, if untrue, might have been expected to invoke a denial by him. First, Defoe does not state that Wesley was present at the Academy when he was a pupil. It is difficult to assume that Wesley was at Newington Green in the period 1675-79 and, therefore, in a position to confirm one way or another that Defoe was present there at that time. According to the National Dictionary of Biography, Wesley attended a grammar school in Dorchester. He was sent away from home to study theology under Theosophilus Gale who died in 1678. Subsequently,

---

[407] BL.1141.i.23. *The Present State of the Parties*, London, 1712.

Wesley attended another grammar school before proceeding to a Dissenting Academy under Edward Veal in Stepney. At some later date he studied at Newington Green. The exact dates are uncertain. It seems probable that Wesley was not at the Newington Academy until the 1680's and could not have been a student there in 1674-1679. Aware of this difficulty, Bastian writes that Samuel Wesley…attended from 1680 or 1681 until 1683…' Bastian is stretching the truth of it by extending dates but by his own analysis Wesley attended the Newington Academy in the early 1680's.

Even if it were to be assumed that they were there at the same time, Defoe might have been able to rely on Wesley's reticence and unwillingness to deny or confirm any such claim. There were reasons for Wesley not being willing to challenge Defoe, assuming he had read *The Present State of the Parties* in the first place. In the 1680's Wesley moved smartly to the right in theological matters and he became a critic of Dissenting Academies. He allied himself with Sacheverell, Defoe's target in the *Shortest Way* and an enemy not only of him but of the Whigs. Wesley had the worst of the public debate. He was savagely attacked by Defoe and described by him in the *Review* as our 'Mighty Champion of this very High Church.'[408] Following this debacle Wesley seems to have resolved not to enter into this type of political debate again.

Wesley had a reputation for being a good poet. By raising Wesley's name in the way he did Defoe was seeking to make a simple point: that Wesley was not superior to him in intellect, integrity or in literature for he, Defoe, had enjoyed a similar education to Wesley as a poet; but that unlike Wesley he had stayed loyal to his religious and political views and in support of the Dissenting Academies – a protestation not strictly true.

Lastly, there is Defoe's statement in his introduction to The *True Collection*, 1703 in which he writes that he gained what *little* (italics mine) education he had received from Charles Morton. Literary critics are quick off the mark. 'There you are', it has been said, 'that proves

[408] *Review*: 11, n. 87, September 22, 1705.

it.' However, I suggest it is always necessary with Defoe to ask two questions before interpreting any statement by him: first what was his purpose in writing and secondly what does he mean? In this publication Defoe is seeking to gain reader approval for works of his that he felt he could acknowledge at the time; and secondly he needed to ride as best he could on Morton's coat-tails in the certain knowledge that otherwise his education could be derided. Defoe seems to have held a physiocratic theory of education: there was a quantity of knowledge at any point of time and a system to become aware of it. Readers will recognise that this being so, Defoe's comment is consistent with my own explanation: that is, Defoe knew something of Morton and might have been helped by him in the early 1680's.

And there the issue lies for readers to make their own choice. I offer the evidence that Defoe was not in London in the 1670's. Even if it were assumed that he was, by my chronology, he would have been too old to attend the Academy as a formal student in 1670-1680. My own judgement is simple to express. Defoe knew of Morton and his work at Newington Green. He may have met Morton after his return to London in 1680. It was important for Defoe to claim a higher education despite having little knowledge of Latin. It is possible that Morton helped him in some ways in his theological studies by suggesting reading matter. There is conjectural evidence that Defoe attended religious meeting houses in 1680-1697 and followed the sermons of leading divines of his time. Both Penn and Defoe had knowledge of Morton and the Newington Academy because they had lived in Stoke Newington at different times and had friends there. It is likely also that Defoe read the sermons and other literature of such men as Collins, Morton and Annesley. Defoe could have been frank about all these matters but he chose not to do so for his own highly complex reasons.

It follows from this analysis of mine that it is incorrect for literary critics to make much of the *limited* knowledge Defoe may have acquired from Morton. He was not a student at Newington Green Academy in 1674-1680.

5. The Worshipful Company of Butchers

It has been advanced as a proof that Defoe was the biological son of James Foe that he applied successfully in January 1687/8 to become a member of The Worshipful Company of Butchers on the grounds of Patrimony.

Paul Dottin writing in 1928 quotes the following entry in the books of the Corporation of Butchers dated January 26: 'At a Court held in Pudding Lane, Daniel Foe, son of James Foe, citizen and butcher of Fore Street, Cripplegate, attended to apply for his admission by patrimony, and was admitted accordingly, and paid in discharge of all offices, L.10 15s.'[409]

However, the actual Admission itself is in the Freedom Admissions Record Book[410] and it reads as follows: 1687/8. Jan 12. Danl. Foe fil Jacobi Foe cet. LL Libre Fact per patrimony & sol. I assume that there was no particular reason for Defoe to attend before the Court on January 26 other that his wish to obtain a discharge of all offices for which he paid. The wording quoted by Paul Dottin signifies that approval was given on that basis.

The Admittance procedures were a good deal more 'free and easy' than is sometimes supposed. In the Admissions Book for the period 1685-1690 there are records of 165 Admissions. Of these one was by redemption (payment of a fee), one hundred and forty-four were admittances by apprenticeship and twenty by Patrimony.

Of the Admissions by Patrimony only seven give the name of the father: that is thirteen did not name a father. There does not appear to be any rhyme or reason for those entries that gave the father's name and those that did not. On one page containing a number of admissions by Patrimony, some included the father's name and some did not, and it is clear that the entries are random. Joshus Widbor, who may well have been known by Defoe, was admitted on Feb.4 1679/80 without any details at all being given about him.

The Worshipful Company of Butchers, in common with most Guilds

---

[409] Dottin, Paul. *Daniel Defoe: The Life and Surprising Adventures*, London, Stanley Paul, 1928, 50.
[410] Worshipful Company of Butchers. CLC/L/B1/C008/MS06446.

at this time, did not keep parental records. There are no baptism records and no mention of people attending Admission interviews or vouching for the parentage of an applicant.

It can be seen, therefore, that there is no evidence that biology entered into membership. Admittedly, there was a sense in which Defoe was admitted as James Foe's 'son'. However, the question to be asked is what was meant by 'son'?

I write in Appendix 3 that previous Defoe biographers have been mistaken in their accounts and understanding of family life in the seventeenth and eighteenth centuries. There has been a belief that nuclear and companionate marriages had become predominant and usual. It was assumed that Defoe was brought up in a strongly Presbyterian family and that it was not unreasonable to conclude, given the Presbyterian attachment to family life, that it was in a nuclear family. However, as I have sought to explain, Defoe was not brought up in a Presbyterian household at any time during his childhood and, even if he had been, it does not follow that it would have been nuclear or companionate as previously supposed.

Recent cultural historians have produced good evidence that family-establishment was the predominant factor in family life up and into the second half of the eighteenth century.[411] In this classification Tadmor suggests there are six basic terms that are most commonly and habitually used in both their narrow and broader meanings. Familial roles are extended to recognise each others kin, sons and daughters, aunts and uncles, nephews and cousins. In a typical seventeenth century family, fatherhood arose from being the senior male in a family and a recognised 'Father'. After the death of his brother Henry in 1674, James was the acknowledged head or 'Father' of the Etton Foe family in general. It would then be entirely natural for Defoe to refer to James Foe as his 'Father' and for him to regard Defoe as his 'Son'. James had no son of his own so the use of the term to describe Defoe was not confusing. We have no knowledge of how he described his nephews John and Richard by the marriage of his sister Mary to Richard

---

[411] Tadmor, Naomi. *Family and Friends*. 133-139.

Lambert. No confusion would have resulted from him calling them his nephews. However, if there had been some confusion, he would have called them son John and son Richard Lambert.

The ambiguous use of this expression 'son' is illustrated by a conversation between Mary Tuffley (the aunt) and the mother (Mary Norton) in *Religious Courtship* that I have described earlier. Asked for the reason for her (Mary Tuffley's) visit at a particular time, the aunt explains that she was worried about her son (Benjamin Norton who was in difficulties at the time. Mary Tuffley had no sons). The Mother exclaims that she (the aunt) had no sons. She received the reply 'not my son but my husband's.' If this usage were to be applied to either the Admission to the Butcher's Guild or to the will of James Foe that made his 'son' Daniel (Defoe) the executor, the answer to any question on what he meant by it, would have been 'not my son but my brother Daniel's son'.

Taken across the London-based Guilds there was a general understanding applied to membership as an Apprentice, but not in Patrimony, that a candidate claiming Admission should be in the direct line of the family concerned: that is, the applicant was not adopted or fostered. This exclusion appears to be a prejudice against bastards and foundlings. Defoe's application for Admission in Patrimony did not require a proof of this kind. However, even if it were assumed that proof was required, he was in fact the biological son of Daniel Foe and thus in the direct line of descent in James Foe's family. This assertion is supported by Defoe's father's will which recognises Defoe as the main beneficiary. Consequently, on both these grounds, the question of whether he was the biological son of James Foe did not and could not arise.

This being so, Defoe although not the biological son of James Foe was correct in describing himself as a 'son'. He did not set out to deceive and no one would have assumed that he had at the time.

Previous biographers are wrong in assuming that by virtue of becoming a Freeman of the Butcher's Guild, James Foe and Defoe were entitled to exercise a vote in elections to the Corporation of

London. The vote was exercised by a small Committee of the Guild elected by the Liverymen.

James Foe died in December, 1706. His will was made in March, 1706 and biographers have been unable to understand it.[412] James Foe described Defoe as his 'son'. He left him nothing but appointed him the Executor. The list of beneficiaries included his daughters and Defoe's children by three women. Defoe's son Daniel received £100. Defoe's elder son and beneficiary, Benjamin Norton was to receive a gold watch to be given to him by Mary Tuffley. As I have explained, it was entirely natural for James to call Defoe his 'son' and he had no other senior male in the family. As the elder 'son' Defoe, if a legitimate biological son, would have expected to inherit and had powerful legal rights to do so. Defoe may not have acted as the Executor. Mary Tuffley in her will proved in 1732 had a gold watch which she bequeathed to Benjamin. If it is the same watch, and I conjecture it was, it had been uncollected over twenty-six years.[413] This long delay would suggest either that Defoe and Mary Tuffley were not in contact in the period, 1706-1731, although their families were, or that she held on to the watch.

---

[412] See *Beyond Belief*, 155, Backscheider, 199-202, Novak, 154-7, Healey, 180.
[413] NA. 11/655/282.

6. The Appearance of Things

He is an 'Old Man [and] a super-annuated *Letter Writer*.

Edmund Curll, bookseller, 1719

The term superannuated as used by Curll meant that he regarded Defoe as retired from work, as being dismissed or discarded as too useless for work, because he was too old. I do not think that Curll would have made the remark if he believed Defoe to be 59 years of age; but it would be credible if he thought him to be 75.

However, I do concede the everyday observation that it would be difficult to accept that a man could be 15-16 years older than he purports to be without people knowing about it. Wouldn't he look older? Wouldn't people, as a matter of common sense, realise his age? There is a related issue. Late in his life, into his eighties, when he was still writing prodigiously, how did Defoe summon the intellectual energy and capacity to write?

I accept also that there are examples of Defoe quoting dates and ages which suggest that he was younger than I argue he was in this account; and also that others described his age at various times and ways consistent with a birth in 1659/1660. All these mentions when given by Defoe or advanced by others fit into a Defoe deception: his decision to hide his origins and his age after returning to England in 1680. It really was quite easy to do this. Others, without direct knowledge, would have used the information given to them.

This work is principally concerned with the life Defoe led in the period 1644-1706. Up to the end of this period, I believe that Defoe had little difficulty in disguising his age. Beyond that time it must have been a problem for him. However, I do not wish to evade the issues of the appearance of old age in the last 25 years of his life during which his written output remained considerable.

General Obscurity

Defoe lived before the registration of births, deaths and marriages were legal requirements. Moreover, he set out to mislead people and hide the basic facts that would enable them to check his age. People are used to guessing ages and taking personal statements on these matters at their 'face value'. Some people look older and others younger than their chronological age. Hence such an expression as 'You're young for your age. I would never have guessed it.' Even now, in our sceptical times, people are inclined to take you at your own estimate give or take off a few years for vanity or effect. For most of the middle period of his life, as described here, Defoe was middle-aged and looked it. *The Concise Oxford Dictionary* defines middle age as 'the period between youth and old age, about 45 to 60'.

Style of Life

Defoe was ubiquitous and restless with many families, homes and lodgings. He was constantly on the move as a salesman, businessman and travel writer: at some time of his life he would have travelled 'Through the Whole Island of Great Britain', Europe, the Caribbean and New England. He ensured that 'one hand did not know what the other was hiding'.

Lying

As I have stated previously, it is difficult for most people to come to terms with systematic lying. Most people have a predisposition to accept that people are telling the truth. It must have come as an unpleasant shock for William Minto to recognise that Defoe was 'a very great liar'. It is easy to quote examples where Defoe lied about his age: for example in his Marriage Licence in December, 1683; and in stating he was 66 years of age when publishing *The Protestant Monastery*, 1726. He was consistent in doing so. People who had not met Defoe took his age to be whatever Defoe said it was.

Dress and Presentation

Defoe presented himself very carefully in public and when having his portrait painted. Contemporaries noted that he was well and even extravagantly dressed in the beauish manner and wore a long wig. When hostile cartoonists wished to derogate him and reduce his public standing they drew him as grey, and balding without a wig. This is how he was presented by artists when appearing in the pillory in July, 1703. He looked very old indeed. A contemporary account of his appearance in the summer of 1706 was given to the Defoe Society by Peter Adamson. He quoted a description given by a John Kelso, a Quaker relative of his, in a letter written to a cousin, John Merrick, at some time after the publication of *Jure Divino* . John Kelso wrote:

> He goes very beauish yet is very sociable and free in discourse, yet not without a due reserve...He is of middle age [45-60] and low stature exactly resembling his Cutt in ye Jure Divino in 8vo. He talks with an admirable Felicity and seems well read in both ancient & modern history. In fine, thou shall find his Discourse like yt of his pen.

He remarked of Defoe that it is not easy to find and meet him, 'for if thou hast read his Satyres wt Dangers he hereby occurs is easily seen'. John Kelso tells the reader that Defoe was in hiding on the supposed grounds of his writings but as I have suggested there were other more probable reasons for him taking refuge.

At this time Defoe was 61 years of age and given that he was 'looking after himself' this description is consistent with a birth in 1644.[414]

Fear of Prosecution

For fifty years of his life Defoe lived in fear of prosecution. He was imprisoned many times and at any moment following his return to England he might have been arrested and killed. He must have thought that the least known about him the better it would be.

Protection

Defoe was protected from prosecution by some of the most powerful men of the age: Sunderland, Harley and Charles De La Faye but even with this protection he had to live furtively. When he moved to his Stoke Newington house, it is said that he barricaded himself in behind secure doors, window shutters and locks. He always carried a sword in public places.

---

[414] Letter to the Defoe Society dated February, 2011.

What Did He Actually Look Like?

There are many images of the adult Defoe almost all of which originate in a short period of time. In her biography Backscheider produces four images made of Defoe taken in 1703-1706 when Defoe was aged 59-62: two portraits by Taverner together with two engravings made from them.[415] The most flattering of these is the portrait made for *Jure Divino* in 1706. The commissioning of these portraits coincided with Defoe's fencing of Captain Avery's diamonds in 1706. He was anxious to display his wealth and importance.

Even in these Taverner portraits, there are tell-tale signs of aging around the eyes and mouth. The engravings tell another story of a much older man. The viewers of these images can but think that if the wig were to be removed they would be looking at a man in his sixties. When Defoe was very old but still active it was extremely difficult for him to disguise his age. Not everyone was fooled. Apart from the means used to conjure up preferred images in painting or engraving there are differences in the points of view of the creators. Engravings and cartoons present cruder and more common place images. Those which convey images of him without a wig, for example when in the pillory, present an aging man going bald with grey hair.

One example of an impression of Defoe's age which seems to be credible is that of Henry Baker's. He writes in a Memorandum that Defoe 'was at least sixty years of age' when he met him. It is assumed that the first meeting which gave rise to this was in 1724 when Defoe was 64 and Baker 75. At this point of time, it is said, Baker was giving a boy aged ten years old, John White, the son of a tenant of Defoe's, lessons to overcome his deafness. However, in a carefully worded proof I show that that John White was born in 1708 and that Defoe met Baker for the first time much earlier than 1724. I estimate the time to be 1716-1718. My belief is that even this date comes some time after the two met and that Defoe knew Baker when he was a child. This being so Defoe was either less than seventy years old, or if a more conservative estimate is taken, between seventy-two and seventy–four years old

---

[415] Backscheider, 190-192.

when he first met Baker.[416] This age spread is within the range of credible doubt and the expression that Defoe was 'at least sixty years old.'

Many People Did Know

Many people in Defoe's life-time knew his real age. His immediate blood relatives knew but other family members may not have done. In 1683 the Special Licence which permitted Defoe to marry Mary Tuffley stated his age to have been about 24 when he would have been 39, fifteen years older and exactly the time, fifteen years, he sought to hide. In reality there was no way for anyone to check Defoe's age. As he kept secret his place of birth and the names of his parents there was no way for anyone to check the baptism record: 'a Gentleman's word was his bond'. Who saw the licence? Perhaps, Charles Lodwick who is named on it and the parish clerk charged with knowing that it existed. Lodwick was a business partner and may have had a vested interest in Defoe getting his hands on the dowry. Mary herself may not have known. It would seem from the correspondence of Henry Baker, who was courting Defoe's daughter Sophia, that she must have been uncertain of Defoe's age. Sophia may not have known. She was the daughter of Mary Norton and may have known little about her father's history.

Many notable people on whom Defoe relied for patronage and protection knew. Robert Spencer, Second Earl of Sunderland and William Penn knew because they went on a version of the Grand Tour together when all were young and carefree at seventeen and nineteen years of age. Robert Spencer may have owed his life to Defoe. Harley, Robert Spencer and Penn must have acquired knowledge of much of Defoe's background. These men had secrets to hide and Defoe knew where 'many of the bodies were hidden'. There was a very real sense that they were all in the business of aggrandisement in the New World together. If Spencer, Penn and Harley knew Defoe's background many others in positions of political power were also in the know.

---

[416] *Beyond Belief*, 268-279, n, 230-240.

In the course of fifteen years a great many people who met and were involved with Defoe made the connection between the man they knew in Portugal, Brazil or New England and the political journalist who emerged in London in the 1680's: merchants, seamen, pirates and buccaneers, planters and government officials. Most were unable to find Defoe and even if they did succeed in doing so were powerless to harm him. Defoe had so many homes and overnight refuges that it was difficult to know where he was at any particular time. I have already mentioned that in *Roxana* Elisabeth White, confronting Mary Norton in Essex, told her, that no matter how hard Defoe tried to avoid her she knew all the places that he might be and that she could find him. She had arrived on Mary Norton's doorstep and like one of Harold Pinter's fictional strangers might have been found watching and waiting at the bottom of the garden. Others could do what Elisabeth White threatened to do if it were important enough for them.

In Essex friends, neighbours and the wider family of Foe's, Wildbore's and Lawrence's knew. Over time they diminished in number. *Moll Flanders* remarks that on a return to Colchester she found that her family had disappeared: dead, moved away, and migrated to New England.

Printers and Other Writers Knew

Defoe had numerous and frequent contact with printers, booksellers and other writers and many of them must have known that he was older than he claimed. The quote at the head of this appendix from Edmund Curll, writing in 1719 when Defoe was seventy-five years of age, illustrates that he knew Defoe was older than generally realised. He was not alone in realising Defoe was old at the time. Gildon, Defoe's most famous literary critic, knew. He could not have made the accusation that *Robinson Crusoe* was an autobiographical account of Defoe's own life unless he recognised that it was Defoe himself who was in exile for at least sixteen years.

Defoe had no difficulty in hiding his age up to 1706 the date at which my chronology of his early life ends. From this date Defoe ceased to present himself in public, limited his public appearances, kept on the road when it suited him and put himself on the other side of bolts and locks when it didn't. Beyond this date there are many Defoe images from a multitude of cartoonists, engravers and publishers making money out of pirating his works. It is clear to the reader that these portraits are not likenesses of Defoe. These images present the creators' points of view on Defoe's character and the significance of his written work.

Attachment 7

Defoe's Paternal
Inheritance

The Cavalier: Defoe's Elder Brother

*My original may be as high as anybody's, for aught I know, for my mother
kept very good company, but that part belongs to her story more than mine.*

Colonel Jack, 1722

*I know no one but Sir John Fenwick here: therefore, I can betray no one to
him.*

Roxana, 1724

Introduction

In an earlier work, I provided a chart of the Foe family of Etton with an
unfilled slot for an elder brother. I was convinced at this time that the
conventional account of Defoe's family background and early history
could not explain the man himself.[417]

As I have pointed out in this work, all the children and grandchildren
in the Foe family of Etton are recorded in the Etton Parish Registers,
except Defoe's father, Daniel Foe.[418] His father died in 1647, twenty-
two years after the birth of Defoe's aunt Mary. He may have died a
comparatively young man; but on the other hand, the absence of a
baptism record may mean that Rose Foe was not Defoe's biological
grandmother. His father may have had previous marriages.

In *Robinson Crusoe*, early in his narrative, Defoe writes about lost
relatives. It reads to me as a marker to a family tradition referencing his
'voyage out'. He wrote in the second paragraph as follows:

---

[417] Beyond Belief, 289.
[418] NRA. Parish Records of Etton, 1587-1712. Baptisms, Marriages and Burials. See
Chart.

> I had two elder Brothers, one of which was Lieutenant Collonel to an English Regiment of Foot in *Flanders*, formerly commanded by the *Coll. Lockhart*, and was killed at the Battle near Dunkirk against the *Spaniards*. What became of my second Brother I never knew any more than my Father or Mother did know what was become of me.[419]

I appreciate that those critics who abide by the 'conventional account' of Defoe's life would think little of this statement; they will think that the dates are wrong for a family link to Defoe and, anyway, it is not possible to conclude that such a comment could constitute an autobiographical fact. However, Defoe's fictions contain many markers of this kind and it is unwise to discredit them in advance of the exploration of their meaning.

Arthur Secord wrote as follows about another marker:

> The difference between *Robinson Crusoe* and *Memoirs of a Cavalier* is not so great as may first seem…their stories have much in common…they are about young men who set out to see the world… and… that Defoe tells his reader that he took his story from a manuscript written sixty years before publication…and found over twenty years before publication.[420]

Following Defoe's helpful hint it can be seen that this statement is supportive of my conclusion that Defoe was born in 1644. The dates work back neatly from the publication of the *Memoirs* in 1722 to 1662 (sixty years), the date Defoe/the *Cavalier* embarked on the Grand Tour; and twenty-four years (over twenty) to the execution of Sir John Fenwick, in 1696. Was this manuscript, or manuscripts, and historical accounts, found in the papers of John Fenwick following his death? To this I would add that Defoe's fictional particulars often turn out to be correct when carefully examined. In the *Cavalier* Defoe describes himself as being a *second* son.

---

[419] *Robinson Crusoe*, 5.
[420] Secord, Arthur. W. *Robert Drury's Journal and Other Studies*, 74.

It is possible to identify the person killed. This 'elder brother' killed in France was Roger Fenwick. The Battle near Dunkirk is called today the Battle of the Dunes, 1658 in which an expeditionary force of some two thousand Commonwealth troops took part. The Military Team of the National Archives have been able to confirm to me that the only Lt Colonel killed in the battle known to them was a Roger Fenwick.[421] There is supporting documentary evidence for his death. A military force of this size might be supposed to consist of five or six regiments each headed by an officer of the brother's rank. It is also reasonable to assume that all such deaths would be reported home 'in despatches'.[422]

Late in research for this work, I decided to test the literal accuracy of *Crusoe's* statement. I was aware that Defoe's disastrous participation in the Portuguese War of Restoration in 1662-1663 as part of an English expeditionary force led by former Commonwealth soldiers may have had determinants for him other than personal recklessness. Perhaps, taking part was influenced by the living out of family traditions and beliefs quite unknown to modern readers of his fiction. And then there were practical considerations. Why would such experienced Cromwellian soldiers in Portugal have been willing to take on so green a youth as Daniel Foe? Obviously, if he had been able to demonstrate that he was the brother of a famous soldier who had fought with them and their former comrades in France, it would have been easy to win their confidence.

The Fenwick Family of Northumberland

The Fenwick families of Northumberland had long played a distinguished role in the county, Scotland, and South Carolina.[423] A letter by an Edward Fenwick to his son Roger dated London, July 27, 1726 states with pride that:

> The name of Fenwick is one of the most ancient names…in England… it had been centred in Wallington [but that the name had branched out] into several other families, who

---

[421] House of Common's Journal, iv 612, vi 435.
[422] Thurloe State Papers, vii, 175.
[423] Armstrong, Angus. *George Fenwick of Brinkburn*, 1603-1656, Armstrong, 2009.

were younger brothers to the House of Wallington, and they were also possessed of good estates, and the chief of these younger families was the House of Stanton ...and this is now the first family of the name because the Wallington family became extinct, at the death of Sir John Fenwick, Bart, who was beheaded in the year 1696...[and who] before his death had sold all his estates and possessions and sent all the money to King James.[424]

The most notable of the Fenwick families in the seventeenth century was that of George Fenwick who was a Member of both the Long and Rump Parliaments, and a successful soldier in the Parliamentary cause. He became the governor of Berwick and Edinburgh castles. Earlier he had founded settlements along the Connecticut River and his descendants settled in America. In particular, they owned property in South Carolina. George Fenwick became one of eight Commissioners appointed to administer Scotland for the English.

It seems possible, therefore, that if Defoe was related to the Fenwick's, it would have given him an entrée to the Scottish aristocracy when there in 1706-1707. Backscheider writes:

At this time in 1707 Defoe's activities and contacts were astonishing. His power to penetrate diverse group's ranks him among the greatest of spies of all time...Defoe formed genuine, mutual friendship with some Scots. His private hours, his investments, his travels around Scotland, and his publications portray a life with complex, intertwined relationships and a number of loyalties.

Defoe's public recognition by the 'great and the good' in Scotland might not have come as a surprise to Harley. Bastian records that Thomas Bell, a distributor to Defoe, and a paid informant of Harley's, wrote to Harley on 1 October, 1706 stating of Defoe that he was already 'publickly knowne in Edinburgh'.[425]

---

[424] Charles Hunter Jackson Web Site.
[425] Bastian, 212, n.31.

Equally famous at a later date, if considerably more notorious, was Sir John Fenwick, Third Baronet – the man who 'lost his head'. Bastian writes that: Defoe was present in Parliament on 13/14th November when [Sir John Fenwick] a notorious Jacobite and conspirator and would-be assassin of William III, was questioned. 'Nine years later he wrote about the trial in the *Review*.'[426]

Defoe has been credited with at least one of the numerous pamphlets written about the attainder hearings and subsequent execution.[427] Sir John Fenwick and his family are ubiquitous in Defoe's written work. Apart from the allusion and mention in the heading to this attachment, there is other naming of Sir John Fenwick in Defoe's ascribed and non-ascribed written work: in the *Tour*, *The Memoirs of Major General Ramikins* and *Memoirs of Captain George Carleton*.

The Fenwick family associations with Defoe do not end with his fiction and biographical accounts. A John Fenwick, a Quaker acting as agent to Edward Billinge, helped found a Quaker settlement in West Jersey. In 1681 he was persuaded to give up his proprietary rights in land there to William Penn in exchange for 150,000 acres of land. In my narrative this is around the time Defoe was giving serious thought to settlement there.

It can be seen, therefore, that Fenwick families are to be found fictionally and in real life in Defoe's written work in diverse places in France, Flanders, Berkshire, Northumberland, Scotland, New Jersey and South Carolina; and on battlefields, in castles, boudoirs, plantations, assembly rooms – and on the scaffold at the Tower. Surely there must be an explanation for such multiplicity?

Who was Roger Fenwick?

A central premise of my literary interpretation of Defoe's fictions is that he is the hero of them all. He is truly 'the hero with a thousand

[426] Bastian, 200, n.124, HCJ, 13 and 14 Nov 1696, *Review*, ii, 388.and Luttrell, iv, 139, 14 Nov. 1696.
[427] *Proceedings against Sir John Fenwick, Bar. Upon a bill of attainder for high Treason...together with a copy of a letter sent to his Lady,...As also of the paper delver'd at the place of his execution.*

faces''[428] This premise guides the articulation of three questions that need answers. They are as follows. Who was the Roger Fenwick who died in France in 1658? How, if at all, was Roger Fenwick related to Daniel Defoe? And thirdly, is Defoe actually telling the reader that he was a *Cavalier* and in what sense?

Roger Fenwick was the son of Edward Fenwick and Sarah (nee Neville) and born March 18, 1632 in Stanton, Northamptonshire. Edward was a son of William Fenwick Second Earl, and John Fenwick, the Jacobite of this story, was William's brother. This John Fenwick succeeded to the Baronetcy because his elder brother was killed in the Battle of Marston Moor. Thus if Defoe was 'truly' a brother to Roger Fenwick then Sir John Fenwick, Third Baronet, would have been his uncle. It is extremely difficult to check whether Defoe was a 'brother' to Roger for Stanton is in the parish of Long Horsley, Northumberland and there are no parish registers before 1668. However, some information is available from secondary sources.[429]

These sources show that Roger Fenwick was born in 1632. He was the first of eleven children, nine boys and two girls. Of the boys, four died young and, apart from Roger, four others survived childhood: William, b.1633, Robert, b.1646; James, b.1648; and Thomas, born later, died 1695.

Crusoe's statement refers to two Elder brothers, one who was killed and another who 'disappeared' and his whereabouts not known even to his Mother and Father. Can this statement be reconciled with what is known now about Roger Fenwick? Roger and William 'were known' in the sense that they could have been born *before* his grandfather moved to Etton and the date of Defoe's birth. Defoe could have *known* about Roger Fenwick while *not knowing* about William. William died in 1675 when Defoe was in Brazil.

On the face of it, there is reason to suppose that Roger's mother

---

[428] Campbell, Joshua. *The Hero with a Thousand Faces*, Fontana Press, 1993
[429] Hodgson, John. *A History of Northumberland*, Part 2, Volume 2. *Stanton Papers* (a collection of deeds for Stanton).

Sarah, the daughter of Francis Nevill of Cheete, married only once. However, given the gap of thirteen years between the date of birth of William and Robert, it may well be that Edward was married before. This speculation is supported by the choice of children's names. It was the practice at the time to name a first son after the father. Edward's known sons do not include an Edward. A deed dated 1659 links Edward Fenwick of Stanton with Sarah, his wife, Francis Neville and Sir William Fenwick (who at this time had become the second Baronet).

How then could Daniel Foe claim that Roger Fenwick was his 'brother' even if the 'broad church' of family terms at the time is taken into account? Could he do so in any way whatsoever? I think he could.

The Fenwick families had separated a little across Northumberland over hundreds of years but remained closely linked by geography, inter-marriage and the ownership of land. I believe Defoe's linkage to these families can be established through the family of Thomas de Lorraine of Kirkdale, near Stanton. Thomas married a woman called Grace and the couple is thought to have had as many as fourteen children, some of whom did not survive their early years. Grace had been married at least once before. Following Thomas's death Grace married Sir John Fenwick, the third Baronet and Jacobite plotter, and had three surviving children by him. At this point in the family narrative, the Houses of Wallington and Stanton were, for a time, re-united. All the children in these two Families had become 'brothers and sisters'. Sir John Fenwick was also married three times. At the time of his death, a Mary Bond was his wife. In the absence of parish records, it is difficult to identify the surviving children of all of these marriages.

The Family of Thomas de Lorraine was domiciled in Britain as far back as the Norman Conquest. However, the Norman Britons retained their family and kinship connections, and some of their allegiances, down through history. In English history the aristocracy and the distinguished in Northumberland retained some of their Roman Catholic and Jacobite sympathies – although others, such as Roger Fenwick, died in the causes of the Commonwealth. It was thought for some time that if the Pretender was to come he would land troops in Northumberland.

Historically, in some unknown way, the family of Thomas de Lorraine must have been historically connected with Philip de Lorraine, who was described as the Chevalier de Lorraine. It is very tempting for a biographer to suggest that Defoe was mimicking in his own life and fiction an understanding of his family heritage. Whether he was or was not may be discoverable, but, alas, not in the time permitted to me in this account.

Defoe is one of the English speaking world's greatest story tellers. As truly awful things were happening to him he was thinking amidst the grief, 'there is a story here that I shall tell in my time'. What was the story in 1696? If Defoe was related through his father to the Fenwick families, and I suggest that he was, does it follow that he had Jacobite sympathies? It is not self-evident. There were distinguished supporters of both the Royalist and Commonwealth causes in the family. The people of Northumberland, and the Fenwick families in particular, did show tolerance to Roman Catholicism and to James II. Did Defoe, in his private and public life, have these sympathies? Were the pamphlets ascribed to him in the period 1701-1713, and thought by contemporaries to denote sympathy for the Pretender, and which urged an end to war with France, a method of his to promote the Pretender's causes? Were these pamphlets a method of keeping the door open to the Pretender while protesting his loyalty? Many commentators in the period denounced Defoe for supporting Jacobitism and Defoe pleaded that there were pro-Jacobites in the administration. Did he mean Harley? In his biography, Novak thought that many of the issues worth discussing about Defoe were his attitudes to Jacobitism. His book has fifty-three indexed references to them.[430] Did Defoe, as instanced in his pamphlet *Mists Closet Broke Open*, share Jacobite sympathies with Nathaniel Mist? Did Defoe seek to help Sir John Fenwick at his last, by organising a letter from his wife Mary in an attempt to save him from the scaffold? Was Defoe's signature to an Oath of Allegiance to

---

[430] Novak, Index, 741.

William III in 1696 an attempt to avoid or deflect criticism of him for possible involvement with the plotters?

Perhaps there were dubious influences and allegiances guiding Defoe's actions. The statement in *Roxana* suggests a betrayal. Is there an issue here of the disclosure of evidence by Defoe of the names of plotters that led to the trial and subsequent execution of Sir John Fenwick? Were Defoe's motives mixed? Was Defoe a 'double agent' working for Harley over the issues raised by the threat of Jacobitism in England and Scotland? Did Defoe make Harley aware that if he were posted to Scotland that, in Backscheider's words, he could be a truly successful spy because he had ready access to the Scottish Jacobites? I do not know the answers to any of these questions – but they can and ought to be addressed.

Bibliography

This book draws upon some 400 written sources. I have restricted the bibliography to 240 cited works including 78 ascribed to Defoe. I concentrate on Defoe's life to 1705/6 and consequential matters although the discussion of his written ouput runs to 1731. Most of the cited books can be obtained through public library systems. Rare books can be read in England at the British Library and other academic libraries throughout the world. The work draws upon material in a large number of archives in Brazil, England, Portugal, Scotland and the USA.

Ascriptions

The following symbols are used:

A. Ascribed by me to Defoe as a result of this work.
AN. A work I believe is best described as an anthology.
E. A work I believe is best described as edited by or contributed to by Defoe.

Defoe's Written Works

Books

Captain Singleton, 1720.
Colonel Jack, 1722.
Compleat English Tradesman, The, 1726.
Conjugal Lewdness, T. Warner, 1727.
The Consolidator, 1705.
Due Preparations for the Plague, 1722.
Essay Upon Projects, An, London, 1697.
Family Instructor, 1715.
Farther Adventures of Robinson Crusoe, 1720.
Historical Collections and Memoires of Passages and Stories Collected from

Severall Authors, 1683 (AN).
History of the Union of Great Britain, The, Edinburgh, 1709.
Journal of The Plague Year, A, 1722.
Jure Divino, 1706.
Memoirs of a Cavalier, 1720.
Moll Flanders, 1722.
The Political History of the Devil, 1726.
Religious Courtship, London, 1722.
Robert Drury's Journal, 1729. (E)
Robinson Crusoe, 1719.
Roxana, or The Fortunate Mistress, 1724.
Serious Reflections of Robinson Crusoe, 1722.
The Storm, The Lay-Man's Sermon upon the Late Storm, an *Essay on the Late Storm*, 1704.
System of Magick, A, 1727.
A Tour Through The Whole Island of Great Britain, 1724-1726.

Pamphlets and Poems

Daniel Defoe's pamphlets and poems are not generally available. In England they can be read at the British Library.

Appeal to Honour and Justice, An, London, 1715.
Argument Shewing that a Standing Army, with Consent of Parliament, is not Inconsistent with a Free Government, London, 1698.
Brief Explanation of a Late Pamphlet, A, 1703.
Case of the Protestant Dissenters in Carolina, The, 1706.
Danger of the Protestant Religion Consider'd, The, 1701.
Enquiry into the Occasional Conformity of Dissenters, in Cases of Preferment, An, 1698.
Essay at Removing National Prejudices against a Union with Scotland, Parts 1, 2 and 3, 1706.
History of the Kentish Petition, The, 1701.
Legion's Memorial, 1701.
Letter from Scotland, A, 1705.(A)

Life and Adventures of Captain Avery, the Famous Pirate, The, 1709 and a play *The Successful Pirate*, 1713. (pseudonym Charles Johnson). (A)
Mists Closet Broke Open; on Several Letters Intercepted, in which Are Contained Some Old Truths New Told, 1728. (A)
Observations: made in England on the Tryal of Captain Green, and the speech at his death, 1705(A).
Original Power of the Collective Body of the People of England, The, 1702.
Pacificator, 1700.
Present State of Jacobitism Considered, The, 1701.
Present State of the Parties, The, 1712.
*Proceedings Against Sir John Fenwick, Bar. ...*1702. (A)
Protestant Monastery, The, 1727.
Reasons Against a War with France, 1701.
Reasons against the Succession of the House of Hanover, 1713.
Remarks on the Bill to Prevent Frauds Committed by Bankrupts, 1706.
Shortest Way With The Dissenters, The, 1702.
Sincerity of the Dissenters Vindicated, The, 1703.
Six Distinguishing Characters of a Parliament Man, The, 1701.
Some Reflections on a Pamphlet Entitled, An Argument Shewing that a Standing Army is Inconsistent with a Free Government, 1697.
Succession to the Crown of England, Considered, The, London, 1701.
True Born Englishman, The, 1701.
Tryal of Captain Green, The, 1705. (A)
Two Great Questions Considered, The, 1700.
Two Great Questions Further Considered, The, 1700.

Defoe Biographies

Most of the books listed in the sections below are available through good bookshops and the public library system. Rare books can be read at the British Library or other academic libraries throughout the world

Abse, Leo. *The Bi-Sexuality of Daniel Defoe, A Psychoanalytic Survey of the Man and His Works*, Karnac, London, 2006.
Backscheider, Paula. *Daniel Defoe: His Life*, Johns Hopkins University Press,

1998.

Bastian, Frank. *Defoe's Early Life*, New Jersey, Barnes and Noble Books, 1981.

Chadwick, William. *The Life and Times of Daniel Defoe*, London, John Russell Smith, 1859.

Chalmers, George. *The Life of Defoe*, London, 1790.

Dottin, Paul. *Daniel Defoe: The Life and Surprising Adventures of Daniel Defoe*, London, Stanley Paul, 1928.

Earle, Peter. *The World of Defoe*, Weidenfeld and Nicholson, 1976. *Monmouths Rebels*, Weidenfeld and Nicholson, 1977.

Gray, John. Ed. *Memoirs of the Life of Sir John Clerk*, Nichols and Sons, London, 1895.

Healey, George Harris. *The Letters of Daniel Defoe*, Clarendon, Oxford University Press, 1955.

Holmes, Richard. *Defoe on Sheppard and Wild*, Harper Perennial, 2004.

Lee, William. *Daniel Defoe: His Life and Hitherto Unknown Writings*, 3 vols., London, Hotten, 1869.

Martin, John. *Beyond Belief*, Accent Press, 2006, 2009. *Alien Come Home*, Anglian Publishing, 2009.

Minto, William. *Daniel Defoe*, London, Macmillan, 1879.

Moore, John Robert. *Daniel Defoe: Citizen of the Modern World*, University of Chicago, 1958.

Novak, Maximillian E. *Daniel Defoe: Master of Fictions*, Oxford University Press, 2001.

Sutherland, James. *Defoe*, London, Methuen, 1937.

Trent, William Peterfield. *A Biographical and Bibliographical Study*. MS biography of Daniel Defoe. Trent Collection, Beinecke Library, New Haven. Conn., c.1900-1927.

Wilson, Walter. *Memoirs of the Life and Times of Daniel De Foe*, 3 vols., Hurst, Chance, London, 1830.

Wright, Thomas. *The Life of Daniel Defoe*, 1894.

Other Relevant Works

Anonymous, *The Welsh Monster or the rise and fall of that late upstart, the*

R-t H-ble *Innuendo Sribble*, 1708.

Armstrong, Katherine. *Defoe: Writer as Agent*, Victoria B.C. English Literary Studies, Univ. of Victoria, 1996.

Becker, Howard S. *Outsiders: Studies in the Sociology of Deviance*, The Free Press, 1973.

Bergler, Edmund. *The Psychology of Gambling*, New York, 1974.

Bingley, Randle. *Journal of the Thurrock Local History, Society*, 1985.

Boem, Christopher. *Moral Origins: The Evolution of Virtue, Altruism and Shame*, Basic Books, May, 2012.

Braithwaite, William C. *The Beginnings of Quakerism*, Cambridge University Press, 1955.

Calamy, Edward. *An Account of the Masters and Fellows of Colleges who were Ejected or Silenced after the Revolution in 1660*, 2nd edition, London, 1713.

Campbell, Joseph. *The Hero with a Thousand Faces*, Fontana Press, 1993.

Congregational History. *A History of the County of Surrey*, 1912.

Cottret, Bernard. *The Huguenots in England: Immigration and Settlement*, Cambridge University Press, 1992.

Dale, Bryan,. *The Annals of Coggeshall*, London, 1860.

Dale, T.C. *The Inhabitants of London in 1638*, Society of Genealogists, 1931.

Dalton, Charles. *A Genuine Narrative of All Street Robberies Committed since October last*, 1728.

Dampier, William. *A Voyage to New Holland*, ed. James Williamson, (1697. Argonaut Press, 1939).

Dunton, John. *Impeachment*, 1704.

Durkheim, Emile. *Suicide: A Study in Sociology*, Routledge Classics, 2002.

English Army Lists, and Commission Registers, Ed. Charles Dalton, Vol.VI, Eyre and Spottiswoode, London, 1904.

Ermath, Elizabeth. *Realism and Consensus in the English Novel*, Princeton University Press, 1983.

Feiling, Keith. *A History of the Tory Party*, 1660-1714, (Oxford at the Clarendon Press), 1965.

Flynn, Carol Houlihan. *The Body in Swift and Defoe*, Cambridge University Press, 1990.

Frank, Katherine. *Daniel Defoe, Robert Knox and the Creation of a Myth*,

Bodley Head, 2011.

Freud, Sigmund. *Family Romances*, 1908, *The Standard Edition of the Complete Works*, London, Hogarth Press, 1959. *Interpretation of Dreams*, Oxford University Press, 1999.

Furbank, P.N. and W.R. Owens. *A Critical Bibliography of Daniel Defoe*, London, Pickering and Chatto, 1998. *The Canonisation of Daniel Defoe*, London, Yale University Press, 1988.

Gadd, Ian Anders. Ed. *Guilds, Society and Economy in London*, Centre for Metropolitan Studies, 2002.

Gilmore, Leigh. *The Limits of Autobiography*, Cornell University Press, 2001.

Guimaraens, A.J.C. *Daniel Defoe and the Family of Foe*, Notes and Queries, March 1912.

Glozier, Mathew. *Marshall Schomberg, 1615-1690*, Sussex Academic Press, Brighton, Sussex.

Gragg, Larry. *The Quaker Community on Barbados, Challenging the Culture of the Planter Class*, University of Missouri Press, 2009.

Habakkuk, H.J. *Marriage Settlements in the Eighteenth Century*, London, 1950.

Hawton, Nick. *The Quest for Radovan Karadzic*, Hutchinson, 2009.

Heidenreich, Hirsch, Arthur and Van Rymbecke, A. Bertrand. *The Huguenots of Colonial South Carolina*, Archon Books, London, 1962.

Horner, Samuel. *Notices on the Ceremony at Bunhill Fields Cemetery.*

Howlett, Peter & Morgan, Mary Sh*ow Well Do Facts Travel?: the dissemination of reliable knowledge*, Cambridge University Press, 2010.

Hunter, J. Paul. *The Reluctant Pilgrim: Defoe's Emblematic Method and Quest for Form in Robinson Crusoe*, Johns Hopkins Press, 1966.

Johnson, *Samuel. Life of Savage*, Oxford University Press, 1971.

Kenyon, J.P., *Robert Spencer, Earl of Sunderland*, Gregg Revivals 1956.

Knox, Robert, *Historical Recollections* and *Autobiography*, 1681, Ed. Paulusz, 2vols. Dehiwla, Sri Lanka, 1989.

Lawrence, D.H. *Studies in Classic American Literature*, 1924.

Lea, B.E.G., *The Individual in the Economy*, Cambridge University Press, 1957.

Lesser, Simon. *Fiction and the Unconscious*, Boston, USA, Beacon Press, 1957.

Locke, John. *An Essay Concerning Human Understanding*, Ed. Alexander Fraser, Clarendon, Oxford University Press, 1894.

Macey, Samuel. *Money and The Novel: Mercenary Motive in Defoe and his Immediate Successors*, Victoria B.C. Sino Nis Press, 1983.

McDonald Wigfield, W. *Monmouth Rebellion*, Moonraker Press, 1980 and *The Monmouth Rebels*, Alan Sutton, 1985.

Makikalli, Aino and Muller, Andreas. *Positioning Daniel Defoe's Non-fiction: Form, Function, Genre*, Cambridge Scholars Publishing, 2010.

McVeigh, John. *Review*, Pickering and Chatto, 2004.

Moore, John Robert. *A Checklist of the Writings of Daniel Defoe*, Indiana University Press, 1960.

Nettleton, Thomas Dr. *Some Thoughts Concerning Virtue and Happiness in* a *Letter to a Clergyman*, London, 1729. *Treatise on Virtue and Happiness*, London, 1736.

Newton, Isaac. Ed. McLachlan H. *Theological Manuscripts*, Liverpool University Press, 1950.

Newton, Theodore F.M. *William Pitts and Queen Anne's Journalism*, Modern Philology 1936.

Peare, Catherine Owen. *William Penn*, Dobson Books, London, 1956.

Penn, William. *No Cross, No Crown*, Collected Works, 1726.

Pepys, Samuel. *Diary of Samuel Pepys*, Bell and Sons, 1970.

Rank, Otto. *The Trauma of Birth*, Martino Publishing, 2010.

Richardson, Humphrey (Pseudonym), *The Secret Life of Robinson Crusoe*, Collectors Publications, 1967.

Richardson, Samuel. *Pamela*, Oxford World's Classics, 2008.

Richetti, John. *Defoe's Narratives, Situations and Structures*, Clarendon, Oxford, 1975.

Ryder, Dudley. *The Diaries of Dudley Ryder, 1715-1716*, 1739.

Satyr Against the French, Anon.

Secord, Arthur. *Robert Drury's Journal and Other Studies*, Kessinger Legacy Reprints, University of Illinois Press, Urbana, 1961.

Schonhorn, Manuel. *Defoe's Politics: Parliament, power, kingship, and Robinson Crusoe*, Cambridge Studies, Cambridge University Press, 1999.

Simpson, William. *Going Naked as a Sign*, 1660.

Souhami, Diana. *Selkirk's Island*, Orion Books, London, 2002.

Spacks, Patricia. *Imagining a Self: Autobiography and the Novel in Eighteenth-Century England*, Cambridge Mass., Harvard University Press, 1976.

Stone, Lawrence. *The Family, Sex, and Marriage in England, 1550-1870*, 1977.

Sutherland, James. *The Restoration Newspaper and its Development*, Cambridge University Press, 1986.

Starr, G.A. *Defoe and Casuistry*, Princeton University Press, 1971.

Tadmor, Naomi. *Family and Friends in Eighteenth Century England: Household, Kinship and Patronage*, Cambridge University Press, 2001.

Theime, John. *Post-Colonial Con-Texts, writing back to the canon*, Continuum, London, 2001.

Thomas, Sir Dalby: *Historical Account of the Rise and Fall of the West Indian Collonies*, London, 1690.

Tomalin, Claire. *Samuel Pepys: The Unequalled Self*, Penguin Books, 2003.

Trevelyan, G M. *English Social History*, Penguin Books, 1944.

Turley, Hans. *Rum, Sodomy and the Lash: Piracy, Sexuality and Masculine Identity*, New York University Press, 1999.

Van der Zee, Henry and Barbara. *William and Mary*, McMillan, 1973.

Walcott, Derek. *Pantomime and Remembrance*, New York, Farrah, Strauss, & Giroux, 1980.

Watt, Ian. *The Rise of the Novel*, University of California Press, 1957.

Weinreb, Ben and Hibbert, Christopher. Eds. *The Corporation of London: Its Origins, Constitution, Powers and Duties*, Oxford University Press, 1950.

Wesley, Samuel. *A Letter to his Friend in London Concerning the Education of the Dissenters, in their Private Academies*, London, 1703.

Woodes Rogers. *A Cruising Voyage Round the World*, 1712,

Index

brick and pantile manufacturer, 181.

hosier in Freeman's Yard, 164, 173.

liveryman, 296.

journalist, 169, 179, 184-202.

merchant, 3, 99-103, 121, 173.

planter, 90-94.

piracy, 97-111.

sailor, 3.

slave trader, 3, 97-11, 158.

soldier, see Illustration of Military Commission, 250.9, commission, 86, military pension, 86.

ships, *Desire* and *Aurangezebe,* 107, 232-250.353.

wine dealer , 73, 108.

education, 36-37, 41, 45, 67-71, 287-295.

EMPLOYMENT

accountant to the Glass Commissioners, 88, 99, 117-119, 146, 180.

hosier, 164.

'intelligence service', 120, 145-148, 218, 462.

journalism, 184-202.

lottery organiser, 199.

oysters and dredging, 173, 303.

propagandist, for Harley, 214-231.

Sunderland, 204, for the Whig administration, 204- 205.

PROPERTY

Colchester, 30, 49, 220.

Hackney, 325.

Tilbury, 45, 152, 187, 198, 201.

Stoke Newington, London, 183, 187, 212, 218, 243-244, 325.

PERSONAL LIFE:

baptism and registration, 5.

birth, date and place, Etton, 5,

change of name, 6.

acquisitiveness and greed, 168.

action, as a relief from stress, 140, 212.

anxiety, 44, 144, 179, 212, 340.

appearance, 42, 447.

attacks on, 41, 101-102, 116

avarice, 43, 164, 168.

character, 61.

courage, bold but prudent, 62.

defects of, 178.

dishonesty and duplicity, 40-41, 63-64, 74, 121, 178, 183, 226, 265, 294, 301-304, 396, 415.

dress, 448.

Other Beliefs.

magic and the spirit world, 258.

martyrdom, 37, 142, 151.

puritanism, 289-290.

Quakerism, see Quakers.

romanticism, 150.

shunamitism, 67.

SOCIETY

Children in society.

abduction of, 43, 61.

abuse within the family, 61, 172.

attitudes to children, 49, 61, 172.

marriage to, 285.

nurses and child keepers, 21.

provision for own children, 49,171, 252.

sex with, 48, 185, 284.

treatment of, 61.

Other

immigration, 10-12.

prostitution, courtesans, male, 201–203, 217.

social contract, 170.

women, treatment of, 29, 171, 252.

WRITTEN WORKS:

Defoe, appearance, 48, 87, 298-

302, 450.

Defoe canon, 9.

Defoe, corpus, 7, bibliography, 250, 390. secrecy/anonymity, 393.

Defoe, aliases, 146, literary characteristics of his writing genre, 252-257; unreliable content, 255-257; defence of fiction, 255-260, lacking realism, and irony, 259-260, narrative tricks, 17, 23, 42, 56, 63, 69, 255, embellishment of actual experience, 256, plagiarism, 71, 150, 174, 258-259, satire, 256.

Defoe Bibliography

An Appeal to Honour and Justice, 146, 184, 192, 215, 221, 248.

A Brief Reply to the History of Standing Armies in England, 188.

An Enquiry into the Occasional Conformity of Dissenters in Cases of Preferment, 142.

An Essay on Projects, 215-216, 219.

www.ingramcontent.com/pod-product-compliance
Lightning Source LLC
Chambersburg PA
CBHW050033170426
42812CB00114B/3292/J